All In One
Rome Guide & Italian Phrasebook

Above: *the Pantheon, Piazza Rotonda*

AA Publishing

Above: *a Swiss Guard at the Vatican*

Find out more about AA Publishing and the wide range of services the AA provides by visiting our website at www.theAA.com

All In One guide first published 2003
Rome Guide written by Jane Shaw

Italian Phrasebook: English edition prepared by First Edition Translations Ltd, Great Britain
Designed and produced by AA Publishing

First published in 1995 as Wat & Hoe Italiaans, © Uitgeverij Kosmos bv - Utrecht/Antwerpen
Van Dale Lexicografie bv - Utrecht/Antwerpen

Published by AA Publishing, a trading name of Automobile Association Developments Limited, whose registered office is Millstream, Maidenhead Road, Windsor SL4 5GD. Registered number 1878835.

A CIP catalogue record for this book is available from the British Library.

ISBN 0 7495 3969 0

The contents of this publication are believed correct at the time of printing. Nevertheless, AA Publishing accepts no responsibility for any errors, omissions or changes in the details given, nor for the consequences of readers' reliance on this information. This does not affect your statutory rights. Assessments of the attractions and hotels and restaurants are based upon the author's own experience and contain subjective opinions that may not reflect the publisher's opinion or a reader's experience.

We have tried to ensure accuracy, but things do change, so please let us know if you have any comments or corrections.

A01882

Colour separation: BTB Digital Imaging, Whitchurch, Hampshire
Printed and bound in Italy by Printer Trento S.r.l.

Contents

About this Book

KEY TO SYMBOLS

- map reference to the maps found in the What to See section (see below)
- address or location
- telephone number
- opening times
- restaurant or café on premises or near by
- nearest underground train station
- nearest bus/tram route
- nearest overground train station
- ferry crossings and excursions by boat
- travel by air
- tourist information
- facilities for visitors with disabilities
- admission charge
- other places of interest near by
- other practical information
- ➤ indicates the page where you will find a fuller description

The ***Rome Guide*** is divided into five sections to cover the most important aspects of your visit to Rome.

Viewing Rome pages 5–14
An introduction to Rome by the author.
Rome's Features
Essence of Rome
The Shaping of Rome
Peace and Quiet
Rome's Famous

Top Ten pages 15–26
The author's choice of the Top Ten places to visit in Rome, each with practical information.

What to See pages 27–90
The two main areas of Rome, each with its own brief introduction and an alphabetical listing of the main attractions.
Practical information
Snippets of 'Did You Know...' information
4 suggested walks
2 suggested tours
2 features

Where To... pages 91–116
Detailed listings of the best places to eat, stay, shop, take the children and be entertained.

Practical Matters pages 117–24
A highly visual section containing essential travel information.

Maps
All map references are to the individual maps found in the What to See section of this guide.
For example, Galleria Borghese has the reference 29D4 – indicating the page on which the map is located and the grid square in which the gallery is to be found.
A list of the maps that have been used in this travel guide can be found in the index.

Prices
Where appropriate, an indication of the cost of an establishment is given by **£** signs:
£££ denotes higher prices, **££** denotes average prices, while **£** denotes lower charges.

Star Ratings
Most of the places described in this book have been given a separate rating:

✪✪✪ Do not miss
✪✪ Highly recommended
✪ Worth seeing

Viewing Rome

Above: *Castel Sant'Angelo*
Right: *shopping by scooter*

Jane Shaw's Rome

Vatican City
Rome is the capital of the Roman Catholic church, for in it lies the Vatican City (Città del Vaticano), covering less than half a hectare, and really a separate state with its own post office, radio and TV stations. Rome abounds in nuns, monks and priests from all over the world who come to study at one of the Catholic universities; in and around St Peter's you can see an exotic array of the habits worn by various religious orders.

Rome has got it all – a climate that gives sunny days at any time of year, a cuisine that has something (and usually a lot of things) for all tastes and some of the best fine art and architecture in the world. This is a city of contrasts; a bustling, modern capital set amid ancient splendour where screeching *motorini* swoop past leisurely pedestrians, classical art competes for attention with high fashion, and a beautiful sunny day can suddenly throw up a sky-blackening storm with thunder like cannon fire and rain that'll soak you in seconds.

It helps to approach it with a flexible attitude. You may not always be able to achieve what you set out to do (museums, shops, restaurants and even occasionally banks sometimes close suddenly for one reason or another), but don't worry. There are plenty of other things to do and even the streetlife, with its constantly changing parade of locals and visitors alike, is worth watching from a pavement or piazza bar. There are intriguing juxtapositions everywhere: in narrow winding streets of terracotta buildings clothes boutiques nestle among family-run grocers, craft studios, art galleries and restaurants.

The weather helps create a relaxed way of life in which even the most simple transaction may need far more time than you would have thought possible. On the other hand, lunch can take all afternoon so you'll probably soon stop worrying that the overseas post takes rather longer than expected. There is notorious bureaucracy and time-consuming public service (but these are improving), but once you adjust to the pace of life, you realise how much of Rome functions extremely efficiently, including the bus service, which gets you where you want in central Rome more or less when you want.

The beauty of Rome is a magnet to artists, tourists and students, many of whom never quite manage to leave it.

St Peter's is impressive even at dusk

Rome's Features

Population

The city of Rome is roughly 2,700 years old. It has a population of over 3 million – up from 200,000 in 1870 when Italy became a unified nation (although there were well over 1 million people living in the city in the days of the empire). There are about 192,000 foreigners resident in Rome. About 10 million people arrive at Fiumicino airport every year. About two-thirds of the working population are in government administration; few work in industry – 100,000, while 600,000 people work in offices. The city covers about 1,500sq km and 12 hills, having expanded somewhat from the original seven hills of Rome.

Climate

The best seasons for visiting are April to June, September and October – also the busiest, although the real peak comes at Easter when pilgrims swell the crowds of tourists who descend on the city. The average annual temperature is 16°C with a high of 38°C and a low of -4°C.

Crime

The bag-snatching and pocket-picking sectors of the Roman criminal community pose the biggest threat to visitors. Here there is good news and bad. 1996 saw bag-snatches, called *scippi* and traditionally committed by masked figures on motor scooters, register a 6 per cent decrease on the year before, at 13,333. But there was a 3 per cent rise in picked pockets, at 85,245.

Carabinieri *police watch the world go by in Piazza Venezia*

In July and August temperatures can reach 40°C and in August a lot of businesses close for the holidays. Early spring and late autumn are the wettest seasons (you can be unlucky at other times as well) – Rome has a similar annual rainfall to London but most falls over a few days. Even in winter the weather can be glorious with maximum daily temperatures around 15 or 16°C but, although it seldom snows, there can be bitingly cold winds in December, January and early February.

Churches and Bars

Central Rome has over 400 churches, 600 bars and less than 40 public toilets (but do not panic, most bars will allow you to use theirs). There are also 150km of holes in the road.

Essence of Rome

Central Rome on both sides of the Tiber (Tevere) is a city of contrasts. This busy modern capital is squeezed into a maze of old streets in which the layers of more than 2,000 years of history are superimposed on each other: ancient columns embedded in Renaissance palaces, baroque façades slapped on to the front of Romanesque churches and 1930s fascist office buildings nestling among it all. Not only is Rome the seat of the Italian government (both the President and the Prime Minister have their official residences here), but it is also a world centre for the film and fashion industries.

Legend has it that Romulus and Remus were breast-fed by a wolf and founded Rome; the beautiful and busy Piazza Navona

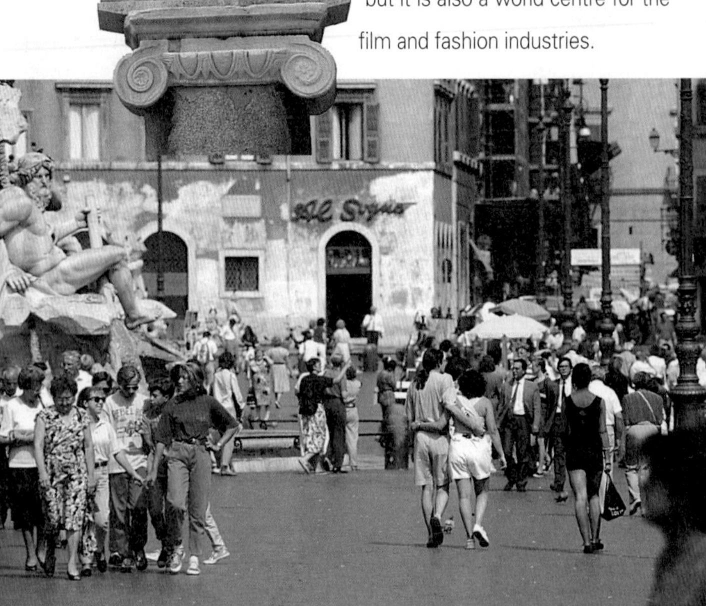

THE 10 ESSENTIALS

If you only have a short time to visit Rome, or would like to get a really complete picture of the city, here are the essentials:

- **Go to the Vatican** and marvel at Michelangelo's masterpieces in the Sistine Chapel (► 24).
- **Look down on Rome from on high** (► 34 for suggested view points), and try to find the flattish dome with a hole in the middle, which is the Pantheon (► 20).

- **Find a bar on Piazza Navona** (► 21) or Campo de' Fiori (► 37), sip a drink and watch life saunter by.
- **See Rome by night,** preferably on foot. Many of the main monuments are floodlit and those that are not have an eerie beauty in the city's soft street lighting.
- **Visit the church of Santa Maria in Cosmedin** (► 68) to test your nerve with your hand in the *Bocca della Verità* (mouth of truth), which will bite if you tell a lie.
- **Walk the streets at the Forum** where Julius Caesar trod (► 22).
- **At St Peter's look on the floor of the central aisle** (► 26) where the lengths of other cathedrals' aisles are marked – see how your local one measures up.
- **Do the historic centre walk** (► 26) to take you past some of the most famous tourist sights in the world.
- **Try to imagine the Colosseum** (► 18) full of raucous crowds with wild animals and hapless humans fighting it out in the ring.
- **Throw a coin into the Trevi Fountain** (► 40) which guarantees your return. Italian currency ends up in the coffers of the town council; foreign coins are donated to the Red Cross.

Illuminated Santa Maria in Trastevere creates an atmospheric meeting place; Piazza Navona's cafés are popular by day

The Shaping of Rome

753 BC
Rome founded by Romulus, the first of seven kings.

616–576 BC
Under Tarquin the Elder the Forum and Circo Massimo are established.

509 BC
Tarquin the Proud, last of the kings, expelled and Brutus establishes the Republic.

312 BC
Via Appia Antica started and Aqua Appia, the first aqueduct.

168 BC
Rome conquers Greece.

149–146 BC
Carthage destroyed in third Punic war.

60 BC
Julius Caesar, Crassus and Pompey form the Triumvirate.

51 BC
Conquest of Gaul.

44 BC
Murder of Julius Caesar.

27 BC
Augustus becomes the first emperor.

AD 64
Fire destroys much of the city (Emperor Nero plays his fiddle).

AD 67
Crucifixion of St Peter and execution of St Paul during first persecution of Christians.

312
Battle of Milvian bridge, Constantine wins control of the Empire.

380
Christianity becomes the Roman Empire's official religion.

395
Empire divided into two parts, Eastern and Western.

410
Rome sacked by Goths.

455
Rome sacked by Vandals.

475
Fall of Western Roman Empire.

778
Charlemagne conquers Italy.

961
King Otto of the Saxons becomes first Holy Roman Emperor.

1300
First Holy Year proclaimed by Pope Boniface VIII.

1309
Pope Clement V moves papacy to Avignon

1347
Cola di Rienzo tries to establish a new Roman Republic.

1377
Papacy returns from Avignon.

1378
Great Schism in papacy, a second 'pope' is established in Avignon.

1409
A third papacy established in Pisa.

1417
Pope Martin V ends the Great Schism.

1453
Fall of Constantinople to the Turks, marking end of Eastern Empire.

1498–1502
Papacy at war with Italian states.

1506
Work starts on new St Peter's.

1508–1512
Papacy at war with Romagna.

1520
Martin Luther's reforming thesis starts the Reformation.

1527
Rome sacked by Charles V and German and Spanish troops.

An impression of the Tiber in ancient times

1545–63
Council of Trent leads to the Counter Reformation to strengthen the Catholic church against reforming Protestants.

1585
Pope Sixtus V plans new city with many new streets and buildings.

1600
Giordano Bruno burned at the stake in Campo de' Fiori.

1626
New St Peter's consecrated.

1797
Napoleon captures Rome.

1801
Concordat between Napoleon and Pope Pius VII.

1806
Holy Roman Empire ends.

1808
Rome occupied by French; Pius VII sent to France in captivity.

1814
Pius VII returns to Rome.

1820
Wars for Italian Unification begin.

1849–66
French troops in Rome protect the Pope from the armies of Unification.

1861
Kingdom of Italy formed under King Vittorio Emanuele.

1870
Rome captured by General Garibaldi's troops; Italian Unification complete.

1922
Mussolini marches on Rome, becomes Prime Minister.

1929
Lateran Treaty between Mussolini and the papacy creates Vatican state.

1940
Italy enters World War II.

1943
Mussolini resigns and Germans take over.

1944
Allies liberate Rome from Germans.

1946
Republic established, King Umberto II exiled.

1957
Treaty of Rome establishes Common Market (now European Union).

1960
Olympic games held in Rome.

1978
Prime Minister Aldo Moro assassinated.

1981
Pope John Paul II shot in St Peter's square.

1993
Anti-corruption movement starts in Italy; two bombs explode – at San Giovanni in Laterano and at San Giorgio in Velabro. Mafia blamed.

2000
Many millions of pilgrims descend on Rome for the Holy Year.

Peace & Quiet

One of the ancient bridges linking Isola Tiberina to the river bank

Rome is not a quiet city. Heavy traffic and vast numbers of tourists combine to make sightseeing a tiring, sometimes stressful, business, particularly in the spring, early summer and autumn. But do not despair, even in the packed historic centre it is possible to come across havens of peace – a little piazza or quiet alley – where you can sit for a moment or two. Some of the sights themselves are often relatively tranquil. The Palatino, Piazza Farnese, the Terme di Caracalla and Circo Massimo, for example, are usually fairly empty, and on the hill above Circo Massimo the town's rose garden will refresh your senses and restore your energy levels.

Parks and Gardens

There are a number of parks and gardens in or near the city centre. The most central of these is Villa Borghese which stretches out behind the Pincio Gardens above Piazza del Popolo (➤ 59). Here there are lakes, flower gardens, trees and rolling hillsides on which to rest. Above the Colosseum is the Colle Oppio, a slightly run-down turn-of-the-century style park which contains the ruins of Nero's Golden House and Trajan's baths as well as some inviting benches. On the other side of the Colosseum is the park of Villa Celimontana (entrance on Piazza della Navicella) laid out as formal gardens for the Mattei family in the 16th century. Off Via di Santa Sabina on the Aventine hill there's the Parco di San Alessio and a most delightful orangery with good views over Trastevere. In Trastevere itself you will find the botanical gardens (on Via Corsini off Via della Lungara), pretty Villa Sciarra (entrance on Via Calandrelli) built on a steep hillside and the massive Villa Doria Pamphili (entrance on Via di San Pancrazio) with its statues, trees, fountains and artificial river.

Wild Cats
Although not exactly wild, Rome is famous for its cats, many of whom live in the streets or among the ruins relying on the goodwill of local people, or informal cat protection organisations, to feed them. The recent increase in these charitable souls may have something to do with the increasing boldness of some of the local rats (although don't worry, you are no more likely to come across a rat than you are in any other major city).

Roman Wildlife

The crumbling masonry of ancient Rome contains a wide array of plants, small animals and birds. In the 19th century, for example, several specific studies of

the flora of the Colosseum were made and hundreds of plant species were identified. Many of these have since disappeared but in spring there is still a flamboyant display of wild and semi-wild flowers sprouting up in the Fori Imperiali (► 40). If you look carefully, you may catch sight of little birds or scuttling lizards, particularly the green-grey Sicilian lizard or even the far rarer green lizard. Geckos, on the other hand, are everywhere. The more exotic birdlife includes the blue rock thrush, the black redstart, little owls and kestrels.

The most famous of the city's trees are the pines of Rome, the aptly named umbrella pine (*Pinus pinea*). Many of the palm trees were planted at the end of the 19th century while orange trees, which sometimes drop their soggy fruit at the feet of passers-by, have long been used to decorate palace and convent gardens.

Finally, a word of warning for hayfever sufferers: the plane trees that line the river and some of the main streets emit a particularly potent pollen in spring.

National Park

Those who want to get right away from the city head off to the Parco Nazionale d'Abruzzo, 400sq km of alpine scenery which includes some of the highest peaks in the Apennine range (2,000m and above) and a network of well sign-posted walking, rambling and hiking routes. The park boasts a spectacular range of (admittedly rather shy) animals and birds including bears, wolves, chamonix, lynx, wild boars (which also feature on some local menus), eagles, falcons and owls. The centre of the park is Pescasseroli reached by bus from Via Tiburtina or car by way of Licenza or Subiaco.

Peaceful today; Circo Massimo was once the site of chariot races and blood sports

Rome's Famous

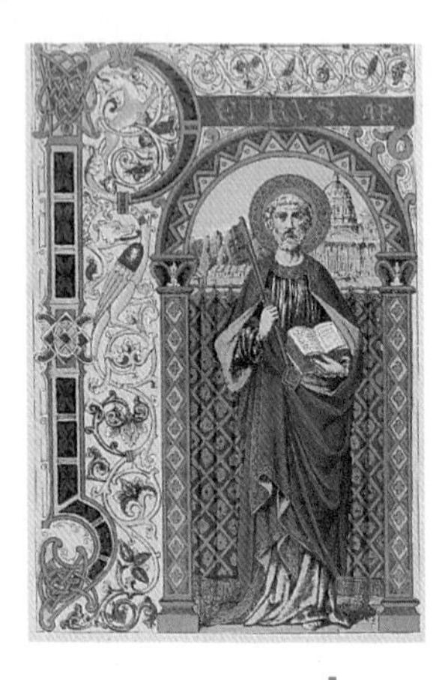

St Peter was martyred here in AD 67

As the former capital of the Roman Empire, the headquarters of the Roman Catholic church and the capital of modern Italy, it is hardly surprising that Rome has attracted a vast array of talented and important people from all professions.

One former resident who went on to true greatness, as guardian of the gates of Heaven, was St Peter. Christ's disciple came to Rome around AD 42. He was one of the first Christian martyrs and was crucified (upside down as he felt unworthy of dying as Christ had) in AD 67 under Emperor Nero.

Artists

The artists who came to Rome include Michelangelo (1475–1564) who was here from 1506. This tempestuous, troubled genius is believed to have been homosexual and always used male models, even when representing women. In contrast, Raphael (1483–1520) who came to Rome in 1508, fell in love with one of his models – the *Fornarina* (baker's daughter) (➤ 19). Caravaggio (1571–1610) was in Rome from 1591 until he had to flee justice in 1606 after killing his tennis opponent in a fight.

Monarchs

Among the monarchs who sought refuge was Queen Christina of Sweden (1626–89) who was welcomed by the Pope after her conversion to Catholicism. In 1715 another Catholic royal, James Edward Stuart (1688–1766), fled here after his unsuccessful attempt to win back the British throne for his family. His son, Charles Edward (Bonnie Prince Charlie), was born here in 1721 and died at Palazzo Balestra near Piazza Venezia in 1788.

Napoleon

Napoleon Bonaparte arrived in Rome at the head of his conquering army in 1797. After his defeat and death in 1821 his family continued to live here.

Writers

Visiting writers include Johann Wolfgang Goethe (1749–1832) who lived on Via del Corso from 1786 to 1788. Henry James (1843–1916) was a frequent visitor, while the English 19th-century poets Keats, Shelley, Byron, Robert Browning and Elizabeth Barrett-Browning all knew the city well. Author Alberto Moravia (1907–90) was born in Rome; many of his novels and stories are set here.

Film Directors

Two of the most famous film-makers of the 20th century set some of their best works in Rome and are still fondly remembered by those who knew them. Federico Fellini's (1920–93) *La Dolce Vita* became synonymous with Rome in the 1960s, especially the scene where Marcello Mastroianni follows Anita Ekberg into the Fontana di Trevi. Pier Paolo Pasolini (1922–75) used a mixture of contemporary and historic settings for his erudite films. He was brutally murdered in 1975 on the coast near Rome.

Top Ten

Above: *The Colosseum*
Right: *Angel, Ponte Sant'Angelo*

1
Campidoglio

28C2

Piazza del Campidoglio

06 6710 2071/
6710 2475

Tue–Sat 9–7, Sun
9–1:30

44, 46, 75, 81, 95, 160,
170, 175, 181, 719 to
Piazza Venezia

None

Moderate; free last Sun
of each month

Piazza del Campidoglio is home to the art and sculpture collections of the Capitoline Museums

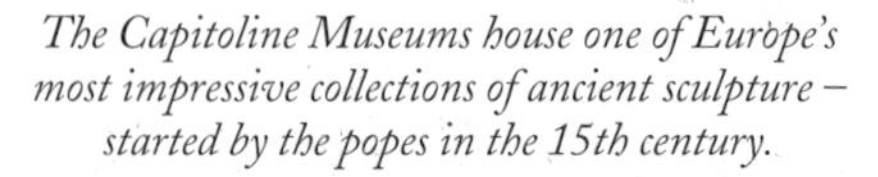

The Capitoline Museums house one of Europe's most impressive collections of ancient sculpture – started by the popes in the 15th century.

Michelangelo designed Rome's magnificent civic centre, although later architects finished the job. Today, only the salmon-pink Palazzo Senatorio is used for political purposes (the mayor's office is here), while the flanking buildings form the Campidoglio (or Capitoline) Museums.

On entering the Palazzo Nuovo, on the left, you are greeted by the enormous 2nd-century AD bronze equestrian statue of Emperor Marcus Aurelius which rested atop the pedestal in the centre of the square until 1981. On the first floor in room 1 (Sala 1), is a superbly modelled, sensual *Dying Gaul*; like many sculptures here, this is a Roman copy in marble of an earlier Greek work. Roman heads abound, including portraits of philosophers (a whole roomful) and eminent citizens with elaborate hair. The erotic *Capitoline Venus* has a chamber to herself.

In the courtyard of the Palazzo dei Conservatori opposite are giant hands, a head and feet – fragments from a colossal statue of Constantine found in the Forum. Upstairs, highlights include the creamy marble *Venus Esquilina* and the delightfully realistic 1st century BC bronze *Spinario*, a young boy extracting a thorn from his foot. The *She-Wolf Suckling Romulus and Remus* in the Sala della Lupa will be familiar to many – the symbol of Rome is reproduced everywhere. The wolf is thought to be an Etruscan bronze of the late 6th to early 5th centuries BC to which the twins were added in the 16th century.

The picture gallery on the second floor provides no relief for the footsore. There are fine works by Pietro da Cortona, Guido Reni, Tintoretto, Rubens, Van Dyck, and others; Caravaggio's sensual *St John the Baptist* in his fully-fledged realist style and Guercino's immense *Burial of St Petronilla* stand out.

2
Castel Sant'Angelo

This powerful monument on the Tiber symbolises almost 2,000 years of Roman history, from Hadrian to Italian Unification.

Castel Sant'Angelo was central to the history of the papacy and the defence of the city until 1886 when it was turned into a museum. It is a labyrinth of a place both literally and historically.

Built by Emperor Hadrian (AD 117–138) as a mausoleum to himself, visitors today enter via the original Roman passageway, up which the funeral procession passed. This joins up with one of the medieval ramps that were added when the tomb was converted into a defensive fortress. The dark ramp finally opens on to a courtyard (originally the funerary garden), where now there is Montelupo's statue of an angel (1544) sheathing a sword, commemorating (along with the monument's name) a legendary event in which an angel was seen over Rome at the end of a plague in 590.

Off the courtyard (with its Michelangelo façade from 1514) is the *Sala di Apollo* (1548), exquisitely decorated with ornate *grotteschi* (frescoes); illuminated windows in the floor give you a view down to the underground corridors that led to a notorious papal prison. Following Medici Pope Clement VII's seven-month siege inside the *Castello* (1527), the popes felt they needed more sumptuous apartments. Farnese Pope Paul III (1534–49) commissioned the magnificent *Sala Paolina*, with its beautiful frescoes and *trompe l'oeil* doors. Off the library (with gorgeous stucco work) is the wood-lined papal treasury, the room believed to have held Hadrian's tomb, although the whereabouts of his remains are a mystery. The tour finishes with a walk around the ramparts.

28B4

Lungotevere Castello 50

06 681 9111

Tue–Sun 9–7

Bar on ramparts (£££)

Lepanto

49, 70, 87, 280, 492, 926 to Piazza Cavour

Moderate

Castel Sant' Angelo has been mausoleum, fortress, papal prison and museum

3
Colosseum (Colosseo)

29D2

Piazza del Colosseo

06 700 4261

Tue–Sat 9 to 1 hour before sunset; Sun, Mon 9–2

Colosseo

75, 81, 85, 87, 175, 673 to Piazza del Colosseo

Very few

Moderate

Pope leads the stations of the cross here on the evening of Good Friday

The Colosseum takes its name from the Colossus of Nero, *a huge bronze statue which once stood close by*

Built in the 1st century AD as a gift to the Romans, this dignified, round monument has become the city's most recognisable symbol.

Emperor Vespasian commissioned the Colosseum to fill the site of a massive lake that his predecessor, Nero, had had excavated for his own private use. The massive circus, with a capacity of more than 55,000, was used for popular, bloodthirsty spectator sports. In spite of centuries of use as an unofficial marble quarry for Renaissance and baroque builders, much of the outer shell has survived showing the four arched tiers (each arch held a statue) behind which staircases and galleries led to the auditorium. Seating was segregated according to sex and status; the emperor's box was at the southern end (opposite today's main entrance) and below him sat the Vestal Virgins.

Nearly all the events staged here guaranteed the bloody death of human participants. Gladiators were usually slaves, prisoners of war or condemned prisoners but the enthusiastic following that a successful gladiator provoked encouraged some upper-class men to train for combat. Other spectacles involved mismatched rivals fighting to the death with nets, tridents and other weapons; fights against wild animals were also popular. The labyrinth of underground passages, lifts and cages through which these unfortunate beasts were channelled into the ring can be seen under the arena. Gladiatorial combat was banned in the 5th century, and changing public tastes led to the Colosseum falling out of use by the 6th century.

4
Palazzo Barberini

A treasure trove of paintings from the 13th to the 16th centuries is housed in one of Rome's grandest baroque palaces.

Carlo Maderno's original design, begun in 1624 for Barberini Pope Urban VIII, was embellished by Bernini and Maderno's nephew Borromini. The latter added the elegant oval staircase and the windows of the upper storey which, using ingenious artificial perspective, preserve the symmetry of the façade while staying in proportion with the size of the actual rooms.

The palace was sold to the Italian state in 1949 and houses, together with Palazzo Corsini (► 53), the national collection of art. There are plans to remove the officers' mess which occupies a large area, expand the gallery and reunite the collection. In the meantime extensive renovations are bringing the main rooms back to their original splendour, the most spectacular of which is the *Gran Salone*, with its elaborate ceiling fresco, *Triumph of Divine Providence*, by Pietro da Cortona.

Magnificent *quattrocento* panel paintings include an ethereal *Annunciation* by Filippo Lippi, and a *Madonna and Saints* by Alunno. The highlights of the collection are the 16th- and 17th-century paintings: Andrea del Sarto's magical *Sacra Famiglia*; Raphael's *La Fornarina* (widely believed to be a portrait of the baker's daughter who was his mistress, although some maintain it is in fact a picture of a courtesan and was painted by Giulio Romano); a portrait of Urban VIII by Bernini (his genius lay more in sculpture and architecture); and works by El Greco, Bronzino, Guido Reni, Guercino and Caravaggio.

The palace itself is as beautiful as the art it houses

- 29D4
- Via Quattro Fontane 13
- 06 481 4591/482 4184
- Tue–Sun 9–7
- Metro Barberini
- 60, 61, 62, 175, 492, 590 to Piazza Barberini; 590 has facilities for passengers with reduced mobility
- None
- Moderate

5
Pantheon

Its massive circular interior, lit only by a round opening in the roof, is one of the most awe-inspiring sights of Rome.

The incredible dome of the Pantheon

 28C3

 Piazza della Rotonda

 06 6830 0230

Mon–Sat 9–6:30, Sun 9–1

 119 to Piazza della Rotonda; 44, 64, 70, 75, 81 to Largo di Torre Argentina

Few

 Free

Sometimes used for concerts and special services

Do not be misled by the inscription, *AGRIPPA FECIT*, over its portals. Agrippa built an earlier version of this temple to all the gods but what we see today was erected by Emperor Hadrian in the early 1st century AD and, in spite of losing many of its opulent trimmings over the centuries, it remains much as he would have remembered it.

The dome is a semi-sphere 43.5m in diameter with walls 6m thick, it was constructed by pouring concrete over a wooden framework. Originally the roof was covered with bronze cladding which was stripped off by Constantine II in the 7th century to decorate Constantinople and, 1,000 years later, Bernini took the remaining bronze from the roof beams to build the canopy (*baldacchino*) in St Peter's (➤ 26). Its huge bronze doors, however, have survived since Roman times. The ornate marble floor is a 19th-century reconstruction of the original design and the interior has been cleaned and touched up to restore its subtly vibrant colours.

It was one of the first Roman temples to be converted into a church (by Pope Boniface IV when Emperor Phocas donated the building to him; consecrated 609) and over the centuries several leading Italians, including the painter Raphael, have been buried here.

6
Piazza Navona

One of the world's most beautiful squares owes its elongated shape to the ancient Roman stadium over which it was built.

Although the best effect can be had by approaching Piazza Navona from the southeast end, whichever of the narrow streets you take, this massive space in the cramped historical centre is always breathtaking. To its north, are remains of the entrance to the stadium that Emperor Domitian built in the 1st century AD.

The piazza's centrepiece is Bernini's spectacular Fontana dei Fiumi (fountain of the rivers, 1651) featuring symbolic representations of the rivers Ganges, Danube, Plate and Nile (blindfolded because its source was then unknown) clinging to a massive artificial cliff-face while sea monsters lurk beneath. The figure at the centre of the fountain to the southeast is another Bernini work, *Il Moro* (the moor); the figures of Neptune and others on the third fountain are 19th-century.

This has always been a hub of Roman social life; there was a market here for centuries and the piazza used to be flooded in August to form a vast watery playground for rich and poor alike. Today it is flooded by musicians, artists, locals and visitors who flock to its bars for hours at a time.

28B3

Piazza Navona

Lots of bars, tend to be expensive but worth it (££)

46, 62, 64 to Corso Vittorio Emanuele II; 70, 81, 87, 115, 186, 492, 628 to Corso del Rinascimento

December Christmas fair (► 116), street performers all year

Bernini's fountain, topped by an obelisk, reigns over Piazza Navona

7
Roman Forum (Foro Romano)

28C3

Via dei Fori Imperiali

06 699 0110

Apr–Sep, Mon 9–2, Tue–Sat 9 to sunset; Oct–Mar, Mon–Sat 9–3, Sun 9–1

Survey the monumental ruins of Classical Rome

This was the social, economic and political centre of ancient Rome, where people came to shop, consult lawyers or gossip.

Before entering the Foro or Forum, look down on it from behind the Campidoglio (➤ 16). To your left is the Arch of Septimius Severus, erected in AD 203 to celebrate his victory over the Parthians; behind it, to the right, is the Column of Phocas, AD 608, erected in honour of the Byzantine Emperor, Phocas, in gratitude after he gave the Pantheon (➤ 20) to the Pope.

Colosseo

85, 87, 175, 186 to Via dei Fori Imperiali; 81 to Piazza del Colosseo; 44, 46, 60, 81, 94, 95, 710, 719 to Piazza Venezia

Few

Moderate (includes entrance to Palatino, ➤ 52)

Guided tours available; booking 06 3908 0730

Left of the public entrance to the Forum is the Basilica Aemilia, a place for business; look for traces of the coins that were fused into the floor when the Basilica was burned down in the 5th century. Next to the Basilica, along the Via Sacra (Sacred Way), is the 3rd-century Curia (rebuilt in the 1930s) where the Senate met; the slightly curved platform outside it is the rostrum on which political speeches and orations were made. Opposite the Curia is the 1st-century BC Basilica Julia and to its left is the Temple of Castor and Pollux, with its three beautiful remaining columns. The round building is the Temple of Vesta, where a fire was kept burning continually by the 16 Vestal Virgins who lived in the elegant villa behind it. On the other side of the Forum are the three massive vaults of the 4th-century Basilica of Maxentius and Constantine much studied by Renaissance artists and architects. To its left is the 4th-century AD Temple of Romulus, under which you can see some dank little rooms, thought to be the remains of a much earlier brothel. The Arch of Titus is near the public exit; it was erected in the 1st century AD to celebrate the Emperor's sack of Jerusalem.

8
San Clemente

A 12th-century church, on top of a 4th-century one, on top of an ancient shrine of Mithras – a walk through Rome's multi-layered history?

29D2

Via di San Giovanni in Laterano

06 7045 1018

9–12:30, 3:30–6:30; Oct–Mar closes at 6

Colosseo

85 to Via di San Giovanni in Laterano; 87, 186 to Via Labicana

Cheap; free to upper church

Even without its hidden depths, San Clemente is one of the prettiest churches in Rome with its 12th-century apse mosaic, *The Triumph of the Cross*, showing details of animals, birds and humans in flower-filled fields and its simple, 6th-century choir stall, originally in the earlier church building. The spiralling column next to the choir stall is a 12th-century cosmati (► 68) mosaic candlestick. To the left of the entrance is the chapel of St Catherine with 15th-century frescoes by Masolini of her life and martyrdom on the original Catherine-wheel.

However, the church's main claim to fame lies underneath where the first layer comprises the remains of a 4th-century church in which some fragments of ancient masonry and 11th-century frescoes, illustrating the life and miracles of St Clemente (martyred by being tied to an anchor and drowned), have been preserved among the foundations of the later church. There is also a large circular well that was probably used as a font.

Descending yet further you come to the ancient Roman level where the highlight is a cramped room with a small altar on which there is a relief of Mithras slaying a bull. The Mithraic cult arrived in Rome from Persia about the same time as Christianity and had a strong following especially among soldiers (women were not allowed to join), involving them in ritualistic banquets.

The route out takes you through the walls of several ancient Roman apartment blocks and even lower, although not open to the public, are some 5th or 6th century catacombs.

View of San Clemente's attractive main façade

9
Sistine Chapel & Vatican Museums

73B1

Viale Vaticano

Vatican tourist office: 06 6988 4947/6988 3333

Easter to mid-Jun, Mon–Fri 8:45–4:45, Sat 8:45–1:45. Rest of year, Mon–Sat 8:45–1:45. All year, last Sun of month 8:45–1:45PM

Choice of restaurants and bars (£)

Above: *a detail from, and (right), the complete Michelangelo masterpiece,* The Last Judgement

Michelangelo's masterpiece is one of today's wonders of the world, fittingly reached via the rooms of one of the world's greatest art collections.

Before reaching the Sistine Chapel you will have to walk for about 20 minutes through the corridors of the Vatican Museums. There is far too much to be absorbed in one visit, but you can select one of several recommended timed routes to see a selection of the highlights. There are: the Museo Gregoriano-Egizio Egyptian collection; the Museo Chiaramonti collection of Roman sculpture; the Museo Pio Clementine, whose classical sculptures include the *Belvedere Apollo* and *Lacoön* and his sons being strangled by snakes; the Museo Gregoriano-Etrusco collection of Greek, Roman and Etruscan art; corridors of tapestries by Pieter van Aelst based on Raphael cartoons; and corridors lined with 16th-century maps of each of the Italian regions, which lead to the Raphael Rooms.

There are four Raphael Rooms, painted between 1508 and 1525 (the last finished by Giulio Romano after Raphael's death in 1520). In the first room the subjects are metaphysical, including the famous *School of Athens* in which many of Raphael's contemporaries are portrayed as Greek philosophers and poets. The second room shows biblical and early Christian events. The third room portrays significant events in papal history, and the final room illustrates the story of Constantine. From here the tour proceeds to the Sistine Chapel.

Michelangelo painted the Sistine Chapel ceiling between 1508 and 1512, crouching for hours on the scaffolding as Pope Julius II chivvied him on from below. A thorough cleaning in the 1980s and 1990s, during which some of the garments that more puritanical popes had had painted on to Michelangelo's scantily clad biblical figures were stripped off along with the dust and grime, restored the original vibrant colours. The ceiling tells the story of the Creation, in which a pink-clad God nips around dividing light from darkness and water from land before going on to create the

sun, the moon, Adam and Eve. The last four panels show the birth of original sin and the story of Noah. On the chapel's end wall is Michelangelo's much later *Last Judgement*. By the time he started this in 1534 he was racked with ill-health and pessimistic thoughts of his own mortality, and it took him until 1541 to complete. The flayed skin held up by St Bartholomew (to Christ's left) is believed to be a self-portrait, while the diabolical figure in the bottom right-hand corner is a portrait of the Pope's secretary, who disapproved of Michelangelo's naturalistic handling of this sacred subject. The other walls of the chapel were painted with episodes from the lives of Christ and Moses by, among others, Botticelli, and Perugino.

Beyond the chapel are: the Vatican library with over one million valuable volumes, many dating from the Middle Ages; a gallery of modern religious art including works by Klee, Munch and Picasso; and collections of pagan and early Christian antiquities. It is definitely worth going into the *Pinacoteca* (picture gallery) which has a marvellous collection of medieval, Renaissance and baroque art including masterpieces by most of the most famous names in European art of the periods.

Ottaviano

23, 49, 81, 492, 907, 991 to Piazza del Risorgimento

Good

Expensive but it covers a lot; free last Sun of month

Guided tours available in a number of languages

10
St Peter's (San Pietro)

73B1

Piazza San Pietro

Vatican tourist office: 06 6988 4947/6988 3333

Apr–Oct, 7–7; Nov–Mar, 7–6

Ottaviano

62, 64 to Piazza San Pietro; 49, 81, 492, 907, 991 to Piazza del Risorgimento

Free to Basilica; moderate for roof

Tours of the necropolis in English must be booked in advance through the Uffizio degli Scavi in St Peter's Square. Papal blessing every Wed morning (unless he is away, as in Jun–Sep) and on Easter and Christmas days.

Whether you find its opulence impressive or over the top, the sheer size of the world's most important church will not leave you unmoved

Emperor Constantine built a shrine to St Peter over his tomb and near where he had been crucified in the Circus of Nero. As the fortunes of Rome and the newly established Christian religion rose and fell, the building saw periods of embellishment fluctuating with sackings and destruction, and had been much altered by the time Pope Nicholas V ordered its restoration in the mid-15th century. Work did not get under way until about 50 years later, however, when Pope Julius II appointed Bramante as the architect for a completely new basilica in 1503. Another 123 years, and interventions from many of the most important architects and artists of the time, were to pass before the new basilica was consecrated. The basic floor plan is more or less as Bramante designed it, 187m long; Michelangelo designed the 132.5m-high dome, Carlo Maderno the façade and Bernini the impressive oval colonnade that surrounds the piazza in front of the basilica.

Inside, on the right, is Michelangelo's *Pietà* of 1499. Other gems include a 13th-century bronze statue of St Peter whose foot has been worn away by the touch of pilgrims; Bernini's massive 20m-high *baldacchino*, or altar canopy (under which only the Pope can celebrate Mass), his monuments to Popes Urban VIII and Alexander VII and the tabernacle in the shape of a temple.

Looking down from the dome designed by Michelangelo

What To See

Above: *dome of St Peter's Basilica*
Right: *detail from the Sistine Chapel ceiling*

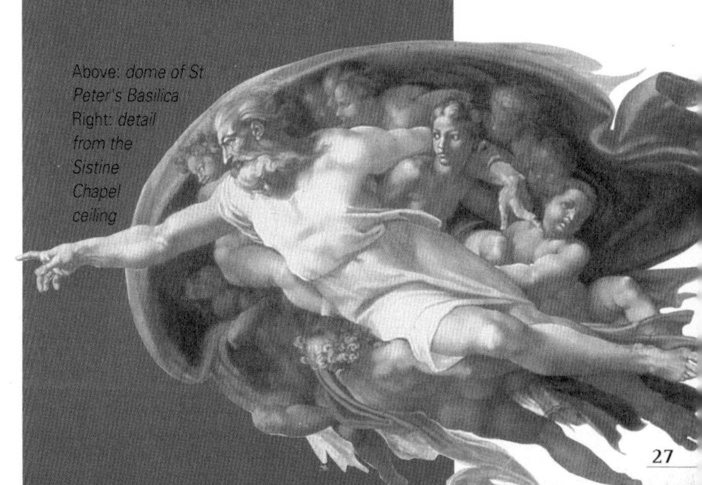

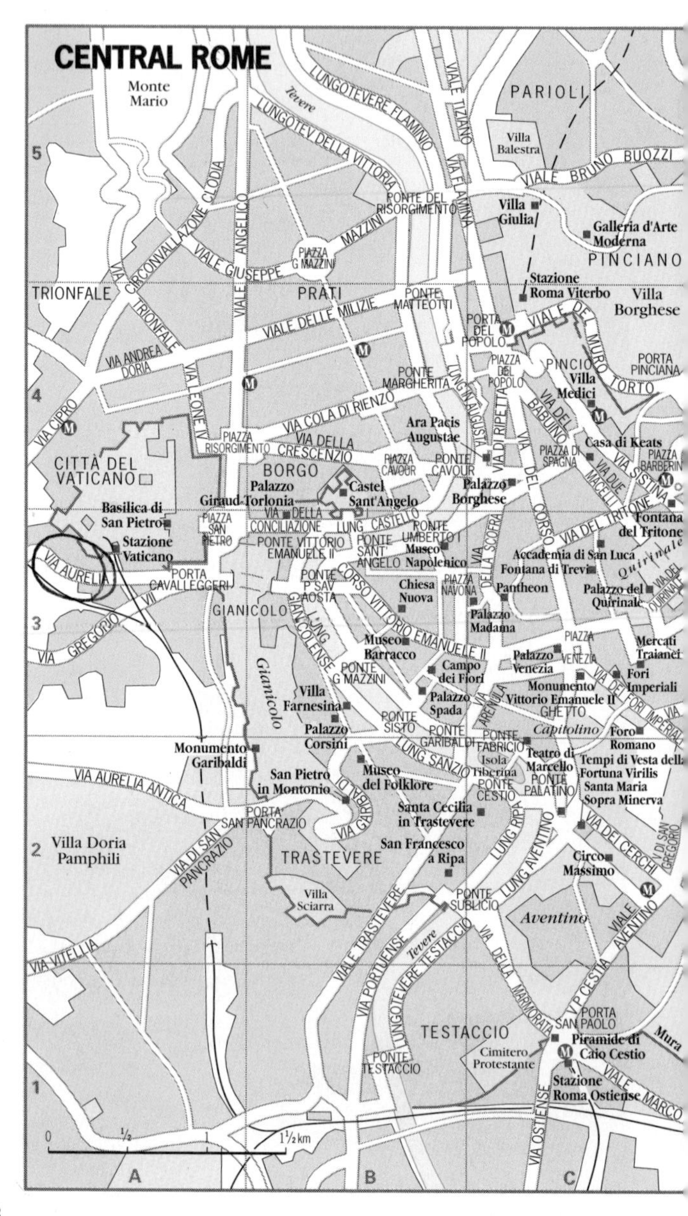
CENTRAL ROME
Monte Mario
Tevere
LUNGOTEVERE FLAMINIO
LUNGOTEV DELLA VITTORIA
VIALE TIZIANO
VIA FLAMINIA
PARIOLI
Villa Balestra
VIALE BRUNO BUOZZI
PONTE DEL RISORGIMENTO
Villa Giulia
Galleria d'Arte Moderna
PINCIANO
VIA CIRCONVALLAZONE CLODIA
VIALE ANGELICO
PIAZZA G MAZZINI
MAZZINI
VIALE GIUSEPPE
TRIONFALE
VIA TRIONFALE
PRATI
PONTE MATTEOTTI
Stazione Roma Viterbo
Villa Borghese
VIALE DELLE MILIZIE
PORTA DEL POPOLO
VIALE DEL MURO TORTO
VIA ANDREA DORIA
VIA LEONE IV
PONTE MARGHERITA
LUNG IN AUGUSTA
PIAZZA DEL POPOLO
PINCIO
Villa Medici
PORTA PINCIANA
VIA CIPRO
VIA COLA DI RIENZO
Ara Pacis Augustae
VIA DI RIPETTA
VIA DEL BABUINO
Casa di Keats
PIAZZA RISORGIMENTO
VIA DELLA CRESCENZIO
PIAZZA CAVOUR
PONTE CAVOUR
PIAZZA DI SPAGNA
VIA DUE MACELLI
VIA SISTINA
PIAZZA BARBERINI
CITTÀ DEL VATICANO
BORGO
Palazzo Giraud-Torlonia
Castel Sant'Angelo
Palazzo Borghese
VIA DEL CORSO
Basilica di San Pietro
PIAZZA SAN PIETRO
VIA DELLA CONCILIAZIONE
LUNG CASTELLO
PONTE UMBERTO I
VIA DEL TRITONE
Fontana del Tritone
Stazione Vaticano
PONTE VITTORIO EMANUELE II
PONTE SANT' ANGELO
Museo Napolenico
VIA DELLA SCOFA
Accademia di San Luca
Fontana di Trevi
Quirinale
VIA AURELIA
PORTA CAVALLEGGERI
PONTE P SAV AOSTA
CORSO VITTORIO EMANUELE II
Chiesa Nuova
PIAZZA NAVONA
Pantheon
Palazzo del Quirinale
VIA DEL QUIRINALE
VIA GREGORIO VII
GIANICOLO
L'UNG GIANICOLENSE
Palazzo Madama
Museo Barracco
PIAZZA VENEZIA
Mercati Traianei
Gianicolo
PONTE G MAZZINI
Campo dei Fiori
Palazzo Venezia
Fori Imperiali
Monumento Vittorio Emanuele II
VIA DEI FORI IMPERIALI
Villa Farnesina
Palazzo Spada
VIA ARENULA
GHETTO
PONTE SISTO
Capitolino
Foro Romano
Palazzo Corsini
PONTE GARIBALDI
PONTE FABRICIO
Monumento Garibaldi
LUNG SANZIO
Isola Tiberina
Teatro di Marcello
Tempi di Vesta della Fortuna Virilis
VIA AURELIA ANTICA
San Pietro in Montorio
Museo del Folklore
PONTE CESTIO
PONTE PALATINO
Santa Maria Sopra Minerva
VIA GARIBALDI
PORTA SAN PANCRAZIO
Santa Cecilia in Trastevere
LUNG RIPA
LUNG AVENTINO
VIA DEI CERCHI
V DI SAN GREGORIO
Villa Doria Pamphili
VIA DI SAN PANCRAZIO
TRASTEVERE
San Francesco a Ripa
Circo Massimo
Villa Sciarra
PONTE SUBLICIO
Aventino
VIALE AVENTINO
VIA VITELLIA
VIALE TRASTEVERE
VIA PORTUENSE
LUNGOTEVERE TESTACCIO
VIA DELLA MARMORATA
V P CESTIA
TESTACCIO
PORTA SAN PAOLO
Mura
Piramide di Caio Cestio
Cimitero Protestante
PONTE TESTACCIO
Stazione Roma Ostiense
VIALE MARCO
VIA OSTIENSE
0
1/2
1 1/2 km
A
B
C
1
2
3
4
5

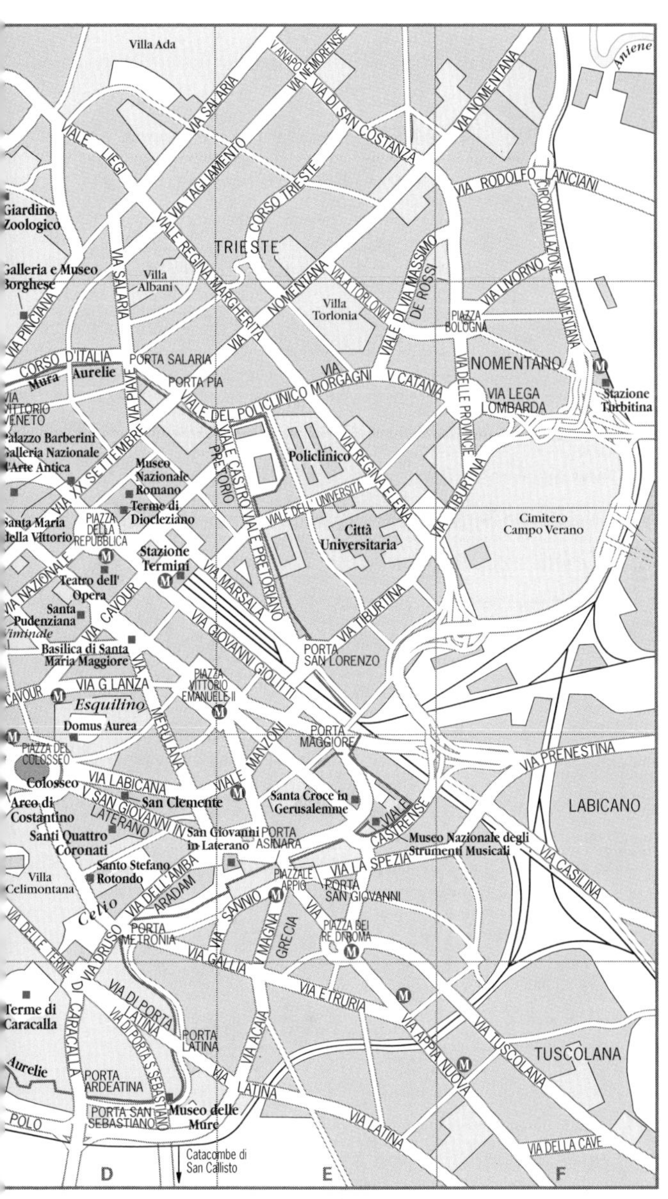

Villa Ada
Aniene
VIA SALARIA
VIA NEMORENSE
V. ANAPO
VIA DI SAN COSTANZA
VIA NOMENTANA
VIALE LIEGI
VIA TAGLIAMENTO
CORSO TRIESTE
VIA RODOLFO LANCIANI
CIRCONVALLAZIONE NOMENTANA
Giardino Zoologico
TRIESTE
VIALE REGINA MARGHERITA
VIA MASSIMO DE ROSSI
VIA LIVORNO
Galleria e Museo Borghese
Villa Albani
VIA SALARIA
VIA NOMENTANA
VIA A TORLONIA
Villa Torlonia
VIALE DI VIA MASSIMO
PIAZZA BOLOGNA
VIA PINCIANA
CORSO D'ITALIA
PORTA SALARIA
VIA MORGAGNI
V. CATANIA
VIA DELLE PROVINCIE
NOMENTANO
Mura Aurelie
PORTA PIA
VIA LEGA LOMBARDA
Stazione Tiburtina
VIA VITTORIO VENETO
VIA PIAVE
VIALE DEL POLICLINICO
VIALE CASTRO PRETORIO
Palazzo Barberini Galleria Nazionale d'Arte Antica
VIA XX SETTEMBRE
Policlinico
VIA REGINA ELENA
VIA TIBURTINA
Museo Nazionale Romano
Terme di Diocleziano
VIALE DELL' UNIVERSITÀ
Santa Maria della Vittorio
PIAZZA DELLA REPUBBLICA
Città Universitaria
Cimitero Campo Verano
Stazione Termini
VIALE PRETORIANO
VIA NAZIONALE
Teatro dell' Opera
VIA MARSALA
VIA CAVOUR
Santa Pudenziana
Viminale
VIA TIBURTINA
VIA GIOVANNI GIOLITTI
Basilica di Santa Maria Maggiore
PORTA SAN LORENZO
VIA G LANZA
PIAZZA VITTORIO EMANUELE II
CAVOUR
Esquilino
VIA MERULANA
Domus Aurea
PORTA MAGGIORE
VIA MANZONI
PIAZZA DEL COLOSSEO
VIA PRENESTINA
Colosseo
VIA LABICANA
VIALE
Santa Croce in Gerusalemme
LABICANO
Arco di Costantino
V. SAN GIOVANNI IN LATERANO
San Clemente
VIALE CASTRENSE
Santi Quattro Coronati
San Giovanni in Laterano
PORTA ASINARA
Museo Nazionale degli Strumenti Musicali
VIA CASILINA
Santo Stefano Rotondo
VIA LA SPEZIA
Villa Celimontana
VIA DELL'AMBA ARADAM
PIAZZALE APPIO
PORTA SAN GIOVANNI
Celio
VIA SANNIO
VIA MAGNA GRECIA
PIAZZA DEI RE DI ROMA
VIA DELLE TERME DI CARACALLA
PORTA METRONIA
VIA GALLIA
VIA DRUSO
VIA ETRURIA
Terme di Caracalla
VIA DI PORTA LATINA
VIA DI PORTA S. SEBASTIANO
PORTA LATINA
VIA ACAIA
VIA APPIA NUOVA
VIA TUSCOLANA
TUSCOLANA
Aurelie
PORTA ARDEATINA
VIA LATINA
PORTA SAN SEBASTIANO
Museo delle Mure
POLO
VIA LATINA
VIA DELLA CAVE
Catacombe di San Callisto
D
E
F

Rome

Rome has been a major city for longer than most other European capitals have existed. First the centre of the Roman Empire, a few centuries later it emerged as the centre of the Roman Catholic faith and finally, in 1870, it became the capital of the newly united Italy. In Rome's museums you can see artworks and artefacts from well over 2,000 years of history – exquisite ancient sculptures, delicate early Renaissance and opulent baroque paintings and much more. Sightseers' Rome breaks into two sections, ancient and Renaissance-baroque, but wherever you are you're likely to suddenly come across some remnant from centuries earlier than its surroundings.

Add the plethora of cool bars, ice-cream shops and restaurants as well as boutiques that attract the fashion-conscious and you've got a place that can guarantee a wonderful visit.

'At each step, a palace, a ruin, a garden, a desert, a little house, a stable, a triumphal arch, a colonnade, and all these so close together that one could draw them on a small sheet of paper.'

J W VON GOETHE
The Italian Journey (1786–8)

The City of Rome

Rome is an ideal city for sightseeing. Nearly all of the main monuments, museums and churches are within walking distance of each other and wherever you look, you are likely to come across some picturesque detail (flower-filled balconies, pristine shirts and sheets hanging out to dry, sleepy cats snoozing on car bonnets, ruined splendour, a little shrine with a portrait of the Madonna and perhaps even a candle) that is guaranteed to charm anybody used to more severe northern cities.

Mornings are the best times for catching opening hours; most churches and museums close at lunchtime and some, but by no means all, reopen at about 4 or 5PM. In summer the middle of the day tends to be too hot for sightseeing anyway so you can use this time for a rest or a leisurely lunch under the awnings of an outdoor restaurant.

The Vatican City, here viewed from across the Tiber, is the world's smallest independent sovereign state, and also the most ancient

What to See in Rome

ACCADEMIA DI SAN LUCA ✪

- 28C3
- Piazza dell'Accademia di San Luca 77
- 06 679 8850
- Mon, Wed, Fri, last Sun of month 10–1
- Barberini
- 52, 53, 56, 58, 60, 62, 71, 95, 115, 175, 492, 590 to Via del Tritone
- Few
- Free

Rome's academy of fine arts was founded by Pope Gregory XIII in 1577. It moved to its present site, the Palazzo Carpegna, in the 1930s when its previous home was cleared to make way for Via dei Fori Imperiali. The building has an unusual inclined spiral ramp (designed by Borromini), instead of stairs, to the upper levels. The collection is predominantly the work of academicians, or was presented by them, with plenty of fine portraits and still lifes. Highlights include a fresco fragment by Raphael, three works attributed to Titian, and paintings by Guido Reni, Van Dyck and Angelica Kauffman, one of the few women members of the academy.

ANTIQUARIO COMUNALE ✪

- 29D2
- Viale del Parco del Celio 22
- 06 700 1569
- Tue–Sat 9–6:30, Sun & hols 9–1. Closed Mon
- Circo Massimo, Colosseo
- 81, 175 to Via Celio Vibenna; tram 13, 30B to Viale del Parco del Celio
- Cheap

Set in a villa on the Celio hill, one of the seven hills of Rome, this small archaeological museum houses delightful artefacts of the area, many of which were unearthed at the end of the 19th century when the city was undergoing expansion. While the grander discoveries found their way into the more important national collections, the exhibits here include more mundane (but therefore perhaps more fascinating) everyday objects: kitchen equipment, tools and other domestic items, including a jointed doll from the 2nd century AD which was found in the tomb of a young girl.

ARA PACIS AUGUSTAE

- 28C4
- Via di Ripeta
- 06 3600 3471
- Tue–Sat 9–7, Sun 9–1
- 81, 115, 119, 125, 590, 913, 926 to Piazza Augusto Imperatore
- None
- Cheap

A modern glass pavilion on the banks of the Tiber houses some of the finest Roman sculpture to have survived. The Ara Pacis (altar of peace) was commissioned by the Senate in 13 BC to celebrate the victories of Emperor Augustus in Spain and Gaul; the outer walls of the enclosure that surrounds it depict a procession in which the faces of the imperial family and other important Romans can be seen. The panels by the entrances represent some symbolic moments from the history and mythology of Rome. Behind the altar is the round mausoleum of Augustus, built by the forward-planning emperor in 28 BC, 42 years before his death.

A marble relief depicting the earth goddess Tellus with animals at her feet

ARCO DI COSTANTINO

Although known as Constantine's Arch, scholars now believe that this magnificent monument outside the Colosseum was originally built in honour of the emperor, Trajan, and adopted by Constantine who made a few alterations and rededicated it to his own triumph over co-emperor Maxentius in AD 315. In any event, many of the carved panels and medallions were scavenged from older monuments, including the figures of Dacian prisoners at the top of the columns, which were almost certainly carved for Trajan.

29D2
Piazza del Colosseo
Colosseo
81, 175, 673 to Piazza del Colosseo
Free

BASILICA DI SAN GIOVANNI E PAOLO

Archaeology meets legend in this church, built over a two-storey Roman house, and containing Roman and medieval frescoes (seen by appointment only). Saints John and Paul were martyred here in 362, and their bodies, discovered only in the 20th century, are now in an ancient porphyry urn under the altar. The inside was modelled in 1718. There is a 13th-century fresco in a small room near the altar which depicts Christ and his Apostles. The church itself is predominantly Byzantine and has one of the most beautiful belltowers in Rome (1150), which was added by the only English pope, Nicholas Breakspeake (Adrian IV) as well as a majestic portico incorporating ancient columns.

29D3
Daily 8–11:30, 3:30–5:30
Piazza dei Santi Giovanni e Paolo
Colosseo
81, 673 to Via della Navicella

Arco di Costantino, like most monuments in Rome, is built in travertine, a white stone from Tivoli

In the Know

If you only have a short time to visit Rome, or would like to get a real flavour of the city, here are some ideas:

10 Ways To Be A Local

Learn a few phrases in Italian for a wonderfully appreciative response.
Be an assertive pedestrian; Roman drivers may look like maniacs but they can have lightning quick reactions and stop if you look determined to cross the road. Make sure you choose a spot where drivers will see you in time, however, and do not take any chances.
Dress comfortably but not scruffily; whether you like the style or not, Italians are nearly always well turned out.
Women, do not be offended by what you may see as invasive male attention – be politely assertive if you do not reciprocate the interest.
Relax; walk at a dignified, leisurely pace. Never rush.
Try not to drink cappuccino after dinner.
Eat ice-cream in the street, but nothing else.
Jaywalk; never use pavements when you can stroll down the middle of the cobbled street.
Do not get drunk. Italians seldom do.

10 Top Places To Have Lunch

Binario 4 (► 93).
Cecilia Metella (► 93).
Enoteca Corsi (► 94).
Frontoni (£) ✉ Viale Trastevere 52–8 ☎ 06 581 2436. A massive range of fillings from which to invent your own pizza.
Insalata Ricca (£) ✉ Piazza di Pasquino 72, and ✉ Largo dei Chiavari 8 ☎ 06 6880 3656. Light pasta dishes and big, meal-in-themselves salads.
Lorodinapoli (► 95).
Panattoni (► 96).
Sora Margherita (► 98).
Volpetti (£) ✉ Via della Scrofa 31 ☎ 06 686 1940. *Tavola calda* plus snacky things to eat on your feet or carry to the cavernous basement sitting area.
La Zucca Magica (► 99).

5 Best Views

- Gianicolo (► 43).
- Palatino (► 52).
- Pincio, Villa Borghese (► 12).
- Ponte Garibaldi
- St Peter's roof (► 26).

10 Top Activities

Explore: hire a *motorino* (scooter) ✉ Happy Rent, Piazza Esquilino 8, ☎ 06 481 8185).
Beach: Spend a day at the beach (► 115).
Football: go to a football match (► 115).
Concerts and films: go to an outdoor concert or film-screening (► 112).
Historic centre: spend half a day wandering around the historic centre, *without a guide book*, or in one of the parks (► 58).
Lunch: spend all afternoon having lunch (see list above or ► 92–99 for suggestions).
The Pope: listen to the Pope's multi-lingual Wednesday morning address in St Peter's Square (not during the summer).

A civilised lunch is important to Romans

Campo de' Fiori Market; romantic Pincio Hill

Coffee: have a really good coffee ⊠ Bar Sant'Eustachio, Piazza Sant'Eustachio 82, ☎ 06 686 1309).
Markets: spend a Sunday morning at Porta Portese flea market, or wander round another of the markets listed (► 109).
Window shop, or buy, in the designer area around Via Condotti (► 77).

5 Best Ice-Creams

- Giolitti (£) ⊠ Via Uffici del Vicario 40 ☎ 06 699 1243. Wide range of flavours.
- Da Mirella (£) ⊠ Trastevere end of Ponte Cestio, Isola Tiberina. *Grattachecha* (grated ice served with flavoured syrups or juice) during the summer.
- Il Palazzo del Freddo (£) ⊠ Via Principe Eugenio 65–7 ☎ 06 446 4740. Hundreds of different chilled desserts.
- San Calisto ⊠ Piazza San Calisto 4. Home-made taste.
- Tre Scalini (£) ⊠ Piazza Navona 28–32 ☎ 06 6880 1996. Rich chocolate *tartufi*.

10 Best Churches

- Gesù (► 43), for baroque opulence.
- Sant'Andrea al Quirinale (► 63), for Bernini.
- San Clemente (► 23), for history.
- San Giovanni in Laterano (► 65), for history.
- Santa Maria in Domnica (► 69), for mosaics.
- Santa Maria Maggiore (► 36), for mosaics and history.
- Santa Maria sopra Minerva (► 69), for art and originality (a Gothic church, rare for Rome).
- Santa Maria del Popolo (► 70), for art.
- Santa Maria in Trastevere (► 70) for mosaics.
- St Peter's (► 26), for size, importance and everything else.

BASILICA DI SANTA MARIA MAGGIORE 

29D3
Piazza di Santa Maria Maggiore
Daily 7–6:50
Termini, Cavour
16, 70, 590, 613, 714, 715 to Piazza Santa Maria Maggiore

On entering you are confronted by the seemingly endless rows of the nave's columns, the sweep of the cosmati floor and a ceiling decorated with the first gold to be brought from the New World. The Sistine (1585) and Pauline (1611) side chapels have opulent works by the most important artists of the day (Maderno, Reni and Ponzio to name but a few). The mosaics are, however, the basilica's glory. On the nave, a 5th-century narrative of the Old Testament and, in the apse, a stunning Glorification of Mary (1295) to whom the church is dedicated, Our Lady herself indicating the site by sending the sign of snowfall in August, an event still celebrated every year. The façade (1743–50) has been restored to its colourful magnificence.

Lavish mosaics at Basilica di San Paolo Fuori le Mura

BASILICA DI SAN PAOLO FUORI LE MURA ✪✪

Off map at 28C1
Via Ostiense 186
Mon–Sat 7:30–6:45, Sun 7–6:45
San Paolo
673, 761, 766 to San Paolo Basilica

Built on the site of St Paul's execution (c67), the present basilica dates from 1874 (Poletti), the original (c386–410) having burnt down in 1823. The only surviving parts are in the transept, the bronze doors (1070), an impressive example of a paschal candlestick (c1190), Arnolfo di Cambio's lovely Gothic *baldacchino* (1285) and the beautiful cloisters (1205–41) with their lavishly decorated mosaic columns (1214, Vassallettis). The general tone, however, is somewhat heavy-handed and 19th-century.

BASILICA DI SAN SEBASTIANO 

Off map at 29D1
Via Appia Antica
Fri–Wed 9–12, 2:30–5
118 to San Sebastiano

The basilica dates from the first half of the 5th century, on the spot where Peter and Paul's bodies were allegedly buried (their names can be seen in the graffiti on the walls of the catacombs beneath) – the present building dates from the early 17th century. The burial chambers (entered on the left of the façade) also contain exquisite Roman frescoes and stucco work. In pride of place, however, is the crypt of St Sebastian, whose image, pierced by the Diocletian guards' arrows, was particularly popular during the Renaissance. His body lies in the calm white-walled basilica above.

CAMPIDOGLIO (➤ 16, TOP TEN)

CAMPO DE' FIORI ✪✪✪

28C3
Piazza Campo de' Fiori
46, 62, 64 to Corso Vittorio Emaneule

Since Renaissance times, this has been one of the most bustling, busiest squares in central Rome and is still a great place to drop by at any time of day. Many of the old, crumbling buildings have been restored but the fascinatingly precarious many-layered Palazzo Pio Righetti, set at the square's northeastern corner, still looks as though one of its plant-covered balconies may be about to drop off. During the morning there is a colourful food market which packs up noisily as people saunter to the outdoor restaurants and bars at lunchtime. The foreboding, hooded figure in the centre of the piazza is Giordano Bruno, a philosopher who was burnt at the stake here in 1600 for heresy – the statue was erected when the popes lost their political control of Rome at Italian Unification. The maze of narrow streets that surround the piazza are full of carpenters' and jewellers' workshops, antique and second-hand clothing shops.

Campo de' Fiori translates as 'field of flowers'; today its market is full of fruit and vegetables

CASTEL SANT'ANGELO (➤ 17, TOP TEN)

CATACOMBS OF SAN CALLISTO ✪

29D1
Via Appia Antica 110
513 6725
Thu–Tue 8:30–12, 2:30–5:30. Closed Wed, Feb
218, 660 to San Callisto
Moderate

In ancient Rome, when Christianity was still very much a minority religion, it was against the law to bury the dead within the city confines. The catacombs of San Callisto, set in rolling parkland off the Via Appia Antica, are among the largest and most visited. Here there are thought to be a total of 20km of underground galleries on four levels lined with niches, or *loculi*, cut into the rock in which the shrouded bodies of the dead were laid to rest behind stone. Many of the early popes were buried here. The guided tours (offered in a range of languages including English, French and German) cover about 1km.

CATACOMBS OF SANTA PRISCILLA 

Off map at 29E5
Via Salaria 430
Tue–Sun 8:30–12, 2:30–5
56, 319 to Santa Priscilla
Moderate

These are probably the most charming of Rome's many catacomb complexes, in the Trieste area, northeast of the centre. The guided tour of the 50m-deep galleries, where 40,000 early Christians were laid to rest, is led by polyglot nuns and includes the earliest-known picture of the Virgin (2nd century AD) and a chapel with frescoes of bible stories. Priscilla was the widow of a Christian who was martyred by Emperor Domitian; the catacombs were dug under the foundations of Priscilla's house.

CHIESA NUOVA 

28B3
Piazza della Chiesa Nuova
8–12, 4.30–7
46, 62, 64 to Piazza della Chiesa Nuova

This was one of the churches which helped to transform the face of Rome in the Catholic resurgence of the 17th century. It is the seat of one of the most important Counter-Reformatory movements, St Phillip Neri's Oratorians. He originally wanted the nave simply whitewashed but did not reckon on the exuberant baroque fresco cycles that were to make their dazzling mark in Roman churches half a century later. The breath-taking example here is Pietro di Cortona's (on the nave ceiling, dome and apse, 1647–56). Next door is the brilliant Borromini's superb Oratory façade (1637–40), which is cunningly detailed.

Did you know ?

Filippo Neri (1515–95), the founder of the Oratorian order for whom Chiesa Nuova was built, was a Florentine banker who had a sudden conversion to Christianity and came to Rome. The emphasis he put on helping the poor, sick, old and young helped him to attract many followers, even though he is said to have made the richer ones humble themselves by dressing in rags.

The Chiesa Nuova set the style for Roman churches in the 17th century

CIRCO MASSIMO

There is not much of this ancient racetrack left but you can make out the tight oval that the charioteers careered round and the sloped side on which there was tiered seating for up to 300,000 spectators. The remains of that seating can still be seen at the circus's southern end, although the tower there is medieval. Chariot races were held here from the 4th century BC until they went out of fashion in the 6th century AD. The site was also used for wild-animal fights, mock sea battles (for which it was flooded), athletics and mass executions.

- 28C2
- Circo Massimo
- Circo Massimo
- 60, 75, 81, 160, 175, 628, 673; trams 13, 30B to Circo Massimo
- Possible
- Free

COLOSSEUM (COLOSSEO) (➤ 18, TOP TEN)

COLUMN OF MARCUS AURELIUS

In the square outside Palazzo Chigi, the prime minister's official residence, and the offices of newspaper *Il Tempo*, is an intricately carved column erected in honour of Emperor Marcus Aurelius after his death in AD 180. It is about 30m high and depicts scenes from the Emperor's successful German campaign. The statue of St Paul at the top of the column replaced the original of Marcus Aurelius on the orders of Pope Sixtus V in 1588.

- 28C3
- Piazza Colonna
- 119 to Piazza Colonna; 56, 60, 62, 81, 85, 95, 160, 175, 492, 628 to Via del Corso

DOMUS AUREA

Reopened to the public in 1999, after nearly 20 years of restoration, the Domus Aurea is Emperor Nero's 'Golden House'. After the great fire of AD 64 destroyed over half the city (and when Nero acquired his fiddling reputation), he built this huge symbol of Imperial power over the ruins. It is adorned with elegant fresco cycles and paintings. Tickets must be booked in advance.

- 29D3
- Via della Domus Aurea, Colle Oppio
- 06 6397 49907
- Daily 9–8
- Colosseo
- 75, 81, 85, 87, 175 to Colosseo
- Moderate

FONTANA DELLE TARTARUGHE

This delightfully delicate fountain, in Piazza Mattei, showing four male nymphs with tantalisingly enigmatic smiles cavorting provocatively around its edges, was the work of Giacomo della Porta and Taddeo Landini in the 1580s. The contrastingly precarious tortoises are believed to have been added by Bernini in the following century According to legend the fountain was erected overnight by the Duke of Mattei who wanted to show his potential father-in-law that he was still capable of achieving great things even though he had just lost his fortune. He also had one of the windows of his palace blocked up so that nobody else would ever see it from that superb vantage point.

- 28C3
- Piazza Mattei
- 44, 56, 60, 75, 170, 181, 710, 719 to Via Arenula

The beautiful Fontana delle Tartarughe is a landmark in one of the most elegant squares in central Rome

28C3
Piazza di Trevi
56, 58, 60, 61, 62, 95, 115, 119, 175, 492, 590 to Via del Tritone; 81, 85, 160, 628 to Via del Corso

FONTANA DI TREVI 

Even without Anita Ekberg, famous for the *Dolce Vita* scene in which she immerses herself in its turbulent waters, this effusively over-the-top fountain is a must for any visitor to Rome (and anyone with any intention of returning to the city should make sure they throw a coin into it). It was designed by Nicolò Salvi in 1762 and shows Neptune flanked by two massive steeds representing the calm and stormy sea bursting out of an artificial cliff-face which contrasts beautifully with the calm orderliness of the Palazzo Poli in whose wall it is built. The panels across the top depict the finding of the spring that feeds the ancient Roman canal leading into the fountain. By the way, the water is now said to contain bleach.

28C3
Via dei Fori Imperiali
Colosseo
85, 87, 175, 186 to Via dei Fori Imperiali

Above: *remains of smaller forums exist alongside the Roman Forum;* Opposite: *the Fontana di Trevi is a must for anyone's agenda*

FORI IMPERIALI 

Opposite and next to the main Roman Forum (► 22) lie the remaining fragments of five other, smaller, forums each built by an emperor to accommodate the overspill when the original forum became too small to cope with the demands of an expanding empire. To the right of the main entrance to the Roman Forum, underneath the Vittorio Emanuele Monument (► 46) is the oldest of these, built by Julius Caesar in AD 51; on the other side of the wide avenue that Mussolini built over other ancient remains to act as a triumphal route up to his Palazzo Venezia headquarters (► 56) are the remains of the forums of Trajan (Mercati Traianei ► 46), Augustus (where you can see some fine columns and friezes), Vespasian and Nerva.

THE FORUM (FORO ROMANO) (➤ 22, TOP TEN)

- 29D4
- Piazzale Scipione Borghese 5, Villa Borghese
- 06 854 8577/328101
- Tue–Sat 9–7, Sun, hol 9–1
- Bar
- Spagna
- 52, 53, 116 to Via Pinciana
- Moderate

GALLERIA BORGHESE ✪✪✪

Finally, after years of restoration work, the whole gallery (both sculpture and painting sections) reopened in summer 1997. The sculpture collection, on the ground floor, includes some important classical works, such as a *Sleeping Hermaphrodite* and a *Dancing Faun*, and the famous Canova sculpture of Paolina Bonaparte Borghese as a reclining Venus. The highlights, however, are the spectacular sculptures by Bernini. Cardinal Scipione Borghese, who had the villa and park built between 1608 and 1615, was Bernini's first patron. Here the sculptor's precocious talent is evident in works such as *The Rape of Proserpine*, *David* (thought to be a self-portrait) and *Daphne and Apollo*. The paintings are on the ground-floor walls and upstairs. Among the celebrated works are a *Deposition* by Raphael, Titian's early masterpiece, *Sacred and Profane Love*, a restored *Last Supper* by Jacopo Bassano, now rich and vibrant, Correggio's erotic *Danae*, and fine works by Guercino, Veronese, Giorgione and Andrea del Sarto. Caravaggio is represented here by six paintings, including one of his most important early works, the luscious *Boy with a Fruit Basket*, the *Sick Bacchus* and also the wonderfully realistic *Madonna of the Serpent*.

Canova's reclining Paolina Bonaparte Borghese

- 28C5
- Viale delle Belle Arti 131
- 06 322981
- Tue–Sat 9–7, Sun, hol 9–1
- Trams 19, 30B to Viale delle Belle Arti
- Moderate
- Villa Giulia (➤ 78)

GALLERIA NAZIONALE D'ARTE MODERNA E CONTEMPORANEA ✪

Cesare Bazzini's *Belle Epoque* palace is one of the few remaining buildings erected for the Rome International Exhibition of 1911 in the northwest area of the park of Villa Borghese. The collection covers the 19th and 20th centuries, mostly Italian artists – De Chirico, the Futurists and the *macchiaioli* (Italy's answer to the French Impressionists) – although there are also works by Gustav Klimt, Paul Cézanne and Henry Moore. Major temporary exhibitions are also staged. The museum has been extensively renovated, long-closed wings are being opened up, there is a new sculpture section, and important contemporary acquisitions have been made.

IL GESÙ ✪✪

This church spans the whole of the baroque: from the floor plan (by Vignola, 1568, and probably based on the ideas of one of Michelangelo's last architectural plans), through the façade (with its triangular pediment and side scrolls) and dome (by Giacomo della Porta, 1575) to Pietro da Cortona's altar of St Xavier (1674) and Andrea Pozzo's almost vulgarly ornate chapel of St Ignatius (1696). This is the central church of the Jesuits, the severe order founded by Ignatius Loyola in the 16th century – its design has been imitated in Jesuit church-building all over the world. Next door are the rooms occupied by Loyola (usually open when the church is) which have a wonderful *trompe l'oeil* fresco by Pozzo.

28C3
Piazza del Gesù
Oct–Mar, 6–12:30, 4:30–7:15; Apr–Sep, 6–12:30, 4–7:30
44, 46, 60, 62, 64, 70, 81, 87, 115, 186, 492, 710 to Largo di Torre Argentina

THE GHETTO ✪✪

The Jewish community in Rome is one of the oldest in Europe and dates from the 1st century BC, although it first settled this area north of Isola Tiberina (➤ 45) in the 13th century. From the mid-16th century until Italian Unification in 1870 Roman Jews were enclosed behind high walls in this warren of narrow, winding alleyways which still house kosher butchers, excellent Jewish restaurants and a baker offering Roman Jewish specialities such as *torta di ricotta* and sweet 'pizzas' made with candied and dried fruit. At the heart of the ghetto was the old fish market held in front of the Portico d'Ottavia, the only remains of a vast shop and temple complex, which was renovated in the 1st century BC and named in honour of Emperor Augustus's sister Octavia.

28C3
Via del Portico d'Ottavia (and the streets north)
44, 46, 60, 62, 64, 70, 81, 87, 115, 492 to Largo di Torre Argentina; 8 to Via Arenula

GIANICOLO ✪✪

The hill that rises between Trastevere and the Vatican to the southwest of the Tiber has some of the best views of central Rome and is a popular lovers' tryst. At its summit is Piazza Giuseppe Garibaldi, where a rousing equestrian statue of Giuseppe Garibaldi commemorates his 1849 victory over the French here when he led the troops of the Roman Republic in the struggle for Italian unification.

28B3
Viale Aldo Fabrizi
870 to Passeggiata del Gianicolo

Below: *Gianicolo hill takes its name from the god Janus*

Gianicolo to the Ghetto

Distance
4km

Time
2 hours, or 4 with stops for coffee and visits

Start point
Piazza Garibaldi
 28B3
41

End point
The Ghetto
28C3
44

Lunch
Sora Margherita (£)
Piazza delle Cinque Scole 30
686 4002

The church of San Bartolomeo stands on the tiny Isola Tiberina

Start at Piazza Garibaldi on the Gianicolo (► 43).

Follow the road southeast, past the busts of heroes of the Risorgimento, to the gateway, turn left down the staircase.

But first look at the monumental baroque Fontana Paola, where people once washed their clothes.

Follow the road down past the Spanish Embassy and turn left on Via Garibaldi. Go to the bottom where, to the left, is Porta Settimiana (1498), the gateway pilgrims used to reach the Vatican. Turn right down Via della Scala.

The church of Santa Maria della Scala dates from the late 16th century. Its plain façade hides a rich, cluttered interior.

Continue straight into Piazza San Egidio, past the Museo del Folklore (► 48), and turn left, passing Vicolo del Piede and the Pasquino cinema, into Piazza Santa Maria in Trastevere.

Here are the church (► 70), with its 12th-century mosaics on the façade, and fountain by Carlo Fontana (1692).

Continue straight through the piazza and follow Via della Lungaretta to Piazza Sonnino.

On the right is the 12th-century bell tower of the ancient church of San Crisogono, rebuilt in the 16th century.

Cross the piazza. The left-corner tower is 13th-century and home to the Dante Society. Go on to Piazza di Piscinula, turn left up a staircase along the side of an old palace and cross the Lungotevere to get to Isola Tiberina (► 45).

Isola Tiberina somewhat resembles a ship and was a strategic point in ancient times being one of the few points at which the Tiber could be easily crossed.

Cross the island to the Ghetto (► 43); on the right is the Synagogue (1874) and a small museum. This area is a good lunch stop.

ISOLA TIBERINA

From the right-hand (Ghetto-) side of the river, Isola Tiberina is reached via the oldest original bridge over the Tiber, the Ponte Fabricio (62 BC). Originally the walls of the buildings rose directly out of the river but, since the end of the 19th century, the island has been surrounded by a wide embankment, now a popular spot for taking early-season sun. The church of San Bartolomeo was built in the 10th century on the site of a 3rd-century BC temple to the god of healing, Aesculapius, and the connection with health has been continued by the Fatebenefratelli hospital which now covers most of the island. Downstream you can see the one remaining arch of the Ponte Rotto (broken bridge) which was the first stone bridge in Rome (142 BC), although it had already fallen down at least twice before this mid-16th-century rebuild collapsed in 1598.

28C2
Isola Tiberina
717, 774, 780 to Lungotevere dei Cenci or to Lungotevere Anguillara

The Landmark Trust
This charity rescues buildings, and lets them out for holidays. When the Keats-Shelley Memorial Association launched an appeal for funds to maintain the Keats-Shelley Memorial House, the Trust took on the 3rd-floor flat, restoring it to its appearance in about 1800. The sitting room overlooks the Spanish Steps. Handbook and prices from: The Landmark Trust, Shottesbrooke, Maidenhead, Berkshire SL6 3SW, UK (01628 825925).

KEATS-SHELLEY MEMORIAL HOUSE

Since 1909 the house at the foot of the Spanish Steps, where Keats died of consumption aged only 25 in February 1821, has been a memorial to Keats, Shelley, Byron and other romantic poets. The rooms which Keats occupied on the first floor now contain a collection of manuscripts, documents and ephemera including Keats's death mask and a lock of his hair. There is also an extensive specialist library. There is a **Landmark Trust** flat on the 3rd floor.

28C4
Piazza di Spagna 26
06 678 4235
Summer, Mon–Fri 9–1, 3–6; winter, Mon–Fri 9–1, 2:30–5:30
Spagna
119 to Piazza di Spagna
Moderate

LARGO ARGENTINA

Behind one of the busiest bus intersections in the Area Sacra at Largo Argentina are the remains of four Republican-era temples, known as temples A, B, C and D (in alphabetical order starting nearest the main bus stop). Temple C is the oldest (4th century BC) while 3rd-century BC Temple A was used as a church during the Middle Ages (remains of two apses); behind it are the drains of a massive public toilet. Julius Caesar was murdered near here in 44BC when the Senate were using the Curia of Pompey as a temporary meeting place while the main senate house was being restored. The area is rarely open to the public.

28C3
Largo di Torre Argentina

Some evenings in summer for guided tours in English and Italian
44, 46, 56, 60, 62, 65, 70, 81, 87, 94, 115, 186, 492, to Largo di Torre Argentina

Right: *This statue stands before the Vittorio Emanuele Monument, built to celebrate the first King of Unified Italy*

Did you know ?

*Until the end of the 19th century, Piazza Venezia was the finishing point of the riderless horse races that were held at Carnevale (the week before Lent begins) down Via del Corso from Piazza del Popolo. The horses were urged on by the use of stimulants, fireworks and ropes studded with nails that were tied around their bodies. The Museo del Folklore (**► 48**) has some contemporary engravings of the event.*

28C3
Clivo Argentario 1, Via di San Pietro in Carcere
06 679 2902
Oct–Mar, 9–12, 2:30–5; Apr–Sep, 9–12, 2:30–6
44, 46, 81, 95, 160, 170, 181, 628, 713, 719 to Piazza Venezia
Donation

MAMERTINE PRISON (CARCERE MAMERTINO)

This dank, dark dungeon dates from the 4th century BC and was where any potential threats to state security, including the leaders of opposing armies, were thrown to starve to death (their bodies were dropped into the main sewer, the Cloaca Maxima). St Peter is said to have been imprisoned here before being crucified and an altar has been built next to the spring that he miraculously created in order to christen other prisoners and two of his guards.

28C3
Via IV Novembre 94
06 679 0048
Tue–Sun 9–7
60, 64, 70, 170 to Via IV Novembre
Limited
Cheap; free last Sun of month

MERCATI TRAIANEI

One of the first shopping malls in the world, Emperor Trajan commissioned this five-level complex of about 150 small shops from the Greek architect Apollodorus of Damascus in the early 2nd century AD. Goods from all over the empire were sold here and shops were probably arranged by area – storage jars found on the first floor suggest that wine and oil were sold here while fruit and flower shops probably occupied the ground floor. The finely carved column next to the markets was erected in AD 113 to celebrate Trajan's campaigns in Dacia (Romania). It is 40m high and originally bore a statue of the emperor which was replaced by the present St Peter in 1587.

28C3
Piazza Venezia
44, 46, 81, 95, 160, 170, 175, 181, 628, 710, 713, 719 to Piazza Venezia

MONUMENTO A VITTORIO EMANUELE II

A monument of many names; *il Vittoriale* was built at the end of the 19th century to honour the first king of the united Italy whose equestrian statue stands out proudly in front. Behind him burns the eternal flame guarded day and night by armed soldiers at the Altar of the Nation while other, less complimentary, ways of referring to this colonnaded mass of white marble include the 'typewriter' and the 'wedding cake'. In any event, you cannot miss it.

Off map south
Viale Lincoln 3, EUR
592 6148

MUSEO DELL'ALTO MEDIOEVO 

This museum houses decorative arts of the 5th to 11th centuries (from the fall of the Roman Empire to the Renaissance). Most of the artefacts were found locally, and include some beautiful jewellery from the 7th century,

fragments of elaborate embroidery from clerical robes and a delicate 5th-century gold fibula found on the Palatine hill. Swords made from gold and silver, intricately carved and decorated, demonstrate how objects made from pure metals can withstand the test of time better than more reactive ones.

Mon–Sat 9–2, Sun, hol 9–1:30
Magliana
714, 715 to Piazzale G Marconi
Cheap

MUSEO DELLE ARTI E TRADIZIONI POPOLARI

A huge collection of fascinating objects relating to Italian folk art and rural traditions. On display are agricultural and pastoral tools, including elaborately decorated carts and horse tack, artisan instruments and handiwork, clothing, furniture, musical instruments, some exquisite traditional jewellery and photographs documenting how the exhibits were used.

Off map south
Piazza G Marconi 8, EUR
06 592 6148
Mon–Sat 9–2, Sun 9–1
Magliana
714, 715
Cheap

MUSEO BARRACCO ✪

28B3
Corso Vittorio Emanuele II 158
06 6880 6848
Tue–Sat 9–7, Sun, hol 9–1
46, 62, 64 to Corso Vittorio Emanuele
None
Cheap

This is one of Rome's most charming museums but often overlooked. The exquisite, small collection of Assyrian, Egyptian, Greek and Roman sculptures (including a series of Roman heads minus their noses) and artefacts was created by Senator Giovanni Barracco and presented to the city in 1902. Underneath the museum (ask the attendants to take you down) are remains of what is said to be a Roman fish shop, complete with counter and a water trough. Fresco fragments (from the 4th century AD) found there are displayed on the ground floor.

MUSEO DELLA CIVILTÀ ROMANA ✪

Off map at 28C1
Piazza Gianni Agnelli 10, EUR
06 592 6041
Tue–Sat 9–7, Sun, hol 9–1
Magliana
714, 715 to Piazza G. Marconi
Moderate
Museo dell'Alto Medioevo, Museo Nazionale delle Arti e Tradizioni Popolari

The models and reconstructions inside this grandly fascist building give a sense of what life was really like in ancient Rome and help put into context the fragments and artefacts that are the treasures of so many of the city's museums. There are busts and statues of the key figures of the day, reproductions of Roman furniture, surgical tools, musical instruments and sundials. The highlight is a giant scale model of Rome in the 4th century AD, at the time of Constantine, showing every building within the circular Aurelian walls.

Models recreate in detail early Roman life for us

MUSEO DEL FOLKLORE E DEI POETI ROMANESCHI 

28B2
Piazza Sant'Egidio 1/b
06 581 6563
Tue–Sat 9–7, Sun 9–1
280 to Lungotevere Sanzio; 64, 70, 71, 87, 492 to Largo Argentina then tram 8 to Viale di Trastevere
Cheap

The museum opened in 1978 in a former Carmelite convent behind the church of Santa Maria in Trastevere. Everyday life in 17th- and 18th-century Italy, including festivals and customs, is illustrated by paintings, prints, reconstructions and waxworks, all among an interesting diversity of artefacts from the period when the popes ruled Rome. There is also memorabilia relating to famous Roman poets including Giuseppe Gioacchino Belli and Carlo Alberto Salustri (better known as Trilussa). Each of these local-dialect poets appropriately has a Trastevere square named after him.

MUSEO NAPOLEONICO ✪

28B3
Via Zanardelli 1
06 6880 6286
Tue–Sat 9–7, Sun, hols 9–1
70, 81, 87, 115, 119, 186, 492, 628 to Via Zanardelli
 Cheap

This collection of art and memorabilia relating to Napoleon includes portraits by David and Gerard, political cartoons, uniforms and the audacious French general's baby teeth. Napoleon was only in Rome for a short time, although his mother and sister Paolina, who married Prince Camillo Borghese, settled here. Paolina was portrayed by Canova as Venus (► 42) and a cast of her breast is on display.

MUSEO NAZIONALE DELLE PASTE ALIMENTARI ✪

A visit to this well-organised museum will tell you everything you ever needed to know about pasta (and a lot more besides). A portable CD player provides commentary (in Italian, English, Japanese, French or German) to the displays. The entire gamut of pasta production is covered, and there are examples of equipment and machinery used over the years, some rather questionable artworks on the pasta theme and photos of Italian and international personalities tucking into steaming plates of the nation's favourite dish.

- 76B1
- Piazza Scanderberg 117
- 06 699 1119
- Mon–Sun 9:30–5:30
- 81, 85, 160, 628 to Via del Corso
- Expensive

MUSEO NAZIONALE ROMANO ✪✪

The beautifully restored Palazzo Massimo is a fine example of how Rome pulled out all the stops for the Holy Year (2000) and gave the national collection of ancient art and sculpture a setting it deserves. The upper floors are bursting with more archaeological goodies from the Roman age (2nd century BC to 4th century AD) such as some exquisite mosaics from Livia's palace and a superb marble statue of a discus thrower (a Roman copy of a 5th-century BC Greek bronze). It's definitely worth equipping yourself with a well-illustrated guidebook from the museum's excellent shop to negotiate your route around the extensive displays.

Spacious and airy rooms open onto a central courtyard, the exhibits are clearly labelled and each room has information sheets in English and Italian. You are greeted by a huge alabaster and basalt statue of Minerva, then follow several rooms of portrait busts from the 3rd to 1st centuries BC, painted friezes, mosaics, sarcophagi and intricately carved pedestals. An extensive collection of coins dating back to the 7th century BC is one of the highlights.

- 29D4
- 67 Piazza dei Cinquecento
- 06 4890 3500
- Tue–Sat 9–7, Sun, hol 9–2
- Termini
- 36, 38, 40, 60, 64, 65, 105, 115, 170, 175, 310, 317, 319, 613, 714, 715, 910 to Termini
- Good
- Moderate

Wander past every type of ancient Roman sculpture in the Museo Nazionale Romano's vast cloister

Food & Drink

Italian cuisine is among the best (and, according to research, the most healthy) in the world. Each region has its own particular specialities, making use of the abundant raw ingredients that grow there, and some typically Roman dishes also owe much to the history of the city and its occupants.

Pasta

Classic Roman pasta dishes are *spaghetti alla carbonara* with bacon, eggs and *pecorino* (matured sheep's milk cheese, often used as an alternative to parmesan); *pasta all'arrabbiata* ('angry pasta' means hot) with tomatoes and fiery hot *peperoncino* (chilli); and *all'Amatriciana*, which is more or less the same with added bacon. *Pasta e ceci* is like a thick soup made with small pasta and chick peas, while *gnocchi* are hunger-busting potato dumplings served with butter and sage or tomato sauce.

Above: *speciality pasta in many shapes and colours*

Below: *making pizza*

Meat and Offal

Tradition has it that, while most of the butchered animal went to the rich, poor Romans had to make do with the left-over offal. This has led to an abundance of dishes using tripe, liver, kidneys, heart, bone marrow (*ossobuco* is a bone out of which the marrow is scooped) and brains. Perhaps the most extreme of these is *pagliata*, which is the intestine of a milk-fed calf, often served with *bucatini*, the thin, tube-like pasta it resembles. The best place for eating offal is in Testaccio where restaurants around the ex-abattoir Mattatoio have a long tradition of this type of cuisine.

Nowadays, however, even the most basic *trattoria* will offer beef and veal steaks, sausages (often with brown lentils) and flavoursome lamb from nearby Abruzzo. *Saltimbocca alla Romana* ('jumps into the mouth') is veal wrapped in raw ham and cooked with sage.

Fish

Apart from the traditional *baccalà* (cod fillets fried in batter and served as a snack or first course in *pizzerie*), the range of fish in Rome is immense and includes seafood such as mussels, clams (especially in *spaghetti alle vongole)*, squid and prawns.

Vegetables and Snack Foods

Some of the vegetables common in Rome make good snacks – courgette flowers fried in batter, artichokes either steamed or baked, potato or spinach croquettes. *Supplì*, rice croquettes with a melted mozzarella filling, are another between-meals filler.

Other vegetables include *fave* (broad beans), often eaten with *pecorino* cheese in spring, spinach, broccoli, rocket and *puntarelle*, a crispy salad vegetable served in a vinegary sauce with anchovies.

Wines and Drinks

In Rome most of the house white wines come from Frascati and the Castelli Romani that surround the city. Orvieto in Umbria is another source of inexpensive white wine. House reds come from slightly further afield, Montepulciano from Abruzzo (not to be confused with the Vino Nobile of Montepulciano in Tuscany, which is a top-quality wine) and Chianti from Tuscany.

As well as wine, Italy has a massive range of drinks to stimulate the appetite before you eat or to help you digest the meal afterwards. *Aperitivi* include Campari and Martini-type aromatics, *prosecco*, a light fizzy white wine and *analcolici*, non-alcoholic versions of Campari and Martini. *Digestivi* include grappas that range from firewater to the smoothest of the smooth and *amari*, those thick, sticky concoctions made with herbs.

Frascati and Orvieto, two local sources for house white wines

Fresh fish on sale at Campo de' Fiori

Dolci

If you don't opt for the ubiquitous *tiramisu*, for which nearly every restaurant has its own subtly different recipe, you could finish your meal with a slice of cake (*torta*); chocolate, fruit or *torta della nonna* with custard and pine kernels. Especially in winter, you'll be offered *crème caramel, crème brulée, panna cotta* ('cooked cream', a thick but light custard often served with berries), or ice-cream.

28C2
Through the Forum or Via di San Gregorio
06 699 0110
(➤ 22) for hours
Colosseo, Circo Massimo
75, 81, 175, 673 to Via di San Gregorio

PALATINO

Attached to the Forum (admission includes both), this is a peaceful, lush, hilly area covered with the remains of the massive palaces that the Roman emperors built for themselves. Most of what is on view dates from the 1st century AD. It can be frustrating to visit because many of the main attractions close at short notice and little is labelled, but there are guaranteed views of the Forum (➤ 22) from the delightful semi-formal Orti Farnesiani (Farnese Gardens), laid out for Cardinal Alessandro Farnese in the 16th century. Underneath the gardens is a long tunnel built by Nero and decorated with stucco reliefs, some of which have survived. He may have intended this as a promenade for hot weather although some researchers believe that it led all the way to his massive palace overlooking the spot where the Colosseum stands today. Other highlights of the Palatine (although not always accessible) include the baths of Septimus Severus, the wall paintings in the house of Livia, traces of an 8th century BC village of huts and the complicated ground floor layouts of the Domus Flavia and the Domus Augustana.

Ruins of Roman palaces cover the Palatine Hill

PALAZZO BARBERINI (➤ 19, TOP TEN)

28C3
Via della Pilotta 17
06 679 4362
Sat 9–1
40, 44, 46, 60, 81, 94, 95, 160, 170, 181, 628, 710, 713, 719 to Piazza Venezia
Expensive

PALAZZO COLONNA

Some of the most beautiful ceiling frescoes in Rome adorn the opulent 18th-century galleries. There are some fine portraits in the first room but the eye automatically wanders through to the lavishly gilded Great Hall with its magnificent ceiling painting representing the life of Marcantonio Colonna. As you step down take care not to trip over the cannonball which became lodged there during the siege of Rome in 1849. Two ornate cabinets – one with inlaid carved ivory panels reproducing works by Raphael and Michelangelo (the central panel is his *Last Judgement* from the Sistine Chapel) – give the Room of the Desks its name. The Apotheosis of the Colonna Pope Martin V decorates the ceiling of the fourth room where Annibale Caracci's delightful *Bean Eater* makes an amusing change from more serious subjects. In the Throne Room a chair is kept ready (turned to the wall) in case of a papal visit.

PALAZZO CORSINI ✪✪

Once the residence of Queen Christina of Sweden (➤ 14), the palace houses part of the national art collection (the more important part is at Palazzo Barberini, (➤ 19). The galleries, decorated with arresting *trompe l'oeil* frescoes, are filled predominantly with paintings from the 16th and 17th centuries. In room 1 Van Dyck's superb *Madonna della Paglia* and Murillo's *Madonna and Child* stand out among many other paintings of the same subject; one by Girolamo Siciolante de Sermoneta is frightening in its awfulness with an over-rosy, muscular baby seeming to choke on its mother's milk. Do not miss the paintings of the Bologna school in room 7, among which Guido Reni's richly coloured and expressive *St Jerome* and melancholy *Salome*, Giovanni Lanfranco's very beautiful *St Peter Healing St Agatha* and the haunting *Ecce Homo* by Guercino are highlights.

- 28B3
- Via della Lungara 10
- 06 6880 2323
- Tue–Fri 9–7, Sat 9–2, Sun 9–1. Closed Mon
- 323, 280 to Lungotevere della Farnesina
- Few
- Expensive
- Villa Farnesina

Looking towards the Palatino from the Forum

28C3
Piazza del Collegio Romano 2
06 679 7323
Daily 10–5; private apartments 10:30–12:30
60, 62, 81, 85, 95, 160, 175, 492, 628 to Via del Corso; 44, 46, 57, 170, 1811, 719, 713, 719 to Piazza Venezia
Few
Moderate

PALAZZO DORIA PAMPHILI

The seat of the noble Roman family since the late Renaissance, Palazzo Doria Pamphili takes up an entire block of Via del Corso. Extensive renovations took place in 1996. In the grand reception rooms, through which you enter, and the original picture galleries with their elaborate frescoed ceilings, the paintings are hung exactly as they were in the 18th century, cluttered side by side from floor to ceiling. Four rooms now house masterpieces from the 15th to 17th centuries including works by Hans Memling, Raphael, Titian, Tintoretto and two early paintings by Caravaggio. The star of the collection is the Velasquez portrait of Doria Pope, Innocent X, resplendent in vermilion robes, majestically positioned in its own chamber. For an extra charge take a guided tour of the fascinating private apartments.

28C3
Via Nazionale 194
06 488 5465/464 5903
10–9. Closed Tue
Bar/café (£)
Repubblica, Cavour
64, 70, 71, 75, 115, 116, 170 to Via Nazionale
Few
Moderate

PALAZZO DELLE ESPOSIZIONI

Rome's purpose-built (1883) palace of the fine arts has had a chequered history. Apart from serving its original brief, the building has housed the Communist Party, been a mess for allied servicemen, a polling station and a public lavatory. After years of restoration it was relaunched in 1990, and is today a vibrant multi-media centre with a strong emphasis on film and video in addition to an active programme of Italian and international exhibitions (both historical and contemporary). Good museum marketing has taken over and there is an excellent shop, a pleasant indoor café and a roof garden.

28B3
Corso del Rinascimento
Sep–Jun; some Sun for guided tours in Italian
70, 81, 87, 115, 186, 492, 628 to Corso del Rinascimento

PALAZZO MADAMA

This pretty little palace has been the seat of the Italian senate since 1871, hence the armed police and military guard. It was built as the Medici family's Roman residence in the 16th century although the Madame after whom it was named was Margaret of Parma, an illegitimate daughter of Emperor Charles V who lived here in the 1560s. The icing-like stucco façade of cherubs and fruit was added in the 17th century.

76A1
Piazza di Montecitorio
Sep–Jun; some Sun for guided tours in Italian
81, 115, 492, 590, 628 to Via del Corso

PALAZZO DI MONTECITORIO

Bernini did the original designs for this concave palace, although all that remains of his work are the clock-tower, the columns and the window sills. In 1871 it became the Chamber of Deputies and had doubled in size by 1918. In the sloping piazza in front of the palace there are often political demonstrations; a strong police presence keeps people at a respectful distance from the main entrance

through which Italy's 630 parliamentarians enter and exit. The obelisk in the piazza was brought from Egypt by Augustus in 10 BC to act as the pointer of a giant (but, due to subsidence, inaccurate) sundial in nearby Campo Marzio. It was re-erected here in 1787.

Palazzo Doria Pamphili is dazzling even by Roman standards

PALAZZO DEL QUIRINALE 

This large orange palace, with the picture-book round look-out tower to its left, is the official residence of the President of the Republic of Italy and is guarded by exotically uniformed *Granatieri* who have been specially selected for their height and good looks. It was built in the 1570s as a papal summer palace for the fresh air on the highest of Rome's seven hills. Opposite, the two massive men with somewhat undersized horses are ancient Roman copies of a 5th-century BC Greek sculpture of Castor and Pollux, the two god-knights who came to Rome's rescue during an early battle. The palace is open to the public on the second and fourth Sunday of the month from September through to July.

28C3
Piazza del Quirinale
64, 70, 75, to Via IV Novembre

Italian Navy band marching out of the Quirinale

Discover Borromini's clever trompe l'oeil *perspective in the courtyard of Palazzo Spada*

28B3
Piazza Capo di Ferro 3
06 686 1158
Tue–Sat 9–7, Sun, hol 9–1
280 to Lungotevere dei Tebaldi; 170 to Via Arenula; 40, 64, 70, 71, 492 to Largo Argentina then tram 8
Moderate

PALAZZO SPADA ✪✪

Built in 1540, the ornate palace was acquired by Cardinal Bernardino Spada in the 17th century. In addition to housing his collection in the Galleria Spada, the palace is the seat of the Italian Council of State and thus under prominent *Carabinieri* guard. Among the 17th- and 18th-century paintings are a jewel-like *Visitation* attributed to Andrea del Sarto and works by Guercino and Rubens. Cardinal Spada also collected Roman sculpture – the restored *Seated Philosopher* is a highlight.

The most delightful aspect of the palace is Borromini's ingenious *trompe l'oeil* perspective in the lower courtyard (ask the attendants or porter to let you in). A long colonnade stretches out to a large statue at the end. Go closer to see that the colonnade is in fact only a quarter of the length it seems, and the statue much smaller than it first appears.

28C3
Via del Plebiscito 118
06 6999 4243
Tue–Sun 9–2
44, 46, 57, 75, 81, 94, 95, 160, 170, 181, 6228, 710, 713, 719 to Piazza Venezia
Few Moderate

PALAZZO VENEZIA ✪✪

Rome's most important collection of medieval decorative arts includes fine examples of Byzantine jewellery, silver work, ceramics, porcelain, tapestries and armour. There is a superb group of intricately carved Florentine wooden marriage chests, some small 16th-century bronzes and fine religious paintings by early Renaissance artists. Palazzo Venezia often hosts special exhibitions in the opulent main halls overlooking the piazza. Mussolini used the impressive, vast Sala del Mappamondo as his office.

PANTHEON (► 20, TOP TEN)

PASQUINO

Physically, Pasquino has seen better days; all that remain of this 3rd-century BC sculpture near Piazza Navona, are a twisted torso and a weather-beaten face. But, for several centuries after he was propped up here in the early 16th century Pasquino played an important role as Rome's most talkative 'talking statue'. During the days of papal rule (until 1870) there were few safe outlets for dissent and those with political or social axes to grind came at dead of night to attach their written complaints to one of the talking statues.

28B3
Piazza di Pasquino
46, 622, 64 to Corso Vittorio Emanuele

PIAZZA BARBERINI 

The traffic-filled square at the foot of Via Veneto, the street that was the hub of the *Dolce Vita* days of swinging Rome in the 1960s, contains two fountains designed by Bernini in the 1640s for the Barberini family. At the join with Via

Bernini's Fontana della Api in Piazza Barberini

Veneto is the Fontana delle Api whose grotesquely large bees (the Barberini family crest) crawl over the unassuming basin. In the centre of the square is the far more dramatic *Tritone*, whose well-muscled body is supported by his own fish-tail legs and four dolphins as he enthusiastically blows water through a vast sea-shell.

28C4
Piazza Barberini
Barberini
60, 61, 62, 492, 590 to Piazza Barberini

PIAZZA DEI CAVALIERI DI MALTA 

Piranesi, famous for his surreal etchings of Roman views, designed this peaceful piazza in 1765 and decorated it with the symbols and devices of the Order of the Knights of Malta whose priory is here. In the door of the priory is a peep-hole which offers a magnificent miniature view of the dome of St Peter's seen beyond the tree-lined avenue of the priory's garden. This part of the city, the Aventine, has always been a genteel residential area.

28C2
Piazza dei Cavalieri di Malta

95, 713, 716 to Lungotevere Aventino

The Historic Centre

Distance
4km

Time
2 hours without stops, 3½ hours with

Start point
Piazza Farnese
28B3
to Corso Vittorio Emanuele

End point
Piazza del Popolo

28C4
Flaminio
to Piazzale Flaminio

Lunch
Hostaria Romanesca (£)
Campo de' Fiori 40
06 686 4024

Combine this walk with visits to the Forum and the Vatican and you can claim to have 'done' Rome.

*From Piazza Farnese take Vicolo dei Baulari into Campo de' Fiori (**➤ 37**), where you can have an early lunch. Go to the far left-hand corner and into Piazza della Cancelleria.*

Palazzo della Cancelleria (now Vatican offices) was built in 1485–1513 for a great-nephew of the Pope.

Turn right on Corso Vittorio Emanuele; cross at the lights. Continue down Via Cuccagna into Piazza Navona. Halfway up the piazza, Corso Agone leads to Palazzo Madama; Via Salvatore runs alongside, to San Luigi dei Francesi on the left. Continue to the Pantheon.

Pause, watch the activity, or have an expensive coffee.

Take the right-hand alley opposite the Pantheon, Vicolo della Maddalena, turn right down Via del Vicario into Piazza del Montecitorio. Follow Via di Guglia, in front of the palazzo, turn left at Via dei Pastini into Piazza di Pietra.

Here there are columns of a 2nd-century AD temple of Hadrian.

Walk past the columns, down Via di Pietra, cross Via del Corso and continue straight up Via di Muratte to the Trevi fountain. Follow Via della Stamperia, right of the fountain, turn right up Via del Tritone, cross and turn left on Via Due Macelli to Piazza di Spagna.

Rest by Bernini's Fontana della Barcaccis to observe the vitality as tourists and shoppers converge.

Climb the Spanish Steps, turn left, past Villa Medici (16th century, now the French Academy), take the path on the right to the Pincio Gardens.

Here are wonderful views over Piazza del Popolo.

PIAZZA FARNESE

Dominated by Palazzo Farnese, which was designed for Farnese Pope Paulo III in the 1530s by – among others – Michelangelo, this spacious, nearly traffic-free square is a peaceful contrast to the nearby buzz of Campo de' Fiori (➤ 37) and a good spot for a quiet rest. The palace is now the French Embassy and at night Caracci's ceiling paintings on the first floor are illuminated. The two vast granite fountains were assembled in the 17th century from bath-tubs found at Caracalla's baths (➤ 75). They are decorated with lilies, the Farnese family crest.

28B3
Piazza Farnese
46, 62, 64 to Corso Vittorio Emanuele

PIAZZA NAVONA (➤ 21, TOP TEN)

PIAZZA DEL POPOLO

For the Grand Tourists of the 18th and 19th centuries this was the first sight of Rome as their luggage-laden carriages trundled through the Porta del Popolo. It was also where condemned criminals were executed (by having their heads smashed with hammers until the more humane guillotine took over in the early 19th century). It is overlooked to the east by the Pincio Gardens, which has marvellous views over the historic city centre and to the Vatican. The two apparently identical churches at the end of Via del Corso were built in the late 17th century by Rainaldi; looks can deceive though and, to fit into the available space, one of them actually has an oval rather than a round dome. Domenico Fontana designed the fountain (1589) around the 3,000-year-old obelisk that Emperor Augustus brought from Egypt.

28C4
Piazza del Popolo
Flaminio
119, 590 to Piazza del Popolo; 95, 125, 490, 495, 926, and tram 225 Piazzale Flaminio

Looking down the Via del Corso from Piazza del Popolo

PIAZZA DELLA REPUBBLICA 

A rather seedy square whose once elegant colonnade is now occupied by adult cinemas and tourist-trapping bars, one side is dominated by the 3rd-century AD remains of the baths of Diocletian, into which Michelangelo incorporated the church of Santa Maria degli Angeli in 1563. The enticingly voluptuous nymphs (1901) of Mario Rutelli's *Fontana delle Naiadi* were greeted with scandalised horror when they were unveiled in 1910, but they have aged badly and their bodies are pock-marked by pollution.

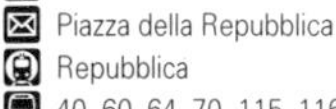

29D3
Piazza della Repubblica
Repubblica
40, 60, 64, 70, 115, 116, 170 to Piazza della Repubblica

28C4
Piazza di Spagna
Spagna
119 to Piazza di Spagna

The perennially popular Spanish Steps afford a bird's-eye view across the city

PIAZZA DI SPAGNA ✪✪✪

The sweeping Spanish Steps, designed in 1720 to connect the piazza with the French church of Trinità dei Monti, are now usually smothered with tourists, Italian soldiers and street-vendors who compete for space with tubs of magnolias in springtime and a life-size nativity scene at Christmas. The piazza gets its name from the Spanish Embassy which was here in the 17th century, and has been a compulsory stop for visitors to Rome since the 18th and 19th centuries when local tradesmen, models, unemployed servants and beggars mingled hopefully with the foreign artists, writers and Grand Tourists who congregated here. Keats lived and died in an apartment here (► 45). The low-

Attractive Ponte Sant'Angelo incorporates arches of Emperor Hadrian's original bridge, the Pons Aelius

lying Fontana della Barcaccia (fountain of the broken boat) at the bottom of the steps was designed by Pietro Bernini, father of the more famous Gian Lorenzo, in 1627 for Barberini Pope Urban VIII; the bees and suns were taken from the Barberini family crest. To the southeast, in Piazza Mignanelli, is a statue of the Virgin Mary on top of a column. This was erected in 1857 when Pope Pius IX proclaimed the doctrine of the Immaculate Conception, holding that the Virgin was the only person ever to have been born without original sin.

PIRAMIDE CESTIA ✪

An engineer could tell you that this is nothing like as well-built as the Egyptian originals that inspired magistrate Caius Cestis (in Italian, *Caio Cestio*) when he was designing his own tomb in the 1st century BC – a time when the fashion for all things Egyptian was at its height. For all that, this 27m-high pyramid has stood the test of time and makes a somewhat surreal landmark next to the Porta San Paolo, one of the original gateways into Rome.

28C1
Piazzale Ostiense
Piramide
57, 75, 175, 673, 716 and trams 13, 30B to Piramide
Protestant Cemetery

PONTE SANT'ANGELO ✪✪

Certainly the most elegant of the bridges over the Tiber, Bernini designed the ten angels which adorn its balustrades, each displaying one of the devices of Christ's passion, in 1667. Their ecstatically swooning expressions earned them the nickname of the 'Breezy Maniacs'. (Two more angels, deemed too beautiful to withstand the rigours of the Roman climate, are on show in the church of Sant'Andrea delle Fratte in Via di Sant'Andrea delle Fratte.) Most of the bridge dates from the 17th and 19th centuries but the central arches are the remains of the bridge that Emperor Hadrian built here in the 1st century AD to lead to his tomb (now Castel Sant'Angelo, ➤ 17).

28B3
Ponte Sant'Angelo
Lepanto
87, 280, 492 to Lungotevere Castello; 49, 70, 926, 990 to Piazza Cavour

Via Appia Antica (The Appian Way)

Distance
9km (3km to tomb of Cecilia Metella)

Time
Whole walk with minimum of stops 3 hours; to tomb of Cecilia Metella 1 hour without stops, 2–3 hours with stops

Start point
Porta di San Sebastiano
 29D1
118

End point
Via Appia Nuova
 29E1
663, 664

Lunch
Cecilia Metella (➤ 93); beyond this there are no bars or restaurants so take your own refreshments.

Via Appia Antica was built in 312 BC by Appius Claudius Caecus

This is a long walk and you may decide to finish at the tomb of Cecilia Metella, about 3km from the start point. Try to go on a Sunday, when the Via Appia is closed to traffic apart from buses and wedding parties.

Go straight through Porta San Sebastiano (➤ 63) and follow the road to the entrance to the Catacombs of San Callisto (➤ 37).

On the left is the church of Domine Quo Vadis, which has the imprints of Christ's feet, left when he appeared to St Peter who was trying to escape from Rome.

Bear right down Via Ardeatina, past the Catacombs of Domitilla to the Fosse Ardeatine.

This is now a moving memorial to the 335 Italians who were shot here by Nazis during World War II.

Follow Vicolo delle Sette Chiese back to the Via Appia and turn right at the Basilica San Sebastiano.

Opposite is the 4th-century tomb of Romulus (son of Emperor Maxentius) and the remains of Maxentius's stadium. Beyond this is the round tomb of Cecilia Metella, wife of a rich 1st-century BC Roman. Stop for lunch here or finish your walk.

From now on the traffic eases as the road, paved with its original vast, uneven cobblestones, cuts straight across the country. The cobbles are of Latium whitish lava stone. The route here is lined by the attractively crumbling tombs of ancient Romans. Along the stretch up to Via Erode Attico there are several modern villas, but beyond that the view gives way to farmland.

The walk finishes at the junction with Via del Casal Rotondo, where another massive round tomb has been converted into a farmhouse.

About half-way along this stretch are the remains of aqueducts and the complex of buildings (including a nyphaeum near the roadside) that made up the 2nd-century AD Villa of the Quintilli.

Turn left at Via del Casal Rotondo and walk until you reach Via Appia Nuova where you can take a bus back into the centre.

PORTA SAN SEBASTIANO ✪

The best-preserved of Rome's ancient gateways, the Porto San Sebastiano, leading to the Via Appia Antica (➤ 62), was rebuilt in the 5th century AD. Today it houses a rather dry museum on the history of the Roman city walls, the highlight of which is a stretch of walkway along the top of the 3rd century AD Aurelian wall.

29D1
Via di Porta San Sebastiano 18
06 7047 5284
Tue–Sat 9–7, Sun 9–1
218, 660 to Porta San Sebastiano
Moderate

PROTESTANT CEMETERY ✪

In fact this serene spot is called the non-Catholic rather than the Protestant cemetery but, in the first years after its establishment in 1738, most of its occupants were Protestant and the name has stuck. A map at the entrance will help you locate the final resting places of, among others, English poets Keats and Shelley, Julius, the son of German poet J W von Goethe, and Antonio Gramsci, the founder of the Italian Communist Party.

28C1
Via Caio Cestio 6
06 574 1141
Mar–Sep, Thu–Tue 8–11:30, 3:20–5:30; Oct–Feb, 8–11:30, 2:20–4:30
57, 75, 175
Donation

SANT'AGOSTINO ✪✪

An important early Renaissance Roman church containing a sculpture of the pregnant Mary by Sansovino (1518–21), an altar with Bernini angels and a Byzantine Madonna. The main attractions are, however, the paintings by Raphael and Guercino and Caravaggio's beautiful *Madonna di Loreto* (painted in 1606, just before he had to flee Rome to escape a murder charge). Caravaggio's realistic portayal of biblical figures as poor people, usually (as here) illuminated in the foreground and forming a strong diagonal across the picture, were criticised for lack of decorum because of their dirty feet, ripped clothes and perhaps too-human Madonna.

28C3
Piazza S. Agostino
8–12, 4.30–7.30
70, 81, 87, 115, 186, 492, 628 to Corso del Rinascimento

Did you know ?

Sant'Agostino was where many of Rome's most sought-after courtesans came to worship, attracting a large following of male admirers. For an attractive, go-getting Renaissance girl, life as the kept woman of a Roman aristocratic (or even a senior church man; many of the popes' so-called nephews were really their sons) could lead to riches and a successful career (like the mother of Lucrezia and Cesare Borgia who bought and ran three hotels).

SANT'ANDREA AL QUIRINALE ✪✪

A theatrical Bernini gem (1628–70) decorated in pink marble. The portico beckons and the interior embraces soothingly. The oval space (imposed by site restrictions), the short distance between entrance and altar, the gold ceiling, dark chapels and four massive richly veined columns all combine to pull one's gaze to the altar and Cortese's marble-framed *Martyrdom* borne by angels. On the pediment above, St Andrew soars to heaven, while garlanded *putti* perch and fishermen recline. The architectural expression of Bernini's sculptural ideals, it was his personal favourite, built for no payment. Also worth noting are the walnut-lined sacristy and chapels of St Stanislao (paintings by Sebastiano del Pozzo, statues by Legros).

29D3
Via del Quirinale 29
10–12, 4–7
71, 115, 116 to Via Milano; 57, 64, 65, 70, 75, 170 to Via Nazionale

28C3
Corso Vittorio Emmanuele
7:30–12, 4:30–7:30
46, 64 to Corso Vittorio Emmanuele; 70, 81, 87, 115, 186, 492, 628 to Corso del Rinascimento

SANT'ANDREA DELLA VALLE ✪

Another great Counter-Reformatory church to put Protestantism on the defensive and accommodate yet another new Order (the Theatines, founded in 1524). Designed by Della Porta (1591), it has a superb and imposing travertine façade (Rainaldi, 1655–63) and Carlo Maderno's impressive dome (1622), which is second only to that of St Peter's and also contains one of the church's important baroque fresco cycles. Other frescoes, by competitors Lanfranco and Domenichino in the dome, and Domenichino's *Scenes from the Life and Death of St Andrew* in the apse, have been recently restored. Opera fans note that this is where the opening scene of Puccini's *Tosca* takes place.

29D3
Via del Quirinale 23 (corner of Via Quattro Fontane)
Mon–Fri, 9:30–12:30, 4–6, Sat 9–1
Repubblica, Barberini
64, 70, 71, 115, 116, 170 to Via Nazionale

SAN CARLO ALLE QUATTRO FONTANE ✪✪

Restored recently, this was Borromini's first major work (1638) after a long apprenticeship under Maderno. It is difficult for modern eyes to appreciate the revolutionary quality of this tortured man's work. He overturned the Renaissance assumptions that architecture was based on the proportions of the human body, designing it instead around geometric units. The manipulation of the minuscule space is ingenious, not least in the swiftly shrinking coffers of the honeycombed dome, which give an illusion of size. The changing rhythms inside are also present on the façade, Borromini's last work (1667). The three bays of the lower half read concave-convex-concave while those above are all concave.

Borromini made the most of a resticted space when he designed the church of San Carlo alle Quattro Fontane

28C2
Piazza Santa Cecilia in Trastevere
10–12, 4–6; Cavallini frescoes, Tue and Thu 10–11:30
44, 75, 170, 181, 280, 710, 717, 719, 774, 780 to Viale Trastevere
Donation expected for Cavallini frescoes and excavations

SANTA CECILIA IN TRASTEVERE ✪✪

Approached through a delightful courtyard, this church contains one of the most beautiful baroque sculptures in Rome (Stefano Maderno, 1599), showing a tiny Saint Cecilia, the patron saint of music. Supposedly in the position of her nasty death (it took her three days to die), her head poignantly turns from our gaze. There are also the great Cavallini's frescoes of the *Last Judgement* (1293), painted in beautifully soft powdery blues, greens and pinks of the trumpeting angels' wings. Underneath the church, the remains of a Roman house and shops, including a mosaic, can still be seen.

SAN CLEMENTE (➤ 23 TOP TEN)

SANTA CROCE IN GERUSALEMME ✪

This church bursts with relics; indeed it was built (1144) for that very purpose. In the Chapel of the Relics are pieces of the True Cross and thorns from Christ's Crown brought to Rome by the Empress Helena in 320, whose crypt is built on soil from Mount Golgotha. The chapel contains some wonderfully ornamental mosaics showing scenes decked with flowers and birds.

29E2
Piazza di Santa Croce in Gerusalemme
Apr–Sep, 6–12:30, 3:30–7:30; Oct–Mar, 6–12:30, 3:30–6:30
9 and trams 13, 30B to Piazza Santa Croce in Gerusalemme

SAN FRANCESCO A RIPA ✪

A 13th-century monastery was built on the site of an inn where St Francis of Assisi supposedly stayed but the present church is baroque (1692, by de' Rossi, working under Bernini). Architecturally uninteresting, it does however house one of Bernini's most splendid works (*The Blessed Ludovica Albertoni*, 1674). Framed in the last left chapel, she is best approached head-on from the nave. Depicted in feverish death throes after her life of good works, the agonised writhings of the deeply cut white folds of her clothes create a powerful impact. The textures of hair, skin or the bed are not differentiated and the whiteness is intensified by the dark foreground drapes, close enough to touch.

28B2
Piazza San Francesco d'Assisi
7–12, 4–7
40, 64, 70, 71, 492 to Largo Argentina then tram 8 to Viale Trastevere

SAN GIOVANNI IN LATERANO ✪✪✪

This was the home of the papacy from Constantine until 1305, and is the present cathedral of Rome. In short, it is an important place. The early buildings suffered from fire and neglect after the Pope's exile to Avignon and the subsequent move to the Vatican, and the present-day San Giovanni dates from the baroque: including Fontana's palace and portico (1585), Gallei's façade and Borromini's nave (1650), which incorporates the columns of the original basilica inside a new and vigorous structure, creating niches for figures of the Apostles. Look out for the 5th-century mosaics in the baptistery apse and the bronze door (1190) of the chapel of St John the Evangelist. The baptistery was damaged by a bomb in 1993.

29E2
Piazza di San Giovanni in Laterano
Apr–Sep, 7–7; Oct–Mar, 7–6
San Giovanni
16, 81, 85, 87, 218, 650, 714, 715 to Piazza di San Giovanni in Laterano

Borromini's nave within Rome's cathedral church

Andrea Pozzo's beautiful and fantastic trompe l'oeil *ceiling in Sant'Ignazio di Layola depicts the saint's entry into Paradise*

29D2
Piazza di San Gregorio Magno
9–1, 4–7
Circo Massimo
81, 175, 673 to Via di San Gregorio

SAN GREGORIO MAGNO

Originally Gregory the Great's monastery (575), from where he set out to take Christianity to England, it is now a feast of baroque, with Soria's masterpiece of a façade (1629) sitting decorously at the top of a splendid flight of stairs. More interesting than the church interior is the (sadly neglected) adjacent Oratory. The first room contains the table (supported by 3rd-century carved griffins) from which Gregory was said to have fed 12 poor people daily. In the central chapel (dedicated to St Andrew) is the lovely misty-coloured fresco by Reni of *St Andrew Adoring the Cross* and Domenichino's even lovelier *Scourging.*

29D3
7:30–12:30
Piazza di Sant'Ignazio
62, 81, 85, 95, 160, 175, 492, 628 to Via del Corso; 119 to Via del Seminario

SANT'IGNAZIO DI LOYOLA

The interior of this second Jesuit church (Il Gesù, ➤ 43) is a late-baroque (1626–50) assault on the senses, epitomised by Jesuit artist, Andrea Pozzo's astonishing fresco in the nave – *Apotheosis of St Ignatius* (1691). An extraordinary feat of perspective, the *trompe l'oeil* architecture becomes indistinguishable from the real. The dome, too, is painted (find the spot, move and watch the perspective distort). Similarly sumptuous are St Aloysius' tomb with its lapis lazuli urn and the altar with Legros' relief sculpture (right transept 1698–9). The friezes are by one of the baroque period's finest, Algardi.

76A2
Piazza San Lorenzo in Lucina
7:30–12:30
60, 62, 81, 85, 95, 160, 175, 492, 628 to Via del Corso

SAN LORENZO IN LUCINA

St Lawrence suffered a gruesome martyrdom (258) by being roasted on the gridiron found in this church. It takes its name from Lucina, one of the Roman matrons who gave her house over to Christian worship, but was rebuilt for Pope Paschal II (*c*1100) with a Romanesque belltower and a cosmati portico of refreshing simplicity, carefully restored. Inside is Bernini's chapel.

A Walk from the Celian Hill

The green and peaceful Celian hill overlooks the Colosseum, and adjoins the Baths of Caracalla and the Circo Massimo.

Starting at San Gregorio Magno (➤ 66), turn right up Via di San Gregorio and take the first right, Clivo di Scauro which runs under the flying buttresses that support Santi Giovanni e Paolo (➤ 33), opposite are the studios of Canale 5 (one of Berlusconi's TV stations). Continue straight up Via di San Paolo della Croce, under the 1st-century AD Arch of Doiabella and past the gateway of San Tommaso in Formis.

San Tommaso in Formis has a 13th-century mosaic of Christ freeing a black and a white slave. To the left is the church of San Stefano Rotondo (➤ 74), and on the right is Santa Maria in Domnica (➤ 69); the fountain was erected in 1931 using a 16th-century sculpture of a boat. Next to the church is the entrance to Villa Celimontana park.

At the bottom of Via della Navicella bear right down Via Druso and turn right along Viale delle Terme di Caracalla, passing the baths (➤ 75) to reach Circo Massimo (➤ 39).

Rest on the grass and let your imagination drift back to the chariot races.

Turn left on Viale Aventino and take the first right up Via di Circo Massimo. Follow this to Piazzale Ugo La Malfa and take the second left, Via di Valle Murcia following it up to the top .

Here there is a small orange garden with views over Rome. Following Via di Santa Sabina you reach Santa Sabina (➤ 73) and Santi Bonifacio e Alessio with its 18th-century façade, cosmati doorway and belltower.

Continue straight to Piazza dei Cavalieri di Malta (➤ 57). Turning left just before the piazza down Via di Porta Lavernale will take you back down to Via Marmorata for buses, but first have lunch near Piramide.

Distance
4km

Time
2 hours without stops,
3 hours with

Start point
San Gregorio Magno
29D2
Circo Massimo
To Circo Massimo Piazza di Colosseo

End point
Via Marmorata
29C2
Ostiense
to Via Marmorata

Lunch
Taverna Cestia (££) (➤ 98).
Viale Piramide Cestia 87
574 3754
Closed Mon
Piramide
13, 30, 75

- 28C3
- Via San Giovanna d'Arco
- Fri–Wed 7:30–12:30, 3:30–7, Thur 7:30–12:30
- 70, 81, 87, 115, 186, 492, 628 to Corso del Rinascimento

SAN LUIGI DEI FRANCESI

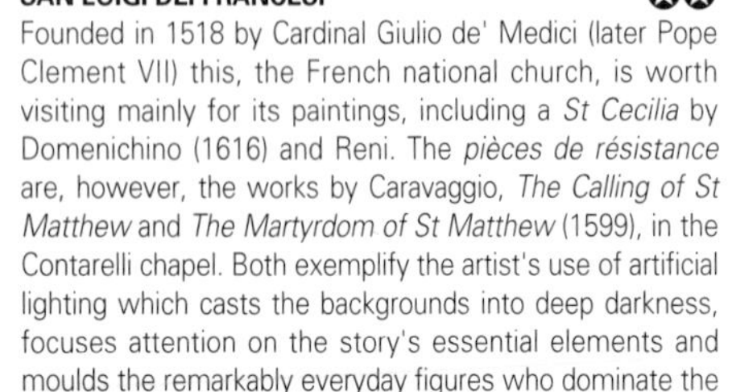

Founded in 1518 by Cardinal Giulio de' Medici (later Pope Clement VII) this, the French national church, is worth visiting mainly for its paintings, including a *St Cecilia* by Domenichino (1616) and Reni. The *pièces de résistance* are, however, the works by Caravaggio, *The Calling of St Matthew* and *The Martyrdom of St Matthew* (1599), in the Contarelli chapel. Both exemplify the artist's use of artificial lighting which casts the backgrounds into deep darkness, focuses attention on the story's essential elements and moulds the remarkably everyday figures who dominate the foreground. This everyday quality was perceived as irreverent and the most notorious example, *St Matthew and the Angel* (1602), is above the altar (note the dirty feet).

- 29D4
- Via Vittorio Veneto 27
- 9–12, 3–6
- Barberini
- 58, 95, 116 to Via Veneto

SANTA MARIA DELLA CONCEZIONE

If you feel like contemplating immortality then visit this little church (1631–8), a Barberini initiative for the Capuchin monks. The sombre theme is spelt out on the tombstone of a Barberini ('here lie dust, ashes and nothing'), but reaches a climax in the musty odour of the bone-lined crypt where dead monks' remains decorate the ceiling and walls. In the church are two major baroque paintings, Pietro da Cortona's *Ananias Healing St Paul of Blindness,* (1631) and Caravaggio's *Meditating St Francis.*

- 29D4
- Piazza della Bocca della Verità
- 9–12, 3–6
- 81, 94, 95, 160, 628, 713, 716 to Piazza della Bocca della Verità

SANTA MARIA IN COSMEDIN

The austere intimacy of this lovingly restored 12th-century basilica in the heart of ancient Rome houses beautiful cosmati works so characteristic of Roman churches of the period. The Cosmati (actually several families but grouped together because of the preponderance of the name Cosma) were builders and designers but are best remembered for their luscious decorations in marble and colourful mosaics. Examples can be seen here in the magnificent nave paving (1123), the raised choir, the paschal candlestick, the bishop's throne and, in particular, the beautiful *baldacchino* (1294). In the portico is the *Bocca della Verità* (mouth of truth) – legend has it that the mouth would bite the hand of he who lied – or more commonly she whose marital fidelity was questioned. In the sacristry are mosaics (706) from old St Peter's.

Beautiful mosaics within the equally lovely medieval church of Santa Maria in Cosmedin

SANTA MARIA IN DOMNICA ✪✪

A haven of calm, this lovely church was rebuilt (817–24) in honour of the Virgin (who takes pride of place in the delightful apse mosaic showing saints striding through meadows). It is also known as *'La Navicella'* on account of the 16th-century copy of a Roman boat in front of the entrance. The boat is a fountain, made from an ancient stone galley; this may have been an offering made by a safely returned traveller. Pope Leo X added the portico and the ceiling. The theme of journeying continues in the 12 images of great delicacy and simplicity on the 11th-century wooden ceiling (among which are the ark, the tree of life and, in the centre, the Medici coat of arms). There is a notable 9th-century mosaic in the apse, which was commissioned by Pope Paschal I. Some excavated Roman remains are exhibited under the altar.

- 29D2
- Piazza della Navicella
- Apr–Sept, 9–12, 3:30–7; Oct–Mar, 9–12, 3:30–6
- Colosseo
- 81, 673 to Via della Navicella

SANTA MARIA SOPRA MINERVA ✪✪✪

Bernini's engaging obelisk-bearing baby elephant (1667) sits in the piazza in front of this typically eclectic church (built in 1280, completed in 1500, modified in the 17th century). Inside there is many a fine work: Bernini's wind-blown richly coloured marble monument to Maria Raggi (1643) and another to G B Vigevano (1617); Michelangelo's *Redeemer with his Cross* (1520); and the rich and lavish Aldobrandini chapel (della Porta and C Maderna, 1600–5) once again bearing witness to important Roman families making their own mark on baroque Rome. The treats, however, are Renaissance, notably the stunning frescoes by Lippi. Saint Valentine was made the patron saint of lovers here in 1465.

- 28C3
- Piazza della Minerva
- 7–12, 4–7
- 40, 44, 46, 60, 662, 64, 70, 81, 87, 115, 186, 492, 710 to Largo di Torre Argentina

Bernini's highly unusual elephant statue in the middle of Piazza della Minerva

SANTA MARIA DEL POPOLO 

28C4
Piazza del Popolo
Mon–Sat 7–1, Sun, hol 8–1:30, 4:30–7
Flaminio
To Piazzale Flaminio

The church is bursting with masterpieces. Part of the façade and interior are by Bernini, whose *Habbakuk* and *Daniel* statues are cramped into small niches in the Renaissance Chigi chapel (Raphael, 1516) along with mosaics. An angel visits Habbakuk and Daniel is praying with arms outstretched. Caravaggio and Carracci, the two dominant forces of baroque painting, are together in the Cerasi chapel (left transept). Caravaggio's *Conversion of St Paul*, so dramatically foreshortened that he seems to fall off the canvas, and the strong diagonals of the *Crucifixion of St Peter* share the space with Carracci's *Assumption of the Virgin* (1601). Pinturicchio (c1485), whose work can be seen in the frescoes, is represented by paintings in the Della Rovere chapel.

The church is worth visiting for any one of these works; to have them all under one roof nestling against the Roman wall in this magnificent piazza is a treat indeed.

Below: *Santa Maria del Popolo's rich interior is crammed with works of art*

SANTA MARIA IN TRASTEVERE 

28B2
Piazza Santa Maria in Trastevere
7–1, 4–7
8 to Viale Trastevere

The 12th-century mosaics on the façade create a magical backdrop to the piazza, the heart and hub of this characteristic quarter, particularly when illuminated. Inside the basilica, is the glorious expanse of gold of the apse mosaic. This is the oldest church in Rome dedicated to Mary (3rd and 4th centuries, rebuilt in the 12th), and she is represented with almost equal stature to Christ in the mosaic's upper panel (c1140) below a fan-like kaleido-

scopic design of luxuriant blue. In the panels below are a series of exquisitely delicate representations of her life (by Pietro Cavallini, working in the late 13th century). There is also a cosmati floor and a ceiling by Domenichino (1617).

SANTA MARIA DELLA VITTORIA

You could be forgiven for leaving Santa Maria della Vittoria off a busy itinerary; its baroque façade and interior are not the best examples in Rome, despite having been worked on by the architects Maderno and Soria and containing paintings by Domenichino, Guercino and Reni. However, it does contain Bernini's Cornaro Chapel and his *Ecstasy of St Teresa*, one of the finest pieces of baroque sculpture, making the church well worth a detour. Recently restored, *St Teresa* embodies Bernini's ideas of capturing the dramatic moment, in this case the saint's religious ecstasy (erotic to modern perceptions) as the Cornaro cardinals watch down from the side chapel.

29D4
Via XX Settembre 17
Sep to mid-Jul, 7:30–12, 4:30–7; mid-Jul to Aug, 7–10:30
Repubblica

SAN PIETRO (ST PETER'S)
(➤ 26, TOP TEN)

SAN PIETRO IN MONTORIO

In the church is Bernini's Raimondi chapel, an important precursor to the Cornaro chapel (➤ Santa Maria della Vittoria, above) for its lighting effects. More significant is Bramante's *tempietto* ('little temple') in the courtyard of the adjoining monastery (1502), a seminal work in the history of architecture. Its perfectly proportioned simplicity and dignity, so in keeping with the commemoration of the (alleged) spot of Peter's crucifixion, expresses the Renaissance ideals of emulating classical architecture.

28B2
Piazza San Pietro in Montorio
9–12, 4–6
41 to Gianicolo

SAN PIETRO IN VINCOLI 

To appreciate Michelangelo's *Moses* without jostling for position in front of the memorial to Julius II, make an early start. Flanked by Leah and Rachel (ironically representing contemplation), he remains remarkably impervious to the clicking cameras and rustling guidebooks, his gaze reaching out to some indeterminate spot across the nave, his hands sagaciously pulling back his abundant beard. Sculpted from a single piece of Carrara marble between 1513 and 1516, Moses is built on a large scale with enormous legs weighing him down and exquisitely moulded musculature; he is a massive expression of power and strength. Nearby, under the altar, lie St Peter's chains.

29D3
Piazza San Pietro in Vincoli
7:30–12:30, 3:30–6
Cavour, Colosseo
75 to Via Cavour

Tradition has it that Santa Pudenziana stands on the site where St Peter once lived

29D3
Via di S. Prassede
7–12, 4–6:30
Termini
16, 70, 71, 75, 590 to Santa Maria Maggiore

SANTA PRASSEDE

Santa Prassede has mosaics unrivalled in medieval Rome. The figure of Christ dominates the vault, flanked by saints and Pope Paschal I (who built the church in 817–24), distinguished by his square halo of the living. The apse mosaics are rich in symbols: the phoenix (resurrection), the eagle, ox, angel and lion (the evangelists) and the four rivers of Eden (earthly paradise). The glimmering intricacy of mosaics can be enjoyed up close in the small, enchanting side Chapel of St Zeno. Behind the altar the saint deposits martyrs' blood and relics down the well beneath the nave. Worth noting is a bust of Monsignor Giovanni Battista Santoni carved by Bernini when a teenager.

29D3
Via Urbana
Mon–Sat 8–12, 3–6, Sun 9–12, 3–6
Termini, Via Cavour
16, 70, 71, 75 to Piazza dell'Esquilino

SANTA PUDENZIANA

The early Christian Basilica (401–17) was erected over ancient Roman baths and a house but tradition supposes this to be the site of the oldest church in Rome (AD 145). It has seen many changes over the centuries; witness the baroque opulence of the Caetani chapel, through which you descend to reach the ancient remains (mornings only; ask). The main impact, comes from the stunning 4th-century apse mosaics set in the nave's serene context.

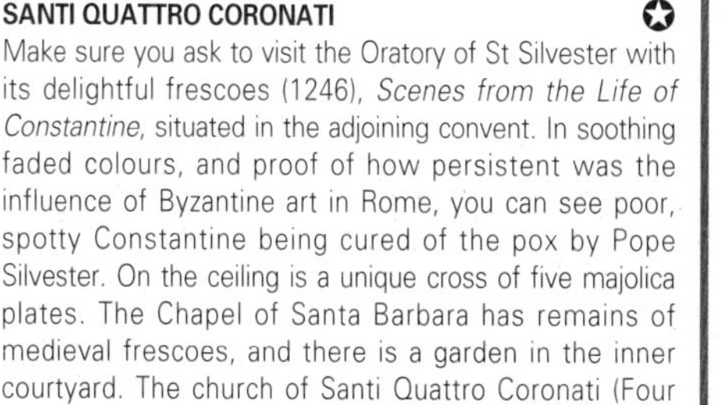

SANTI QUATTRO CORONATI ✪

Make sure you ask to visit the Oratory of St Silvester with its delightful frescoes (1246), *Scenes from the Life of Constantine*, situated in the adjoining convent. In soothing faded colours, and proof of how persistent was the influence of Byzantine art in Rome, you can see poor, spotty Constantine being cured of the pox by Pope Silvester. On the ceiling is a unique cross of five majolica plates. The Chapel of Santa Barbara has remains of medieval frescoes, and there is a garden in the inner courtyard. The church of Santi Quattro Coronati (Four Crowned Saints) has a typically long and complicated history; originally 4th-century, it was rebuilt in the 12th, as you can see from the belltower and cosmati paving. It more resembles a castle than a church.

29D2
Via dei Santi Quattro Coronati 20
9:30–12, 4:30–6
13, 15, 30, 85, 118 to Via San Giovanni in Laterano

SANTA SABINA ✪✪

The light-bathed interior of this perfect, serene early Christian basilica was built for Peter of Illyria (422–32), the belltower and cloisters were added in 1218 when the church was given to St Dominic and his newly formed order. Dominic's orange tree can be peeked at through a small gap in the portico. The church is named after the Roman Sabina martyred in Hadrian's time. Inside, the beautifully proportioned antique columns with their delicately carved Corinthian capitals support the nave arcading and 5th-century frieze. Unfortunately, the 5th-century mosaics on the apse and arch have not survived; the fresco reproductions are 15th-century. There is also a cosmati choir.

28C2
Piazza Pietro d'Illiria 1
7–12:20, 3:30–7
95, 713, 716 to Lungotevere Aventino

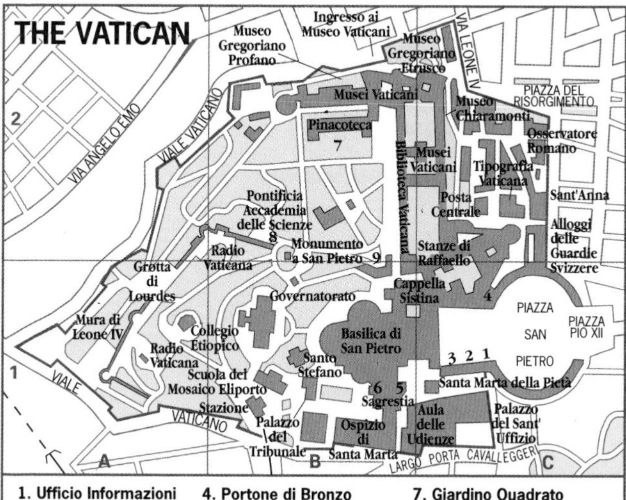

1. Ufficio Informazioni
2. Ufficio Postale
3. Arco delle Campane
4. Portone di Bronzo
5. Ufficio Scavi
6. Museo Storico Artistico
7. Giardino Quadrato
8. Fontana dell'Aquilone
9. Fontana del Sacramento

SANTO STEFANO ROTONDO ✪

29D2
Via di Santa Stefano 7
9–1
81, 673 to Via della Navicella

Beset by the usual problems of funding, Santo Stefano (one of the oldest round churches in Rome, c470) is in a constant state of restoration. Originally, the outer walls were further out, with circular and cross-shaped windows, and there were eight entrances. No evidence of an altar has been found (the present one is 13th-century); the two central columns supporting the lofty white-washed dome are also later additions. To the left of the present-day entrance a section of the original flooring has been painstakingly recreated using excavated marble fragments. Faded representations of gruesome martyrdoms (by Pomerancio and others c1600) adorn the walls.

SISTINE CHAPEL AND THE VATICAN MUSEUMS (➤ 24, TOP TEN)

TEATRO DI MARCELLO ✪✪✪

28C2
Via del Teatro di Marcello
81, 95, 160, 628, 713, 716 to Via del Teatro di Marcello

Here 2,000 years of Roman history can be seen at a glance. The lower part of the multi-levelled and many-styled building comprises the surviving two levels of a three-storey theatre that Julius Caesar started. Augustus finished the theatre in the 1st century BC and named it after one of his nephews. The elegant 16th-century palace, dramatically built on top of these crumbling remains (which served as, among other uses, a medieval fortress) and now divided into luxury apartments, was built by Baldassarre Peruzzi. The strange, reddish coloured protuberance stuck on the southern end is a 1930s Fascist addition, supposedly in keeping with the style of the theatre. To the north are three delicate Corinthian columns, part of a Temple of Apollo which was rebuilt in the 1st century BC. In summer, classical music concerts are held outside the theatre (➤ 114).

Above: *the Temple of Vesta;*
Right: *Terme di Caracalla*

TEMPI DI VESTA E DELLA FORTUNA VIRILIS ✪✪

Neither of these photogenic, small but perfectly formed temples have anything to do with Vesta or *Fortuna Virilis* (manly fortune). The round one, which dates from the 1st century BC and is the same shape as the temple of Vesta in the Forum (➤ 22), was dedicated to Hercules. The rectangular one, dating from the 2nd century BC, was dedicated to Portunus, the god of harbours; this was the port area of ancient Rome. Across the piazza from the temples is the 4th-century double arch of Janus, named after the two-headed guardian of the underworld.

28C2
Piazza della Bocca della Verità
81, 95, 160, 628, 713, 716 to Piazza della Bocca della Verità

TERME DI CARACALLA ✪✪✪

Ancient Romans did not go to the baths just to keep clean but to relax, meet each other, discuss politics, exercise and even study. Even bathing itself was not merely a soak in a tub; the Romans started off with a sauna, followed by a scrape down, a hot bath, a tepid bath and, finally, a dive into the cold bath. The serene ruins of the baths that Caracalla built in the 3rd century AD include remains of each of these types of bath as well as gyms, a library and a complicated underfloor heating system. They are used for summer outdoor opera performances (➤ 114).

29D1
Via delle Terme di Caracalla 52
06 575 8626
Tue–Sat 9 to 2 hours before sunset, Sun–Mon 9–1
Circo Massimo
160, 613, 628, 714
Few
Moderate

28B1
Area between Via Marmorata and Lungotevere Testaccio
95, 716 to Via Marmorata; 713 to Lungotevere Testaccio

TESTACCIO

Although well-known to Romans, who flock to its traditional restaurants and less-traditional nightclubs in the evenings, the Testaccio area is off the main tourist track. Most of its buildings are tall, courtyarded residential blocks, dating from the end of the 19th century and designed to include schools, crèches and shops, but it is the area around Monte Testaccio that sees the action, especially at night and during the summer (➤ 114–15). The *monte* is made up of millions of broken *amphorae*, dumped here by ancient Roman dockers when this was the port area where ships unloaded their cargo, including

Exclusive shopping on the Via Condotti

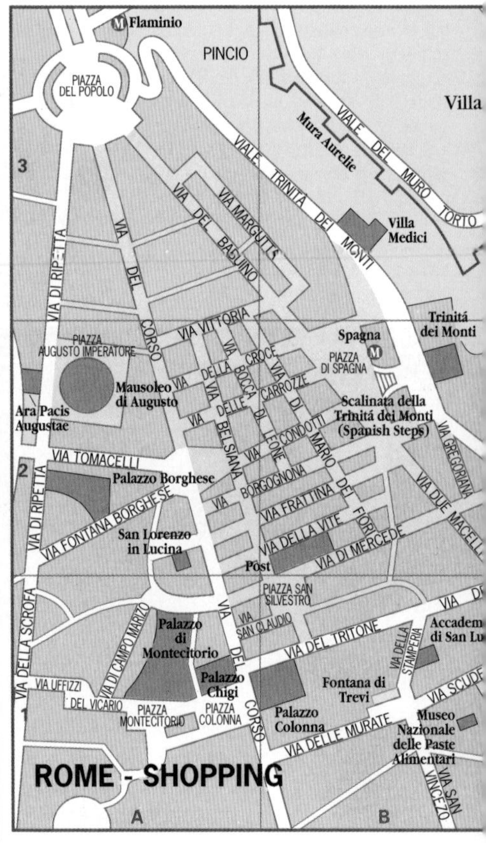

the oil that was transported in these clay pots. Opposite the hill is the old *mattatoio* – the most sophisticated abattoir in Europe when it opened in 1891 – now used for concerts, art exhibitions and other cultural events.

VIA CONDOTTI

Usually packed with well-heeled fashion victims and tourists, this elegant street is the heart of designer Rome, and most of the big Italian names have shops here or on the adjoining streets (➤ 108). It runs from Via del Corso to Piazza di Spagna and has an excellent view of the Spanish Steps. Keats and Liszt visited Caffè Greco at number 86.

76B2
Via Condotti
Spagna
81, 90, 90b, 119 to Via Condotti

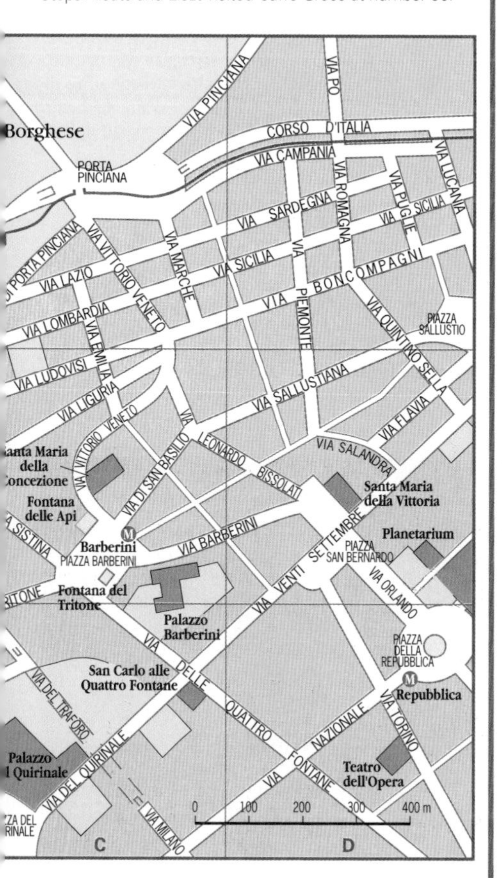

From high above, the designer delights of the Via Condotti are as yet unseen

Below: *the Sale delle Prospettive, and (inset) Raphael's fresco of Cupid, Villa Farnesina;*
Right: *view across rooftops to St Peter's*

VILLA FARNESINA

- 28B3
- Via della Lungara 230
- 06 6880 1767
- Tue–Sat 9–1
- 280 to Lungotevere della Farnesina
- Free; moderate for temporary exhibitions

Baldassare Peruzzi built this delicate little villa in 1508 for the rich banker Agostino Chigi, who was also a patron of Raphael. Now it is used for temporary exhibitions although its otherwise empty rooms are also worth visiting for their spectacular frescoes by Raphael, whose *Triumph of Galatea* is on the ground floor along with the *Loggia di Psiche* which he designed, and Sodoma, whose seductive fresco of the *Marriage of Alexander the Great and Roxanne* is painted against a *trompe l'oeil* background of views of contemporary Rome.

VILLA GIULIA

- 28C5
- Piazzale di Villa Giulia 9
- 06 322 6571
- Tue–Sat 9–7, Sun, hol 9–2
- Trams 19, 30B to Piazza Thorwaldsen
- Few
- Moderate
- Galleria Nazionale d'Arte Moderna e Contemporanea (➤ 42)

This charming palace with its shady courtyards houses the national collection of Etruscan art, although it was originally built in 1550–5 as a summer residence for Pope Julius III. The central loggia and *nymphaeum*, decorated with frescoes and mosaics, were frequently copied in later 16th-century Italian villas.

The Etruscans arrived in Italy towards the end of the 8th century BC and settled between the Arno and the Tiber, the area known as Etruria (present day Lazio, Umbria and southern Tuscany). The objects unearthed from Etruscan tombs in the region bear witness to the sophistication of the civilisation. The highlight of the collection is the 6th-century BC terracotta sarcophagus of a husband and wife reclining on a divan (in room 9) found at the necropolis of Cerveteri. Have a look at some of the jewellery, and you will see that design has not necessarily changed all that much since.

Excursions from the City

Just as all roads lead to Rome, they also lead from it. To escape the chaos, crowds or summer heat dozens of destinations are within easy reach. Heading south are the fascinating excavations of Ostia Antica; further towards Naples are the sandy beaches of Sperlonga and Gaeta. To the southeast the Castelli Romani offer a fine combination of history and gastronomy, while to the northwest the tombs of the Etruscans are waiting to be discovered. Viterbo, to the north, offers medieval charm, hot springs and Renaissance architectural extravagances, while you can only marvel at the extensive ruins of Hadrian's villa to the northeast. Stopping for lunch at a local trattoria or selecting ingredients for a gourmet picnic is half the fun. But beware if you are driving, especially on Sundays. Romans are addicted to what they refer to as the *gita fuori porta* or day trip out of town and the traffic returning from these outings can be a nightmare.

'...[the Campagne Romana] is the aptest and fittest burial ground for the Dead City. So sad, so quiet, so secret in its covering up of great masses of ruin.'

CHARLES DICKENS
Pictures from Italy (1846)

ARICCIA: PALAZZO CHIGI

Alessandro Chigi was the pope who gave Rome its baroque face. This was his summer retreat, the centrepiece of Bernini's exercise in town-planning that is Ariccia. Sold by the Chigi family in the 1980s and opened to the public since 1999, his magnificent *palazzo* (built in 1672) has been beautifully restored to its original pale-blue colour. It is bursting with paintings and furniture from centuries of the family history. Particularly noteworthy are the pharmacy, with miniature portraits of the family from the 16th century onwards, and the *Salada Pranzo d'Estate*.

- Off map
- Piazza di Corte
- 06 933 0053
- Tours: Tue–Fri 11:30, 4:30, 5:30, Sat–Sun 10–7 on the hour
- COTRAL bus from Anagnina to Ariccia or from terminal to Albano Laziale then bus

BOMARZO

The *Sacro Bosco* or *Parco dei Mostri* (Park of Monsters) at Bomarzo near Viterbo was created in the mid-1500s by Prince Vicino Orsini. While other nobles were building refined villas and laying out Renaissance gardens, the prince had anonymous sculptors craft grotesque figures, including a life-size elephant crushing a Roman soldier with its trunk and a screaming face with a mouth big enough to hold several people. Inscriptions encourage today's visitors to 'eat, drink and be merry for after death there is no pleasure'. It was a favourite with Salvador Dali.

- Off map
- Sacro Bosco, 01020 Bomarzo (VT)
- (0761) 924029
- Apr–Sep, 8:30–7; Oct–Mar, 8:30–5
- Restaurant, bar
- COTRAL bus from Saxa Rubra to Viterbo, then to Bomarzo.
- Expensive
- Viterbo (► 90)

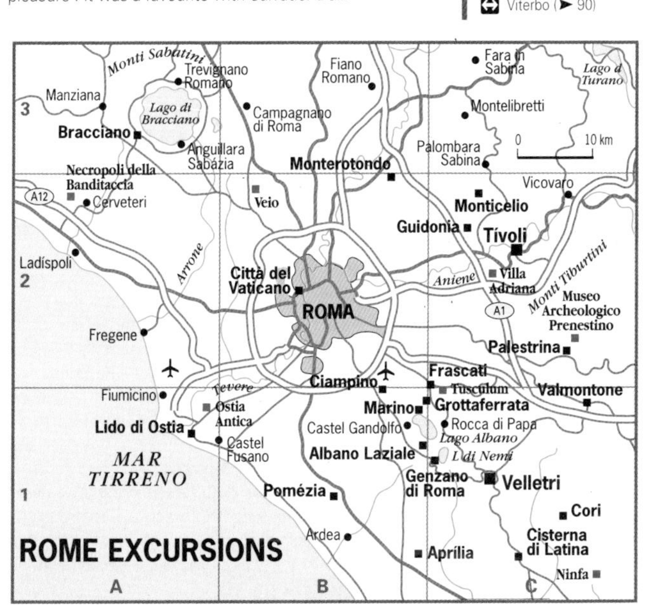

Off map
Piazza Farnese, 01032 Caprarola (VT)
(0761) 646052
Apr–Sep, 8:45–6:45; Oct–Mar, 9–4
COTRAL bus from Saxa Rubra to Caprarola. **By car**: 80km SS2 bis (Cassia bis) from Rome, then SS2 to Sutri, then follow signs to Caprarola
None Cheap

CAPRAROLA: VILLA FARNESE

One of the high points of Italian Mannerism, the imposing Villa Farnese, built by Antonio di Sangallo the Younger for Pierluigi Farnese, dwarfs the little town of Caprarola. Cardinal Alessandro Farnese took up residence in 1559, hiring one of the most competent architects of the late Renaissance, Vignola, to modify his home. Retaining the original and unusual pentagonal floor plan, Vignola turned the entire town of Caprarola into a setting for the palace, raising and extending the approach road and burying the lower storeys of the existing houses.

The *piano nobile* is the only floor open to the public. It is approached by Vignola's monumental spiral staircase of stone columns and frescoes up which Alessandro Farnese used to ride on his horse. Frescoes recording significant moments in the Farnese family history decorate all the rooms, except for the *Sala del Mappamondo*, where there are instead huge paintings of maps of the world (as it was known in the 16th century) and wonderful frescoes of constellations on the ceiling. The gardens outside are also worth a close look.

Villa Farnese

81A2

Banditaccia Necropolis/ Museo Nazionale di Cerveteri
06 994 0001
Banditaccia Necropolis: Tue–Sun 9 to 1 hour before sunset. Museo Nazionale di Cerveteri: Tue–Sun 8:30–7:30
COTRAL bus from Lepanto
From Termini, Tiburtina, Ostiense or Trastevere to Cerveteri-Ladispoli station (6km from town centre)
Local bus runs from main piazza in Cerveteri to necropolis in summer only. **By car**: 44km by A12 or Via Aurelia (SS1)
Necropolis moderate; museum free

CERVETERI

Founded by the Etruscans in the 8th century BC, ancient Caere was one of the great trading centres of the Mediterranean between the 7th and 5th centuries BC. In the **Banditaccia Necropolis**, a couple of kilometres from the main piazza of modern Cerveteri, the tombs of the inhabitants of the prosperous city are laid out in the form of a town, with streets and squares – a real city of the dead.

A map on sale at the entrance to the necropolis, which is set among Roman pines and cypress trees, is a useful guide to the tombs. Do not miss the 6th-century Tomba dei Capitelli carved from light volcanic rock to resemble Etruscan houses and the Tomba dei Rilievi decorated with painted reliefs of cooking utensils and other household objects. The Tomba degli Scudi e delle Sedie outside the main gate has chairs carved out of the tufo and unusual reliefs of shields decorating the walls.

The **Museo Nazionale di Cerveteri** in the town centre displays interesting pottery and sarcophagi from Cerveteri and the nearby port of Pyrgi, although most of the best discoveries are in the Vatican Museums (► 24) and Villa Giulia (► 78).

Etruria

Although little remains of Etruscan cities in the area of northern Lazio referred to as Etruria, many tombs, which contained reproductions of their occupants' luxuries and favourite things, have survived and give a fascinating insight into Etruscan civilisation. The Etruscans were clever, perhaps too clever for their own good. One historical account tells the story of an Etruscan man who set off for Gaul with his belongings and ample quantities of good wine. The precious nectar convinced the Gauls to come down to Italy, where they subsequently wiped out the Etruscan race.

Distance
230km

Time
1 day

Start/end point
Rome
28C3

Lunch
Le Due Orfanelle (££)
Via di Porta Tarquinia 11a, Tarquinia
(0766) 856276
Closed Tue

Head out of Rome on the Via Aurelia (SS1), which joins the autostrada A12. After a visit to the necropolis of Cerveteri (➤ 82), continue north up the A12.

Civitavecchia, one of Rome's ports, is worth a detour. Established by Emperor Trajan in AD 106, the town regained importance as a papal stronghold in the 16th century, when Michelangelo designed the fortress.

Continuing on the A12 up the coast you reach Tarquinia.

This is thought to have been founded in the 12th century BC, an important economic and political centre for the Etruscans. The painted tombs at the necropolis of Monterozzi are a must. The Museo Nazionale di Tarquinia has a collection of artefacts.

The Roman aqueduct at Tarquinia

Turn right onto a minor road after Tarquinia and head inland for about 20km until you reach Tuscania.

This became a leading Etruscan city after the 4th century BC. Lovely sarcophagi are on display in the Museo Archeologico. However it is the post-Etruscan civilisation which makes an impression – especially the churches of San Pietro and Santa Maria Maggiore, built in the 8th century AD with 11th- and 12th-century additions.

Return to Rome by the same route or taking the Via Cassia (SS2) from Vetralla to Rome.

81C2

Frascati tourist office (06 942 0331)

Villa Aldobrandini

Piazzale Marconi, Frascati

06 942 2560

Mon–Fri 10–7

Train from Termini station, 30 min. **By car:** Via Tuscolana from Rome for about 25km

Free (the tourist office in Piazzale Marconi issues passes to the garden of Villa Aldobrandini).

FRASCATI

Situated 25km from Rome, Frascati is the nearest of the Castelli Romani – the towns dotted along the volcanic Alban Hills. Frascati suffered severe damage during World War II, but many of the buildings have since been restored, including the cathedral of San Pietro in Piazza San Pietro and the church of the Gesù designed by Pietro da Cortona, which is decorated with fresco perspectives.

Frascati is renowned for both its white wine (this can be sampled fresh from the barrel in the numerous cellars around the town) and its Renaissance villas. The magnificent **Villa Aldobrandini**, designed by Giacomo della Porta between 1598 and 1603 for Cardinal Pietro Aldobrandini, a nephew of Pope Clement VIII, dominates the town. On a clear day the views of Rome from the terrace can be breathtaking.

Frascati, with other Castelli towns, was once part of the ancient city of Tusculum, which dates back as far as the 9th century BC. It was a favourite spot for Roman dignitaries, many of whom had villas there. The archaeological remains of Tusculum are scant: there is a Roman road leading up to the former city, the ruins of the villa of Emperor Tiberius and – best-preserved of all – a small amphitheatre now somewhat notorious after reports of black masses being held there. For directions refer to Castelli Romani drive (► 85).

Renaissance villas of Frascati

Castelli Romani

The Castelli Romani are small towns which grew up in ancient times and developed during the Middle Ages along the slopes of the Alban Hills. The name probably comes from the palaces built there by popes and noble Roman families. Each has its own history and attractions.

From Frascati's Piazza G. Marconi, follow the signs to Tusculum (➤ 84).

Grottaferrata is 3km south of Frascati and is famous for its 11th-century abbey. Castelli wines are high on the list of popular Italian table wines. Even in Roman times they were regarded as 'unstable'. Today locals insist that the wine is better drunk on the spot. Test the theory by quaffing from the barrel in the wine shops in the towns.

Following route 215, you reach Marino, whose white wine is regarded as the region's best after Frascati. From Marino the scenic Via dei Laghi runs along the eastern rim of Lago Albano. Just after the lake, turn left on SS218 to Monte Cavo (the second highest of the Alban Hills) and Rocca di Papa, at 680m.

This is the highest of the Castelli towns and one of the most picturesque with its medieval quarter.

Return to Via dei Laghi until the turnoff on the right to Nemi. Nemi, positioned above the volcanic lake of the same name, is famous for its wild strawberries. It is an attractive place that gets busy at weekends. On the other side of Lake Nemi the panoramic SS7 continues to Genzano di Roma, Ariccia and Albano Laziale.

Ariccia is renowned for its main square ornamented by Bernini and for its *porchetta,* or stuffed roast pork. Albano Laziale has majestic Etruscan and Roman ruins.

From Albano Laziale take the picturesque Galleria di Sopra to Castel Gandolfo.

This is the summer residence of the Pope. He gives a blessing at 12:00 every Sunday, June to September.

Return to Rome on the Via Appia Antica.

Distance
90km

Time
Half a day

Start/end point
Rome
81C2

Lunch
Taberna Mamilius (££))
Viale Balilla 1, Frascati
06 942 1559

OSTIA ANTICA

- 81A1
- 06 5635 8099
- Excavations Oct–Mar, 9–5; Apr–Sept, 9–6. Museum 9–2
- Il Monumento (££)
  - Piazza Umberto I 18
  - 06 565 0021
- Closed Mon
- Metro B to Magliana, then the Ostia Lido train to Ostia Antica. **By car**: 25km. Via del Mare (SS8 bis) from Rome
- Moderate

Visit Ostia Antica's famously well-preserved Roman town for a good idea of what life was like in Italy BC

Founded at the mouth of the river Tiber by the Romans in the 4th century BC, Ostia Antica was the port of ancient Rome. Populated by merchants and sailors, the city was a strategically important centre of defence and trade until its decline in the 4th century AD.

After Pompeii and Herculaneum, Ostia Antica is the best-preserved Roman town in Italy. Its park-like setting is a refreshing change from the chaos of Rome, and should be enjoyed at a leisurely pace. Allow a good few hours to explore the **excavations** which are as fascinating (if not quite so grand) as those at the Roman Forum and give a good impression of what day-to-day life in a working Roman town was like.

The ruins span both sides of the kilometre-long main street, the Decumanus Maximus, from the Porta Romana to the Porta Marina at the other end (which once opened on to the seafront). On the right just after the Porta Romana are the Terme di Nettuno (baths of Neptune), best viewed by climbing the stone stairs at the front. Further on is the impressive amphitheatre which could hold 2,700 people. It was restored in 1927 and is used as a theatre in summer (➤ 113). Behind the theatre is the town's commercial centre, Piazzale delle Corporazioni, surrounded by offices and shops with decorative mosaics announcing the trades practised by each business.

Picturesque Sperlonga has a harbour as well as a very popular beach

Returning to the Decumanus Maximus, the ruins of the forum are to the left. Off to the right are the remains of some *horrea* (warehouses) that once stood all over the city. Also on the right is the well-preserved Casa di Diana and the *Thermopilium*, a Roman bar complete with a marble counter and frescoes of the available fare. Just beyond, to the northeast, is the museum which houses statues, mosaics and other artefacts found at the site.

Before you leave, look at the medieval *borgo* (village) of Ostia, a stone's throw from the archaeological site, where there are some characteristic cottages which once housed workers from the nearby salt plains and a fortified castle built for future Pope Julius II in 1483–6.

SPERLONGA ✪

With its whitewashed houses and narrow streets, the popular resort town of Sperlonga, built on a high, rocky promontory on the coast south of Terracina, is possibly more Greek than Italian in feel. Cars are banned from the old centre, which is made up of winding alleys and stone stairways. In the summer the spectacular beach is filled with wealthy Romans vying for a place in the front row of the beach-umbrella/sunbed operations (there is a small stretch of non-paying public beach but this seems to get smaller every year). Food and drink can be bought from the many beachside bars.

The archaeological museum located 2km from the town displays artefacts found among the ruins of the nearby villa of Emperor Tiberius, including reconstructions of larger-than-life-size sculpture groups illustrating the adventures of Ulysses, erected between AD 4 and 26 for Tiberius in his nearby cliff-face grotto.

Off map

Lido da Rocco (£–££) Via Spiaggia Angelo 22 (0771) 54493

Naples train from Termini station to Fondi

Local bus to Sperlonga from Fondi should coincide with the train. Taxis also available. The return bus leaves from the central piazza at the top of the hill. **By car**: 120km. Take the SS148 south out of Rome (follow signs to Latina and Terracina). From Terracina take the SS213 to Sperlonga

The delightful grounds of Tivoli's Villa d'Este offer respite from the summer heat

TIVOLI ✪✪

Tivoli was a country retreat for Roman patricians and a summer playground for the monied classes during the Renaissance. The town has long been famous for its Travertine marble and the quarries that line the road from Rome testify to this continuing flourishing trade. Easily reached by car or public transport, Tivoli is one of the most popular day trips from Rome. The Villa d'Este and Villa Adriana are the best-known sights, but it is worth having a look at the Rocca Pia, a 15th-century castle built by Pope Pius II at the top of the town, and wandering around the labyrinthine streets of the historical centre, stopping at the Romanesque church of San Silvestro (where there are some interesting early medieval frescoes) and the 17th-century cathedral of San Lorenzo.

There is a sense of faded splendour about the Renaissance pleasure palace **Villa d'Este** created in 1550 by Cardinal Ippolito d'Este, grandson of Borgia Pope Alexander VI. Some of the remaining Mannerist frescoes in the villa have recently been restored and deserve a look, but the residence is totally upstaged by the gardens – an almost entirely symmetrical series of terraces, shady pathways and spectacular fountains, powered solely by gravitational force and including one that once played the organ and another that imitated the call of birds. Sadly neither of these are functional today, but you can still get a sense of the fantastic creation that the garden once was, and there are delightful features such as the long terrace of grotesque heads, all spouting water, and the Rometta fountain (on the far left going down the terraces) which has reproductions of Rome's major buildings. From 1865 to 1886 the villa was home to Franz Liszt and inspired his *Fountains of the Villa d'Este*.

The waterfalls and gardens of Tivoli's **Villa Gregoriana** were created when Pope Gregory XVI diverted the flow of the Aniene river to put an end to the periodic flooding in the area. There are two main waterfalls: the large Grande Cascata on the far side and a smaller one at the neck of the gorge, designed by Bernini. Shady paths surrounded by lush vegetation wind down to various viewpoints over the waterfalls and across to two exceptionally well-preserved Roman temples, the circular Temple of Vesta and the rectangular Temple of the Sibyl, which date from the Republican era.

81C2
Cinque State (££)
Largo Sant'Angelo
(0774) 20281
Metro to Rebibbia, then COTRAL bus to Tivoli. Buses leave every 10 minutes (Mon–Sat), 15–20 minutes (Sun). **By car:** 40km east of Rome on Via Tiburtina SS5 or Rome-L'Aquila autostrada A24

Villa d'Este
Piazza Trento
(0774) 312070
9 to 1 hour before sunset
Moderate

Villa Gregoriana
Largo S. Angelo
(0774) 334522
Apr, 9:30–6; May–Aug, 10–7:30; Sep, 9:30–6:30; Oct–Mar, 9:30–4:30
Cheap

VILLA ADRIANA ✪✪✪

Constructed between AD 118 and 134, Villa Adriana was the largest and most sumptuous villa ever built in the Roman Empire. It was the country palace of Emperor Hadrian and later used by other emperors. After the fall of the empire it was plundered for building materials. Many of its decorations were used to embellish the Villa d'Este.

A model near the entrance gives you some idea of the scale of the complex. The site is enormous and you will need several hours to see it properly. Hadrian travelled widely and was a keen architect, and parts of the villa were inspired by buildings he had seen around the world. The massive *Pecile*, through which you enter, was a reproduction of a building in Athens and the Canopus, on the far side of the site, is a copy of the sanctuary of Serapis near Alexandria, and the long canal of water, originally surrounded by Egyptian statues, reproducing the Nile.

Highlights include the fishpond (probably used less for keeping fish than for creating reflections and plays of light) encircled by an underground gallery where the emperor took his walks, the baths, and Hadrian's private retreat, the Teatro Marittimo, a small circular palace on an island in a pool, which could be reached only by a retractable bridge. There are *nymphaeums*, temples, barracks and a museum. Archaeologists have found features such as a heated bench with steam pipes under the sand, and a network of subterranean service passages for horses and carts.

- 81C2
- Via di Villa Adriana, Tivoli
- (0774) 530203
- Nov–Jan, 9–5; Feb, Oct, 9–6; Mar, Sept, 9–6:30; Apr, 9–7; May–Aug, 9–7:30. Tickets sold until one hour before closing
- Villa Esedra (£) Via di Villa Adriana 51 (0774) 534716 Closed Tue
- 32km. Local bus from Tivoli's Piazza Garibaldi to Villa Adriana. COTRAL bus can drop you on main road to Rome (1km to villa).
- Moderate

In its day, the Villa Adriana, built by Emperor Hadrian, was the most lavish of its kind

VITERBO 

Off map
Richiastro (£) Via Della Marrocca 16–18 (0761) 223 609 Closed Mon–Wed, Sun eve
COTRAL bus from Saxa Rubra station to Viterbo.
From Termini station (also Tiburtina, Ostiense, Trastevere stations) to Viterbo (2 hours). **By car:** Cassia bis (SS2 bis) from Rome (1½ hours). Pay parking.

Founded by the Etruscans and later taken over by Rome, Viterbo developed into an important medieval centre and in the 13th century became the residence of the popes. Although badly bombed during World War II, it remains Lazio's best preserved medieval town and its historical quarter, San Pellegrino, is such a perfect architectural ensemble that it is often used as a movie set. The natural hot springs close by are an additional attraction.

From the rather oddly named but lovely Piazza della Morte (Death Square) a bridge leads over to Piazza San Lorenzo and the black-and-white striped cathedral of the same name which dates from the 12th century. Inside are magnificent cosmati tiled floors and the tomb of Pope John XXI, who died in 1277 when the floor of his room collapsed. Next door is the 13th-century Palazzo Papale. Have a peek at the 'new' roof. The original one was removed in 1271, during the first conclave in Viterbo, to speed up the election of the pope. The cardinals, slow to elect the new pontiff, were locked inside the palace, next the roof was removed and finally, in desperation, the cardinals were put on a starvation diet. It was 33 months before Gregory X was finally elected.

The pretty Romanesque church of Santa Maria Nuova, with its outdoor pulpit from which St Thomas Aquinas preached and its cloister at the back, is also worth a look, before you head up towards Piazza del Plebiscito, which is dominated by the 16th-century Palazzo Comunale. Stop for a rest in Piazza delle Erbe by the fountain or for refreshments at the 15th-century Caffe Schenardi.

San Pellegrino, the oldest quarter of medieval Viterbo, is often used for film locations

Where To...

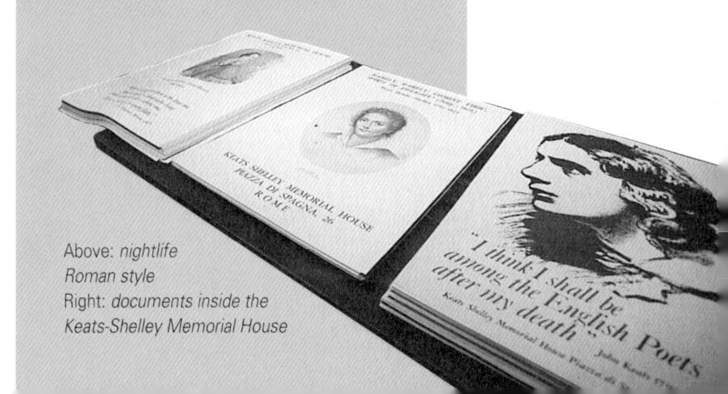

Above: *nightlife Roman style*
Right: *documents inside the Keats-Shelley Memorial House*

Rome

How Much will it Cost?

The price brackets used here are for a three-course meal for one without drinks or service – a half litre of house wine will often not make that much difference to the bill especially in cheaper places:

£ = up to €20
££ = €20–€35
£££ = more than €35

The bill will usually include a small cover charge (about €1–2 per person) and some restaurants add service (10–15 per cent); otherwise tipping is usually about 10 per cent.

Agata e Romeo (£££)

Near the Basilica of Santa Maria Maggiore, this intimate, elegant restaurant is renowned for its cosy and convivial atmosphere, its excellent Roman and southern Italian dishes, and equally a wine list that pays tribute to the quality of the food.

Via Carlo Alberto 45 06 446 5842 Closed Sun Vittorio Emanuele 70, 71

Alberto Ciarla (£££)

The classic Rome restaurant for serious fish lovers – fresh fish in its stark simplicity or as a sublimely creative dish, accompanied by a perfect match from the extensive wine list. There are intimate candlelit tables, a dramatic red-and-black decor, and refined and impeccable service.

Piazza San Cosimato 40 06 581 8668 Closed Sun, lunch 44, 75, 170, 181

Albistrò (££)

This is a central restaurant near Corso Vittorio to which you can flee after an overdose of the ubiquitous Roman cuisine. Swiss, oriental and regional Italian dishes are all prepared with ingenuity, subtle flavours and delicate combinations. An inspiration.

Via dei Banchi Vecchi 140a 06 686 5274 Closed Wed; Sun, Mon, Tue lunch To Corso Vittorio Emanuele

Alfredo a Via Gabi (££)

Comfortable local trattoria with pavement tables for outside eating in summer. Traditional and innovative specialities from Rome and the Marches, Roman dishes, especially on Saturday. A family atmosphere and cordial, attentive service. Remember to book at weekends.

Via Gabi 36 06 7720 6792 Closed Tue Re di Roma 4, 87

Al 34 (trentaquattro) (££)

Seasonal vegetables and herbs characterise the predominantly southern Italian fish and meat dishes of this very popular central restaurant. There is a comfortable, intimate atmosphere, and efficient service. Book to avoid inevitable disappointment in the evening.

Via Mario de' Fiori 34 06 679 5091 Closed Mon Spagna To Via del Tritone

Augusto (£)

This historic Roman trattoria has characteristic paper-covered tables (outside in summer). Happy confusion reigns here and service may be slapdash but the Roman cooking is genuine. Go early to enjoy the best dishes.

Piazza de' Renzi 15 06 580 3798 Closed Sun To Piazza Sonnino

Il Bacaro (££)

A candle-lit romantic little restaurant especially popular with young people both for its atmosphere and its location (near the Pantheon). It is particularly appealing in summer with outside tables. Innovative Italian dishes and affable service.

Via degli Spagnoli 27 06 686 4110 Closed Sun, lunch in Winter To Largo di Torre Argentina

Da Baffetto (£)
Immensely popular central pizzeria, recognisable from afar due to the crowd jostling to get past the door. Service however is swift and efficient, the pizzas are well worth the wait. Not a place for lingering. Open late.
Via del Governo Vecchio 11 06 686 1617 Closed Sun, lunch To Corso Vittorio Emanuele

Binario 4 (£)
A welcome arrival near the Colosseum: an updated version of the genuine local 'osteria'. There are carefully executed traditional dishes itemised daily on a strategically placed blackboard. Informal bonhomie. No rules for eating – have as little or as much as you like. Open late.
Via San Giovanni in Laterano 32 06 700 5561 Always open Colosseo To Piazza del Colosseo

Cecilia Metella (££)
At the top of a winding drive, a shower of tables in a delightful garden setting, complete with fountain. Large, open-fire interior for winter. Cheerful, bustling waiters. Stress-free parking.
Via Appia Antica 12 06 511 0213 Closed Mon 118

Al Ceppo (££)
Skilfully recreated regional dishes from the Marches alongside creative variations on more local dishes are to be savoured in this elegant salon that has long enjoyed the exacting patronage of its local Parioli regulars. There is also a discerning wine list.
Via Panama 2 06 841 9696 Closed Mon To Piazza Ungheria

Checchino dal 1887 (£££)
In the heart of Testaccio, this cool vaulted restaurant vaunts the experience of over 100 years. Quintessential Roman cuisine based on the once lowly offerings from the old slaughterhouse opposite. A superb natural wine cellar complements the meal.
Via di Monte Testaccio 30 06 574 3816 Closed Sun eve, Mon, Christmas Piramide 13, 27, 30

Ciak (££)
A rustic Tuscan bistro for lovers of game, roast meats and inimitable local specialities: checked tablecloths, engaging informal service, enthusiastic diners, friendly seating arrangements and an open grill all add to the enjoyment.
Vicolo del Cinque 21 06 589 4774 Closed Mon, lunch To Piazza Sonnino

Colline Emiliane (££)
An old-fashioned family trattoria which adheres strictly to the well-established genuine traditions of the rich cuisine of the northern region of Emilia Romagna. Excellent homemade pasta, particularly *tortellini*, boiled meats and no frills.
Via degli Avignonesi 22 06 481 7538 Closed Fri Barberini To Piazza Barberini

Il Convivio (£££)
A prime choice for a special gourmet occasion: creative cuisine spiced with a touch of genius and true professionalism. Both the well-balanced set menus and the *à la carte* dishes are tantalising in their range and variety; a comparable wine list.
Via dell'Orso 44 06 686 9432 Closed Sun, Mon lunch To Corso del Rinascimento

Opening and Closing
In general, restaurants are open for lunch from about 12 until 3 and from about 8 until 11 for dinner. Most remain closed one day a week and many are closed two or more weeks in August and/or for up to a month in November or January, on Christmas day, Labour Day (1 May) and other public holidays.

What to Eat

A full Italian lunch or dinner starts with *antipasti* (raw and cooked vegetables, cold meats, sea-food) followed by the *primo* (first) course of pasta, rice or soup. *Secondi* are the main courses of meat or fish accompanied, or followed, by *contorni* (vegetables and salad). The meal finishes with *dolce* and coffee with digestive liqueurs. Although you do not have to eat your way through all of these, most restaurants expect you to have at least a couple of courses.

Ditirambo (££)

The two beamed rooms with tiled floors have the tranquillity of an old country inn; innovative Italian dishes are based on genuine ingredients and subtle combinations. Homemade bread, pasta and desserts; excellent (house) wine. Informative staff.

Piazza della Cancelleria 74 06 687 1626 Closed Mon To Corso Vittorio Emanuele

Il Drappo (££)

The kitsch ceiling drapes (hence the name '*il drappo*') of this restaurant off Via Giulia envelop diners voluptuously together; the authentic Sardinian cuisine is a rare beacon in the capital. Set-price menu and booking obligatory.

Vicolo del Malpasso 9 06 687 7365 Closed Sun, lunch To Corso Vittorio Emanuele

Enoteca Corsi (£)

An old-fashioned and comfortable central spot for a plain and simple lunch. No pretensions here – genuine Roman food, informal service and friendly diners eager to share their table space. Informal service. Adjoining wine shop also recommended.

Via del Gesù 88 06 679 0821 Closed Sun, eves To Largo di Torre Argentina

Est! Est! Est! dei Fratelli Ricci (£)

Subdued but much loved central pizzeria with neither brashness nor pretensions. Diners will find simple wooden tables, minimal decor, excellent flat and crispy Roman pizzas, tap beer and regional Italian wines. An experience.

Via Genova 32 06 488 1107 Closed Mon, lunch Repubblica To Piazza della Repubblica

Fiaschetteria Beltramme (££)

Try to get here early after shopping in the centre. A nostalgic survivor of past glories, this tiny trattoria is beginning to suffer from too much superstar visibility, so catch the lingering atmosphere. Share your table, jostle with the famous and enjoy genuine Roman cooking in suitably uninhibited cramped conditions.

Via della Croce 39 None Closed Sun Spagna To Via del Corso

Fornarina (££)

Dine romantically in summer in the ancient walled candlelit courtyard garden and bask in the atmosphere of the home of Raphael's famous mistress and model ('*La Fornarina*'). Almost as atmospheric in winter. Roman cuisine.

Via di Porta Settimiana 8 06 581 8284 Closed Mon To Lungotevere della Farnesina

Da Gino (£)

Central, cheerful, chaotic, crowded and cheap! Politicians and journalists jostle for a seat to enjoy homemade pasta and each day's traditional dish: *gnocchi* and *ossobuco* (Thu), *baccalà* (Fri), *trippa* (Sat). Wonderful tiramisù has to be eaten to be believed.

Vicolo Rosini 4 06 687 3434 Closed Sun To Via del Corso

Gioia mia (Pisciapiano) (£)

A useful spot after a hard day's shopping, offering menus for all palates and purses: from pizzas to full-blown meals. Noisy and chaotic but enjoyable nonetheless. (*Pisciapiano*, for those with linguistic curiosity, actually refers to a Tuscan wine with diuretic

qualities, hence the emblematic cherub relieving himself.)
Via degli Avignonesi 06 488 2784 Closed Sun Barberini To Piazza Barberini

Girarrosto Toscano (£££)
This large, bustling restaurant is a sure culinary oasis in the residential area near St Peter's. Book to ensure your enjoyment of quality Tuscan T-bone steaks, mountain ham, homemade pasta, delicious bread and the company of other dedicated diners.
Via Germanico 58 06 3972 5717 Closed Mon Ottaviano To Piazza del Risorgimento

Grappolo d'Oro (£)
A stone's throw from Campo de' Fiori, this pleasant trattoria continues to offer typical basic Roman fare at prices that are more than reasonable for such a location. Discreet, cordial service and guaranteed satisfaction.
Piazza della Cancelleria 80 06 686 4118 Closed Sun To Corso Vittorio Emanuele

Hostaria Romana (££)
Close to the Trevi Fountain and familiarly known to locals as 'Sergio and Ada'. Hot pizza bread, a wide variety of appetizers, great bowls of steaming pasta, fresh fish and Roman meat dishes ensure a dedicated and happy clientele. There are also inexpensive set menus.
Via del Boccaccio 1 06 474 5284 Closed Sun To Via del Corso

L'Isola Felice (££)
Cheerful home-from-home tiny welcoming trattoria with good plain regional Italian cooking, based on skilful combinations of seasonal products and unexpected individual touches. Delicious homemade desserts. Some tables outside in summer. Excellent wine list.
Vicolo del Leopardo 39a 06 581 4738 Closed Sun, lunch To Piazza Sonnino

Ivo a Trastevere (£)
Go early to avoid the evening queue. Savour a classic Roman pizza and join the scores of contented customers who can say that they have eaten at this institution. Polluted tables outside for those who are non-environmentalists. Open late.
Via San Francesco a Ripa 158 06 581 7082 Closed Tue, lunch To Piazza Sonnino, Viale Trastevere

Lorodinapoli (££)
This popular new Neapolitan restaurant is based on an astute winning formula: a concise lunch menu and an inspirational evening one, which changes every day according to available ingredients and the creativity of the chef. Essential to book ahead. Open late.
Via Fabio Massimo 101 06 323 5790 Closed Sat lunch, Sun eve, Mon Ottaviano To Piazza del Risorgimento

Da Lucia (£)
Catch the last glimpses of the fading splendours of one of old Trastevere's culinary historic spots. Genuine Roman dishes are traditionally and carefully prepared and served without undue ceremony, as is the wine. Sit outside in summer and take in the local atmosphere.
Vicolo del Mattonato 2b 06 580 3601 Closed Mon, 2 weeks at Christmas To Piazza Sonnino

Piatti di Buon Ricordo
Some restaurants take part in the *piatto del buon ricordo* (literally, 'plate of good memory') scheme, in which anybody ordering the special dish of the house will be presented with a plate to take home with them. At Agata e Romeo, for example, the *piatto del buon ricordo* is *pasta e broccoli in brodo di arzilla* (pasta and broccoli).

Snacking
Rome has several eating alternatives if you are in a hurry or only want a snack. *Enoteche* (wine bars) often have cheeses, cold meats and sometimes pasta dishes to accompany their wine lists. *Birrerie* sell beer and basic dishes such as hamburgers. *Pizza al taglio* sell slices of freshly made pizza to take away. Bars have sandwiches and sometimes a *tavola calda*, with one or two hot *primi* and *secondi*. Finally, *alimentari* (grocers) fill rolls with whatever is in stock.

McDonald's (£)
The best of the chain, now spawning offspring throughout the city. There is something for everyone – an upstairs bar serving ice-cream and pastries and, in the spacious basement, a mouthwatering range of fresh mixed salads for the diet-conscious (alongside calorific desserts), as well as the usual US specials.
Piazza di Spagna 46 06 6992 2400 Always open Spagna To Via del Tritone

Margutta Vegetariano (£)
A good vegetarian restaurant and a place to drop in, at any time of day, for a drink, a snack or a complete meal. Good selection of Mediterranean vegetable dishes and a recommended delicate *fritto misto*.
Via Margutta 118 06 3600 1805 Always open Flaminio To Piazzale Flaminio

Le Maschere (££)
A rustic basement restaurant, glowing with wall masks, within a splendid 17th-century Roman palace. Almost impossible to resist the vast colourful display of fresh vegetable dishes and appetizers at the entrance. Fiery Calabrian cuisine and magnificent pizzas. The wines are predominantly Calabrian wines.
Via Monte della Farina 29 06 687 9444 Closed Mon, lunch To Largo di Torre Argentina

Trattoria Monti (££)
A delightful family-run local trattoria recommended for its carefully executed traditional dishes from the Marches and regular daily favourites: *gnocchi* on Thursday, *baccalà* on Friday, *trippa* on Saturday, baked lasagne (*vincisgrassi*) and roasts on Sunday. Commendable wines. Booking advisable.
Via di San Vito 13a 06 446 6573 Closed Tue Termini To Santa Maria Maggiore

Der Pallaro (£)
Democratic authentic Roman family-run restaurant near Campo de' Fiori with no ordering involved – each course of the changing daily menu is brought swiftly to your table. Some tables outside when the sun shines. Open late.
Largo del Pallaro 15 06 6880 1488 Closed Mon To Corso Vittorio Emanuele

Panattoni (£)
A hugely popular Trastevere pizzeria nicknamed 'the coffin-maker' (*cassamortaro*) for its characteristic marble-topped tables. Watch the chef's flamboyant flipping of pizzas at the large oven inside, scramble for a pavement table in summer. Open late.
Viale Trastevere 53 06 580 0919 Closed Wed, lunch To Viale Trastevere

Papà Baccus (££)
An eminently reliable welcoming restaurant in the often daunting Via Veneto area. From his native mountainous Tuscany, the owner offers traditional country soups, ham, salami, grilled meats and fish, homemade desserts. Informal service, seats outside in summer.
Via Toscana 36 06 4274 2808 Closed Sat lunch, Sun, 2 weeks at Christmas Barberini To Via Vittorio Veneto

Da Paris (££)
Satisfied customers return again and again to attest to the winning formula of Trastevere's prime Roman-

Jewish restaurant: unchanging traditional dishes and a sapient use of fresh ingredients. Delicate *vegetable fritto misto*, fresh fish. Small terrace in front, lofty rooms within. Well-selected wine list.
Piazza San Calisto 7a
06 581 5378 Closed Sun eve, Mon To Viale Trastevere

Peccati di Gola (££)

Set in a scenic quiet piazza of Trastevere, and particularly atmospheric in summer, this elegant little restaurant (aptly named after culinary over-indulgence) specialises in Mediterranean and Calabrian fish dishes. Various reasonable set menus. Friendly, attentive service.
Piazza de' Ponziani 7a
06 581 4529 Closed Mon To Viale Trastevere

Perilli a Testaccio (££)

A popular, noisy and crowded trattoria making no concessions to fashionable décor, thriving on its reputation for gargantuan portions of honest Roman specialities. Locals rub shoulders with the famous and everybody really enjoys themselves. Booking ahead is essential.
Via Marmorata 39
06 574 2415 Closed Wed Piramide To Via Marmorata

Piperno (£££)

At the heart of the Jewish Ghetto, the name Piperno has been synonymous with the best (and not cheap) Roman-Jewish cuisine for over 100 years. Time really does seem to stand still in this restaurant: the old-fashioned decor is a sombre backdrop, the waiters exude an olde-worlde chivalry and the classic food is consistently genuine.
Monte de' Cenci 9
06 6880 2772 Closed Sun eve, Mon To Via Arenula, Lungotevere de' Cenci

Pizzaré (£)

Worth a stop, especially at lunchtime, for true large-format Neapolitan pizzas in nearly 40 different combinations. Set menus at ludicrously low prices; also pasta, meat, salads and desserts.
Via di Ripetta 14
06 321 1468 Closed Sun lunch To Lungotevere in Augusta

Trattoria Priscilla (£)

A useful place after trekking around the catacombs and one that is not hard on the pocket. Simple family-run trattoria offering classic Roman fare with no concessions to *haute cuisine* but happy to serve a plate of pasta and a glass of wine.
Via Appia Antica 68
06 513 6379 Closed Sun 118

Nel Regno di Re Ferdinando II (£££)

A new location in Testaccio for this highly acclaimed Neapolitan restaurant, serving all kinds of regional fish, meat and vegetable dishes and superb pizzas from the wood oven.
Via di Monte Testaccio 39
06 578 3725 Closed Sun Piramide To Via Marmorata

Li Rioni (£)

An original street-like pizzeria, complete with tiled courtyard, streetlights and balconies. The atmosphere plus the excellent choice of pizzas have made it a local hot spot. Very popular so be prepared to queue.
Via Santissimi Quattro 24
06 7045 0605 Closed Tue, lunch To Piazza del Colosseo

Pizzas

The best pizzas have a hint of charcoal around the edges. This is caused by being cooked in wood ovens (*forno a legna)*, which create temperatures that seem unbearable in summer. Not all pizzas are the same; Roman ones have a thin, crisp base while, in Naples, pizzas come on a thick, bready base, which is more filling; *calzone*, a particularly appetite-satisfying option, are made from folded over pizza dough stuffed with the filling you choose.

Rome & Excursions from the City

Vegetarians
In Rome there is a dearth of restaurants catering exclusively to vegetarians but that should not stop you from eating well. Even if you do not eat any animal products at all, wherever you go you are likely to find a good selection of delicious meat-, fish- and egg-free pasta dishes, which you can follow with a selection of vegetables *(contorni)* or cheese.

Romolo nel Giardino della San Teodoro (££)

Stumble across this enticing and elegant little trattoria in its romantic setting and you will be treated to a memorable experience, especially in summer. Grilled meats, fresh fish and Roman specialities. Informal, welcoming. Good wines.

Via dei Fienili 49 06 678 0933 Always open To Piazza Bocca della Verità

Sora Lella (££)

A legendary Roman institution on the enchanting Tiber Island, embued with the shades of Sora Lella, a charismatic Roman personality. The food is, naturally, Roman; the diners may be illustrious. Charming, informative service.

Via del Ponte Quattro Capi 16 06 686 1601 Closed Sun To Lungotevere de'Cenci, Lungotevere Anguillare

Sora Margherita (£)

Little more than a hole in the wall, this tiny, unpretentious, sparse and spartan trattoria in the Jewish Ghetto merits a lunchtime stop for its few, selected daily dishes. Genuine home cooking (and fresh pasta) at mouth-watering prices.

Piazza delle Cinque Scole 30 06 686 4002 Closed Sat, Sun, eves To Via Arenula, Lungotevere de' Cenci

La Tana del Grillo (££)

The northern region of Emilia, and Ferrara in particular, offers its inimitable hospitality in this relaxed and understated restaurant, where the customer is made to feel immediately at home and dishes are wholesome and comforting. Affable, attentive service.

Via Alfieri 4 (ang. Via Merulana) 06 7045 3517 Closed Sun, Mon lunch To Via Merulana

Taverna Angelica (££)

A restaurant near St Peter's for romantic, intimate candle-lit dining until the small hours. Creative regional cuisine, both fish and meat, excellent cheeses and imaginative desserts (with well-matched dessert wines by the glass). Courteous and efficient service.

Piazza delle Vaschette 14a 06 687 4514 Closed Sat lunch, Sun Ottaviano To Piazza del Risorgimento

Taverna Cestia (££)

A quality-for-money restaurant enjoying favour with many of the foreign residents working for the nearby UN agency. An extensive menu of Italian dishes, competently executed, together with crisp Roman pizzas. Terrace outside.

Viale Piramide Cestia 67 06 574 3754 Closed Mon Piramide 11, 13, 27, 30

Tito e Quirino Fazioli (£)

A consistently good bet in an area that is notorious for tourist traps. Just behind Piazza Navona, this capacious and good-value trattoria turns out a succession of inspirational fish dishes and a variety of luscious desserts. Worthy wine list.

Via Santa Maria dell'Anima 8 06 686 8100 Closed Sun, lunch in summer To Corso Vittorio Emmanuele

La Zucca Magica (£)
Dulcis in fundo – a vegetarian restaurant patronised by non-vegetarians for the culinary delights that only a chef of genius can produce. Each dish is painstakingly described – vegetables will never seem the same again. Tiny, cosy bordering on kitsch, a jewel of a central eating place. Recommended for lunch (after 1PM).
Via dei Barbieri 23 06 683 3207 Closed Sun, Mon To Largo Vittorio Emanuele

Bracciano

Trattoria del Castello (££)
Classic, local cuisine, adapting medieval recipes to create special fish and meat dishes. Homemade pasta and an extensive wine list.
Piazza Mazzini 1 06 9980 4339 Closed Wed

Frascati

Cacciani (£££)
Classic, consistently reliable spacious restaurant in the Castelli Romani with a large panoramic terrace from which to view Rome's urban conglomeration. Classic meat and fish dishes from Rome and Lazio. Try the regional white Frascati wine.
Via A Diaz 13 06 942 0378 Closed Mon

Taberna Mamilius (££)
Friendly, elegant atmosphere with touches of rusticity. The menu, of mainly local dishes, changes daily according to the best of the season's ingredients that are available.
Viale Balilla 1, Frascati 06 942 1559 Closed Wed/Sun eve

Ostia Antica

Il Monumento (££)
Simple, well-made fish and seafood dishes are the mainstay of this trattoria in the village near the ancient remains of Ostia. The house speciality, '*spaghetti monumento*', is a wonderful mix of seafood and prawns.
Piazza Umberto I 18 06 565 0021 Closed Mon

Sperlonga

Agli Archi (£££)
All the dishes at this little restaurant are delicious, from the *antipasto* of hot and cold seafood, to the homemade puddings. The menu changes daily to take advantages of that day's catches and *mozzarella di bufala* (produced in the area) is another highlight. There is a good-value wine list.
Via Ottaviano 17 (0771) 548300 Closed Wed, except in Jul and Aug

Villa Adriana

Villa Esedra (£)
The *antipasti* and *primi*, of risotto or home-made pasta, offer a range of dishes that are slightly out of the ordinary for a *trattoria*. Secondi and puddings are more standard but still pretty good. Take a table outside in summer.
Via di Villa Adriana 51 (0774) 534716 Closed Tue

Viterbo

Aquilanti (£££)
This huge restaurant, in a 17th-century building, has a range of traditional Viterbo dishes, such as *I lombrichelli all viterbese* and bean soup with wild chicory.
Via del Santuario 4 (0761) 341701 Closed Tue, Sun eve

Richiastro (£)
Traditional local dishes that you will not find in many other places, using simple ingredients such as bread with a spread made from eggs and peppers, lentil and chick-pea soups, and tripe.
Via della Marrocca 16–18 (0761) 223609 Closed Mon–Wed, Sun eve

What's in a Name?
In general, a *trattoria* is an unpretentious, family-run concern often with a regular clientele of local people who drop in when they do not want to cook for themselves. *Ristoranti* are usually more formal and expensive places for a special occasion. *Osterie* used to be the most basic of all, where simple dishes were washed down with jugs of local wine, but beware – recently the name has been adopted by some of the most expensive or touristy establishments.

Rome

Prices
Hotels in Rome are not cheap. The price brackets used here are for a double room – rooms in the mid and upper price ranges nearly always have private bathrooms. Those in the lower range do not always, but nearly all hotels will have at least a few rooms with private bathrooms.
£ = up to €80
££ = €80–€130
£££ = more than€130

Aberdeen (££)
This friendly 26-roomed hotel (all with bathrooms) lies opposite the Ministry of the Interior, two steps from Santa Maria Maggiore. It was refurbished in 1996. English, French and German spoken.
Via Firenze 48 06 482 3920 To Via Nazionale

Campo dei Fiori (££)
Situated in one of the loveliest quarters of the centre, this hotel (terrace overlooks Roman rooftops) is in a flaking ochre-coloured street. Pleasant decor and multi-lingual staff.
Via del Biscione 6 06 688 06865/687 6003 To Corso Vittorio, Largo Argentina

Campo Marzio (£)
If you want a no-frills place to rest your head then this low-cost family-run *pensione*, although a little drab, is clean and superbly situated two steps from parliament and the Pantheon.
Piazza Campo Marzio 7 06 688 01486 To Largo di Torre Argentina

Canova (£££)
Completely refurbished in the summer of 1996 this 3-star, comfortably appointed hotel is situated in a lovely, quiet and safe street near the station at Santa Maria Maggiore.
Via Urbana 10/a 06 487 3314/481 9123 Cavour To Via Cavour

Caravaggio (££)
The lovely wooden-framed door gives the impression of a private club and the atmosphere of this refurbished, centrally located hotel is as welcoming as you might expect .
Via Palermo 73 06 485 915/474 7363 Repubblica To Via Nazionale

Della Conciliazione (££)
Situated in one of the lovely streets tucked away behind the Vatican. The rooms are a little small but they are pleasantly furnished. Friendly service from a multi-lingual staff.
Via Borgo Pio 164 06 686 7910/6880 1164 To Piazza del Risorgimento

Coppedè (££)
A recently refurbished small establishment a little out of the centre in the much sought-after residential area designed by the weird and wonderful architect from which the hotel takes its name. Excellent value for price category.
Via Chiana 88 06 854 9535/854 9535 To Via Po

Corot (££)
Right next to the station so perfectly placed for getting to all sights both in and out of town, this hotel offers comfortable rooms and a hospitable and multi-lingual staff.
Via Marghera 15/17 06 4470 0900/4470 0905 Termini To Termini

Cosmopolita (££)
Large, marble-floored rooms, courteous English and French-speaking staff, located right in the centre (so ask for inward-facing rooms). All facilities. Buffet breakfast included.
Via IV Novembre 114 06 6994 1349 To Piazza Venezia

D'Inghilterra (£££)
A very classy place, situated in a most elegant area of the city. Over a century old it boasts former guests such as Hemingway and Liszt.
Via Bocca di Leone 14
06 69 981/6992 2243
To Piazza San Silvestro

Eliana (££)
At the bottom end of the medium-price range, this 2-star hotel still offers great value for money. Not a great street to be on at night but a great jumping-off point for daytime sightseeing.
Via Gioberti 30 **06 446 5392** **Termini**
To Termini

Elite (££)
A moderately priced, very comfortable small hotel in an expensive area. It also has air-conditioning, an important consideration in the centre in the summer.
Via F. Crispi 49 **06 678 3083/679 1761** **Barberini**
To Via del Tritone

Emmaus (££)
This fourth-floor 25-roomed hotel (some of the rooms have a view of St Peter's dome) is excellent value for this category. It has satellite TV and, unusually, wheelchair access.
Via delle Fornaci 23 **06 635 331** **To Via Gregorio VII**

Enrica (£)
This cheap hotel near Rome's student quarter is run by a friendly multi-lingual ex-sailor and his wife. It has its own lovely garden.
Viale Castro Pretorio **06 445 3742** **Castro Pretorio**
To Via Castro Pretorio

Esquilino (££)
On the 'clean' side of the station, this lovingly refurbished hotel is run by two professional hoteliers. Some rooms look out at Santa Maria Maggiore but the courtyard is quieter.
Piazza dell'Esquilino 29
06 474 3454 **Termini**
To Piazza dell'Esquilino

Excelsior (£££)
Probably the most prestigious hotel in Rome with a luxury and service reminiscent of the days before mass travel.
Via Vittorio Veneto 125
06 47081 **Barberini**
To Vittorio Veneto

Fiorella (£)
Exceptional value on Rome's elegant antiques street. It is small (book early) and the bathrooms are shared; rooms spotless and airy.
Via del Babuino 196 **06 361 0597** **Spagna** **To Via del Corso**

Firenze (££)
Completely restored at the end of 1995, on the first floor of a chic but busy street (near the Spanish Steps) so get a courtyard room.
Via Due Macelli 106 **06 679 7240/678 5636** **Barberini**
To Via del Tritone

Grifo (££)
Tunisian family-run establishment, located in a lovely street in a quiet enclave near the Colosseum. Some rooms have delightful private terraces. Also available is a self-catering option on the top floor.
Via del Boschetto 144
06 487 1395 **To Via Nazionale**

Hassler Villa Medici (£££)
One of the grandest old-style luxury hotels in the heart of the most elegant part of the centre with a view to die for from the elegant roof terrace and restaurant.
Piazza Trinità dei Monti 6
06 678 2651/6994 1607
Spagna **To Via del Tritone**

Booking
There are some 700 hotels in Rome but early booking is still advisable. Even the most modest places may want a telephone booking backed up by a deposit (a credit card will usually, but not always, be enough). If you do book, the local EPT tourist offices will help. There is an office in the centre (Via Parigi, 5; 06 4889 9253), at the station (06 487 1270) and at Fiumicino airport (06 6595 6074) with multi-lingual staff.

Rome & Excursions from the City

Special Needs
Italian culture and society may not accommodate special requirements formally, but the flexibility and initiative of the people means you could encounter extraordinary gestures of generosity (alternatively, you may find your path irremediably blocked). For example, hotels with no night porter often provide a key for guests who want to stay out late; those without breakfast may miraculously produce coffee. Unfortunately, the nature of Roman building does not lend itself to wheelchairs, but, whatever the official line, check with the individual establishment first.

Madrid (££)
At the top end of the moderate-price category in an expensive area, this 26-roomed hotel has all the amenities and a delightful inside courtyard-terrace.
Via Mario de' Fiori 89
06 699 1510/679 1653
To Piazza San Silvestro

Manara (£)
Very basic, also very cheap, with the distinct advantage of being located in lovely Trastevere, one of the best places to be of an evening.
Via Luciano Manara 25
06 581 4713 **To Viale Trastevere**

Michelangelo (££)
A hotel with 4-star facilities (including air-conditioning) but at 3-star prices within a stone's throw of the Vatican.
Via Stazione di S Pietro 14
06 622 412/632 359 **To Via Stazione di San Pietro**

Perugia (£)
Modest with no frills, but with a friendly multi-lingual staff and most of the 11 rooms have bathrooms. Two steps from the Colosseum.
Via del Colosseo 7 **06 679 7200/678 4635** **Colosseo**
To Via Cavour, Colosseo

Ponte Sisto (££)
An enormous hotel for the area (130 rooms). It offers all the basic amenities and a terrace in a beautiful part of the historical centre.
Via dei Pettinari 64
06 686 8843/6830 8822
To Via Arenula

Portoghesi (££)
Tucked away in a lovely side street in one of the prettiest areas. Tastefully furnished, with a roof terrace.
Via dei Portoghesi 1 **06 686 4231/687 6976** **To Corso del Rinascimento**

San Paolo (£)
Basic but clean and bright on a lovely street, with friendly staff. Twenty rooms (many with own bathroom). Group discounts available.
Via Panisperna 95 **06 474 5213/474 5217** **Cavour**
To Via Cavour

Sant'Anselmo (££)
A lovely reasonably priced hotel in a villa with garden in the heart of ancient Rome; wheelchair facilities.
Piazza Sant'Anselmo 2
06 578 3214 **Circo Massimo** **To Via Aventino**

Shangri la' Corsetti (££)
Situated out of the centre beyond EUR. Every amenity including a good restaurant.
Viale Algeria 141 **06 591 6441** **EUR Fermi**
To Palazzo dello Sporto

Sole al Pantheon (£££)
Next to the Pantheon with some rooms looking over it, this hotel has had some illustrious guests not least Ariosto, one of the greats of Italian literature.
Piazza della Rotunda 63
06 678 0441 **To Largo di Torre Argentina**

Self-Catering

Ripa (£££)
One of the main service-apartment options is in Trastevere. All amenities, including a restaurant. Book early, as popular with visiting Italians working in Rome.
Via Luigi Gianniti **06 586 611/581 4550** **To Viale Trastevere**

EUR Torrino Residence (££)
A new service-apartment complex near the business district which it serves. Somewhat sterile in the evenings but well-connected to the centre; reasonable prices.
✉ Via Decima 245 ☎ 06 529 7570 Ⓜ Palasport (then bus)

Villa Tassoni (££)
This huge turn-of-the-19th-century mansion was built by a general for his family. Now it has been converted into smart studio flats with centralised services. The attractive location of Monte Mario is convenient for the Vatican and the city centre.
✉ Via delle Medaglie d'Oro 134–8 ☎ 06 355 899/3545 4188 🚌 To Vatican

Youth Hostels

YWCA (£)
The safe women-only hostel near the central station is the perfect option if you are in Rome for early starts and serious sightseeing. There is an evening curfew.
✉ Via Cesare Balbo 4 ☎ 06 488 0460 Ⓜ Termini 🚌 To Via Cavour

Ostello de la Gioventù Foro Italico (£)
Members of the Youth Hostel Association can stay in this Youth Hostel a little way from the centre. Bed and breakfast, half and full board options.
✉ Viale delle Olimpiadi 61 ☎ 06 324 2571 🚌 To Viale delle Olimpiadi

Campsites

Parco del Lago (£)
A tranquil campsite set on the edge of Lake Bracciano. All necessary amenities, and popular with Romans who come to get away from it all. Book early. Summer only.
✉ Strada Provinciale Anguillara Trevignano Km 4,100 ☎ 06 9980 2003 🚌 To Anguillara/Trevignano

Flaminio (£)
A large and reasonably priced campsite within reach of the city, offering cabins among its options. There is a swimming pool. Open March to December.
✉ Via Flaminia Nuova Km 8,200 ☎ 06 333 2604 🚌 Bus or train to Due Ponti

Castelfusano Country Club (£)
This is actually one of the two campsites near the not-so-clean but long and wide Roman beaches. In Ostia, so Rome is easily reached by public transport. Open all year.
✉ Piazza di Castelfusano 1 ☎ 06 566 2394 Ⓜ To Castelfusano

Subiaco

Italia (££)
Open December to March, June to September this hotel with gardens and tennis courts is situated in an off-the-beaten-track area of Lazio in the mountains, yet only 90 minute's drive from Rome. Wonderful local restaurants.
✉ Via Monte Livata ☎ (0774) 826014 🚌 Coach to Subiaco

La Torraccis

Tarquinia Lido (££)
An option which is not-too-distant from Rome and near the Estruscan ruins. Every room has a terrace.
✉ Viale Mediterraneo 45 ☎ (0766) 864 375/8642 🚆 To Tarquinia

Tivoli

Delle Terme (££)
This 3-star hotel with its own gardens and restaurant, conveniently placed for the villas of Tivoli, is a fine alternative to staying in the centre, not least because the price goes down by half for the privilege of being in a small attractive countryside town
✉ Piazza B della Quiete ☎ (0774) 371010 🚆 To Tivoli

The Cost of a Star
The Italian star-rating system can make it difficult to know what you are getting, as it is based exclusively on facilities offered. This means, for example, a charmingly furnished atmospheric 2-star affair may cost less than a grotty run-down 3-star business. This is further complicated by a fewer-stars-less-tax situation with some hoteliers happy not to upgrade themselves.

Antiques, Art, Books Toys & Fashion

Where to Find Antiques
If you are looking for antiques (from an old print of Rome to furniture) the most prestigious shops are on Via del Babuino. Another safe and reliable destination is Via Guilia. At the end of May and October, just before and after the blistering heat, Via dei Coronari, which has only antiques, holds its fair. The shops open late, the street is carpeted red and lined with candles. It is a magical atmosphere, perfect for a evening stroll.

Antiques

Arnaboldi
For the more serious collector, this antiques dealer a little out of the centre has everything from porcelain to Russian icons.
Via Gregorio VII 110
06 393 76878 To Via Gregorio VII

Art Import
A slightly unprepossessing name but a treasure trove if you are after antique silver. They also stock porcelain, an interesting collection of *objéts d'art* and modern Italian Barbini glass vases.
Via del Babuino 150
06 3600 2189 Spagna
To Piazzale Flaminio

Ramoni
This shop, established in 1930, on another of the important Roman antiques streets, sells everything from furniture to work in silver and bronze. Also an interior design service.
Via Governo Vecchio 76
06 6880 2003 To Corso Vittorio Emmanuele

Art

Aldo di Castro
Definitely the shop to visit for authentic prints. It stretches far back off the street and is lined with prints of all price ranges. A great selection of framed or unframed Roman scenes.
Via del Babuino 71
06 361 3752 Spagna
To Piazza San Silvestro, Via del Tritone

Ciambrelli
For a classy canvas or print of pre-20th-century views of Rome at a reasonable price, this charming and courteous family-run establishment will satisfy your needs.
Via dei Coronari 143
06 6880 1024 To Corso del Rinascimento

Books

The Corner Bookshop
This small but well-stocked English bookshop in Trastevere offers a good selection of classic and recent fiction and non-fiction, as well as a wide range of books on Italy.
Via del Moro 48 06 583 6942 To Piazza Sonnino

Feltrinelli
The best-stocked bookshop chain in Rome (with a new international outlet near Piazza della Repubblica). Conveniently located branches and easy-to-understand merchandising. Also cards, specialist magazines, posters, videos and CD-Roms.
Via VE Orlando 84/6
06 482 7878
Repubblica To Via Nazionale

Libri D'Arte
Out-of-print and rare books not only in Italian, specialising in art books, and posting to anywhere in the world. A little off the beaten track near the Italian TV (RAI) headquarters.
Via Caposile 6 06 361 3156 To Piazza Mazzini

Mel Bookshop
One of the largest, newest bookshops in Rome. 'Mel' has a good English section. It sells everything from kids' books to CDs and even has a

café in the art department.
Via Nationale 254/5
06 488 5405
Repubblica
To Via Nazionale

Touring Viaggi
This bookshop and travel agent of the Touring Club Italiano stocks all you need in terms of maps and guides as well as a small selection of tasteful postcards.
Via del Babuino 20
06 3609 5801 **Spagna, Flaminio** **To Piazzale Flaminio**

Children's Clothes and Toys

La Cicogna
Somewhat pricey but chic high-quality Italian kids' fashion and elegantly practical maternity clothes. Some great bargains if you catch the sales.
Via Cola di Rienzo 268
06 689 6557 **To Piazza Cavour**

Città del Sole
An inspired selection of top-of-the-range educational toys and books for children of all ages. A pretty hands-on, child-friendly approach.
Via della Scrofa 65
06 687 5404 **To Corso del Rinascimento**

Al Sogno
Sogno means dream but this shop could be a parent's nightmare given the prices of the wonderful stock, which sometimes resembles museum pieces. Particularly tempting are the soft toys.
Piazza Navona 53
06 686 4198 **To Corso del Rinascimento**

Invicta
No self-respecting Italian schoolkid can be seen without an 'Invicta' knapsack, so established that it is now officially part of the Italian language. The new shop includes brand-stretching clothes.
Via del Babuino 27/8
06 3600 1737 **Spagna**
To Piazzale Flaminio, Piazza San Silvestro

Fashion: designer

Giorgio Armani
The beautifully cut, hand-finished simplicity of the Milanese designer resides in the prestigious Via Condotti. Look for the off-the-peg *Emporio* line which is round the corner on Via del Babuino.
Via Condotti 77 **06 699 1460** **Spagna** **Via del Corso**

Arsenale
Owner Patrizia Pieroni's outlet for her own romantic designs which are an interesting mix between classic and original, and they incorporate the most wonderful velvets, silks, linens and lace.
Via del Governo Vecchio 64
06 686 1380 **To Corso Vittorio Emanuele**

Cenci
High quality, classic and classy. Davide Cenci is synonymous in Rome with low-key tailored elegance and is as refined as an old-style English outfitters. The prices are to match.
Via Campo Marzio 1/7
06 699 0681 **To Largo di Torre Argentina, Via del Corso**

Fendi
There are fur coats, shoes and ready-to-wear clothes, but it is the much-copied signature handbag with the discreet 'F' in the design that is the classic purchase for both Romans and visitors.
Via Borgognona 36–9
06 679 7641 **Spagna**
To Piazza Augusto Imperatore

Opening and Closing
Shop opening hours are beginning to change with more all-day and Sunday openings and the traditional August shut-down is weakening as Romans begin to take shorter holidays. Generally, however, it is a Monday to Saturday set-up with a break from 1PM to 4PM. Food shops close on Thursday afternoons and others on Monday mornings.

Fashion, Interiors, Jewellery, Leather & Stationery

Prices

Prices in Rome are not low, a state of affairs that is not helped by the preponderance of small shops, which has made for an inefficient retailing system. The tradition is hard to kill. Italian life is public and the local shop, particularly the foodstore, is a place to chat, have things put aside for you, receive discounts and even credit. As a visitor you can expect to be excluded.

VAT Refunds

Non-EU citizens spending more than €155 are entitled to VAT refunds, so be sure to buy from those shops displaying the sticker. You will be furnished with a form to present to customs on leaving Italy along with the *scontrino* (receipt). Do not use or wear the goods first.

Il Discount dell' Alta Moda

Last season's designer clothes, shoes and accessories for men and women at half their original price. A must for bargain hunters.

Via Gesu' e Maria 16A 06 361 3791 To Via del Corso

Fendissime

Fendi's 'diffusion' label aimed at younger women, has a range of easy to wear, fun clothes, original shoes and classy leather goods, at reasonable prices.

Via della Fontanella di Borghese 56a 06 696661 To Via del Corso, Piazza Augusto Imperatore

Gucci

Another classic Italian fashion-house offers inimitable wares in a soothing creamy-beige outlet on the most chic street in Rome.

Via Condotti 8 06 678 9340 Spagna To Via del Corso

Missoni

The multi-coloured elegance of the inspired tapestry-like knitwear is almost outrageous. The beach towels offer a taste of the style, if you can not stretch to a sweater.

Piazza di Spagna 78 06 679 2555 Spagna To Via del Corso

Max Mara

The affordable end of designer land, Max Mara offers wonderfully crisp shapes and clean colours in various branches.

Via Nazionale 28–31 06 488 5870 Repubblica To Via Nazionale

Valentino

Rome's own has his boutique on Via Condotti just two steps from the wonderful headquarters in Piazza Mignatelli. The casual wear 'Oliver' is round the corner on Via del Babuino.

Via Condotti 13 06 678 3656 Spagna To Via del Corso

Fashion: 'non-label'

Citoni

Trendy up-to-the-minute fashions for men and women in their twenties and thirties. Lines include the currently highly popular Dolce e Gabbana.

Via Due Macelli 92–4 06 679 5006 Barberini To Via del Tritone

Clark

'Safe' fashions for the twenties upwards. Nothing spectacular but it has good quality at reasonable prices.

Via Appia Nuova 103 a/b 06 049 2552 San Giovanni, Re di Roma To Via Appia Nuova

Gente

One of the best women's clothes shops in Rome, on the city's most popular shopping street. 'Gente' sells lots of wearable styles (including many designer labels). Other branches in the historic centre.

Via Cola di Renzo 277 06 321 1516 To Piazza Cavour

Lei

For good-quality, fairly pricey but seriously wearable young adult fashions go here. Among others they stock the

smart, simple French label Tara. Some shoes and accessories.
Via dei Gubbonari, 103 06 687 5432 To Via Arenula

Interior Design

Azi
An Aladdin's cave of stainless steel, glass and blue and white ceramics for kitchens, bathrooms and the rest of the house. Most of the stock comes from Italy and France.
Via San Francesco a Ripa 06 588 3303 To Viale Trastevere

Bagagli
A veritable field-day is to be had in this cobblestoned shop if you want tableware. Villeroy and Boch and the wonderful Alessi designs, which are among the best-quality ranges on offer.
Via di Campo Marzio 42 06 687 1406 To Via del Corso

Cucina
A beautifully merchandised basement shop that stocks top-of-the-range kitchen equipment with impeccable design. Buy your pasta pan here.
Via del Babuino 118–a 06 679 1275 Spagna To Via del Corso, Piazza San Silvestro

Frette
The queen of household linens. The bed linen and towels, often inspired by classical designs, are quite beautiful, as are the prices unless your trip happens to coincide with the sales.
Via Nazionale 84 06 488 2641 To Via Nazionale

Spazio Sette
By no means cheap but quite easily the best home shop in the centre selling everything from glassware to hardware, postcards to furniture. The buying philosophy seems to be 'If it is designer...'.
Via dei Barbieri 7 06 686 9747 To Largo di Torre Argentina

Jewellery

Boncompagni
Nìcola Boncompagni is a fine shop on a fine street selling a delectable range of antique jewellery.
Via del Babuino 83 06 678 3847 Spagna To Via del Corso

Raggi
A fine shop for its wide selection at reasonable prices, with several branches in the city. This branch is on one of the best shopping streets in Rome.
Via Cola di Rienzo 250 06 689 6601 To Piazza Cavour

Vestroni
A small jeweller's which includes in its stock delightful Brugiotti watches reproducing old ceramics on their faces.
Via del Pantheon 42 06 687 5813 To Largo di Torre Argentina

Leather

Bertoletti
With a strong reputation among Romans, this shop is one of the classiest in Rome selling sheepskins, furs and leatherwear.
Via Sistina 42 06 678 9625 Barberini To Via del Tritone

Castello D'Auria
A lovely little drawer-lined shop with a small but excellent selection of leather gloves; they also sell hosiery.
Via Due Macelli 55 06 679 3364 Spagna To Via del Tritone

Department Stores
Department stores are not the Italian style. If they are yours, the less touristy Piazza Fiume (not far from Via Veneto) is the best bet. Here you will find the larger of the Rinascente (the other is on Via del Corso) with kitchenware, furnishings and a café and, nearby, the old Peroni beer factory has been lovingly converted into Coin.

Shoes, Souvenirs & Markets

Souvenir Shopping
Characteristic Roman souvenirs consist of copies of the main sights or bronze reproductions of Etruscan artefacts, all of which can be found in most tobaccanists at half the price of the stalls near the sights themselves. Ecclesiastical memorabilia is to be had in the shops in and around Borgo Pio, while shops supplying the religious community are on Via dei Cestari near the Pantheon.

Red and Blue
An excellent place to go if you are looking for top-quality leatherwear in the classic styles reflected by its other merchandise, (for example Burberry). Also children's clothes.
Via due Macelli 57 06 679 1933 Spagna To Via del Tritone

Accessories

Borsalino
An old-fashioned hat shop which is the most famous in Rome for its classic men's headwear and more changeable women's styles.
Via IV Novembre 157b 06 679 4192 To Piazza Venezia

Marissa Padovani
The ultimate place to buy swimming costumes – as well as a good range of ready-to-wear, you can have your bikini or one-piece made to measure.
Via delle Carrozze 81 06 679 3946 Spagna To Via del Corso

Vision Optika
A massive range of classic and fashion sunglasses, including the latest designer collection (John Paul Gaultier, Police, Sting) which will be altered to fit your face. The shop is also an opticians' studio and can make up prescription lenses.
Via di S. Claudio 87/a/b 06 678 5983 To Piazza San Silvestro

Stationery

Campo Marzio Penne
Specialises in antique, calligraphic and major-brand pens (and restoration). The new Vatican collection pen is based on designs by Raphael in the Vatican museums.
Campo Marzio 41 06 6880 7877 To Via del Corso

Pantheon
A gorgeous little shop which sells hand-marbled paper, notebooks and photo albums as well as a great selection of writing paper and cards.
Via della Rotonda 15 06 687 5313 To Largo di Torre Argentina

Vertecchi
A serious and modern stationery shop selling an excellent selection of pens, writing paper (also by the sheet in a variety of colours). There is a large artist's section.
Via della Croce 74 06 679 0100 Flaminio To Via del Corso

Shoes

Dominici
A pristine white-tiled shop in which this Roman designer's original shoes are displayed in neat rows. The prices are good and the styles a bit out of the ordinary without being over the top.
Via del Corso 14 06 361 0591 To Via del Corso

Impronta
A small shop but with a good collection of young fashion styles. It is on the piazza at the beginning of this atmospheric shopping street.
Via del Governo Vecchio 1 06 689 6947 To Corso Vittorio Emmanuele

Italya
Tucked away in a side

street near St Lorenzo in Lucina; ladies' own-brand shoes in styles appealing to most age-groups and tastes. There is also a nice selection of bags.
Via della Torretta 69 06 687 1026 To Via del Corso

Bruno Magli
These incredibly elegant, classic Italian shoes for ladies and gentlemen can be found near the other classic Italian fashion shops.
Via del Gambero 06 679 3802 To Piazza San Silvestro

Ramirez
Part of a chain and thus competitively priced, this shop can boast a wide selection of shoe styles for both sexes as well as all age groups.
Via Frattina 85–a 06 679 2012 To Via del Corso

Fausto Santini
The ultimate in modern Roman shoe design, Fausto Santini's styles are original and elegant and you won't find anything quite like them elsewhere.
Via Frattina 120 06 678 4114 Spagna To Via del Corso

Souvenirs and Religious Gifts

Gini O Graphics
This sells some great mugs, T-shirts and watches on Roman themes by young designers. There is also fine-art inspired memorabilia, pens and notebooks.
Via Nazionale 185 06 474 6872 To Via Nazionale

Soprani
One of the many shops around the Vatican dedicated to serious religious artefacts and more commercially minded souvenirs of your trip to the Holy City; images of the Pope and Christ can be printed on almost everything.
Via del Mascherino 29 06 6880 1404 To Piazza del Risorgimento

Markets

Campo de' Fiori
Probably the loveliest food market in central Rome thanks to the wonderful piazza hosting it. Open every morning except Sundays, the wall of flower-sellers can be found all day.
Piazza Campo dei Fiori To Corso Vittorio

Vittorio Emmanuele
The largest food market in Rome, often criticised for lowering the tone of this splendid piazza with its recently gentrified central garden, is also the cheapest food market. There is a wonderful array of fish and fruit and vegetables.
Piazza Vittorio Emmanuele Vittorio To Piazza Vittorio Emmanuele

Porta Portese
This market is famous throughout Italy. It takes over the streets in and around Porta Portese every Sunday morning and is jam-packed. You can buy almost everything imaginable from clothes (beware of fake labels) to books and antiques.
Via Porta Portese To Viale Trastevere

Via Sannio
Popular with Romans for new and second-hand clothes. The leather jackets are excellent value and a couple of the shoe stands are good (only if you have the right shoe size). Some real bargains in the piles at the back if you have an eye.
Via Sannio San Giovanni To Via Appia Nuova

Ancient Sights, Museums & Theme Parks

Christmas
From the beginning of December until Epiphany (6 January) Rome is decorated with delicate street lighting and, on some streets, red carpets. Piazza Navona is taken over by a massive Christmas market selling an exotic range of gaudy sweets, cheap toys and Christmas decorations. In addition many churches have *presepi* (nativity scenes), often with valuable old models placed in realistic Renaissance street scenes.

Ancient Sights

To help get to grips with ancient Rome, the souvenir stands outside the major sights sell little books that show many of the ancient remains as they are now and as they were when they were intact. The gaudy souvenirs on sale here should also appeal to children.

Colosseo (Colosseum)
See the corridors through which lions came on their way to eat Christians. (➤ 18).

Largo Argentina
Full of serene cats and the remains of a massive public toilet (➤ 45).

Museo della Civiltà Romana
Models of what ancient Rome was really like (➤ 48).

Ostia Antica
Well-preserved remains of an ancient Roman seaside town (➤ 86).

Via Appia Antica
The road ancient Romans travelled on their way to the sea, west to Ostia, east to the other side of Italy (➤ 62).

Churches

San Clemente
Underneath this pretty mosaic-filled church are secret corridors leading to ancient remains (➤ 23).

Sant'Ignazio di Loyola
Here you really can see up to heaven by looking at the magnificent *trompe l'oeil* ceiling (➤ 66).

Santa Maria della Concezione
The macabre crypt is decorated with the bones of defunct monks (➤ 68).

Santa Maria in Cosmedin
Put your hand into the mouth of truth, which was originally an ancient Roman drain cover and probably represented the sun (➤ 68).

The Catacombs
Definitely not for the faint-hearted child – these kilometres-long underground passages are lined with the tombs of early Christians (➤ 38).

Other Sights

Castel Sant'Angelo
This tomb-come-fortress-come-palace has some wonderful *trompe l'oeils* and lots of winding, secret corridors, gloomy guardrooms and good views (➤ 17).

Galleria Spada
Visit the Galleria in Palazzo Spada particularly for its spectacular three-dimensional *trompe l'oeil*, whose fake perspective will make even the smallest child seem tall (➤ 56).

Museo delle Cere
The surreality of some of the tableaux may appeal more to adult senses of humour than to children used to Madame Tussaud's, but it is still worth going to see what Leonardo and his contemporaries might have looked like.
Piazza dei Santi Apostoli 67 **06 679 6482** **Apr–Sept, 9–9. Oct–Mar, 9–8** **To Piazza Venezia**

Museo del Folklore e dei Poeti Romaneschi
As well as paintings of what Rome looked like when all these artists were strolling around, there are some amusing waxworks of Roman and rustic life in the 18th century (➤ 48).

Outdoor: Parks and Shows

Aquafelix
A water park with an exotic range of themed rides and slides involving getting wet and screaming – most children under five may find it a little too much. There are also shops, a bar and a self-service restaurant.
Autostrada Roma–Civitavecchia at the Civitavecchia Nord Exit (0766) 32221 Jun–Sep, 10–6 daily

Aquapiper
An outdoor swimming pool complex with a children's pool complete with a slide, an adult/older children's pool with a wave machine and its own more exciting (or terrifying, depending on your point of view) slide. There are also ponies and camels, a picnic area, a bar and a games room.
Via Maremmana Inferiore Km 29, Guidonia (0774) 326 538 First week Jun to first week Sep, Mon–Fri 9–6:30, Sat & Sun 9–7 From Ponte Mammolo to Palombara

Bioparco
Rome's zoo underwent a transformation in the late 1990s to re-emerge as a champion of environmental awareness. In place of the old museum mentality, visitors are encouraged to learn more about the natural habitats of the animals and to play an active part in their conservation.
Piazzale del Giardino Zoologico, Villa Borghese 06 360 8211 8:30–6 To Piazza Ungheria

Piazza Navona
There is always plenty to see here; you can pose for a portrait or caricature, buy a helium-filled balloon or eat ice-cream. There is Bernini's wonderful fountain to set your imagination flying (➤ 21).

Puppet Shows
Although these are in Italian (and a fairly dialectic Italian at that) they are more or less comprehensible to anybody, being variations on the traditional 'Punch and Judy' theme. There are also fairground-type stalls and a roundabout nearby.
Piazza Garibaldi Summer weekday eve, all year Sun AM To Gianicolo A hat is passed around

Luna Park
This 30-year-old funfair is the nearest that Rome gets to a theme park. Most of its attractions are fairly traditional – a hall of mirrors, a ferris wheel, roller-coasters and merry-go-rounds – but recent additions include some more ambitious contraptions and stage-sets based on American theme-park rides.
Via delle Tre Fontane 592 5933 Jun–Sep, Mon–Fri 5–12, Sat 3–1, Sun 3–12; Sept–Jun, Mon, Wed–Fri 3–7, Sat 3–1, Sun 10–1, 3–10 Magliana To Via delle Tre Fontane

Carnevale
Carnevale takes place the week before Shrove Tuesday and children dress up as cartoon or historical characters, animals and so on to walk through the streets with their parents, letting off fire crackers and throwing confetti.

Cinema, Theatre, Music & Opera

Hollywood on the Tiber
Rome has had an active film industry since 1937 when Mussolini opened the studios at Cinecittà. The heyday of 'Hollywood on the Tiber' was in the 1950s and 1960s when many American producers and directors came here to make films such as *Ben Hur*, *Cleopatra* and, of course, the famous spaghetti westerns. Things have quietened down a bit since then but the studios are still used by Italian film and TV makers and guided tours are sometimes arranged (phone to check).
Via Tuscolana 1055
06 722931
Cinecittà 502, 503, 504, 506, 551, 558, 561

Cinema

Italy is proud of its high standard of dubbing and most foreign films are dubbed into Italian. Cinema screenings are usually at 4:30, 6:30, 8:30 and 10:30. In the summer (June to September), there are several open-air cinemas, showing mainly classics or the previous season's most successful releases.

L'Alcazar

Recent releases in Trastevere. Films shown in English or with English sub-titles on Mondays.
Via Cardinal Merry del Val 14 06 588 0099
To Viale Trastevere, Piazza Sonnino

Majestic

Mainstream cinema near Piazza Venezia. Shows films in English on Mondays.
Via Santi Apostoli 20
06 679 4908 To Piazza Venezia

Nuovo Sacher

This cinema belongs to film-maker Nanni Moretti (of *Caro Diario* fame) and is named after his favourite cake. It shows slightly offbeat new releases (which appeal to the proprietor) and screens them in original language (which can be anything) on Mondays and Tuesdays. There is an outdoor arena where films are shown during the summer.
Largo Ascianghi 1
06 581 8116 To Viale Trastevere

Pasquino

The new management recently overhauled 'Pasquino', the first English language cinema in Rome. The 2 cinemas show English-language films only (usually with Italian sub-titles).
Vicolo del Piede 19
06 580 3622 To Viale Trastevere, Piazza Sonnino

Warner Village Moderno

Five large screens in this ultra-modern complex – new releases in English every Thursday. Great sound and comfy seats.
Piazza della Repubblica 45/6 06 477791
Repubblica 40, 60, 64, 170 to Piazza della Repubblica

Outdoor Cinema

Massenzio

The main summer cinema venue, which has no official fixed abode but has recently been on the park opposite the entrance to the Palatino. Three films a night, ranging from the previous season's releases to erudite festivals by international stars of the film-making world. There is a lively jazz and music festival going on at the same time.
Parco del Celio, entrance on Via di San Gregorio.

Piazza Vittorio

Weekly original-language (usually English) films in the pristine Piazza Vittorio gardens. Also holds other events, including activities for children from Jul–Sep.
Piazza Vittorio 06 445 1208/291

Theatre and Dance

Agorà

This theatre hosts visiting theatre companies from the rest of Europe. Plays in

Italian, English, French, Spanish and so on depending on who is here.
Via della Penitenza 33 06 687 4167 To Lungotevere Farnesina

dell'Angelo
A fairly recent-comer to the theatre scene. Productions include some avant-garde Italian and foreign companies. There is also an interesting programme of contemporary and jazz music.
Via Simon de San Bon 17 06 3600 2640 Ottaviano To Largo Trionfale

Argentina
A beautiful, restored 19th-century gem which occasionally hosts TV spectaculars. Home to the Rome Theatre Company, who do good (if slightly traditional) productions of ancient and modern classics.
Largo di Torre Argentina 52 06 6880 4601 To Largo di Torre Argentina

Colosseo
One of the best venues for seeing works by young Italian directors and playwrights.
Via Capo d'Africa 5a 06 700 4932 Colosseo 81, 85

Olimpico
A vast barn of a place where international dance and musical productions are staged. It is also where the Rome Philharmonic Orchestra holds its concerts.
Piazza Gentile da Fabriano 17 06 323 4890 To Piazza Mancini

Sistina
This is the place to come for musicals, either homegrown or Italianised versions of London and New York hits.
Via Sistina 129 06 482 6841 Barberini To Piazza Barberini

Valle
One of two venues for the National Italian Theatre company. Excellent productions of modern classics such as Pirandello, Beckett and Pinter.
Via del Teatro Valle 23a 06 6880 3794 To Corso Vittorio Emanuele

Vascello
As well as hosting some of the most interesting theatre companies in Italy, this is a venue for ballet, contemporary and ethnic dance.
Via Giacinto Carini 72 06 588 1021 41, 44, 75

Music: Classical and Opera

Auditorio di Santa Cecilia
The Accademia has one of Rome's best chamber and symphony orchestras, who perform here, often under the baton of top-class visiting conductors.
Via della Conciliazione 4 06 6880 1844 To Piazza del Risorgimento

Teatro Olimpico
Where the Filarmonica di Roma, and its visiting performers and ensembles, perform. (➤ Theatre and Dance, above).

Teatro dell'Opera
The winter season of the Rome opera and ballet company takes place here. In summer performances are staged in the Piazza di Siena, in the Villa Borghese.
Via Firenze 72 06 481601 Termini To Termini,

Music: Jazz, Rock

Alexanderplatz
The place for jazz in Rome. A restaurant and cocktail bar.
Via Ostia 9 06 3974 2171 Ottaviano To Largo Trionfale

Ancient Theatre
For an authentic ancient Roman theatre experience head down to the well-preserved ancient Roman theatre at Ostia Antica (➤ 86) in July and August when the Teatro Romano produces classical Roman and Greek plays. Alternatively, at the Vatican end of the Gianicolo (➤ 43) lies the little amphitheatre of Tasso's Oak, where ancient and less ancient classics are performed against the backdrop of wonderful views of the city.

Anfiteatro della Quercia del Tasso
Passegiata del Gianicolo (07) 575 0827 Jul–Sep 41, 44 Teatro Romano di Ostia Antica Ostia Antica 06 687 7390 Jul–Aug Train to Ostia Antica

Music, Clubs, Bars & Sport

Outdoor Music
During the summer there are plenty of outdoor classical musical events, including a series of Sunday morning concerts given by the orchestras of various branches of the armed forces on the Pincio. For a combination of world-class performers and a staggeringly beautiful setting, head to Villa Giulia (➤ 78) which is where the Accademia di Santa Cecilia hosts its summer season. Other top-quality performers can be heard under the remains of Teatro di Marcello (➤ 74).

Teatro di Marcello
✉ Via del Teatro di Marcello 44
☎ Information about the concerts: 06 481 4800
🕐 Jun–Oct
🚌 To Via del Teatro di Marcello

Terme di Caracalla
✉ Via della Terme di Caracalla 52
☎ Information about the concerts: 06 575 8626
🕐 Jun–Oct
🚌 160, 613, 628, 714
♿ Few

Villa Giulia
✉ Piazzale di Villa Giulia 9
☎ Information about the concerts: 06 678 6428
🕐 Jul 🚌 19, 19b, 30, 30b, 225, 926

Alpheus
Three separate areas: one catering for jazz, one for rock and the other for dancing to records.
✉ Via del Commercio 36 ☎ 06 574 7826 🚇 Piramide 🚌 To Via Ostiense

Big Mama
Sub-titled 'the home of the blues in Rome', Big Mama has an interesting programme of live music performed by Italian and international musicians, including the occasional legend.
✉ Vicolo San Francesco a Ripa 18 ☎ 06 581 2551 🚌 To Viale Trastevere

Bossanova
One of the Latin-American venues, with a mixture of live and recorded music and dancing.
✉ Via degli Orti di Trastevere 43 ☎ 06 581 6121 🚌 To Viale Trastevere

Circolo degli Artisti
Some of the most recent big names from the international music scene play here. It is also a good place for dancing and organises nights of 1960s, African and so on music, as well as hosting visiting DJs from the rest of Europe.
✉ Via Lamarmora 28 ☎ 06 446 4968

Il Locale
Small, friendly venue near Piazza Navona with mainly Italian live music.
✉ Vicolo del Fico 3 ☎ 06 687 9075 🚌 To Corso Vittorio Emanuele

Palladium
A converted cinema that now hosts largeish-scale rock concerts as well as specialised dance and other music events.
✉ Piazza Bartolomeo Romano 8 ☎ 06 511 0203 🚇 Garbetella 🚌 92, 770

Saint Louis Music City
Another fun, jazz venue with strongly American-themed decor.
✉ Via del Cardello 13a ☎ 06 474 5076 🚇 Cavour 🚌 To Via Cavour, Via dei Fori Imperiali

Stadio Olimpico
A sports stadium that hosts the very biggest Italian and foreign rock names to come to Rome.
✉ Via dei Gladiatori ☎ 06 323 7333 🚌 To Lungotevere Maresciallo Cadorna

Stazione Ouagadougou
A new-comer offering live and recorded African music in a spectacularly furnished venue.
✉ Via della Lungaretta 75 ☎ 06 581 2510 🚌 To Viale Trastevere

Nightclubs and Bars

Alibi
A hetero-friendly gay club in the throbbing Testaccio area.
✉ Via di Monte Testaccio 44 ☎ 06 574 3448 🚇 Piramide 🚌 To Via Marmorata

Alien
Vast mainstream disco with *cubistes* (scantily clad girls, and a few boys, who dance on top of columns for those who cannot be bothered to move themselves).
✉ Via Velletri 13 ☎ 06 841 2212 🚌 To Piazza Fiume

Caffè Latina
One of the earliest of the Testaccio clubs to open. In spite of its name you're as likely to hear jazz, blues or rock music as you are Latin American.
Via di Monte Testaccio 96

06 574 4020 Piramide
To Via Marmorata

Gilda
The establishment place to bop (or watch others), frequented by, among others, right-wing politicians and TV personalities.
Via Mario de' Fiori 97
06 679 7396 To Piazza San Silvestro

Jonathan's Angels
A beautifully decorated cocktail bar, covered with the paintings of its biker owner, Jonathan.
Via della Fossa 16
06 689 3426 To Corso del Rinascimento, Corso Vittorio Emanuele

Piper
The place of the Dolce Vita 1960s; now a non-threatening club for those who do not do much clubbing.
Via Tagliamento 9
06 855 5398 56, 57, 319

La Vineria
In summer, the clients of this little wine bar spill out into Campo de' Fiori. Popular with trendy foreigners.
Campo de' Fiori 15
06 6880 3268 To Corso Vittorio Emanuele

Sport

ATAC Dopolavoro
The city bus company employees' social club rents out its tennis courts to the public.
Lungotevere Thaon di Revel 11–13 06 702 2637
Mon–Sat 8AM–11PM; Sun 8–8; book the day before
To Piazza Mancini

Cavalieri Hilton
At a price you can enjoy the luxury of the Hilton's outdoor swimming pool.
Via Cadlolo 101
06 35091 May–Sept: 9–7 907, 913, 991, 999

Foro Italico
The annual International Tennis Tournament, the Italian Open, is held here for two weeks in mid-May.
Viale dei Gladiatori 31
Information: 06 321 9064
Lungotevere Maresciallo Cadorna

Ippodromo delle Campanelle
This is Rome's horse-racing track. Races are held from September to June.
Via Appia Nuova 1255
06 718 8750 663, 664

Piazza Siena
The elegant horse show takes place in the little arena in Villa Borghese every May.
Villa Borghese
Information: 06 3974 0789
To Piazzale Flaminio

Piscina delle Rose
Aptly named public swimming pool where you can hire sun-beds and umbrellas. There is also a bar.
Viale America 20 06 592 6717 EUR Palasport
To Piazzale dello Sport

Roman Sport Centre
Daily membership allows you access to the gyms of one of Rome's most exclusive sports and fitness clubs.
The car park underneath Villa Borghese 06 320 1667
Mon–Sat 9AM–10PM, Sun 9–3 Spagna To Via Veneto

Stadio Olimpico
Both the football teams, AS Roma and Lazio play here.
Via dei Gladiatori 06 3685 7520 To Lungotevere Maresciallo Cadorna

Swim, Sun, Sand
It may not be the best way to escape the crowds, but a day at the beach is a good break from sightseeing, especially during the week. Entrepreneurs sometimes limit beach access to those renting sunbeds and parasols, but this is not always the case. Bars and restaurants offer lunch. The nearest beaches are at Ostia (metro from Magliana), Fregene and Torvaianica. Further afield are Sperlonga (► 87) to the south and Santa Marinella to the north.

What's On When

Villaggio Globale
The old abattoir in the centre of Testaccio has been taken over and converted into the Villagio Globale, a cultural centre for exhibitions, concerts and dance events. In the summer the vast central courtyard (originally used for herding animals) is given over to an excellent festival of world music with side stalls and an interesting range of international refreshment stands.
✉ Lungotevere Testaccio ☎ 06 5730 0329 🚌 27, 92

January
New Year's Day: public holiday.
6 Jan: Epiphany, public holiday. Traditionally the *befana* (witch) leaves presents for children.

February
Week leading up to Shrove Tuesday: *Carnevale* (➤ 111), streets full of adults and children in fancy dress.
Shrove Tuesday: *Martedi grasso* celebrations (in costume) in Piazza Navona (➤ 21) and elsewhere.

March/April
9 Mar: cars, buses and taxis blessed at the church of San Francesca Romana (the patron saint of motorists) in the Forum (➤ 22).
Mid-Mar onwards: Spanish Steps (➤ 60) decorated with huge azalea plants.
Good Friday: Pope leads the ceremony of the Stations of the Cross at the Colosseo (Colosseum) (➤ 18).
Easter Sunday: papal address at St Peter's.
Easter Monday: public holiday.
21 Apr: Rome's birthday, bands and orchestras perform at Campidoglio, (➤ 16) Piazza di Spagna (➤ 60) and elsewhere.
25 Apr: Liberation Day, public holiday to commemorate the Allies' liberation of Rome from the Nazis in 1944.

May
1 May: Labour Day, public holiday, no public transport, huge free rock concert in Piazza di San Giovanni in Laterano.
Early May: horse show at Piazza di Siena.
Mid-May to Oct: rose garden above Circo Massimo (➤ 39) open to the public.
Mid-May: International Tennis Tournament (➤ 115).

June/July
Mid-Jun to Sep: outdoor concerts, cinemas, fairs and other arts events all over the city.
End-Jun to mid-Sep: *Estate Romana*. The ever expanding festival offering open-air cinema, music, theatre and arts events around the city.
Mid to late Jul: *Festa de Noantri*, stalls, concerts and other cultural events in Trastevere.

August
15 Aug: *Ferragosto*, public holiday, lots of shops, restaurants, bars and businesses close for a week or more.

October
Early Oct: wine festivals in towns near Rome, and a small one in Trastevere.

November
1 Nov: All Saints, public holiday.
Mid-Nov: the new season's vini novelli ready for drinking.

December
Beginning Dec to 6 Jan: Christmas fair in Piazza Navona (➤ 21, 110).
8 Dec: Immaculate Conception, public holiday.
Christmas time: *presepi* (nativity scenes) on show in churches and main piazzas.
25 Dec: Christmas Day, public holiday, papal address in St Peter's Square.
31 Dec: New Year's Eve celebrations, fireworks and concerts in Piazza del Popolo and elsewhere in the city.

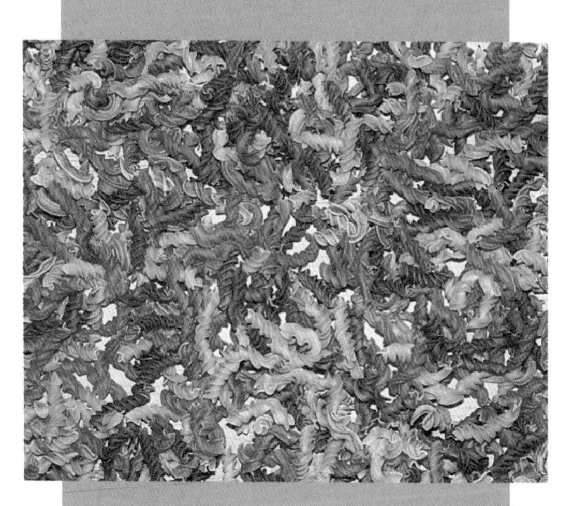

Practical Matters

Above: *fusilli pasta*
Below: *Roman police*

TIME DIFFERENCES

GMT	Rome	Germany	USA (NY)	Netherlands	Spain
12 noon	1PM	1PM	7AM	1PM	1PM

BEFORE YOU GO

WHAT YOU NEED

● Required
○ Suggested
▲ Not required

Some countries require a passport to remain valid for a minimum period (usually at least six months) beyond the date of entry – contact their consulate or embassy or your travel agent for details.

	UK	Germany	USA	Netherlands	Spain
Passport orNational Identity Card where applicable	●	●	●	●	●
Visa	▲	▲	▲	▲	▲
Onward or Return Ticket	▲	▲	▲	▲	▲
Health Inoculations	▲	▲	▲	▲	▲
Health Documentation (reciprocal agreement document) (➤ 123, Health)	●	●	▲	●	●
Travel Insurance	○	○	○	○	○
Driving Licence (national)	●	●	●	●	●
Car Insurance Certificate (if own car)	○	○	○	○	○
Car Registration Document (if own car)	●	●	●	●	●

WHEN TO GO

Rome

High season

Low season

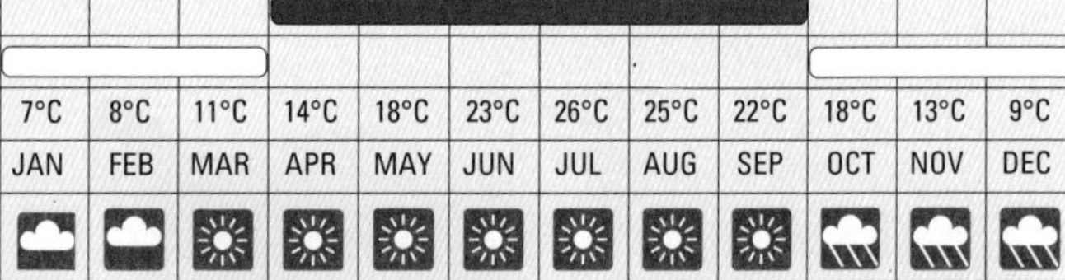

7°C	8°C	11°C	14°C	18°C	23°C	26°C	25°C	22°C	18°C	13°C	9°C
JAN	FEB	MAR	APR	MAY	JUN	JUL	AUG	SEP	OCT	NOV	DEC

 Wet   Cloud  Sun

TOURIST OFFICES

In the UK
Italian State Tourist Board
1 Princes Street
London W1R 8AY
☎ 020 7408 1254
Fax: 020 7493 6695

In the USA
Italian State Tourist Board
630 Fifth Avenue
Suite 1565
New York NY 10111
☎ 212/245 4822
Fax: 212/586 9242

Italian State Tourist Board
12400 Wilshire Boulevard
Suite 550
Los Angeles, CA 90025
☎ 310/820 1959
Fax: 310/820 6357

POLICE 113 CARABINIERI 112

FIRE 115

ANY EMERGENCY (including AMBULANCE) 113

ROAD ASSISTANCE (ACI) 116

WHEN YOU ARE THERE

ARRIVING

There are direct flights from Europe and North America. Alitalia (☎ 06 65631) is the national airline. Rome has two airports: Leonardo da Vinci, also known as Fiumicino (☎ 06 65951), is the larger and handles scheduled flights, while Ciampino (☎ 06 794941) caters mostly for charter flights.

Leonardo da Vinci (Fiumicino) Airport
Kilometres to city centre

26 kilometres

Journey times	
Train	30 or 45 minutes
Bus	50 minutes
Car	40 minutes

Ciampino Airport
Kilometres to city centre

13 kilometres

Journey times	
Train	20 minutes after bus
Bus	15 minutes (to train)
Car	30 minutes

MONEY

The monetary unit of Italy is the lira (plural lire), abbreviated to Lit or L. The denominations are: coins of 50, 100, 200, 500 and 1,000 lire and notes of 1,000, 2,000, 5,000, 10,000, 50,000, 100,000 and 500,000 lire. In 1999 the lira became a denomination of the euro. Lira notes and coins continue to be legal tender during a transitional period. Euro bank notes and coins are due to be introduced by January 2002.

TIME

Italy is one hour ahead of Greenwich Mean Time (GMT+1), but from late March, when clocks are put forward one hour, to late September, Italian Summer Time (GMT+2) operates.

CUSTOMS

YES
From another EU country for personal use (guidelines):
800 cigarettes, 200 cigars,
1 kilogram of tobacco
10 litres of spirits (over 22%)
20 litres of aperitifs
90 litres of wine, of which 60 litres can be sparkling wine
110 litres of beer

From a non-EU country for your personal use, the allowances are:
200 cigarettes OR
50 cigars OR 20 grams of tobacco
1 litre of spirits (over 22%)
2 litres of intermediary products (e.g. sherry) and sparkling wine
2 litres of still wine
50 grams of perfume
0.25 litres of eau de toilette
The value limit for goods is 175 euros

Travellers under 17 years of age are not entitled to the tobacco and alcohol allowances

NO
Drugs, firearms, ammunition, offensive weapons, obscene material, unlicensed animals.

EMBASSIES

UK
482 5441

Germany
884741

USA
46741

Netherlands
322 1141

Spain
580 0144

WHEN YOU ARE THERE

TOURIST OFFICES

Ente Provinciale Tourismo (Rome Provincial Tourist Board)

Offices:

- Via Parigi 5
  ☎ 06 4889 9253
  Mon–Sat 8:15–7
- Leonardo da Vinci (Fiumicino) Airport
  ☎ 06 6595 6074
  Mon–Sat 8:15–7
- Stazione Termini (Main Railway Station)
  ☎ 06 487 1270
  daily 8:15–7.15

Info-Tourism Kiosks:
Tue–Sat 10–6; Sun 10–1

- Largo Carlo Goldoni, Via del Corso
  ☎ 06 6813 6061
- Via Nazionale
  ☎ 06 4782 4525
- Fori Imperiali
  Piazza del Tempio della Pace ☎ 06 6902 4307
- Piazza Navona
  Piazza Cinque Lune
  ☎ 06 6880 9240
- Santa Maria Maggiore
  Via dell'Olmata
  ☎ 06 4788 0294

NATIONAL HOLIDAYS

J	F	M	A	M	J	J	A	S	O	N	D
2		1	2	1			1			1	3

1 Jan	New Year's Day
6 Jan	Epiphany
Mar/Apr	Easter Monday
25 Apr	Liberation Day, 1945
1 May	Labour Day
15 Aug	Assumption of the Virgin
1 Nov	All Saints' Day
8 Dec	Immaculate Conception
25 Dec	Christmas Day
26 Dec	St Stephen's Day

Banks, businesses and most shops and museums close on these days. Rome celebrates its patron saint (St Peter) on 29 June, but generally most places remain open.

OPENING HOURS

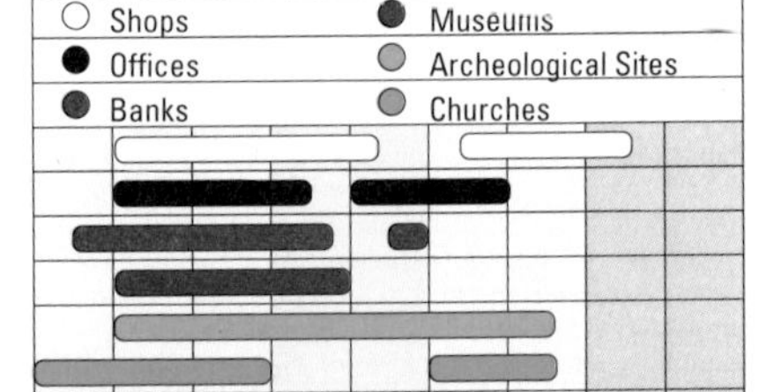

Day
Mid day

In addition to the times in the chart, department stores, some supermarkets, plus shops in tourist areas may not close lunchtime, and sometimes remain open until later in the evening. Some shops shut Monday morning and in summer may close Saturday afternoon. Most shops close Sunday. Some banks open until 2PM and do not reopen in the afternoon. All are closed weekends.
Some museums also open in the afternoon (usually 5–8PM). Many museums close early on Sunday (around 1PM) and most are closed Mondays.

PUBLIC TRANSPORT

Internal Flights Services throughout the country are provided by Alitalia – the national airline (☎ 06 65641), and its associated companies ATI (☎ (020) 8709 1111) and Avianova (☎ 06 655 1617). The flight time to Rome from Milan is 65 minutes; from Florence 75 minutes; and from Naples 45 minutes.

Trains Italian State Railways (Ferrovie dello Stato, or FS) provide an efficient service. Almost all long-distance trains to Rome arrive and depart from Stazione Termini (some fast trains use Stazione Roma Tiburtina). Stazione Termini is shut from midnight to 5AM, then trains stop at other city stations. Timetable information ☎ 147 888088

Long Distance Buses There is no national bus company but COTRAL (☎ 06 591 5551) has the major presence in Rome, serving the Lazio region. Buses depart from numerous points throughout the city, depending on their destinations. For details of who goes where, ask at the nearest tourist information office.

Urban Transport Buses (yellow), plus in the outer districts trams, are the best way to get around, though the complexity of the routes can be daunting. Bus or tram stops (*fermata*) have yellow signs. You must have a ticket before boarding at the rear (*salita*) and your ticket stamped in the machine there. Exit through the middle door (*uscita*). The underground (*Metropolitana* or *Metrò*) – entrances: white 'M' on red – has only two lines: *Linea A* (red) runs from Battistini to Anagnina in the southeast. *Linea B* (blue) runs from Rebibbia in the northeast to EUR in the southwest. Tickets from machines at stations.

CAR RENTAL

Car hire (*autonoleggio*) is at airports, the main railway station, and city offices, but driving in Rome is not recommended and not cheap. Small local firms offer the best rates but cars can only be booked locally. Air or train travellers can benefit from inclusive deals.

TAXIS

Taxis can be hailed on the street, found at a taxi rank (stations and major piazze), or phoned 06 3570, 3875, 4994 or 8433). There is an initial charge and a rate for each kilometre. Traffic can mean stiff meter increases and there are Sunday and late-night supplements.

DRIVING

Speed limits on motorways (*autostrade*), which have tolls: **130kph**

Speed limits on main roads: **110kph**; secondary roads: **90kph**

Speed limits on urban roads: **50kph**

Must be worn in front seats at all times and in rear seats where fitted.

Random breath-testing is frequent. Limit: 80mg per 100ml blood.

Petrol (*benzina*) is more expensive in Italy than in Britain and most other European countries. All except small garages in out-of-the-way places sell unleaded petrol (*senza piombo*). Outside urban areas filling stations open 7AM to 12:30PM and 3 to 7:30PM. Motorway service stations are open 24 hours. Credit cards are rarely accepted.

In the event of a breakdown, ring 116, giving your registration number and type of car and the nearest ACI (Automobile Club d'Italia) office will be informed to assist you. You will be towed to the nearest ACI garage. This service is free to foreign-registered vehicles or cars rented from Rome or Milan airports (you will need to produce your passport).

PERSONAL SAFETY

In Rome, petty theft (bag and neck-chain snatching, pick-pocketing and car break-ins) is the main problem. The police (*polizia*) to whom thefts should be reported wear light-blue trousers and dark-blue jackets. Some precautions:

- Carry shoulder bags not *on* your shoulder but slung *across* your body.
- Scooter-borne bag-snatchers can be foiled if you keep on the *inside* of the pavement.
- Do not put anything down on a café or restaurant table.
- Lock car doors and never keep valuables in your car.

Police assistance:
☎ **113 from any call box**

TELEPHONES

Almost every bar in Italy has a telephone, plus many in public places. Phonecards are available from SIP (state telephone company) offices, tobacconists, stations and other public places.

International Dialling Codes	
From Rome to:	
UK:	**00 44**
Germany:	**00 49**
USA:	**00 1**
Netherlands:	**00 31**
Spain:	**00 34**

POST

Post Offices
The city's main post office is on Piazza San Silvestro.
8.25AM–7.40PM (8.20–11.50AM Sat). Closed: Sun
☎ 160
Vatican City has its own postal system, with a post office in St Peter's Square.
8.30AM–7PM (6PM Sat)
Closed: Sun ☎ 69 82

ELECTRICITY

The power supply is: 220 volts (in parts of Rome: 125 volts).

Type of socket: Round two- or three-hole sockets takings plugs of two round pins, or sometimes three pins in a vertical row. British visitors should bring an adaptor; US visitors a voltage transformer.

TIPS/GRATUITIES

Yes ✓ No ✕		
Hotels (if service not included)	✓	10–15%
Restaurants (if service not included)	✓	10–15%
Cafés/bars	✓	€1 min
Taxis	✓	15%
Porters	✓	€1
Chambermaids	✓	€2 weekly
Cinema/theatre usherettes	✓	10 cents min
Hairdressers	✓	€2
Cloakroom attendants	✓	€1
Toilets	✓	10 cents min

PHOTOGRAPHY

Light: The light in Rome is good: neither the glare of the south nor the hazier light of the north of the country.

Where you can photograph: Most museums and certain churches will not allow you to photograph inside; check first.

Film and developing: A roll of film is called a *pellicola*, but 'film' should get you understood. Film and developing are much more expensive in Italy than in the UK or USA.

HEALTH

Insurance

Nationals of EU and certain other countries receive reduced cost medical (including hospital) treatment and pay a percentage of prescribed medicines. You need a qualifying document (Form E111 for Britons). Private medical insurance is still advised.

Dental Services

Nationals of EU and certain other countries can obtain dental treatment at a reduced cost at dentists within the Italian health service. A qualifying document (Form E111 for Britons) is needed. Private medical insurance is still advised.

Sun Advice

In summer, particularly in July and August, it can get oppressively hot and humid in the city. If 'doing the sights' cover up or apply a sunscreen (or dive into the shade of a museum), plus take in plenty of fluids.

Drugs

A pharmacy (*farmacia*), recognised by a green cross sign, will possess highly trained staff able to offer medical advice on minor ailments and provide a wide range of prescribed and non-prescribed medicines and drugs.

Safe Water

Rome is famed for its drinking water, which is generally safe, even from outdoor fountains (unless you see a sign saying *acqua non potabile*). However, Romans prefer the taste of bottled mineral

CONCESSIONS

Students/Youths Holders of an International Student Identity Card (ISIC), and for those under 26 an International Youth Card (IYC) – available from student organisations – can take advantage of discounts on transport, accommodation, museum entrance fees, car hire and in restaurants. Nationals (under 18) of EU and certain other countries receive free admission to state museums.

Senior Citizens Citizens aged over 60 of EU and a number of other countries with which Italy has a reciprocal arrangement (not including the USA) may gain free admission to communal and state museums and receive discounts at other museums and on public transport on production of their passport.

CLOTHING SIZES

Italy	UK	Rest of Europe		
46	36	46	36	Suits
48	38	48	38	
50	40	50	40	
52	42	52	42	
54	44	54	44	
56	46	56	46	
41	7	41	8	Shoes
42	7.5	42	8.5	
43	8.5	43	9.5	
44	9.5	44	10.5	
45	10.5	45	11.5	
46	11	46	12	
37	14.5	37	14.5	Shirts
38	15	38	15	
39/40	15.5	39/40	15.5	
41	16	41	16	
42	16.5	42	16.5	
43	17	43	17	
38	8	34	6	Dresses
40	10	36	8	
42	12	38	10	
44	14	40	12	
46	16	42	14	
48	18	44	16	
38	4.5	38	6	Shoes
38	5	38	6.5	
39	5.5	39	7	
39	6	39	7.5	
40	6.5	40	8	
41	7	41	8.5	

- Contact the airport or airline on the day prior to leaving to ensure the flight details are unchanged.
- The airport departure tax, payable when you leave Italy, is included in the cost of the airline ticket.
- Check the duty-free limits of the country you are travelling to before departure.

LANGUAGE

Italian is the native language but Romans speak a dialect with its own particular stresses, intonations and vocabulary, of which they are fiercely proud. Many Romans speak English but you will be better received if you at least attempt to communicate in Italian. Italian words are pronounced phonetically. Every vowel and consonant (except 'h') is sounded. The accent usually (but not always) falls on the penultimate syllable. Below is a list of a few words that may be helpful. More extensive coverage can be found in the AA's *Essential Italian Phrase Book* which lists over 2,000 phrases and 2,000 words.

hotel	*albergo*	breakfast	*prima colazione*
room	*camera*	toilet	*toilette*
..single/double	*....singola/doppia*	bath	*bagno*
..one/two nights	*per una/due notte/i*	shower	*doccia*
		balcony	*balcone*
..one/two people	*....per una/due persona/e*	reception	*reception*
		key	*chiave*
reservation	*prenotazione*	room service	*servizio da camera*
rate	*tariffa*	chambermaid	*cameriera*

bank	*banco*	bank note	*banconota*
exchange office	*cambio*	coin	*moneta*
post office	*posta*	credit card	*carta di credito*
cashier	*cassiere/a*	traveller's cheque	*assegno turistico*
foreign exchange	*cambio con l'estero*	cheque book	*libretto degli assegni*
foreign currency	*valuta estera*		
pound sterling	*sterlina*	exchange rate	*tasso di cambio*
American dollar	*dollaro*	commission charge	*commissione*

restaurant	*ristorante*	starter	*il primo*
café	*caffè*	main course	*il secondo*
table	*tavolo*	dish of the day	*piatto del giorno*
menu	*menù/carta*	dessert	*dolci*
set menu	*menù turístico*	drink	*bevanda*
wine list	*lista dei vini*	waiter	*cameriere*
lunch	*pranzo/colazione*	waitress	*cameriera*
dinner	*cena*	the bill	*conto*

aeroplane	*aeroplano*	..single/return	*....andata sola/ andata e ritorno*
airport	*aeroporto*		
train	*treno*	...first/second class	*....prima/seconda classe*
..station	*....stazione ferroviaria*	ticket office	*biglietteria*
bus	*autobus*	timetable	*orario*
..station	*....autostazione*	seat	*posto*
ferry	*traghetto*	non-smoking	*vietato fumaro*
ticket	*biglietto*	reserved	*prenotato*

yes	*sì*	help!	*aiuto!*
no	*no*	today	*oggi*
please	*per favore*	tomorrow	*domani*
thank you	*grazie*	yesterday	*ieri*
hello	*ciao*	how much?	*quanto?*
goodbye	*arrivederci*	expensive	*caro*
goodnight	*buona notte*	open	*aperto*
sorry	*mi dispiace*	closed	*chiuso*

INDEX

Acknowledgements
The Automobile Association wishes to thank the following libraries, photographers and associations for their assistance in the preparation of this book.

BRIDGEMAN ART LIBRARY/Vatican Museums and Galleries, Vatican City, Italy 24, 25, 27b; JOHN HESELTINE 90; MARY EVANS PICTURE LIBRARY 11,14; M R I BANKERS' GUIDE TO FOREIGN CURRENCY 119; SPECTRUM COLOUR LIBRARY 60, 89; THE STOCK MARKET, INC 27a; WORLD PICTURES LTD 12/3, 87.

The remaining transparencies are held in the Association's own library (**AA PHOTO LIBRARY**) with contributions from: **J Holmes F/cover (b) woman, (c) sculptured hand, (f) scooter, B/cover Romulus and Remus, 5a, 5b, 12, 16, 18, 26, 34, 35b, 39, 44, 47, 48, 49, 51a, 52, 55b, 57a, 57b, 59, 61, 65, 70, 72, 76; D Mitidieri F/cover (d) plaque, 7, 8a, 8b, 9a, 9b, 20, 23, 32, 35a, 36, 38, 42, 43, 56, 64, 66, 68, 69, 71, 74, 75a, 75b, 78a, 78b, 84a, 91a, 91b; C Sawyer F/cover (bottom) statue, 1,15b, 17, 21, 22, 31, 33, 41, 50a, 86, 117b; L B Smith 122a; T Souter F/cover (e) Swiss Guard, 40, 53, 82, 83, 84b, 88, 117a; P Wilson F/cover (a) Colosseum, (g) sculptured head, 2, 6, 15a, 19, 37, 45, 50b, 55a, 62, 77, 79.**

Author's Acknowledgements
Jane Shaw wishes to thank Fiona Benson for expertise on churches, shops and hotels, Roberta Mitchell for expertise on restaurants and food and Sally Webb for expertise on museums and excursions.

The Automobile Association wishes to thank Marco De Pellegrin for his insight and invaluable assistance.

Contributors
Copy editor: Pat Pierce **Verifier:** Teresa Fisher **Researcher (Practical Matters):** Colin Follett
Indexer: Marie Lorimer **Revision management:** Outcrop Publishing Services, Cumbria

Dear Essential Traveller

Your comments, opinions and recommendations are very important to us. So please help us to improve our travel guides by taking a few minutes to complete this simple questionnaire.

You do not need a stamp (unless posted outside the UK). If you do not want to cut this page from your guide, then photocopy it or write your answers on a plain sheet of paper.

Send to: **The Editor, AA World Travel Guides, FREEPOST SCE 4598, Basingstoke RG21 4GY.**

Your recommendations...

We always encourage readers' recommendations for restaurants, nightlife or shopping – if your recommendation is used in the next edition of the guide, we will send you a ***FREE*** **AA *Essential* Guide** of your choice. Please state below the establishment name, location and your reasons for recommending it.

____

____

____

____

Please send me **AA *Essential*** ______________________

(*see list of titles inside the front cover*)

About this guide...

Which title did you buy?

AA *Essential* ______________________

Where did you buy it? ______________________

When? m m / y y

Why did you choose an AA *Essential* Guide? ______________________

____

____

____

____

Did this guide meet your expectations?

Exceeded ☐ Met all ☐ Met most ☐ Fell below ☐

Please give your reasons ______________________

____

____

____

continued on next page...

Were there any aspects of this guide that you particularly liked? ___

___

___

___

Is there anything we could have done better? ___

___

___

___

___

About you...

Name (*Mr/Mrs/Ms*) ___

Address ___

___

___ Postcode ___

Daytime tel nos ___

Which age group are you in?

Under 25 ☐ 25–34 ☐ 35–44 ☐ 45–54 ☐ 55–64 ☐ 65+ ☐

How many trips do you make a year?

Less than one ☐ One ☐ Two ☐ Three or more ☐

Are you an AA member? Yes ☐ No ☐

About your trip...

When did you book? m m / y y When did you travel? m m / y y

How long did you stay? ___

Was it for business or leisure? ___

Did you buy any other travel guides for your trip?

If yes, which ones? ___

___

Thank you for taking the time to complete this questionnaire. Please send it to us as soon as possible, and remember, you do not need a stamp (*unless posted outside the UK*).

Happy Holidays!

The AA and the Automobile Association Limited, their subsidiaries and any other companies or bodies in which either has an interest ('the AA Group') may use information about you to provide you with details of other products and services, by telephone or in writing. The AA Group as a matter of policy does not release its lists to third parties.

If you do not wish to receive further information please tick the box... ☐

AA Publishing

Contents

Introduction

● **Welcome to the AA's Italian Phrasebook, which contains everything you'd expect from a comprehensive language guide. It's concise, accessible and easy to understand, and you'll find it indispensable on your trip abroad.**

The guide is divided into 15 themed sections and starts with a pronunciation table which gives you the phonetic spelling to all the words and phrases you'll need to know for your trip, while at the back of the book is an extensive word list and grammar guide which will help you construct basic sentences in Italian.

Throughout the book you'll come across coloured boxes with a beside them. These are designed to help you if you can't understand what your listener is saying to you. Hand the book over to them and encourage them to point to the appropriate answer to the question you are asking.

Other coloured boxes in the book – this time without the symbol – give alphabetical listings of themed words with their English translations below.

For extra clarity, we have put all English words and phrases in black, foreign language terms in red and their phonetic pronunciation in italic.

This phrasebook covers all subjects you are likely to come across during the course of your visit, from reserving a room for the night to ordering food and drink at a restaurant and what to do if your car breaks down or you lose your traveller's cheques and money. With over 2,000 commonly used words and essential phrases at your fingertips you can rest assured that you will be able to get by in all situations, so let the AA's Italian Phrasebook become your passport to a secure and enjoyable trip!

Pronunciation table

The imitated pronunciation should be read as if it were English, bearing in mind the following main points:

Consonants

b, d, f, l, m, n, p, q, t, vk, j, w	as in English rarely appear in Italian			
c	• before **e** and **i**, like **ch** in **ch**ip	***ch***	cinema	***chee****naymah*
	• elsewhere, like **c** in **c**at	***k***	casa	***ka****hzah*
ch	like **c** in **c**at	***k***	chi	***kee***
g	• before **e** and **i**, like **j** in **j**et	***j***	giro	***jee****ro*
	• elsewere, like **g** in **g**o	***g***	gatto	***gah****tto*
gh	like **g** in **g**o	***gh***	funghi	*foon****ghee***
gl	• like **lli** in mi**lli**on	***lly***	figlio	*fee****lly****o*
	• (rarely) like **gl** in En**gl**ish	***gl***	inglese	*een****glay****say*
gn	like **ni** in o**ni**on	***n***	bagno	*bah****nee****o*
h	always silent		ho	***o***
r	trilled like Scottish **r**	***r***	riso	***ree****zo*
s	• generally like **s** in **s**it	***s***	sette	***say****ttay*
	• sometimes like **z** in **z**oo	***z***	rosa	*ro****zah***
sc	• before e and i, like **sh** in **sh**ot	***sh***	pesce	*pay****shay***
	• elsewhere, like **sk** in **sk**ip	***sk***	fresco	*fray****sko***
z,zz	• generally like **ts** in bi**ts**	***ts***	grazie	*grahts****eeay***
	• sometimes like **ds** in moo**ds**	***dz***	zero	***dzay****ro*

Vowels

a	like **a** in c**a**r	***ah***	**pasta**	***pahstah***
e	like **ay** in w**ay**	***ay***	**sera**	***sayrah***
i	like **ee** in m**ee**t	***ee***	**vini**	***veenee***
o	like **o** in n**o**t	***o***	**notte**	***no****ttay*
u	like **oo** in f**oo**t	***oo***	**uno**	***oo****no*

Stressing of words

Stress tends to be on the last syllable but one, e.g. fratello = frah**tay**llo; ragazza = rah**gah**tzah; italiano = eetahlee**ah**no. A number of words have a written accent on the last syllable, to indicate that the final vowel is stressed, e.g. città = cheet**tah**; caffè = kahf**fay**; lunedì = loonay**dee**.

Useful lists

Useful lists

1.1 Today or tomorrow?

What day is it today?	Oggi, che giorno è? *Odjee kay jorno ay?*
Today's Monday	Oggi è lunedì *Odjee ay loonaydee*
– Tuesday	Oggi è martedì *Odjee ay mahrtaydee*
– Wednesday	Oggi è mercoledì *Odjee ay mahrkolaydee*
– Thursday	Oggi è giovedì *Odjee ay jovaydee*
– Friday	Oggi è venerdì *Odjee ay vaynahrdee*
– Saturday	Oggi è sabato *Odjee ay sahbahto*
– Sunday	Oggi è domenica *Odjee ay domayneekah*
in January	in gennaio *een jaynnaheeo*
since February	da febbraio *dah faybbraheeo*
in spring	in primavera *een preemahvayrah*
in summer	in estate/d'estate *een aystahtay*
in autumn	in autunno *een ahootoonno*
in winter	in inverno/d'inverno *een eenvayrno/deenvayrno*
1997	millenovecentonovantasette *meellay/novaychaynto/novahntasayttay*
the twentieth century	il novecento *eel novaychaynto*
What's the date today?	Quanti ne abbiamo oggi? *Kwahntee nay abbeeahmo odjee?*
Today's the 24th	Oggi è il ventiquattro *Odjee ay eel vaynteekwahttro*
Monday 3 November 1998	lunedì, tre novembre millenovecentonovantotto *loonaydee, tray novaymbray meellay/novaychaynto/novahntotto*
in the morning	la mattina *lah mahtteenah*
in the afternoon	il pomeriggio *eel pomayreedjo*
in the evening	la sera *lah sayrah*
at night	la notte *lah nottay*
this morning	stamattina *stahmahtteenah*

this afternoon	oggi pomeriggio *odjee pomayreedjo*
this evening	stasera *stahsayhrah*
tonight	stanotte *stahnottay*
last night	la notte scorsa *lah nottay skorsah*
this week	questa settimana *kwaystah saytteemahnah*
next month	il mese prossimo *eel maysay prosseemo*
last year	l'anno scorso *lahnno skorso*
next...	...prossimo/prossima *...prosseemo/prosseemah*
in...days/weeks/ months/years	fra...giorni/settimane/mesi/anni *frah...jornee/saytteemahnay/mayzee/ahnnee*
...weeks ago	...settimane fa *...saytteemahnay fah*
day off	giorno libero *jorno leebayro*

 .2 Bank holidays

- **The most important** Bank holidays in Italy are the following:

January 1	New Year's Day	Capodanno
January 6	Epiphany	Epifania
March/April	Easter and Easter Monday	Pasqua/Lunedì dell'Angelo
25 April	Liberation Day	Anniversario della Liberazione (1945)
1 May	Labour Day	Festa del lavoro
15 August	Feast of the Assumption	Assunzione (Ferragosto)
1 November	All Saints' Day	Ognissanti
8 December	Feast of the Immaculate Conception	Immacolata Concezione
25 December	Christmas Day	Natale
26 December	Feast of Santo Stefano	Santo Stefano

Most shops, banks and government institutions are closed on these days. Individual towns also have public holidays to celebrate their own patron saints.

 .3 What time is it?

What time is it?	Che ore sono? *Kay oray sono?*
It's nine o'clock	Sono le nove *Sono lay novay*
– five past ten	Sono le dieci e cinque *Sono lay deeaychy ay cheenkway*
– a quarter past eleven	Sono le undici e un quarto *Sono lay oondeechee ay oon kwahrto*
– twenty past twelve	E' mezzogiorno e venti *Ay maydzojorno ay vayntee*

– half past one	E' l'una e mezza *Ay loonah ay maydzah*
– twenty–five to three	Sono le due e trentacinque *Sono lay dooay ay trayntahcheenkway*
– a quarter to four	Sono le quattro meno un quarto *Sono lay kwahttro mayno oon kwahrto*
– ten to five	Sono le cinque meno dieci *Sono lay cheenkway mayno deeaychee*
It's midday (twelve noon)	E' mezzogiorno *Ay maydzojorno*
It's midnight	E' mezzanotte *Ay maydzahnottay*
half an hour	una mezz'ora *oonah maydzorah*
What time?	A che ora? *Ah kay orah?*
What time can I come round?	A che ora potrei venire? *Ah kay orah potraèe vayneeray?*
At...	Alle... *Ahllay...*
After...	Dopo le... *Dopo lay...*
Before...	Prima delle... *Preemah dayllay...*
Between...and...(o'clock)	Fra le...e le... *Frah lay...ay lay...*
From...to...	Dalle...alle... *Dahllay...ahllay...*
In...minutes	Fra...minuti *Frah...meenootee*
– an hour	Fra...un'ora *Frah...oonorah*
–...hours	Fra...ore *Frah...oray*
– a quarter of an hour	Fra un quarto d'ora *Frah oon kwahrto dorah*
– three quarters of an hour	Fra tre quarti d'ora *Frah tray kwahrtèe dorah*
too early/late	troppo presto/tardi *troppo praysto/tahrdee*
on time	in orario/puntuale *een orahreeo/poontooahlay*
summertime (daylight saving)	ora legale *orah laygahlay*
wintertime	ora invernale *orah eenvayrnahlay*

 .4 One, two, three...

0	zero	*dzayro*
1	uno	*oono*
2	due	*dooay*
3	tre	*tray*
4	quattro	*kwahttro*
5	cinque	*cheenkway*
6	sei	*sayèe*
7	sette	*sayttay*
8	otto	*otto*
9	nove	*novay*
10	dieci	*deeaychèe*
11	undici	*oondeechee*
12	dodici	*dodeechee*
13	tredici	*traydeechee*
14	quattordici	*kwahttordeechee*
15	quindici	*kweendeechee*
16	sedici	*saydeechee*
17	diciassette	*deechahssettay*
18	diciotto	*deecheeotto*
19	diciannove	*deechahnnovay*
20	venti	*vayntee*
21	ventuno	*vayntoono*
22	ventidue	*vaynteedooay*
30	trenta	*trayntah*
31	trentuno	*trayntoono*
32	trentadue	*trayntahdooay*
40	quaranta	*kwahrahntah*
50	cinquanta	*cheenkwahntah*
60	sessanta	*sayssahntah*
70	settanta	*sayttahntah*
80	ottanta	*ottahntah*
90	novanta	*novahntah*
100	cento	*chaynto*
101	centouno	*chayntooono*
110	centodieci	*chayntodeeaychee*
120	centoventi	*chayntovayntee*
200	duecento	*dooaychaynto*
300	trecento	*traychaynto*
400	quattrocento	*kwahttrochaynto*
500	cinquecento	*cheenkwaychaynto*
600	seicento	*saychaynto*
700	settecento	*sayttaychaynto*
800	ottocento	*ottochaynto*
900	novecento	*novaychaynto*
1,000	mille	*meellay*
1,100	millecento	*meellaychaynto*
2,000	duemila	*dooaymeelah*
10,000	diecimila	*deeaycheemeelah*
100,000	centomila	*chayntomeelah*
1,000,000	un milione	*oon meeleeonay*

1st	primo	*preemo*
2nd	secondo	*saykondo*
3rd	terzo	*tayrtzo*
4th	quarto	*kwahrto*
5th	quinto	*kweento*
6th	sesto	*saysto*
7th	settimo	*saytteemo*
8th	ottavo	*ottahvo*
9th	nono	*nono*
10th	decimo	*daycheemo*
11th	undicesimo	*oondeechayzeemo*
12th	dodicesimo	*dodeechayzeemo*
13th	tredicesimo	*traydeechayzeemo*
14th	quattordicesimo	*kwahttordeechayzeemo*
15th	quindicesimo	*kweendeechayzeemo*
16th	sedicesimo	*saydeechayzeemo*
17th	diciassettesimo	*deechahsayttayzeemo*
18th	diciottesimo	*deechottayzeemo*
19th	diciannovesimo	*deechahnovayzeemo*
20th	ventesimo	*vayntayzeemo*
21st	ventunesimo	*vayntoonayzeemo*
22nd	ventiduesimo	*vaynteedooayzeemo*
30th	trentesimo	*trahntayzeemo*
100th	centesimo	*chayntayzeemo*
1,000th	millesimo	*meellayzeemo*
once	una volta	*oonah voltah*
twice	due volte	*dooay voltay*
double	il doppio	*eel doppeeo*
triple	il triplo	*eel treeplo*
half	la metà	*lah maytah*
a quarter	un quarto	*oon kwahrto*
a third	un terzo	*oon tayrtzo*
some/a few	alcuni	*ahlkoonee*
2 + 4 = 6	due più quattro fa sei *dooay peeoo kwahttro fah sayèe*	
4 - 2 = 2	quattro meno due fa due *kwahttro mayno dooay fah dooay*	
2 x 4 = 8	due per quattro fa otto *dooay payr kwahttro fah otto*	
4 ÷ 2 = 2	quattro diviso due fa due *kwahttro deeveezo dooay fah dooay*	
even/odd	pari/dispari *pahree/deesparee*	
total	(in) totale *(een) totahlay*	
6 x 9	sei per nove *sayèe payr novay*	

1.5 The weather

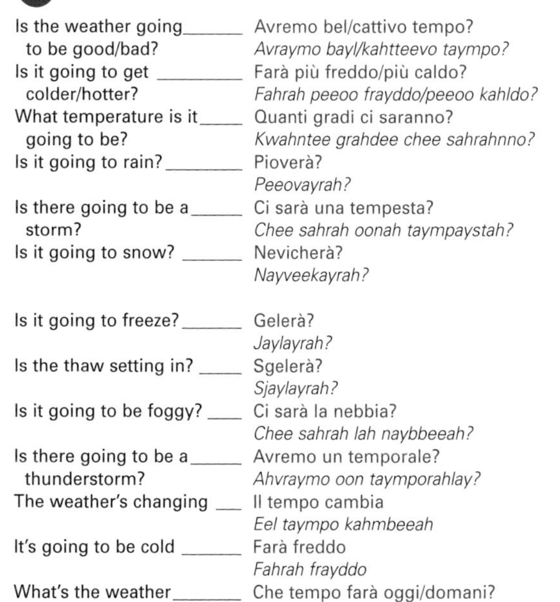

Is the weather going to be good/bad?	Avremo bel/cattivo tempo? *Avraymo bayl/kahtteevo taympo?*
Is it going to get colder/hotter?	Farà più freddo/più caldo? *Fahrah peeoo frayddo/peeoo kahldo?*
What temperature is it going to be?	Quanti gradi ci saranno? *Kwahntee grahdee chee sahrahnno?*
Is it going to rain?	Pioverà? *Peeovayrah?*
Is there going to be a storm?	Ci sarà una tempesta? *Chee sahrah oonah taympaystah?*
Is it going to snow?	Nevicherà? *Nayveekayrah?*
Is it going to freeze?	Gelerà? *Jaylayrah?*
Is the thaw setting in?	Sgelerà? *Sjaylayrah?*
Is it going to be foggy?	Ci sarà la nebbia? *Chee sahrah lah naybbeeah?*
Is there going to be a thunderstorm?	Avremo un temporale? *Ahvraymo oon taymporahlay?*
The weather's changing	Il tempo cambia *Eel taympo kahmbeeah*
It's going to be cold	Farà freddo *Fahrah frayddo*
What's the weather going to be like today/tomorrow?	Che tempo farà oggi/domani? *Kay taympo fahrah odjee/domahnee?*

afoso	sweltering/muggy
assolato	sunny
bello	fine
brina	frost/frosty
caldissimo	very hot
diluvio	heavy rain
forza del vento moderata/forte/molto forte	moderate/strong/very strong winds
freddo umido	cold and damp
fresco	cool
gelido	bleak
gelo	frost
gelo notturno	overnight frost
ghiaccio	ice/icy
giornata di sole	sunny day
... gradi (sotto/sopra zero)	... degrees (below/above zero)
grandine	hail
mite	mild
nebbia	fog/foggy
neve	snow
nuvolosità	cloudiness
ondata di caldo	heatwave
pioggia	rain
raffiche di vento	gusts of wind
rovescio di pioggia	downpour
sereno/nuvoloso/coperto	clear skies/cloudy/overcast
sereno	fine/clear
soffocante	stifling
tempesta	storm
umido	humid
uragano	hurricaine
vento	wind
ventoso	windy

1.6 Here, there...

See also 5.1 Asking for directions

here, over here / there, over there	qui, qua/lì, là *kwee, kwah/lee, lah*
somewhere/nowhere	da qualche parte/da nessuna parte *dah kwahlkay pahrtay/dah nayssoonah pahrtay*
everywhere	dappertutto *dahppayrtootto*
far away/nearby	lontano/vicino *lontahno/veecheeno*
(on the) right/(on the) left	a destra/a sinistra *ah daystrah/ah seeneestrah*
to the right/left of	a destra di/a sinistra di *ah daystrah dee/ah seeneestrah dee*
straight ahead	dritto *dreetto*
via	per *payr*
in/to	in/a *een/ah*
on	su/sopra *soo/soprah*
under	sotto *sotto*
against	contro *contro*
opposite/facing	di fronte a *dee frontay ah*
next to	accanto a *ahkkahnto ah*
near	presso/vicino a *praysso/veecheeno ah*
in front of	davanti a/dinanzi a *dahvahntee ah/deenahnzee ah*
in the centre	al centro *al chayntro*
forward	avanti *ahvahntee*
down	(in) giù *(een) joo*
up	(in) su *(een) soo*
inside	dentro *dayntro*
outside	fuori *fworee*
behind	(in)dietro *(een) deeayhtro*
at the front	davanti *dahvahntee*
at the back/in line	in fondo/in fila *een fondo/een feelah*
in the north	nel nord *nayl nord*

to the south	al sud *ahl sood*
from the west	dall'ovest *dahllovayst*
from the east	dall'est *dahllayst*
to the...of	a... di *ah... dee*

.7 What does that sign say?

See 5.4 Traffic signs

a noleggio
for hire
acqua calda/fredda
hot/cold water
acqua (non) potabile
(no) drinking water
affittasi
for rent
albergo
hotel
alt
stop
alta tensione
high voltage
aperto
open
attenti al cane
beware of the dog
attenzione
danger
biglietteria
ticket office
cambio
exchange
carabinieri
police
cassa
cash desk/pay here
chiuso (per ferie/restauro)
closed (for holiday/ refurbishment)
completo
full
divieto di caccia/ pesca
no hunting/fishing
entrata
entrance
esaurito
sold out
freno d'emergenza
hand brake
fuori uso
not in use
gabinetti
lavatories/toilets
guasto
out of order
in vendita
for sale
informazioni
information
ingresso (libero)
entrance (free)
non disturbare/ toccare
please do not disturb/touch
occupato
engaged
orario
timetable
ospedale
hospital
pedoni
pedestrians
pericolo (d'incendio/ di morte)
danger/fire hazard/ danger to life
polizia stradale
traffic police
pronto soccorso
first aid/accident and emergency (hospital)
riservato
reserved
sala d'attesa
waiting room
scala di sicurezza/mobile
fire escape/escalator
spingere
push
tirare
pull
ufficio informazioni turistiche
tourist information bureau
ufficio postale
post office
uscita (di emergenza)
(emergency) exit
vendesi
for sale
vernice fresca
wet paint
vietato fumare/ gettare rifiuti
no smoking/no litter
vietato l'accesso/ l'ingresso
no access/no entry
vigili del fuoco
fire brigade
vigili urbani
(municipal) police

1.8 Telephone alphabet

Pronouncing the alphabet, e.g. A as in Ancona

a	*ah*	come Ancona	*komay Ankonah*
b	*bee*	come Bologna	*komay Bolonyah*
c	*chee*	come Como	*komay Komo*
d	*dee*	come Domodossola	*komay Domodossolah*
e	*ay*	come Empoli	*komay Empolee*
f	*ayffay*	come Firenze	*komay Feeraynzay*
g	*jee*	come Genova	*komay Jaynovah*
h	*ahkkah*	come Hotel	*komay Hotayl*
i	*ee*	come Imola	*komay Eemolah*
j	*ee loongo*	come Jersey	*komay Jayrsay*
k	*kahppah*	come Kursaal	*komay Koorsaal*
l	*ayllay*	come Livorno	*komay Leevorno*
m	*aymmay*	come Milano	*komay Meelahno*
n	*aynnay*	come Napoli	*komay Nahpolee*
o	*o*	come Otranto	*komay Otrahnto*
p	*pee*	come Padova	*komay Pahdovah*
q	*koo*	come Quarto	*komay Kwahrto*
r	*ayrray*	come Roma	*komay Romah*
s	*ayssay*	come Savona	*komay Sahvonah*
t	*tee*	come Torino	*komay Toreeno*
u	*oo*	come Udine	*komay Oodeenay*
v	*voo*	come Venezia	*komay Vaynaytzyah*
w	*doppeeovoo or voodoppeeo*	come Washington	*komay Washington*
x	*eex*	come Xeres	*komay Xayrays*
y	*eepseelon*	come York, yacht	*komay York, yahcht*
z	*dzayhtah*	come Zara	*komay Dzahrah*

1.9 Personal details

surname	cognome *koneeomay*
first/forename	nome *nomay*
initials	iniziali *eeneetzeeahlee*
address (street/number)	indirizzo (via/numero) *eendeereetzo (veeah/noomahro)*
post code/town	codice postale/residenza *kodeechay postahlay/rayseedayntzah*
sex (male/female)	sesso (m/f) *saysso (m/f)*
nationality/citizenship	nazionalità/cittadinanza *nahtzeeonahleetah/cheettahdeenahntzah*
date of birth	data di nascita *dahtah dee nahsheetah*
place of birth	luogo di nascita *loo-ogo dee nahsheetah*
occupation	professione *profaysseeonay*
marital status	stato civile *stahto cheeveelay*

married, single	coniugato/a, celibe (m) nubile (f) *konyoogahto/tah, chayleebay/ noobeelay*
widowed	vedovo (m), vedova (f) *vaydovo, vaydovah*
(number of) children	(numero di) figli *(noomahro dee) feelly*
passport/identity card/driving licence number	numero del passaporto/della carta di identità/della patente *noomayro dayl pahssahporto/dayllah cahrtah deedaynteetah/dayllah pahtayntay*
place and date of issue	luogo e data di rilascio *loo-ogo ay dahtah dee reelahshyo*
signature	firma *feermah*

Courtesies

Courtesies

● **It is usual in Italy** to shake hands on meeting and parting company. Female friends and relatives may kiss each other on both cheeks when meeting and parting company. For men, this is also quite usual. It is also polite to say *Signore* and *Signora* quite systematically as part of a greeting, i.e. *Buongiorno/arrivederLa, signora.*

.1 Greetings

Hello/Good morning Mr Williams	Buongiorno signor Williams	*Bwonjorno seeneeor Williams*
Hello/Good morning Mrs Jones	Buongiorno signora Jones	*Bwonjorno sineeorah Jones*
Hello, Peter	Ciao Peter	*Chaho Peter*
Hi, Helen	Ciao Helen	*Chaho Helen*
Good morning, madam	Buongiorno signora	*Bwonjorno seeneeorah*
Good afternoon, sir	Buongiorno signore	*Bwonjorno seeneeoray*
Good afternoon/evening	Buona sera	*Bwona sayrah*
Hello/Good morning	Buongiorno	*Bwonjorno*
How are you?/How are things?	Come va?	*Komay vah?*
Fine, thank you, and you?	Bene, grazie, e Lei?	*Baynay, grahtzeeay, ay layee?*
Very well, and you?	Benissimo, e Lei?	*Bayneesseemo, ay layee?*
In excellent health/ In great shape	In ottima forma	*Een otteemah formah*
So-so	Così così	*Cozee cozee*
Not very well	Non molto bene	*Non molto baynay*
Not bad	Non c'è male	*Non chay mahlay*
I'm going to leave	Me ne vado	*May nay vahdo*
I have to be going someone's waiting for me	Devo andarmene. Mi aspettano	*Dayvo ahndahrmaynay. Mee ahspettahno*
Goodbye	Ciao!	*Chaho!*
Good-bye/Good-bye (formal)/See you later	Arrivederci/ArrivederLa/Ci vediamo	*Ahrreevaydayrchee/ahrreevaydayrlah/chee vaydeeahmo*
See you soon	A presto	*Ah praysto*
See you later	A più tardi	*Ah peeoo tahrdee*
See you in a little while	A fra poco	*Ah frah poko*

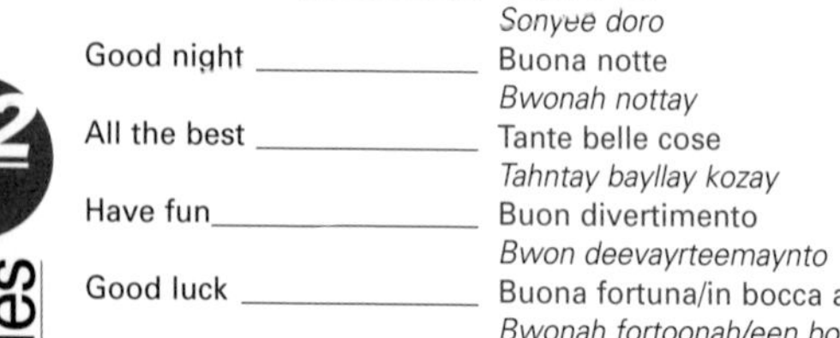

Sweet dreams	Sogni d'oro *Sonyee doro*
Good night	Buona notte *Bwonah nottay*
All the best	Tante belle cose *Tahntay bayllay kozay*
Have fun	Buon divertimento *Bwon deevayrteemaynto*
Good luck	Buona fortuna/in bocca al lupo *Bwonah fortoonah/een bokkah al loopo*
Have a nice holiday	Buone vacanze/buone ferie *Bwonay vahkahntzay/bwonay fayreeay*
Bon voyage/Have a good trip	Buon viaggio *Bwon veeahdjo*
Thank you, the same to you	Grazie, altrettanto *Grahtzeeay, ahltrayttahnto*
Say hello to/Give my regards to (formal)....	Mi saluti... *Mee sahlootee...*
Say hello to (informal)	Salutami... *Sahlootahmee...*

2.2 How to ask a question

Who?	Chi? *Kee?*
Who's that?/Who is it?/Who's there?	Chi è? *Kee ay?*
What?	Che (cosa)? *Kay (kosah)?*
What is there to see?	Che c'è da vedere? *Kay chay dah vaydayray?*
What category of hotel is it?	Che tipo di albergo è? *Kay teepo dee ahlbayrgo ay?*
Where?	Dove? *Dovay?*
Where's the toilet/bathroom?	Dov'è il bagno? *Dovay ay eel bahneeo?*
Where are you going? (formal)	Dove va? *Dovay vah?*
Where are you from?	Da dove viene? *Dah dovay veeayhnay?*
What?/How?	Come? *Komay?*
How far is that?	Quanto è lontano? *Kwahnto ay lontahno?*
How long does that take?	Quanto tempo ci vorrà? *Kwahnto taympo chee vorrah?*
How long is the trip?	Quanto tempo durerà il viaggio? *Kwahnto taympo doorayrah eel veeahdjo?*
How much?	Quanto? *Kwahnto?*
How much is this?	Quanto costa? *Kwahnto kostah?*
What time is it?	Che ore sono? *Kay oray sono?*
Which one/s?	Quale?/Quali? *Kwahlay?/Kwahlee?*

Which glass is mine?	Qual è il mio bicchiere? *Kwahlay eel meeo beekkeeayray?*
When?	Quando? *Kwahndo?*
When are you leaving? (formal)	Quando parte? *Kwahndo pahrtay?*
Why?	Perchè? *Payrkay?*
Could you...? (formal)	Potrebbe...? *Potraybbay..?*
Could you help me/give me a hand please?	Potrebbe darmi una mano, per piacere? *Potraybbay dahrmee oonah mahno, payr peeahchayray?*
Could you point that out to me/show me please?	Potrebbe indicarmelo? *Potraybbay eendeekahrmayhlo?*
Could you come with me, please?	Potrebbe accompagnarmi, per favore? *Potraybbay ahkkompahnyahrmee, payr fahvoray?*
Could you reserve/ book me some tickets please?	Mi potrebbe prenotare dei biglietti, per piacere? *Mee potraybbay praynotahray day beellyayttee, payr peeahchayray?*
Could you recommend another hotel?	Saprebbe consigliarmi un altro albergo? *Sahpraybbay konseellyahrmee oonahltro ahlbayrgo?*
Do you know...? (formal)	Saprebbe...? *Saprebbay...?*
Do you know whether...?	Sa se...? *Sah say...?*
Do you have...? (formal)	Ha...? *Ah...?*
Do you have a.... for me?	Ha un/una...per me? *Ah oon/oona.....payr may?*
Do you have a vegetarian dish, please?	Ha per caso un piatto vegetariano/senza carne? *Ah payr kahzo oon pyahtto vayjaytahryahno/saynzah kahrnay?*
I would like...	Vorrei... *Vorrayee...*
I'd like a kilo of apples, please	Vorrei un chilo di mele *Vorrayee oon keelo dee mayhlay*
Can/May I?	Posso...? *Posso...?*
Can/May I take this away?	Posso portare via questo? *Posso portahray veeah kwaysto?*
Can I smoke here?	Si può fumare qui? *See pwo foomahray kwee?*
Could I ask you something?	Posso farLe una domanda? *Posso fahrlay oonah domahndah?*

2.3 How to reply

Yes, of course	Sì certo *See chayrto*
No, I'm sorry	No, mi dispiace *No, mee deespeeahchay*
Yes, what can I do for you?	Sì, che cosa desidera? *See, kay kosah dayzeederah?*
Just a moment, please	Un attimo, per favore *Oon attymo payr fahvoray*
No, I don't have time now	No, purtroppo ora non ho tempo *No, poortroppo orah non o taympo*
No, that's impossible	No, non è possibile *No, non ay posseebeelay*
I think so/I think that's absolutely right	Credo di sì/Credo proprio di sì *Kraydo dee see/Kraydo propreeo dee see*
I think so too/I agree	Lo penso anch'io *Lo paynso ahnkeeo*
I hope so too	Lo spero anch'io *Lo spayro ankeeo*
No, not at all/Absolutely not	No, niente affatto *No, neeayntay ahffahtto*
No, no-one	No, nessuno *No, nayssoono*
No, nothing	No, niente *No, neeayntay*
That's right	Esatto *Ezahtto*
Something's wrong	C'è qualcosa che non va *Chay kwahlkosah kahy non vah*
I agree (don't agree)	(Non) sono d'accordo *(Non) sono dahkkordo*
OK/it's fine	Va bene *Vah bayhnay*
OK, all right	D'accordo *Dahkkordo*
Perhaps/maybe	Forse *Forsay*
I don't know	Non lo so *Non lo so*

2.4 Thank you

Thank you	Grazie *Grahtzeeay*
You're welcome	Di niente/nulla *Dee neeayntay/noollah*
Thank you very much/ Many thanks	Mille grazie *Meellay grahtzeeay*
Very kind of you	Molto gentile *Molto jaynteelay*
My pleasure	E' stato un piacere *Ay stahto oon peeahchayray*
I enjoyed it very much	Mi è piaciuto moltissimo *Mee ay peeacheeooto molteesseemo*
Thank you for...	La ringrazio di... *Lah reengrahtzeeo dee...*

You shouldn't have/That was so kind of you	E stato veramente gentile/da parte sua *Ay stahto vayrahmayntay jaynteelay/dah pahrtay sooah*
Don't mention it!	Ma si figuri! *Mah see feegoory!*
That's all right	Prego *Praygo*

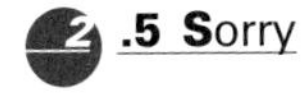

.5 Sorry

Excuse me/pardon me/sorry (formal)	Scusi! *Skoozee!*
Excuse me/pardon me/sorry (informal)	Scusa! *Skoozah!*
Sorry, I didn't know that....	Scusi, ma non sapevo che... *Skoozee, mah non sahpayvo kay...*
Excuse/pardon me (formal)	Mi scusi *Mee skoozee*
I do apologise (formal/informal)	La/ti prego di scusarmi *Lah/tee praygo dee scoosahrmee*
I'm sorry	Mi dispiace *Mee deespeeahchay*
I didn't mean it/It was an accident	Non l'ho fatto apposta *Non lo fahtto appostah*
That's all right/Don't worry about it (formal)	Non si preoccupi *Non see prayokkoopee*
Never mind/Forget it (informal)	Non importa *Non eemportah*
It could happen to anyone	Può succedere a tutti *Pwo sootchaydayray ah tootty*

2.6 What do you think?

Which do you prefer/like best (formal)	Cosa preferisce? *Kosah prayfayreeshay?*
What do you think? (informal)	Che ne pensi? *Kay nay pensee?*
Don't you like dancing? (formal/informal)	Non le/ti piace ballare? *Non lay/tee peeahchay bahllahray?*
I don't mind	Per me è uguale *Payr may ay oogwahlay*
Well done! (m.sing/f.sing/m.plu/f.plu)	Bravo/brava/bravi/brave! *Brahvo/brahvah/brahvee/brahvay!*
Not bad!	Niente male! *Neeayntay mahlay!*
Great!/Marvellous!	Che meraviglia! *Kay mayrahveellyah!*
Wonderful!	Stupendo! *Stoopayndo!*
How lovely!	Che bello! *Kay bayllo!*
I am pleased for you (formal/informal)	Mi fa piacere per Lei/te *Mee fah peeahchayay payr layee/tay*
I'm (not very happy) delighted to/with...	(Non) sono molto contento/a di... *(Non) sono molto contaynto/ah dee...*
It's really nice here!	È proprio un bel posto *Ay propreeo oon bayl posto*

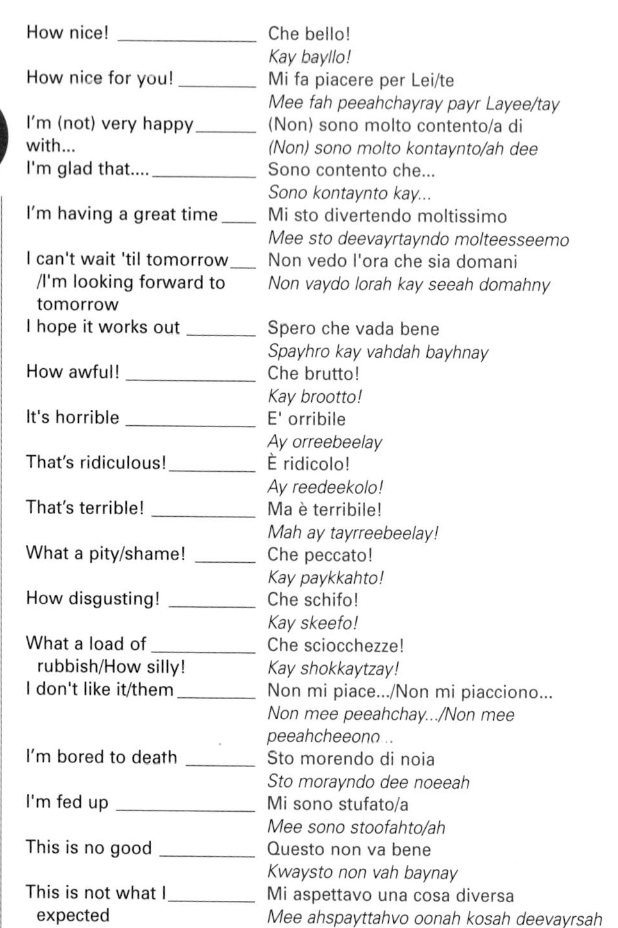

How nice!	Che bello! *Kay bayllo!*
How nice for you!	Mi fa piacere per Lei/te *Mee fah peeahchayray payr Layee/tay*
I'm (not) very happy with...	(Non) sono molto contento/a di *(Non) sono molto kontaynto/ah dee*
I'm glad that....	Sono contento che... *Sono kontaynto kay...*
I'm having a great time	Mi sto divertendo moltissimo *Mee sto deevayrtayndo molteesseemo*
I can't wait 'til tomorrow /I'm looking forward to tomorrow	Non vedo l'ora che sia domani *Non vaydo lorah kay seeah domahny*
I hope it works out	Spero che vada bene *Spayhro kay vahdah bayhnay*
How awful!	Che brutto! *Kay brootto!*
It's horrible	E' orribile *Ay orreebeelay*
That's ridiculous!	È ridicolo! *Ay reedeekolo!*
That's terrible!	Ma è terribile! *Mah ay tayrreebeelay!*
What a pity/shame!	Che peccato! *Kay paykkahto!*
How disgusting!	Che schifo! *Kay skeefo!*
What a load of rubbish/How silly!	Che sciocchezze! *Kay shokkaytzay!*
I don't like it/them	Non mi piace.../Non mi piacciono... *Non mee peeahchay.../Non mee peeahcheeono...*
I'm bored to death	Sto morendo di noia *Sto morayndo dee noeeah*
I'm fed up	Mi sono stufato/a *Mee sono stoofahto/ah*
This is no good	Questo non va bene *Kwaysto non vah baynay*
This is not what I expected	Mi aspettavo una cosa diversa *Mee ahspayttahvo oonah kosah deevayrsah*

Conversation

Conversation

3.1 I beg your pardon?

I don't speak any/ I speak a little...	Non parlo/Parlo un po' di... *Non parlo/Parlo oon po dee...*
I'm English	Sono inglese *Sono eenglaysay*
I'm Scottish	Sono scozzese *Sono skotzaysay*
I'm Irish	Sono irlandese *Sono eerlahndaysay*
I'm Welsh	Sono gallese *Sono gahllaysay*
Do you speak English? (formal)	Lei parla inglese? *Layee pahrlah eenglaysay?*
Is there anyone who speaks...?	C'è qualcuno che parla...? *Chay kwahlkoono kay pahrlah...?*
I beg your pardon/ What?	Come? *Komay?*
I (don't) understand	(Non) capisco *(Non) kahpeesko*
Do you understand me? (formal)	Mi capisce? *Mee kahpeeshay?*
Could you repeat that, please?	Potrebbe ripetermelo? *Potraybbay reepayhtayrmaylo?*
Could you speak more slowly, please?	Potrebbe parlare un po' più lentamente? *Potraybbay pahrlahray oon po peeoo layntahmayntay?*
What does that mean?/that word mean?	Che cosa significa/Che cosa significa quella parola? *Kay kosah seeneeteekah/Kay kosah seeneefeekah kwayllah pahrolah?*
It's more or less the same as...	E' più o meno lo stesso di...? *Ay peeoo o mayno lo staysso dee..*
Could you write that down for me, please?	Potrebbe scrivermelo? *Potraybbay skreevayrmaylo?*
Could you spell that for me, please?	Come si scrive? *Komay see skreevay?*

(See 1.8 Telephone alphabet)

Could you point that out in this phrase book, please?	Potrebbe indicarmelo in questo frasario? *Potraybbay eendeekahrmaylo een kwaysto frahzahreeo?*
Just a minute, I'll look it up	Un attimo che lo cerco *Oon ahtteemo kay lo chayrko*
I can't find the word/the sentence	Non riesco a trovare la parola/la frase *Non reeaysko ah trovahray lah pahrolah/lah frahzay*
How do you say that in...?	Come si dice in...? *Komay see deechay een...?*
How do you pronounce that?	Come si pronuncia? *Komay see pronoonchah?*

3.2 Introductions

May I introduce myself?	Permette che mi presenti? *Payrmayttay kay mee praysayntee?*
My name's...	Mi chiamo... *Mee keeahmo...*
I'm...	Sono... *Sono...*
What's your name? (formal/informal)...	Lei, come si chiama?/Come ti chiami? *Lay, komay see keeahmah?/Komay tee keeahmee?*
May I introduce...? (formal/informal)...	Permette, Le presento.../Permetti, ti presento... *Payrmayttay, lay praysaynto.../Payrmayttee, tee praysaynto...*
This is my wife/husband (formal/informal)	Le/ti presento mia moglie/mio marito *Lay/tee praysaynto meeah mollyay/meeo mahreeto*
This is my daughter/son (formal/informal)	Le/ti presento mia figlia/mio figlio *Lay/tee presento meeah feellyah/meeo feellyo*
This is my mother/father (formal/informal)	Le/ti presento mia madre/mio padre *Lay/tee praysaynto meeah mahdray/meeo pahdray*
This is my fiancée/fiancé (formal/informal)	Le/ti presento la mia fidanzata/il mio fidanzato *Lay/tee praysaynto lah meeah feedahntzahtah/eel meeo feedahntzahto*
This is my friend (f/m) (formal/informal)	Le/ti presento un'amica mia/un amico mio *Lay/tee praysaynto oonahmeekah meeah/oonahmeeko meeo*
How do you do	Piacere *Peeahchayray*
Hi, pleased to meet you (informal)	Ciao, piacere di conoscerti *Chahoo, peeahchayray dee konoshayrtee*
Pleased to meet you (formal)	Piacere di conoscerLa *Peeahchayray dee konoshayrlah*
Where are you from? (formal/informal)	Lei, di dov'è?/Di dove sei? *Layèe dee dovay ay?/Dee dovay sayee?*
I'm English	Sono inglese *Sono eenglaysay*
What city do you live in?	In quale città abita? *Een kwahlay cheettah ahbeetah?*
In...near....	Abito a... vicino a... *Ahbeeto ah... veecheeno ah...*
Have you been here long?	E' molto che sta qui? *Ay molto kay stah kwee?*
A few days	Qualche giorno *Kwahlkay jorno*
How long are you staying here?	Quanto tempo rimarrà? *Kwahnto taympo reemahrrah?*
We're (probably) leaving tomorrow/ in two weeks	Partiremo (probabilmente) domani/fra due settimane *Pahrtyraymo (probahbeelmayntay) domahny/frah dooay sayttymahnay*
Where are you (m/f) staying?	Dov'è alloggiato/a? *Dovay ay ahllodjahto/ah?*

I'm staying in a hotel/an apartment	Sono alloggiato in un albergo/ appartamento *Sono ahllodjahto een oon ahlbayrgo/ahppahrtahmaynto*
At a campsite	Sono in campeggio *Sono een kahmpaydjo*
I'm staying with friends/relatives	Sono ospite di amici/sono a casa di parenti *Sono ospeetay dee ahmeechee/sono ah kasa dee pahrayntee*
Are you (m/f) here on your own? Are you here with your family?	E' da solo/a?/E' con la Sua famiglia? *Ay dah solo/ah?/Ay con lah sooah fahmeellyah?*
I'm on my own	Sono da solo/a *Sono dah solo/ah*
I'm with my partner/wife/husband	Sono con il mio partner/la mia partner/mia moglie/mio marito *Sono con eel meeo pahrtnayr/lah meeah pahrtnayr/meeah mollyay/meeo mahreeto*
– with my family	Sono con la mia famiglia *Sono con lah meeah fahmeellyah*
– with relatives	Sono con i miei parenti *Sono con ee meeayee pahrayntee*
– with a friend/friends (m.sing/f.sing/m. plu/ f.plu)	Sono con un amico/un'amica/degli amici/delle amiche *Sono con oonahmeeko/oonahmeekah/ daylyee ahmeechee/daylly ahmeekay*
Are you married? (m/f)	Lei è sposato/a? *Layèe ay sposahto/ah?*
Are you engaged?/ Do you have a steady boy/ girlfriend?	È fidanzato/È fidanzata? *Ay feedahntzahto/Ay feedahntzahtah?*
That's none of your business (formal/informal)	Questo non La/ti riguarda per niente *Kwaysto non lah/tee reegwahrdah payr nee-ayntay*
I'm married (m/f)	Sono sposato/a *Sono spozahto/ah*
I'm single (m. only)	Sono scapolo *Sono skahpolo*
I'm not married (m/f)	Non sono sposato/a *Non sono sposahto/ah*
I'm separated (m/f)	Sono separato/a *Sono saypahrahto/ah*
I'm divorced (m/f)	Sono divorziato/a *Sono deevortzeeahto/ah*
I'm a widow/widower	Sono vedova/o *Sono vaydovah/o*
I live alone (m/f)/with someone	Vivo da solo/a/Vivo con il mio partner/la mia partner *Veevo dah solo/ah/Veevo con eel meeo pahrtnayr/lah meeah pahrtnayr*
Do you have any children/grandchildren?	Ha figli/nipoti? *Ah feelly/neepotee?*
How old are (formal/informal) you?	Quanti anni ha/hai? *Kwahnty ahnnee ah/ahee?*
How old is she/he?	Quanti anni ha (lei/lui)? *Kwahnty ahnnee ah (lahee/looee)?*

I'm... (years old)	Ho...anni	*O...ahnnee*
She's/he's...(years old)	Ha...anni	*Ah...ahnnee*
What do you do for a living? (formal/informal)	Che lavoro fa/fai??	*Kay lahvoro faah?/faee?*
I work in an office	Lavoro in ufficio	*Lahvoro een ooffeecho*
I'm a student (m/f)	Sono uno studente/una studentessa	*Sono oono stoodayntay/oona stoodayntayssah*
I am unemployed (m/f)	Sono disoccupato/a	*Sono deesokkoopahto/ah*
I'm retired	Sono pensionato/a	*Sono paynseeonahto/ah*
I'm on a disability pension	Sono invalido/a al lavoro	*Sono eenvahleedo/ah ahl lahvoro*
I'm a housewife	Sono casalinga	*Sono kahsahleengah*
Do you like your job? (formal/informal)	Le/ti piace il Suo/tuo lavoro?	*Lay/tee peeahchay eel soo-o/too-o lahvoro?*
Most of the time	Per lo più sì	*Payr lo peeoo see*
Mostly I do, but I prefer holidays	Il più delle volte sì, però le vacanze mi piacciono di più	*Eel peeoo dayllay voltay see, payro lay vahkahntzay mee peeahchono dee peeoo*

.3 Starting/ending a conversation

Could I ask you something? (formal/informal)	Posso chiederLe/ti una cosa?	*Posso keeaydayrlay/tee oonah kosah?*
Excuse/Pardon me (formal/informal)	Mi scusi/scusami	*Mee skoozee/skoozahmee*
Could you help me please?	Scusi, mi può aiutare?	*Skoozee, mee pwo aheeootahray?*
Yes, what's the problem?	Sì, che cosa c'è?	*See, kay kosah chay?*
What can I do for you?	Di che cosa ha bisogno?	*Dee kay kosah ah beezoneeo?*
Sorry, I don't have time now	Mi dispiace, non ho tempo	*Mee deespeeahchay, non o taympo*
Do you have a light? (formal/informal)	Ha/hai da accendere?	*Ah/ay dah ahtchayndayhray?*
May I join you?	Posso farLe compagnia?	*Posso fahrlay compahnee-ah?*
Could you take a picture of me/us?	Mi/ci potrebbe fare una foto?	*Mee/chee potraybbay fahray oonah photo?*
Leave me alone (formal/informal)	Mi lasci/lasciami in pace	*Mee lahshee/Lahshahmee een pahchay*
Get lost (formal/informal)	Se ne vada/Vattene	*Say nay vahdah/Vahttenay*
Go away or I'll scream	Se non se ne va subito, strillo	*Say non say nay vah soobeeto, streello*

3.4 Congratulations and condolences

Happy birthday/many happy returns/happy name day	Tanti auguri, buon compleanno/buon onomastico *Tahntee owgooree, bwon complayahnno/bwon onomahsteeko*
Please accept my condolences.	Le mie condoglianze *Lay meeay condollyahnzay*
My deepest sympathy	Mi dispiace moltissimo *Mee deespeeahchay molteesseemo*

3.5 A chat about the weather

See also 1.5 The weather

It's so hot/cold today!	Che caldo/freddo oggi! *Kay kahldo/frayddo odjee!*
Isn't it a lovely day?	Che bella giornata! *Kay bayllah jornahtah!*
It's so windy/ what a storm!	Che vento/temporale! *Kay vaynto/taymporahlay!*
All that rain/snow!	Che pioggia/neve! *Kay peeodjah/nayhvay!*
It's so foggy!	Che nebbia! *Kay naybbeeah!*
Has the weather been like this for long?	E' da parecchio che avete questo tempo? *Ay dah pahraykkeeo kay ahvaytay kwaysto taympo?*
Is it always this hot/cold here?	Fa sempre tanto caldo/freddo qui? *Fah saympray tahnto kahldo/frayddo kwee?*
Is it always this dry/ humid here?	E' sempre tanto secco/umido qui? *Ay saympray tahnto saykko/oomeedo kwee?*

3.6 Hobbies

Do you have any hobbies?(formal/informal)	Ha/hai qualche hobby? *Ah/ay kwahlkay obby?*
I like knitting/ reading/photography/ DIY	Mi piace lavorare a maglia/leggere/la fotografia/il fai-da-te *Mee peeahchay lahvoraray ah mahllyah/ledjayray/lah fotograhfeeah/eell fahee dah tay*
I enjoy listening to music	Mi piace ascoltare la musica *Mee peeahchay ahskoltahray lah moozeekah*
I play the guitar/the piano	Suono la chitarra/il pianoforte *Swono lah keetahrrah/eel peeahnofortay*
I like the cinema	Mi piace andare al cinema *Mee peeahchay ahndahray ahl cheenaymah*
I like travelling/playing sport/going fishing/going for a walk	Mi piace viaggiare/fare dello sport/andare a pesca/fare passeggiate *Mee peeahchay veeahdjahray/fahray dayllo sport/ahndahray ah payskah/fahray pahssaydjahtay*

3.7 Being the host(ess)

See also 4 Eating out

Can I offer you a drink? (formal/informal)	Le/ti posso offrire qualcosa da bere? *Lay/tee posso offreeray kwahlkosah dah bayray?*
What would you like to drink? (formal/informal)	Cosa beve?/Cosa bevi? *Kozah bayvay?/Kozah bayvee?*
Something non-alcoholic, please.	Vorrei una bibita analcolica *Vorrayèe oonah beebeetah ahnahlkoleekah*
Would you like a cigarette/cigar	Vuole una sigaretta/un sigaro? *Vwolay oonah seegahrayttah/oon seegahro?*
I don't smoke	Non fumo *Non foomo*

3.8 Invitations

Are you doing anything tonight? (formal/informal)	Ha/hai qualcosa da fare stasera? *Ah/ay kwahlkosah dah fahray stahsayhrah?*
Do you have any plans for today/this afternoon/tonight? (formal/informal)	Che intende/intendi fare oggi/questo pomeriggio/stasera? *Kay eentaynday/eentayndee fahray odjee/kwaysto pomayreedjo/stahsayrah?*
Would you like to go out with me? (formal/informal)	Le/ti piacerebbe uscire con me? *Lay/tee peeahchayraybbay oosheeray con may?*
Would you like to go dancing with me? (formal/informal)	Le/ti piacerebbe andare a ballare con me? *Lay/tee peeahcherebbay ahndaray ah bahllahray con may?*
Would you like to have lunch/dinner with me? (formal/informal)	Le/ti piacerebbe venire a pranzo/a cena con me? *Lay/tee peeahchayraybbay vayneeray ah prahnzo/ah chaynah con may?*
Would you like to come to the beach with me? (formal/informal)	Le/ti piacerebbe venire alla spiaggia con me? *Lay/tee peeahchayraybbay vayneeray allah spee-ahdjah con may?*
Would you like to come into town with us? (formal/informal)	Le/ti piacerebbe venire in città con noi? *Lay/tee peeahchayraybbay vayneeray een cheettah con noee?*
Would you like to come and see some friends with us? (formal/informal)	Le/ti piacerebbe venire con noi a trovare degli amici? *Lay/tee peeahchayraybbay veneeray con noee ah trovahray daylly ahmeechee?*
Shall we dance?	Balliamo? *Bahlleeahmo?*
– sit at the bar?	Ci sediamo al bar? *Chee saydeeahmo ahl bahr?*
– get something to drink?	Beviamo qualcosa? *Beveeahmo kwahlkosah?*
– go for a walk/drive?	Vogliamo fare due passi? Facciamo un giro in macchina? *Vollyahmo fahray dooay pahssee? Fahtcheeahmo oon jeero een mahkkeenah?*
Yes, all right	Sí, va bene *See, vah baynay*

Good idea	E' una buona idea *Ay oonah bwonah eedayah*
No thank you	No grazie *No, grahtzeeay*
Maybe later	Più tardi, forse *Peeoo tahrdy, forsay*
I don't feel like it	Non mi va *Non mee vah*
I don't have time	Purtroppo non ho tempo *Poortroppo non o taympo*
I already have a date	Ho già un altro appuntamento *O jah oonahltro ahppoontahmaynto*
I'm not very good at dancing/volleyball/ swimming	Non so ballare/giocare a pallavolo/nuotare *Non so bahllahray/jokahray ah pahllahvolo/nwotahray*

3.9 Paying a compliment

You look great! (formal/informal)	Sta/stai proprio bene! *Stah/stahee propreeo bayhnay!*
I like your car!	Che bella macchina! *Kay bayllah mahkkeenah!*
I like your ski outfit!	Che bel completo da sci! *Kay bayl complayto dah shee!*
You are very nice (formal/informal)	È/sei molto gentile *Ay/say molto jaynteelay*
What a good boy/girl!	Che bambino/a buono/a! *Kay bahmbeeno/ah bwono/ah!*
You're (formal) a good dancer	(Lei) balla molto bene *(Layee) bahllah molto bayhnay*
You're (formal) a very good cook	(Lei) cucina molto bene *(Layee) koocheenah molto bayhnay*
You're (formal) a good footballer	(Lei) sa giocare molto bene a calcio *(Layee) sah jokahray molto bayhnay ah kahlcheeo*

3.10 Chatting someone up

I like being with you	Mi piace stare con te *Mee peeahchay stahray con tay*
I've missed you so much	Mi sei mancato/a tanto *Mee say mahnkahto/ah tahnto*
I dreamt about you (m/f)	Ti ho sognato/a *Tee o sonyahto/ah*
I think about you all day	Tutto il giorno penso a te *Tootto eel jorno paynso ah tay*
I've been thinking about you all day	Ho pensato a te tutto il giorno *O paynsahto ah tay tootto eel jorno*
You have such a sweet smile	Hai un bel sorriso *Ahee oon bayl sorreezo*
You have such beautiful eyes	I tuoi occhi sono bellissimi *Ee too-oee okkee sono baylleesseemee*
I love you (I'm fond of you)	Ti voglio bene *Tee vollyo bayhnay*
I'm in love with you (m/f)	Sono innamorato/a di te *Sono eennahmorahto/ah dee tay*

I'm in love with you too (m/f)	Anch'io sono innamorato/a di te *Ankeeo sono eennahmorahto/ah dee tay*
I love you	Ti amo *Tee ahmo*
I love you too	Anch'io ti amo *Ahnkeeo tee ahmo*
I don't feel as strongly about you	I miei sentimenti verso di te non sono così intensi *Ee meeay saynteemayntee vayrso dee tay non sono kozee eentaynsee*
I already have a girlfriend/boyfriend	Sono già fidanzato/a *Sono jah feedahntzahto/ah*
I'm not ready for that	Me dispiace, non me la sento *Mee deespeeahchay, non may lah saynto*
I don't want to rush into it	Non voglio precipitare le cose *Non volleeo praycheepeetahray lay cosay*
Take your hands off me	Non toccarmi *Non tokkahrmee*
Okay, no problem	O.k., non c'è problema *O.K., non chay problaymah*
Will you spend the night with me?	Rimani con me stanotte? *Reemahnee con may stahnottay?*
I'd like to go to bed with you	Vorrei andare a letto con te *Vorrayee ahndahray ah laytto con tay*
Only if we use a condom	Soltanto con un preservativo *Solo kon oon praysayrvahteevo*
We have to be careful about AIDS	Dobbiamo stare attenti a causa dell'aids *Dobbyahmo stahray ahttayntee ah kaoosah dayll aheèids*
That's what they all say	Questo lo dicono tutti *Kwaysto lo deekono toottee*
We shouldn't take any risks	Non possiamo correre rischi *Non posseeahmo korrayray reeskee*
Do you have a condom?	Hai un preservativo? *Ahee oon praysayrvahteevo?*
No? Then the answer's no	No? Allora lasciamo perdere *No? Ahllorah lahshyahmo payrdayray*

3.11 Arrangements

When will I see you again?	Quando La/ti rivedrò? *Kwahndo lah/tee reevaydro?*
Are you (informal) free over the weekend?	Sei libero/a al fine-settimana? *Say leebayro/ah ahl feenay saytteemahnah?*
What's the plan, then?	Come rimaniamo d'accordo? *Komay reemahnyahmo dahkkordo?*
Where shall we meet?	Dove ci vediamo? *Dovay chee vaydyahmo?*
Will you pick me/us up?	Mi/ci verrà a prendere? *Mee/chee vayrrah ah prayndayray?*
Shall I pick you (formal) up?	La passo a prendere? *Lah pahsso ah prayndayray?*
I have to be home by...	Devo essere a casa alle... *Dayvo ayssayray ah cahsah ahllay...*
I don't want to see you (formal) anymore	Non voglio più rivederLa *Non volleeo peeoo reevaydayrlah*

.12 Saying goodbye

Can I take you (formal) home?	Posso accompagnarLa a casa? *Posso ahkkompahneeahrlah ah kahsah?*
Can I write/call you (formal)?	Posso scriverLe/chiamarLa? *Posso skreevayrlay/keeahmahrlah?*
Will you (formal) write to me/call me?	Lei mi scriverà/chiamerà? *Layeeh mee skreeverrah/keeahmaheerah?*
Can I have your address/phone number?	Mi dà il Suo indirizzo/numero di telefono? *Mee dah eel sooo eendeereetzo/ noomayro dee taylayfono?*
Thanks for everything	Grazie di tutto *Grahtzeeay dee tootto*
It was a lot of fun	E' stato molto divertente *Ay stahto molto deevayrtayntay*
Say hello to (informal)...	Salutami... *Sahlootahmee...*
All the best	Tante belle cose *Tahntay bayllay kosay*
Good luck	Auguri *Owgooree*
When will you (informal) be back?	Quando tornerai? *Kwahndo tornayrahee?*
I'll be waiting for you (informal)	Ti aspetterò *Tee ahspayttayrro*
I'd like to see you again	Vorrei rivederti *Vorrayee reevaydayrtee*
I hope we meet again soon	Spero che ci rivedremo presto *Spayro kay chee reevaydraymo praysto*
Here's our address. If you're ever in England... (formal)	Ecco il nostro indirizzo. Casomai venisse in Inghilterra... *Aykko eel nostro eendeereetzo. Kahzomahee vayneessay een Eengeelltayrrah*
You'd be more than welcome (formal)	Saremo lieti di ospitarLa *Sahrraymo leeaytee dee ospeetarlah*

Eating out

4 Eating out

- **Eating establishments:**

Trattoria: middle-price restaurant
Ristorante: prices vary but with better service than a *Trattoria*
Tavola calda: cheap, self-service style
Rosticceria: large selection of mainly take-away meals
Pizzeria: specialising in pizza
Osteria: small trattoria or wine bar
Gelateria: specialising in icecream
Bar/Caffè: café also serving alcohol and snack food
Birreria: bar specialising in beer

- **Mealtimes:**

In Italy people usually have three meals:
1 *(Prima) colazione* (breakfast), is eaten sometime between 7.30 and 10 a.m., often standing up in a bar. It generally consists of *caffelatte* (white coffee) and biscuits or *cappuccino* with a *brioche* (croissant).
2 *Pranzo* (lunch), traditionally eaten at home between 1 and 2.30 p.m., includes a hot dish and is considered to be the most important meal of the day. Offices and shops often close and, unless enroled in a special afternoon programme, school children generally return home at lunchtime. Lunch usually consists of three courses:
- pasta or risotto
- main course of meat or fish with a vegetable or salad
- cheese and/or fruit

Antipasti (hors d'oeuvres preceding the pasta course), cakes and desserts are usually eaten on Sundays or on special occasions.
3 *Cena* (dinner), at around 8 or 9 p.m., is a light meal, often including soup, usually taken with the family.
At around 5 p.m., *merenda* (a snack) is often served to children and consists of bread and cured meats and/or cake.

- **In restaurants:** Most trattorias and restaurants have a cover charge (*coperto*) which includes bread, and a service charge.

4.1 On arrival

I'd like to book a table for seven o'clock, please	Vorrei prenotare un tavolo per le sette? *Vorrayee praynotahray oon tahvolo payr lay sayttay?*
A table for two, please	Un tavolo per due, per favore *Oon tahvolo payr dooay payr fahvoray*
We've (We haven't) booked	(Non) abbiamo prenotato *(Non) ahbbeeamo praynotahto*

Ha prenotato?	Do you have a reservation?
A che nome?	What name, please?
Prego, da questa parte	This way, please
Questo tavolo è prenotato	This table is reserved
Fra un quarto d'ora ci sarà un tavolo libero	We'll have a table free in fifteen minutes.
Le dispiace aspettare nel frattempo?	Would you mind waiting?

Is the restaurant open yet?	Il ristorante è già aperto? *Eel reestorahntay ay jah ahpayrto?*
What time does the restaurant open?/What time does the restaurant close?	A che ora apre il ristorante/A che ora chiude il ristorante? *Ah kay orah ahpray eel reestorahntay?/Ah kay orah keeooday eel reestorahntay?*
Can we wait for a table?	Possiamo aspettare che si liberi un tavolo? *Possyahmo ahspayttahray kay see leebayree oon tahvolo?*
Do we have to wait long?	Dobbiamo aspettare parecchio? *Dobbyahmo ahspayttahray pahraykkeeo?*
Is this seat taken?	E' libero questo posto? *Ay leebayro kwaysto posto?*
Could we sit here/there?	Possiamo accomodarci qui/lì? *Possyahmo ahkkomodahrchee kwee/lee?*
Can we sit by the window?	Possiamo sedere vicino alla finestra? *Possyahmo sayhdayray veecheeno ahllah feenaystrah?*
Are there any tables outside?	Si può mangiare anche fuori? *See pwo mahnjahray ahnkay fworee?*
Do you have another chair for us?	Ha un'altra sedia? *Ah oonahltrah saydyah?*
Do you have a highchair?	Ha un seggiolone (per bambini)? *Ah oon saydjolonay (payr bahmbeenee)?*
Is there a socket for this bottle-warmer?	C'è una presa di corrente per lo scaldabiberon? *Chay oonah praysah dee corrayntay payr lo skahldahbeebayron?*
Could you warm up this bottle/jar for me? (in the microwave)	Potrebbe riscaldare questo biberon/vasetto (nel forno a microonde)? *Potraybbay reeskahldahray kwaysto beebayron/vahzaytto (nayl forno ah meekro-onday)?*
Not too hot, please	Non bollente, per favore *Non bollayntay payr fahvoray*
Is there somewhere I can change the baby's nappy?	C'è un posto dove posso cambiare il bambino/la bambina? *Chay oon posto dovay posso kahmbeeahray eel bahmbeeno/lah bahmbeenah?*
Where are the toilets?	Dove è il bagno? *Dovay ay eel bahnyo?*

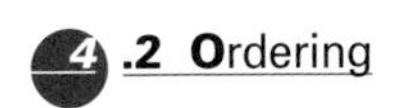

4.2 Ordering

Waiter/Waitress!	Cameriere/a! *Kahmayreeayray/ah!*
Madam!	Signora! *Seeneeorah!*
Sir!	Signore! *Seeneeoray!*
We'd like something to eat/drink	Vorremmo mangiare/bere qualcosa *Vorraymmo mahnjahray/bayhray kwahlkosah*
Could I have a quick meal?	Potrei mangiare qualcosa rapidamente? *Potray mahnjahray kwahlkosah rahpeedahmayntay?*

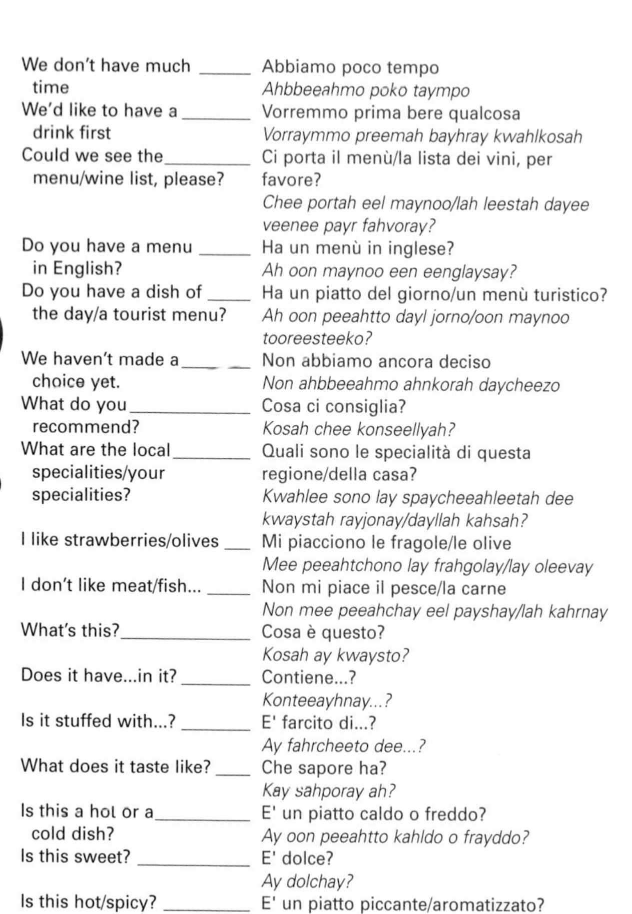

We don't have much time	Abbiamo poco tempo *Ahbbeeahmo poko taympo*
We'd like to have a drink first	Vorremmo prima bere qualcosa *Vorraymmo preemah bayhray kwahlkosah*
Could we see the menu/wine list, please?	Ci porta il menù/la lista dei vini, per favore? *Chee portah eel maynoo/lah leestah dayee veenee payr fahvoray?*
Do you have a menu in English?	Ha un menù in inglese? *Ah oon maynoo een eenglaysay?*
Do you have a dish of the day/a tourist menu?	Ha un piatto del giorno/un menù turistico? *Ah oon peeahtto dayl jorno/oon maynoo tooreesteeko?*
We haven't made a choice yet.	Non abbiamo ancora deciso *Non ahbbeeahmo ahnkorah daycheezo*
What do you recommend?	Cosa ci consiglia? *Kosah chee konseellyah?*
What are the local specialities/your specialities?	Quali sono le specialità di questa regione/della casa? *Kwahlee sono lay spaycheeahleetah dee kwaystah rayjonay/dayllah kahsah?*
I like strawberries/olives	Mi piacciono le fragole/le olive *Mee peeahtchono lay frahgolay/lay oleevay*
I don't like meat/fish...	Non mi piace il pesce/la carne *Non mee peeahchay eel payshay/lah kahrnay*
What's this?	Cosa è questo? *Kosah ay kwaysto?*
Does it have...in it?	Contiene...? *Konteeayhnay...?*
Is it stuffed with...?	E' farcito di...? *Ay fahrcheeto dee...?*
What does it taste like?	Che sapore ha? *Kay sahporay ah?*
Is this a hot or a cold dish?	E' un piatto caldo o freddo? *Ay oon peeahtto kahldo o frayddo?*
Is this sweet?	E' dolce? *Ay dolchay?*
Is this hot/spicy?	E' un piatto piccante/aromatizzato? *Ay oon peeahtto peekkahntay/ ahromahteedzahto?*

Desidera?	What would you like?
Ha scelto?	Have you decided?
Vuole un aperitivo?	Would you like a drink first?
Cosa prende da bere?	What would you like to drink?
... sono finiti/e	We've run out of.....
Buon appetito	Enjoy your meal/Bon appetit
Tutto bene?	Is everything all right?
Posso sparecchiare?	May I clear the table?

Do you have anything else, by any chance?	Avrebbe magari qualcos'altro? *Ahvraybbay mahgahree kwahlkosahltro?*
I'm on a salt-free diet	Non posso mangiare sale *Non posso mahnjahray sahlay*
I can't eat pork	Non posso mangiare carne di maiale *Non posso mahnjahray kahrnay dee maheeahlay*
I can't have sugar	Non posso mangiare zuccheri *Non posso mahnjahray dzookkayree*
I'm on a fat-free diet	Non posso mangiare grassi *Non posso mahnjahray grahssee*
I can't have spicy food	Non posso mangiare cibi piccanti *Non posso mahnjahray cheebee peekkahntee*
We'll have what those people are having	Vorremmo un piatto uguale al loro *Vorraymmo oon peeahtto oogwahlay ahl loro*
I'd like...	Vorrei... *Vorrayee...*
We're not having antipasto/a pasta dish	Passiamo subito al primo/secondo piatto *Pahsseeahmo soobeeto ahl preemo/ saykondo peeahtto*
Could I have some more bread, please?	Mi porta un altro po' di pane, per favore? *Mee portah oonahltro po dee pahnay payr fahvoray?*
Could I have another bottle of water/wine, please?	Mi porta un'altra bottiglia di acqua/di vino, per favore? *Mee portah oonahltrah botteelleeah dee ahkwah/dee veeno payr fahvoray?*
Could I have another portion of...please?	Mi porta un'altra porzione di..., per favore? *Mee portah oonahltrah portzeeonay dee..., payr fahvoray?*
Could I have the salt and pepper, please?	Mi porta il sale e il pepe, per favore? *Mee portah eel sahlay ay eel paypay, payr fahvoray?*
Could I have a napkin, please?	Mi porta un tovagliolo, per favore? *Mee portah oon tovallyolo, payr fahvoray?*
Could I have a teaspoon, please?	Mi porta un cucchiaino, per favore? *Mee portah oon kookkeeaheeno payr fahvoray?*
Could I have an ashtray, please?	Mi porta un portacenere, per favore? *Mee portah oon portahchaynayray, payr fahvoray?*
Could I have some matches, please?	Mi porta dei fiammiferi, per favore? *Mee portah dayee feeahmmeefayree payr fahvoray?*
Could I have some toothpicks, please	Mi porta degli stuzzicadenti, per favore? *Mee portah daylly stootzeekahdayntee payr fahvoray?*
Could I have a glass of water, please?	Mi porta un bicchiere d'acqua, per favore? *Mee portah oon beekkeeayray dahkwah payr fahvoray?*
Could I have a straw please?	Mi porta una cannuccia, per favore? *Mee portah oonah kahnnootchah payr fahvoray?*
Enjoy your meal/Bon appetit!	Buon appetito! *Bwon ahppayteeto!*

You too!	Grazie, altrettanto! *Grahtzeeay, ahltrayttahnto!*
Cheers!	Cin cin! *Cheen cheen!*
The next round's on me	La prossima volta offro io *Lah prosseemah voltah offro eeo*
Could we have a doggy bag, please?	Potremmo portare via gli avanzi per il nostro cane? *Potraymmo portahray veeah lly ahvahntzee payr eel nostro kahnay?*

4.3 The bill

See also 8.2 Settling the bill

How much is this dish?	Quanto costa questo piatto? *Kwahnto kostah kwaysto peeahtto?*
Could I have the bill, please?	Ci porti il conto *Chee portee eel konto*
All together	Tutto insieme *Tootto eensee-aymay*
Everyone pays separately/ let's go Dutch	Facciamo alla romana *Fahtcheeahmo ahllah romahnah*
Could we have the menu again, please?	Ci porta di nuovo il menu? *Chee portah dee nwovo eel maynoo?*
The...is not on the bill	Ha dimenticato di mettere il/la... sul conto *Ah deemaynteekahto dee mayttayray eel/lah...sool konto*

4.4 Complaints

It's taking a very long time	C'è ancora molto da aspettare? *Chay ahnkorah molto dah ahspayttahray?*
We've been here an hour already	E' un'ora che stiamo qui *Ay oonorah kay steeahmo kwee*
This must be a mistake	Senz'altro è uno sbaglio *Saynzahltro ay oono sbahleeo*
This is not what I ordered	Non ho ordinato questo piatto *Non o ordeenahto kwaysto peeahtto*
I ordered...	Ho chiesto... *O keeaysto...*
There's a dish missing	Manca un piatto *Mahnkah oon peeahtto*
This is broken/not clean	Questo è rotto/non è pulito *Kwaysto ay rotto/non ay pooleeto*
The food's cold	Il piatto è freddo *Eel peeahtto ay frayddo*
The food's not fresh	Il cibo non è fresco *Eel cheebo non ay fraysko*
The food's too salty/ sweet/spicy	Il piatto è troppo salato/dolce/ aromatizzato *Eel peeahtto ay troppo sahlahto/dolchay/ahromahteedzahto*
The meat's too rare	La carne è poco cotta *Lah kahrnay ay poko kottah*

The meat's overdone ______ La carne è troppo cotta
Lah kahrnay ay troppo kottah

The meat's tough ________ La carne è dura
Lah kahrnay ay doorah

The meat is off/has gone bad __ La carne è andata a male
Lah kahrnay ay ahndahtah ah mahlay

Could I have something else instead of this? ___ Invece di questo, mi potrebbe dare un'altra cosa?
Eenvayhchay dee kwaysto mee potraybbay dahray oonahltrah kosah?

The bill/this amount is not right _____ Il conto non torna
Eel konto non tornah

We didn't have this ________ Non abbiamo preso questo
Non ahbbeeahmo prayso kwaysto

There's no paper in the toilet ____ Manca la carta igienica nel bagno
Mahnkah lah kahrtah eejayneekah nayl bahneeo

Will you call the manager, please? __________ Mi chiama il capo-servizio, per favore?
Mee keeahmah eel kahpo-sayrveetzeeo payr fahvoray?

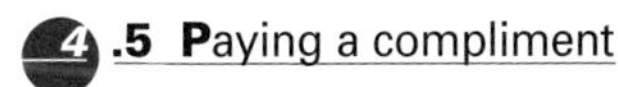

4.5 Paying a compliment

That was a wonderful meal _____ Abbiamo mangiato molto bene
Ahbbeeahmo mahnjahto molto bayhnay

The food was excellent ____ Il cibo era ottimo
Eel cheebo ayrah otteemo

The...in particular was delicious _____ Soprattutto... era squisito/a
Soprahttootto...ayrah skweezeeto/ah

4.6 The menu

antipasti
starter/hors d'oeuvres
cacciagione
game
carne
meat
contorni
side dishes/vegetables
coperto
cover charge
digestivo
liqueur (after dinner)
dolci
cakes/desserts
formaggio
cheese
frutta
fruit
gelati
icecream
insalata
salad
I.V.A.
VAT
minestra
soup
pane
bread
pasta(sciutta)
pasta
pesce
fish
pizza
pizza
pollame
fowl
primo piatto
first course
secondo piatto
main course
servizio (compreso)
service charge (included)
specialità
specialities
spuntini
snacks
verdure
vegetables

4.7 Alphabetical list of drinks and dishes

acciuga
anchovy
acqua (minerale)
(mineral) water
affettati
sliced cured meats
affumicato
smoked
aglio
garlic
agnello
lamb
amatriciana, all'
(with) bacon, chilli and tomato sauce (for pasta)
anatra
duck
anguilla (carpionata)
eel (soused)
aranciata
orange juice/ade
arista
roast pork
arrabbiata, all'
(with) chilli and tomato sauce (for pasta)
arrosto
roast
asparago
asparagus
bianco (in)
without seasoning
birra
beer
bistecca
steak
bollito
boiled meat
braciola
minute steak
brasato
braised
brodo
broth
bruschetta
toasted bread with garlic topping
budino
pudding
burro
butter
cacciatora, alla
(with) mushroom sauce (esp. for chicken)
caffè corretto/macchiato
laced or flavoured coffee/coffee with a drop of milk
caffè freddo
iced coffee
caffè (lungo/ristretto)
coffee (weak/strong)
caffellatte
Café au lait/milky coffee
calamaro
squid
cannelloni
cannelloni (pasta tubes)
cappero
caper
cappuccino
cappuccino (coffee with frothy milk)
carbonara, alla
(with) cream, bacon, egg, black pepper and parmesan sauce (for pasta)
carciofo
artichoke
carota
carrot
carpa
carp
carrettiera, alla
(with) tomato, garlic, chilli and parsley sauce (for pasta)
casalingo
home-made
cassata
cassata (Sicilian fruited icecream)
cavolfiore
cauliflower
cavolini di Bruxelles
Brussels sprouts
cavolo
cabbage
ceci
chick peas
cervello
brains
cervo
venison
cetriolino
gherkin
cetriolo
cucumber
cicoria
chicory
cinghiale
boar
cioccolata
chocolate
cipolla
onion
coda di bue
oxtail
condito
dressed
coniglio
rabbit
coscia
leg (of chicken, of lamb)
cotoletta
cutlet
cozze
mussels
crema
custard
crostini
canapé with savoury topping/croutons
crudo
raw
digestivo
liqueur (after dinner)
erbe aromatiche
herbs
fagiano
pheasant
fagioli
beans
fagiolini
green beans
faraona
guinea fowl
farcito
stuffed

fegato
liver

alla brace
barbequed/grilled

fetta/fettina
slice/thin slice

filetto
fillet

finocchio
fennel

forno, al
baked

frappé
milk-shake

frittata
omelette

fritto
fried

frizzante
fizzy

frullato
milk-shake/whisked

frutti di mare
seafood

funghi
mushrooms

gamberetto
shrimp

gambero
crayfish

gelato
icecream

ghiaccio (con)
(with) ice

giardiniera, alla
(with) vegetable sauce

gnocchi
potato dumplings

granchio
crab

gran(o)turco
corn

grappa
eau de vie

griglia, alla
grilled

imbottito
stuffed

infuso
infusion (tea)

intingolo di lepre
hare sauce

involtino
roulade

latte
milk

lepre
hare

limone (al)
(with) lemon

lingua
tongue

liquore
liqueur

lombata/lombo
loin

luccio
pike

lumache
snails

maccheroni
macaroni (pasta)

macedonia di frutta
fruit salad

manzo
beef

marinato
marinated/pickled

melanzana
eggplant/aubergine

merluzzo
cod

miele
honey

minestrone
minestrone soup

molluschi
shellfish

noce
walnut

noce moscata
nutmeg

olio
oil

oliva
olive

ossobuco
veal shin

ostrica
oyster

pancetta
bacon

pane (integrale/tostato)
bread (wholemeal/ toasted)

panino (imbottito)
bread-roll (filled)

panna (montata)
(whipped) cream

parmigiano
parmesan (cheese)

passata
sieved or creamed

pasta
pasta

pastasciutta
pasta (with sauce)

pasta sfoglia
puff pastry

pasticcio
(sort of) pie (often made of pasta)

patate fritte
chips

pecora
sheep/mutton

pecorino
sheep's milk cheese

penne
pasta quills

peperoncino
chilli

peperone
(green, red, yellow) pepper

pesto
basil,pine-nut and parmesan sauce

petto
breast

piccione
pigeon

piselli
peas

pizzaiola, alla
(with) mozzarella cheese, oregano and tomato sauce

pollo
chicken

polpetta
meatball

pomodoro
tomato

porchetta
suckling pig

porcini
(porcini) mushrooms

porto
Port (wine)

prezzemolo
parsley

prosciutto
cured ham

puttanesca, alla
(with) spicy tomato sauce

quaglia
quail
rapa
turnip
ragù
meat (Bolognese) sauce
riccio di mare
see urchin
rigatoni
rigatoni (large pasta tubes)
ripieno
stuffed
riso
rice
risotto
risotto
rognone
kidney
rosbiff
roast beef
salame
salami
salmone
salmon
salsa
sauce
salsiccia
sausage
saltimbocca
veal with prosciutto and sage
salumi
cured meats
sambuca
sweet aniseed liqueur
sarda, sardina
sardine
scaloppina
escalope
scampi
prawns
secco
dry
sedano
celery
sel(t)z
soda water
selvaggina
game
semifreddo
icecream cake
senape
mustard
seppia
cuttle fish
sogliola
sole
sottaceti
pickles
spalla
shoulder
spezzatino
stew
spiedo, allo
on the spit
spina, alla
draught (beer)
spinaci
spinach
spremuta
(freshly squeezed) juice
spumante
sparkling wine
S.Q. secondo quantità
according to weight
stracciatella
soup: broth with beaten egg
stufato
stew
succo di frutta
fruit juice
sugo
sauce
tacchino
turkey
tagliatelle
tagliatelle (flat ribbon pasta)
tartaruga
turtle
tartufo
truffle
tè
tea
testa (di vitello)
head (of veal)
tonno
tuna
torta
pie/cake
tortellini
tortellini (kind of stuffed pasta)
trippa
tripe
trita(ta)
minced or ground (usually herbs or meat)
trota
trout
uova strapazzate
scrambled eggs
uovo affogato/in camicia
poached egg
uovo al tegame/fritto
fried egg
uovo, all'
(with) egg
uovo alla coque/da bere/sodo
soft boiled/fresh/hard boiled egg
vaniglia
vanilla
verdura
green vegetables
vino bianco/rosso/rosato
white/red/rosé wine
vitello
veal
vongola
clam
zabaione
zabaglione (sweet custard sauce made with egg and Marsala)
zucchero
sugar
zucchino
courgette (small marrow, squash)
zuppa
soup
zuppa alla pavese
kind of broth
zuppa inglese
kind of trifle

On the road

5 On the road

5.1 Asking for directions

Excuse me, could I ask you something?	Mi scusi, potrei chiederLe una cosa? *Mee skoozee potray keeaydayrlay oonah kozah?*
I've lost my way	Mi sono perso/a *Mee sono payrso/ah*
Is there a(n)... around here?	Sa se c'è un/una...da queste parti? *Sah say chay oon/oonah...dah kwaystay pahrtee?*
Is this the way to...?	E' questa la strada per...? *Ay kwaystah lah strahdah payr...*
Could you tell me how to get to....?	Mi può indicare la strada per...? *Mee pwo eendeekahray lah strahdah payr...*
What's the quickest way to...?	Qual'è la strada più diretta per...? *Kwahlay ay lah strahdah peeoo deerayttah payr...?*
How many kilometres is it to...?	A quanti chilometri è...? *Ah qwahntee keelomaytreeay....?*
Could you point it out on the map?	Me lo può indicare sulla mappa? *May lo pwo eendeekahray soollah mahppah?*

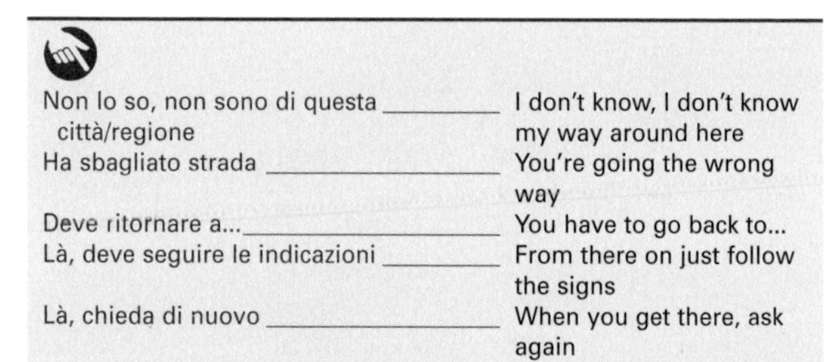

Non lo so, non sono di questa città/regione	I don't know, I don't know my way around here
Ha sbagliato strada	You're going the wrong way
Deve ritornare a...	You have to go back to...
Là, deve seguire le indicazioni	From there on just follow the signs
Là, chieda di nuovo	When you get there, ask again

Vada dritto Go straight ahead	la strada the road/street	il fiume the river
Giri a sinistra Turn left	il semaforo the traffic light	il viadotto the flyover
Giri a destra Turn right	la galleria the tunnel	il ponte the bridge
Volti a destra/sinistra Turn right/left	il cartello/segnale stradale di 'dare la precedenza' the "give way" sign	il passaggio a livello the level crossing
Segua Follow	il palazzo the building	le indicazioni per... the signs pointing to....
Attraversi Cross	all'angolo at the corner	la freccia the arrow
l'incrocio the intersection/ crossroads		

5.2 Customs

By law you must always carry with you an identification document and, if driving, your driving licence.

- **Border documents:** valid passport. Citizens of EU countries may enter Italy using a national identity card. Strictly speaking, visitors planning to stay at the same address for more than one week need a *permesso di soggiorno*, obtained from the *questura* (police station) and requiring a visa stamp. This only becomes a necessity if you plan to study, work or live in Italy.
- **For car and motorbike:** valid driving licence (non-EU licences require an Italian translation or an International Driving Permit); vehicle registration document; third party international insurance document (Green Card).
- **Caravan:** same registration numberplate and Green Card.

A warning triangle is compulsory (bulb kit, fire extinguisher and first-aid kit are recommended).

- **Import and export specifications:**

– Foreign currrency:	no restrictions on the import of lire.
– Alcohol:	1 lt spirits or liquor, 2 lts wine or fortified wine.
– Tobacco:	200 cigarettes, 50 cigars, 250g tobacco
– Perfume:	50g perfume, 250ml eau de toilette
– Coffee:	500g
– Tea:	100g

You must be aged 17 to import alcohol and tobacco and 15 to import coffee and tea. The above restrictions are relevant to all alcohol and tobacco purchased in duty-free shops and will apply until 30/6/99.

Il passaporto, prego	Your passport, please
La carta verde, prego	Your green card, please
Il libretto d'immatricolazione, prego	Your vehicle documents, please
Il visto, prego	Your visa, please
Dove va?	Where are you going?
Quanto tempo intende rimanere?	How long are you planning to stay?
Ha qualcosa da dichiarare?	Do you have anything to declare?
Per favore, mi apra questo/a	Open this, please

My children are entered on this passport	I miei figli sono su questo passaporto *Ee meeayee feelly sono soo kwaysto pahssahporto*
I'm travelling through	Sono di passaggio *Sono dee pahssahdjo*
I'm going on holiday to...	Passerò le vacanze a... *Pahssayhro lay vahkahntzay ah...*
I'm on a business trip	Sono in viaggio d'affari *Sono een veeahdjo dahffahree*
I don't know how long I'll be staying	Non so quanto tempo rimarrò *Non so kwahnto taympo reemahrro*
I'll be staying here for a weekend	Rimarrò qui un weekend *Reemahrro kwee oon weekend*
I'll be staying here for a few days	Rimarrò qui qualche giorno *Reemahrro kwee kwahlkay jorno*

I'll be staying here a week	Rimarrò qui una settimana *Reemahrro kwee oonah saytteemahnah*
I'll be staying here for two weeks	Rimarrò qui due settimane *Reemahrro kwee dooay saytteemahnay*
I've got nothing to declare	Non ho niente da dichiarare *Non o neeayntay dah deekeeahrahray*
I have...	Ho... *O...*
– a carton of cigarettes	– una stecca di sigarette *– oonah staykkah dee seegahrayttay*
– a bottle of...	– una bottiglia di... *– oonah botteellyah dee...*
– some souvenirs	– qualche souvenir *– kwahlkay sovayneer*
These are personal effects	Sono oggetti personali *Sono odjayttee payrsonahlee*
These are not new	Questa roba non è nuova *Kwaystah robah non ay nwovah*
Here's the receipt	Ecco lo scontrino *Aykko lo skontreeno*
This is for private use	E' per uso personale *Ay payr oozo payrsonahlay*
How much import duty do I have to pay?	Quanto devo pagare di tassa d'importazione? *Kwahnto dayvo pahgahray dee tahssah deemportahtzeeonay ?*
May I go now?	Posso andare adesso? *Posso ahndahray ahdaysso?*

5.3 Luggage

Porter!	Facchino! *Fahkkeeno!*
Could you take this luggage to...?	Per favore, potrebbe portare questi bagagli a... *Payr fahvoray, potraybbay portahray kwaystee bahgahlly ah...*
How much do I owe you?	Quanto Le devo? *Kwahnto lay dayvo?*
Where can I find a trolley?	Dove posso trovare un carrello? *Dovay posso trovahray oon kahrrello?*
Could you store this luggage for me?	E' possibile lasciare in consegna questi bagagli? *Ay posseebeelay lahsheeahray een konsayneeah kwaystee bahgahlly?*
Where are the luggage lockers?	Dove sono le cassette per la custodia dei bagagli? *Dovay sono lay kahssayttay payr lah koostodeeah dayee bahgahlly?*
I can't get the locker open	Non riesco ad aprire la cassetta *Non ree-aysko ahdahpreeray lah kahssaytta*
How much is it per item per day?	Quanto costa al giorno ogni collo? *Kwahnto kostah ahl jorno onyee kollo?*
This is not my bag/suitcase	Non è la mia borsa/valigia *Non ay lah meeah borsah/vahleejah*

There's one item/bag/ suitcase missing	Manca un collo/una borsa/una valigia *Mahnkah oon kollo/oonah borsah/oonah vahleejah*
My suitcase is damaged	La mia valigia è danneggiata *Lah meeah vahleejah ay dahnnaydjahtah*

 5.4 Traffic signs

accendere i fari (in galleria)
switch on headlights (in the tunnel)
alt
stop
area/stazione di servizio
service station
attenzione
beware
autocarri
heavy goods vehicles
banchina non transitabile
impassable verge
caduta massi
beware, falling rocks
cambiare corsia
change lanes
chiuso al traffico
road closed
corsia di emergenza
emergency lane
curve
bends
deviazione
detour
disco orario (obbligatorio)
parking disk (compulsory)
divieto di accesso
no entry
divieto di sorpasso/di sosta
no overtaking/no parking
diritto di precedenza a fine strada
right of way at end of road
galleria
tunnel
incrocio
intersection/ crossroads
(isola/zona) pedonale
traffic island/ pedestrian precinct
lasciare libero il passo/passaggio
do not obstruct
lavori in corso
roadworks
pagamento/ pedaggio
toll payment
parcheggio a pagamento/ riservato a...
paying carpark/parking reserved for...
parcheggio custodito
supervised carpark
passaggio a livello
level crossing
altezza limitata a...
maximum head room...
passo carrabile
driveway
pericolo(so)
danger(ous)
pioggia o gelo per km....
rain or ice for...kms
precedenza
right of way
rallentare
slow down
senso unico
one way
senso vietato
no entry
soccorso stradale
road assistance (breakdown service)
sosta limitata
parking for a limited period
strada deformata/in dissesto
broken/uneven surface
strada interrotta
road closed
strettoia
narrowing in the road
tenere la destra/sinistra
keep right/left
traffico interrotto
road blocked
transito con catene
snow-chains required
uscita
exit
velocità massima
maximum speed
vietato l'accesso/ai pedoni
no access/no pedestrian access
vietato l'autostop
no hitch-hiking
vietato svoltare a destra/sinistra
no right/left turn
zona disco
disk zone
zona rimozione (ambo i lati)
tow-away area (both sides of the road)

The parts of a car

(the diagram shows the numbered parts)

1	battery	batteria	*bahttayreeyah*
2	rear light	il fanale posteriore	*eel fahnahlay postayry-oray*
3	rear-view mirror	lo specchietto retrovisore	*lo spaykkeeaytto raytroveezoray*
	reversing light	la luce di retromarcia	*lah loochay dee raytromahrcheeah*
4	aerial	antenna	*ahntaynnah*
	car radio	autoradio (f)	*ahootorahdeeo*
5	petrol tank	serbatoio carburante	*sayrbahtoeeo kahrboorahntay*
6	sparking plugs	le candele	*lay kahndaylay*
	fuel pump	pompa della benzina	*pompah dayllah bayndzeenah*
7	wing mirror	lo specchietto retrovisore esterno	*lo spaykkeeaytto raytroveezoray aystayrno*
8	bumper	il paraurti	*eel pahrah-oortee*
	carburettor	il carburatore	*eel kahrboorahtoray*
	crankcase	basamento del motore	*bahsahmayhnto dayl motoray*
	cylinder	cilindro	*cheeleendro*
	ignition	accensione (f)	*ahtchaynseeonay*
	warning light	spia luminosa	*spee-ah loomeenohzah*
	dynamo	la dinamo	*lah deenahmo*
	accelerator	acceleratore (m)	*ahtchayllayrahtoray*
	handbrake	freno a mano	*frayno ah mahno*
	valve	valvola	*vahlvolah*
9	silencer	marmitta	*mahrmeettah*
10	boot	cofano	*kofahno*
11	headlight	faro	*fahro*
	crank shaft	albero a gomiti	*ahlbayro ah gomeetee*
12	air filter	filtro dell aria	*feeltro dayllahreea*
	fog lamp	faro fendinebbia	*fahro fayndeenaybbeeah*
13	engine block	monoblocco	*monoblokko*
	camshaft	albero a camme	*ahlbayro ah kahmmay*
	oil filter/pump	filtro/pompa dell'olio	*feeltro/pompah daylloleeo*
	dipstick	indicatore (m) di livello dell'olio	*eendeekahtoray dee leevayllo daylloleeo*
	pedal	il pedale	*eel paydahlay*
14	door	portiera	*porteeayrah*
15	radiator	il radiatore	*eel rahdeeahtoray*
16	brake disc	disco del freno	*deesko dayl frayno*
	spare wheel	ruota di scorta	*rwohtah dee skortah*
17	indicator	indicatore (m) (di direzione)	*eendeekahtoray (dee deeraytzeeonay)*
18	windscreen wiper	tergicristallo	*tayrjeekreestahllo*
19	shock absorbers	ammortizzatore (m)	*ahmmorteedzahtoray*
	sunroof	tetto apribile	*taytto ahpreebeelay*
	spoiler	lo spoiler	*lo spoeelayr*
	starter motor	motorino di avviamento	*motoreeno dee ahvveeahmaynto*

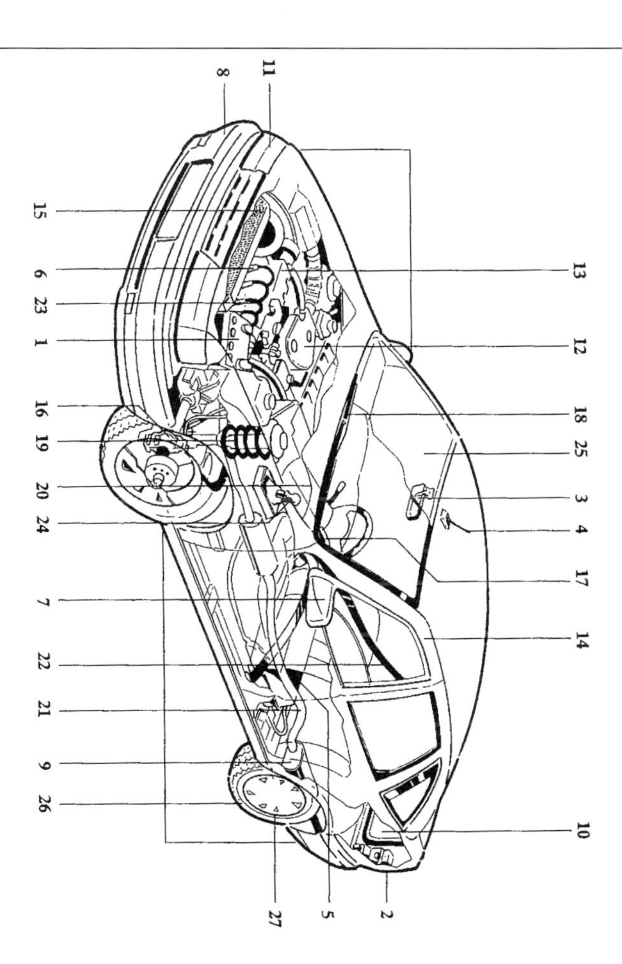

20	steering column	il piantone dello sterzo	*eel peeahntonay dayllo stayrtzo*
	steering wheel	il volante	*eel volahntay*
21	exhaust pipe	tubo di scarico	*toobo dee skahreeko*
22	seat belt	cintura di sicurezza	*cheentoorah dee seekooraytzah*
	fan	il ventilatore	*eel vaynteelahtoray*
23	distributor cables	i cavi del distributore	*ee kahvee dayl deestreebootoray*
24	gear lever	leva del cambio	*layvah del kahmbeeo*
25	windscreen	il parabrezza	*eel pahrahbrayzah*
	water pump	pompa dell'acqua	*pompah dayllahkkwah*
26	wheel	ruota	*rwotah*
27	hubcap	coprimozzo	*kopreemotzo*
	piston	il pistone	*eel peestonay*

5.5 The car

See the diagram on page 51.

- **Particular traffic regulations:**

Speed limits: on *autostradas* 130 km/h for cars of 1100cc or more; 110km/h for smaller cars and motorbikes under 350cc.
On all main, non-urban highways 110 km/h; on secondary, non-urban highways 90 km/h; in built-up areas 50 km/h.
Give way to vehicles coming from the right unless otherwise indicated.
– towing: prohibited to private drivers.

5.6 The petrol station

- **The cost of petrol** in Italy is very high (around L. 1,500/litre), slightly less for unleaded.

How many kilometres to the next petrol station, please?	A quanti chilometri sta il prossimo distributore di benzina? *Ah kwahntee keelomaytree sta eel prossemo deestreebootoray dee baynzeenah?*
I would like...litres of	Vorrei...litri di *Vorrayee...leetree dee*
– super	Vorrei...litri di super *Vorrayee... leetree dee soopayr*
– leaded	Vorrei...litri di normale *Vorrayee... leetree dee normahlay*
– unleaded	Vorrei...litri di benzina senza piombo *Vorrayee...leetree dee baynzeenah saynzah peeombo*
– diesel	Vorrei...litri di gasolio *Vorrayee... leetree dee gahzoleeo*
... lire worth of gas	Vorrei...lire di benzina *Vorrayee...leeray dee baynzeenah*
Fill her up, please	Mi faccia il pieno per favore *Mee fahtchah eel peeayno payr fahvoray*
Could you check...?	Può controllarmi...? *Pwo controllahrmee...?*
– the oil level	– il livello dell'olio *– eel leevayllo daylloleeo*
– the tyre pressure	– la pressione delle gomme *– lah praysseeonay dayllay gommay*
Could you change the oil, please?	Può cambiarmi l'olio? *Pwo kahmbeeahrmeo loleeo?*
Could you clean the windscreen, please?	Può lavarmi il parabrezza? *Pwo lahvahrmeo eel pahrahbraydzah?*
Could you give the car a wash, please?	Può lavarmi la macchina? *Pwo lahvahrmee lah mahkkeenah?*

5.7 Breakdown and repairs

I have broken down Could you give me a hand?	Sono rimasto/a in panne. Mi potrebbe dare una mano? *Sono reaymahsto/ah een pahnnay. Mee potraybbay dahray oonah mahno?*

I (m/f) have run out of petrol	Sono rimasto/a senza benzina *Sono reaymahsto/ah saynzah bayndzeenah*
I've locked the keys in the car	Ho chiuso le chiavi in macchina *O keeoozo lay keeahvee een mahkkeenah*
The car/motorbike/ moped won't start	La macchina/la moto (cicletta)/il motorino non parte *Lah mahkkeenah/lah moto(cheeklayttah)/eel motoreeno non pahrtay*
Could you contact the breakdown service for me, please?	Può chiamarmi il soccorso stradale? *Pwo keeahmahrmee eel sokkorso strahdahlay?*
Could you call a garage for me, please?	Può chiamarmi un garage? *Pwo keeahmahrmee oon gahrahj?*
Could you give me a lift to...?	Mi darebbe un passaggio fino... ? *Mee dahraybbay oon pahssahdjo feeno...?*
– to the nearest garage?	– al prossimo garage? *– ahl prosseemo gahraj?*
– to the nearest town?	– fino alla prossima città? *– feeno ahllah prosseemah cheettah?*
– to the nearest telephone booth?	– fino al prossimo telefono pubblico? *– feeno ahl prosseemo taylayfono poobbleeko?*
– to the nearest emergency phone?	– fino al prossimo telefono di emergenza? *– feeno ahl posseemo taylayfono dee aymayrjayntzah?*
Can we take my moped?	Può caricare il mio motorino? *Pwo kahreekahray eel meeo motoreeno?*
Could you tow me to a garage?	Può trainarmi a un garage? *Pwo traheenahrmee ah oon gahrahj?*
There's probably something wrong with...(See 5.5)	Probabilmente si è guastato/a/si sono guastati/e... *Probahbeelmayntay see ay gwahstahto/ah see sono gwahstahtee/ay...*
Can you fix it?	Me lo potrebbe aggiustare? *May lo potraybbay ahdjoostahray?*
Could you fix my tyre?	Mi potrebbe aggiustare la gomma? *Mee potraybbay ahdjoostahray lah gommah?*
Could you change this wheel?	Potrebbe cambiare questa ruota? *Potraybbay kahmbeeahray kwaystah rwotah?*
Can you fix it so it'll get me to...?	Me lo potrebbe aggiustare in modo da poter arrivare fino a...? *May lo potraybbay ahdjoostahray een modo dah potayr ahrreevahray feeno ah...?*
Which garage can help me?	Quale altro garage potrebbe aiutarmi? *Kwahlay ahltro gahrahj potraybbay aheeootahrmee?*
When will my car/ bicycle be ready?	La mia macchina/bicicletta, quando sarà pronta? *Lah meeah mahkkeenah/beecheeklettah kwahndo sahrah prontah?*
Have you already finished?	Ha già finito? *Hah djah feeneeto?*
Can I wait for it here?	Posso restare qui ad aspettare? *Posso raystahray kwee ahdahspayttahray?*
How much will it cost?	Quanto verrà a costare? *Kwahnto vayrrah ah costahray?*

The parts of a bicycle

(the diagram shows the numbered parts)

1	rear lamp	fanalino posteriore	*fahnahleeno postayreeoray*
2	rear wheel	ruota posteriore	*rwotah postayreeoray*
3	(luggage) carrier	il portapacchi	*eel portahpahkkee*
4	fork	forcella	*forchayllah*
5	bell	campanello	*kahmpahnayllo*
	inner tube	camera d'aria	*kahmayrah dahreeyah*
	tyre	gomma	*gommah*
6	peddle crank	pedivella	*payhdeevayllah*
7	gear change	cambio	*kahmbeeo*
	wire	filo	*feelo*
	dynamo	la dinamo	*lah deenahmo*
	bicycle trailer	carrello	*kahrrayllo*
	frame	telaio	*tayllahee-oh*
8	wheel guard	il pararuota	*eel pahrah-rwohtah*
9	chain	catena	*kahtaynah*
	chain guard	il copricatena	*eel kopreekahtaynah*
	odometer	il contachilometri	*eel kontahkeelomayhtree*
	child's seat	il seggiolino	*eel saydjholeeno*
10	headlamp	il fanale	*eel fahnahlay*
	bulb	lampadina	*lahmpahdeenah*
11	pedal	il pedale	*eel paydahlay*
12	pump	pompa	*pompah*
13	reflector	il catarifrangente	*eel kahtahreefrahndjayhntay*
14	brake pad	pastiglia	*pahsteelleeah*
15	brake cable	cavo del freno	*kahvo dayl frayno*
16	anti-theft device	antifurto (m)	*ahnteefoorto*
17	carrier straps	le cinghie del portapacchi	*lay cheengeeay dayl portahpahkkee*
	tachometer	tachimetro	*tahkeemaytro*
18	spoke	raggio	*rahjeeo*
19	mudguard	parafango	*pahrahfahngo*
20	handlebar	manubrio	*mahnoobreeo*
21	chain wheel	ruota dentata	*rwotah dayntahtah*
	toe clip	il fermapiede	*eel fayrmahpeeayday*
22	crank axle	albero delle pedivelle	*ahlbayro dayllay paydeevayllay*
	drum brake	freno a tamburo	*frayno ah tahmbooro*
23	rim	il cerchione	*eel chayrkeeonay*
24	valve	valvola	*vahlvolah*
25	gear cable	cavo del cambio	*kahvo dayl kahmbeeo*
26	fork	forcella	*forchayllah*
27	front wheel	ruota anteriore	*rwotah ahntayreeoray*
28	seat	sellino (sella)	*saylleeno (sayllah)*

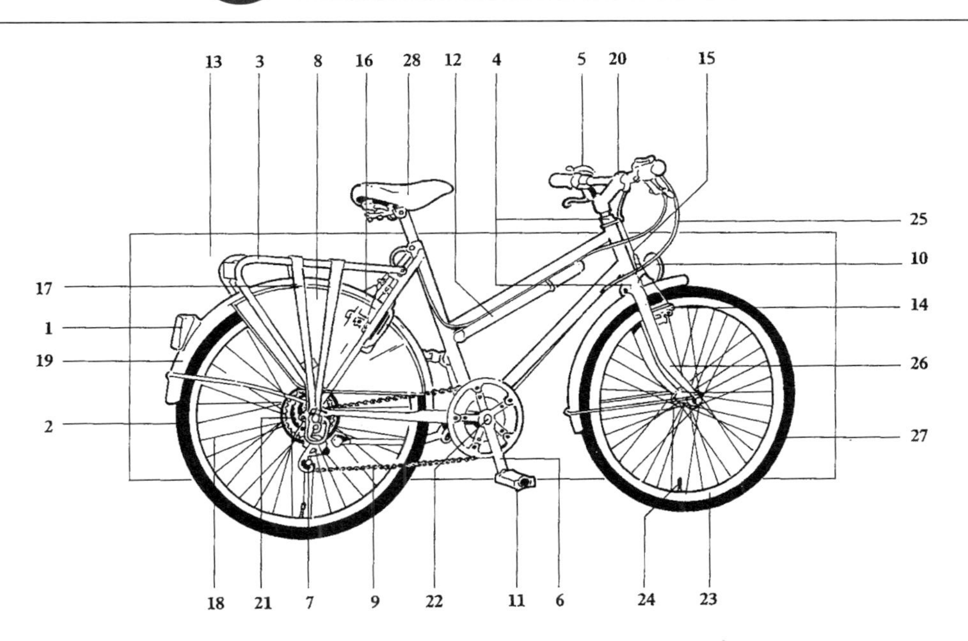
13
3
8
16
28
12
4
5
20
15
17
1
19
2
25
10
14
26
27
18
21
7
9
22
11
6
24
23

Could you itemise the bill?	Mi potrebbe dettagliare il conto? *Mee potraybbay dayttahllyahray eel konto?*
Could you give me a receipt for insurance purposes?	Mi potrebbe dare una ricevuta per l'assicurazione? *Mee potraybbay dahray oonah reechayvootah payr lahsseekoorahtzeeonay?*

5.8 The bicycle/moped

See the diagram on page 55.

● **Cycle paths** are rare in Italy. Bikes can be hired in most Italian towns. Not much consideration for bikes should be expected on the roads. The maximum speed for mopeds is 40 km/h but you should be aged 14 and over. A crash helmet is compulsory up to the age of 18, and a new law is being considered to make helmets compulsory for anyone. This should be checked when you arrive.

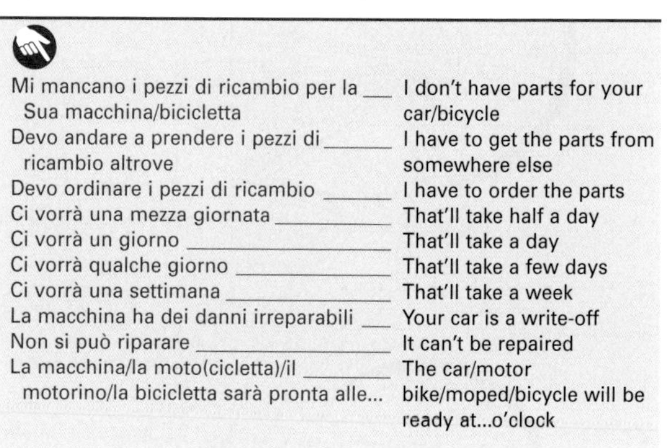

Mi mancano i pezzi di ricambio per la Sua macchina/bicicletta	I don't have parts for your car/bicycle
Devo andare a prendere i pezzi di ricambio altrove	I have to get the parts from somewhere else
Devo ordinare i pezzi di ricambio	I have to order the parts
Ci vorrà una mezza giornata	That'll take half a day
Ci vorrà un giorno	That'll take a day
Ci vorrà qualche giorno	That'll take a few days
Ci vorrà una settimana	That'll take a week
La macchina ha dei danni irreparabili	Your car is a write-off
Non si può riparare	It can't be repaired
La macchina/la moto(cicletta)/il motorino/la bicicletta sarà pronta alle...	The car/motor bike/moped/bicycle will be ready at...o'clock

5.9 Renting a vehicle

I'd like to rent a...	Vorrei noleggiare un/una... *Vorray nolaydgeeahray oon/oonah...*
Do I need a (special) licence for that?	Mi occorre una patente speciale? *Mee okkorray oonah pahtayntay spaych-eeahlay?*
I'd like to rent the...for...	Vorrei noleggiare il/la... per... *Vorrayee nolaydgeeahray eel/lah...payr...*
the...for a day	il/la...per un giorno *eel/lah...payr oon jorno*
the...for two days	il/la...per due giorni *eel/lah...payr dooay jornee*
How much is that per day/week?	Quanto costa al giorno/alla settimana? *Kwahnto kostah ahl jorno/ahllah saytteemahnah?*
How much is the deposit?	Quant'è la cauzione? *Kwahnto ay lah kahootzeeonay?*

Could I have a receipt for the deposit?	Mi potrebbe dare una ricevuta per la cauzione? *Mee potraybbay dahray oonah reechayhvootah payr lah kahootzeeonay?*
How much is the surcharge per kilometre?	Quant'è il supplemento di prezzo al chilometro? *Kwahnto ay eel soopplaymaynto dee praytzo ahl keelomayhtro?*
Does that include petrol?	E' compresa la benzina? *Ay kompraysah lah bayndzeenah?*
Does that include insurance?	E' compresa l'assicurazione? *Ay compraysah laysseekoorahtzeeonay?*
What time can I pick the...up?	A che ora potrei venire a prendere il/la...? *Ah kay orah potrayee vayneeray ah prayndayray eel/lah...?*
When does the...have to be back?	A che ora dovrò riportare il/la...? *Ah kay orah dovro reeportahray eel/lah...?*
Where's the petrol tank?	Dov'è il serbatoio? *Dovay eel sayrbahtoeeo?*
What sort of fuel does it take?	Quale carburante occorre? *Kwahlay kahrboorahntay okkorray?*

5.10 Hitchhiking

Where are you heading?	Dove va? *Dovay vah?*
Can you give me a lift?	Mi dà un passaggio? *Mee dah oon pahssahdjo?*
Can my friend (m/f) come too?	Darebbe un passaggio anche al mio amico/alla mia amica? *Dahraybbay oon pahssahdjo ahnkay ahl meeo ahmeeko/ahllah meeah ahmeekah?*
I'd like to go to...	Voglio andare a... *Vollyo ahndahray ah...*
Is that on the way to...?	Si trova sulla strada per...? *See trovah soollah strahda payr...?*
Could you drop me off...?	Mi potrebbe far scendere...? *Mee potraybbay fahr shayndayray...?*
Could you drop me off here?	Mi potrebbe far scendere qui? *Mee potraybbay fahr shayndayray kwee?*
– at the entrance to the motorway?	– all'entrata dell'autostrada? *– ahll'ayntrahtah dayllowtostrahdah?*
– in the centre?	– al centro? *– ahl chayntro?*
– at the next intersection?	– al prossimo incrocio? *– ahl prosseemo eenkrocheeo?*
Could you stop here, please?	Si potrebbe fermare qui per favore? *See potraybbay fayrmahray kwee payr fahvoray?*
I'd like to get out here	Vorrei scendere qui *Vorrayee shayndayray kwee*
Thanks for the lift	Grazie per il passaggio *Grahtzeeay payr eel pahssahdjo*

Public transport

Public transport

6.1 In general

● **Bus tickets** are purchased at tobacconists, newspaper stands and automatic vending machines at major bus stops, then validated in a machine as you enter the bus. Single tickets be bought in blocks of 4. Milan and Rome also have an underground train (*metropolitana*). Venice is served by a water-bus (*vaporetto*). Tickets are purchased from booths at most landing stations and validated before you get on the boat. A 24-hour ticket is good value for unlimited travel. Venice also has a gondola service (*traghetto*) crossing the Grand Canal, costing very little.

Il treno per...delle ore...viaggia con un ritardo di (circa)...minuti	The [time] train to...has been delayed by (about)...minutes
E' in arrivo sul binario...il treno per...	The train to...is now arriving at platform...
E' in arrivo sul binario...il treno proveniente da...	The train from...is now arriving at platform...
E' in partenza dal binario...il treno per...	The train to...will leave from platform...
Oggi il treno per... delle ore...partirà dal binario...	Today the [time] train to...will leave from platform...
La prossima stazione è...	The next station is...

Where does this train go to?	Dove va questo treno? *Dovay vah kwaysto trayno?*
Does this boat go to...?	Questo traghetto va a...? *Kwaysto trahgaytto vah ah...?*
Can I take this bus to...?	Posso prendere questo autobus per andare a...? *Posso prayndayray kwaysto ahootoboos payr ahndahray ah...?*
Does this train stop at...?	Questo treno si ferma a...? *Kwaysto trayno see fayrmah ah...?*
Is this seat taken/free /reserved?	E' occupato/libero/prenotato questo posto? *Ay okkoopahto/leebayro/praynotahto kwaysto posto?*
I've booked...	Ho prenotato... *O praynotahto...*
Could you tell me where I have to get off for... ?	Mi potrebbe indicare la fermata per...? *Mee potraybbay eendeekahray lah fayrmahtah payr...?*
Could you let me know when we get to...?	Mi potrebbe avvisare quando arriviamo a...? *Mee potraybbay ahvveezahray kwahndo ahrreeveeahmo ah...?*

Could you stop at the next stop, please?	Si potrebbe fermare alla prossima fermata? *See potraybbay fayrmahray ahllah prosseemah fayrmahtah?*
Where are we?	Dove siamo? *Dovay seeahmo?*
Do I have to get off here?	Devo scendere adesso? *Dayvo shayndayray ahdaysso?*
Have we already passed...?	Abbiamo già passato...? *Ahbbeeahmo jah pahssahto ..?*
How long have I been asleep?	Quanto tempo ho dormito? *Kwahnto taympo o dormeeto?*
How long does the train stop here?	Quanto tempo si fermerà il treno? *Kwahnto taympo see fayrmayrah eel trayno?*
Can I come back on the same ticket?	Questo biglietto è valido anche per il viaggio di ritorno? *Kwaysto beellyaytto ay vahleedo ahnkay payr eell veeahdjo dee reetorno?*
Can I change on this ticket?	Posso cambiare con questo biglietto? *Posso kahmbeeahray con kwaysto beellyaytto?*
How long is this ticket valid for?	Quanto tempo è valido questo biglietto? *Kwahnto taympo ay vahleedo kwaysto beellyaytto?*
How much is the supplement for the high speed train?	Quant'è il supplemento rapido? *Kwahntò ay eel soopplaymaynto rahpeedo?*

6.2 Questions to passengers

Ticket types

Prima o seconda classe?	First or second class?
Andata o andata e ritorno?	Single or return?
Fumatori o non fumatori?	Smoking or non-smoking?
Vicino al finestrino?	Window seat?
In testa o in coda?	Front or back (of train)?
Un posto o una cuccetta?	Seat or couchette?
Sopra, in mezzo o sotto?	Top, middle or bottom?
Classe turistica o prima classe?	Economy or first class?
Una cabina o un posto a sedere?	Cabin or seat?
Una cabina singola o per due?	Single or double?
Quanti siete a viaggiare?	How many are travelling?

Dove va?	Where are you travelling?
Quando parte?	When are you leaving?
La partenza è alle...	Your...leaves at...
Deve cambiare	You have to change
Deve scendere a...	You have to get off at...
Deve passare per...	You have to go via....
L'andata è il...	The outward journey is on...
Il ritorno è il...	The return journey is on...
Deve imbarcarsi entro...	You have to be on board by....(o'clock)

Inside the vehicle

Biglietti prego	Tickets, please
La prenotazione prego	Your reservation, please
Passaporto prego	Your passport, please
Ha sbagliato posto	You're in the wrong seat
Ha sbagliato...	You have made a mistake/You are in the wrong...
Questo posto è prenotato	This seat is reserved
Deve pagare un supplemento	You'll have to pay a supplement
Il/la... viaggia con un ritardo di... minuti	The...has been delayed by...minutes

6.3 Tickets

Where can I...?	Dove posso...? *Dovay posso...?*
– buy a ticket?	Dove posso comprare un biglietto? *– komprahray oon beellyaytto?*
– reserve a seat?	Dove posso prenotare un posto? *– praynotahray oon posto?*
– book a flight?	Dove posso prenotare un volo? *– praynotahray oon volo?*
Could I have...for... please?	Mi può dare...per...per favore *Mee pwo dahray...payr...payr fahvoray*
A single to...please	Un'andata per...per favore *Oonahndahtah payr...payr fahvoray*
A return ticket, please	Un'andata e ritorno, per favore *Oonahndahtah ay reetorno payr fahvoray*
first class	prima classe *preemah klahssay*
second class	seconda classe *saykondah klahssay*
economy class	classe turistica *klahssay tooreesteekah*

I'd like to book a seat/couchette/cabin	Vorrei prenotare un posto/una cuccetta/una cabina *Vorrayee praynotahray oon posto/oonah cootchayttah/oonah kahbeenah*
I'd like to book a top/middle/bottom berth in the sleeping car	Vorrei prenotare un posto nella carrozza letto in alto/in mezzo/in basso *Vorrayee praynotahray oon posto nayllah kahrrotzah laytto een ahlto/een maydzo/een bahsso*
smoking/no smoking	fumatori/non fumatori *foomahtoree/non foomahtoree*
by the window	vicino al finestrino *veecheeno ahl feenaystreeno*
single/double	singola/per due *seengolah/payr dooay*
at the front/back	nella parte davanti/in fondo *nayllah pahrtay dahvahntee/een fondo*
There are...of us	Siamo in... *Seeahmo een...*
We have a car	Abbiamo una macchina *Ahbbeeahmo oonae makkeenah*
We have a caravan	Abbiamo una roulotte *Ahbbeeahmo oonah roolot*
We have...bicycles	Abbiamo...biciclette *Ahbbeeahmo...beecheeklayttay*
Do you have a...	Ha un/una ? *Ah oon/oonah...?*
– travel card for 10 trips?	Ha una tessera valida dieci corse? *Ah oonah tayssayrah vahleedah deeaychee corsay?*
– weekly travel card?	Ha un abbonamento settimanale *Ah oon ahbbonahmaynto saytteemahnahlay?*
– monthly season ticket?	Ha un abbonamento mensile? *Ah oon ahbbonahmaynto maynseelay?*
Where's-?	Dov'è ? *Dovay ay?*
Where's the information desk?	Dov'è l'ufficio informazioni? *Dovay ay looffeecheeo eenformahtzeeonee?*

6.4 Information

Where can I find a timetable?	Dov'è l'orario delle partenze/degli arrivi? *Dovay ay lorayryo dayllay pahrtayntzay/daylly ahrreevee?*
Where's the...desk?	Dov'è il banco di... *Dovay eel bahnko dee...*
Do you have a city map with the bus/the underground routes on it?	Avrebbe una pianta della città con le linee degli autobus/del metrò? *Ahvraybbay oonah peeahntah dayllah cheettah kon lay leenayay daylly ahootoboos/dayl maytro?*
Do you have a timetable?	Avrebbe un orario? *Ahvraybbay oon orayreeo?*
Will I get my money back?	Le spese mi saranno rimborsate? *Lay spaysay mee sahrahnno reemborsahtay?*

I'd like to confirm/cancel/change my booking for/trip to...	Vorrei confermare/annullare/cambiare la prenotazione per... *Vorrayee confayrmahray/ahnnoollahray/kahmbyahray lah praynotahtzeeonay payr...*
I'd like to go to... What is the quickest way to get there?	Vorrei andare a...Qual'è il modo più rapido per andarci? *Vorrayee ahndahray ah...Kwahlay ay eel modo peeoo rahpeedo payr ahndahrchee?*
How much is a single/return to...?	Quanto costa un'andata/un'andata e ritorno per...? *Kwahnto kostah oonahndahtah/oonahndahtah ay reetorno payr...?*
Do I have to pay a supplement?	Devo pagare un supplemento? *Dayvo pahgahray oon soopplaymaynto?*
Can I break my journey with this ticket?	Posso interrompere il viaggio con questo biglietto? *Posso eentayrrompayray eel veeahdjo con kwaysto beellyaytto?*
How much luggage am I allowed?	Quanti chili di bagaglio posso portare ? *Kwahntee keely dee bahgahllyo posso portahray?*
Is this a direct train?	E' un treno diretto? *Ay oon trayno deeraytto?*
Do I have to change? Where?	Devo cambiare? Dove? *Dayvo kahmbeeahray? Dovay?*
Does the plane touch down anywhere?	L'aereo fa scalo da nessuna parte? *Lahayrayo fah skahlo dah nayssoonah pahrtay?*
Will there be any stopovers?	Ci saranno soste intermedie? *Chee sahrahnno sostay eentayrmaydeeay?*
Does the boat stop at any other ports on the way?	Il traghetto fa scalo ad altri porti? *Eel trahgaytto fah skahlo ahdahltree portee?*
Does the train/bus stop at...?	Questo treno/autobus si ferma a...? *Kwaysto trayno/ahootoboos see fayrmah ah...?*
Where do I get off?	Dove devo scendere? *Dovay dayvo shayndayray?*
Is there a connection to...?	C'è una coincidenza per...? *Chay oonah coeencheedayntzah payr...?*
How long do I have to wait?	Quanto tempo devo aspettare? *Kwahnto taympo dayvo ahspayttahray?*
When does...leave?	Quando parte...? *Kwahndo pahrtay...?*
What time does the first/next/last...leave?	A che ora parte il/la primo/a/il/la prossimo/a/l'ultimo/a...? *Ah kay orah pahrtay eel/lah preemo/ah eel/lah prosseemo/ah/loolteemo/ah...?*
How long does...take?	Quanto tempo impiega...? *Kwahnto taympo eempeeaygah...?*
What time does...arrive in...?	A che ora arriverà...a...? *Ah kay orah ahrreevayhrah...ah...?*
Where does the...to... leave from?	Da dove parte il/la...per...? *Dah dovay pahrtay eel/lah...payr...?*
Is this the train/bus...to...?	E' questo il treno/l'autobus per...? *Ay kwaysto eel trayno/lahootoboos payr...?*

6.5 Aeroplanes

● **On arrival** at an Italian airport (*aeroporto*), you will find the following signs:

accettazione check-in	internazionale international	voli domestici domestic flights
arrivo arrivals	partenze departures	

6.6 Trains

● **Train travel** in Italy is simple and cheap. *The Ferrovie dello Stato* (FS) is the state rail system. There are several types of trains: the *regionale* stops at all stations and is slow; the *interregionale* travels between regions; the *diretto* means you reach your destination without having to change; the *espresso* stops at major stations. The ETR450, or *Pendolino*, is an espress service between Rome, Florence, Bologna and Milan; the *Intercity* services major cities and the *EuroCity* connects major European cities. Tickets must be punched by a validation machine at the entrance to platforms.

6.7 Taxis

● **There are plenty of taxis** in Italian cities but they are quite expensive. They can be found on ranks, especially at train and bus stations, or you can phone the radio-taxi numbers from a rank or any telephone. Rates vary and there is a supplement from 10 pm to 7am and on Sundays and bank holidays. Check for airport supplements.

libero for hire	occupato occupied	posteggio dei taxi taxi rank

Taxi!	Taxi! *Tahxee!*
Could you get me a taxi, please?	Mi potrebbe chiamare un taxi? *Mee potraybbay keeahmahray oon tahxee?*
Where can I find a taxi around here?	Dove posso prendere un taxi qui vicino? *Dovay posso prayndayray oon tahxee kwee veecheeno?*
Could you take me to..., please?	Mi porti a... per favore *Mee portee ah...payr fahvoray*
Could you take me to this address, please	Mi porti a questo indirizzo per favore *Mee portee ah kwaysto eendeereetzo payr fahvoray*
– to the...hotel, please	Mi porti all'albergo...per favore *Mee portee ahllahlbayrgo...payr fahvoray*
– to the town/city centre, please	Mi porti al centro per favore *Mee portee ahl chayntro payr fahvoray*
– to the station, please	Mi porti alla stazione per favore *Mee portee ahllah statzeeonay payr fahvoray*

– to the airport, please	Mi porti all'aeroporto per favore *Mee portee ahllahayroporto payr fahvoray*
How much is the trip to...?	Quanto costa una corsa fino a...? *Kwahnto kostah oonah korsah feeno ah...?*
How far is it to...?	Quanto è lontano...? *Kwahnto ay lontahno...?*
Could you turn on the meter, please?	Può accendere il tassametro, per piacere? *Pwo ahtchayndayray eel tahssahmaytro, payr peeahchayray?*
I'm in a hurry	Ho fretta *O frayttah*
Could you speed up/ slow down a little?	Può andare più veloce/piano? *Pwo ahndahray peeoo vayhlochay/peeahno?*
Could you take a different route?	Può prendere un'altra strada? *Pwo prayndayray oonahltrah strahdah?*
I'd like to get out here, please.	Mi faccia scendere adesso *Mee fahtchhah shayndayray ahdaysso*
Go -	Vada *Vahdah*
You have to go...here	Deve andare... qui *Dayvay ahndahray... kwee*
Go straight ahead	Vada dritto *Vahdah dreetto*
Turn left	Vada a sinistra *Vahda ah seeneestra*
Turn right	Vada a destra *Vahdah ah daystrah*
This is it/We're here	Siamo arrivati *Seeahmo ahrreevahtee*
Could you wait a minute for me, please?	Mi potrebbe aspettare un attimo? *Mee potraybbay ahspayttahray oon ahtteemo?*

Overnight accommodation

Overnight accommodation

7.1 General

● **There is a great variety** of overnight accommodation in Italy and prices vary according to the season.

A hotel or *albergo* can be awarded up to five stars while a *pensione* will usually be one-three star quality. *Locande* are similar to *pensioni*, and *alloggi* or *affittacamere* are usually cheaper and are not part of the star classification system. Youth hostels, *ostelli per la gioventù*, are often in beautiful locations. Some hostels offer family rooms. *Agriturismo* is the increasingly popular practice of staying in farmhouses, at a restaurant with rooms to rent or perhaps in a restored medieval farm complex. Some religious institutions, *casa religiosa di ospitalità*, offer accommodation equivalent to a one-star hotel. There is a network of *rifugi* offering dormitory accommodation in the Alps, Appenines or other mountains in Italy. Campsites range from large complexes with swimming pools, tennis courts, restaurants etc. to simple grounds. Free camping is generally not permitted in Italy and you need the permission of the landowner if you want to camp on private property.

Quanto tempo vuole rimanere?	How long will you be staying?
Mi compili questo modulo, per favore	Fill out this form, please
Potrei avere il Suo passaporto?	Could I see your passport?
Deve pagare una caparra	I'll need a deposit
Deve pagare in anticipo	You'll have to pay in advance

My name is...I've made a reservation	Il mio nome è...Ho prenotato *Eel meeo nomay ay...O praynotahto*
How much is it per night/week/ month?	Quanto costa per una notte/alla settimana/al mese? *Kwahnto kostah payr oonah nottay/ahllah saytteemahnah/ahl maysay?*
We'll be staying at least...nights/weeks	Vogliamo rimanere minimo...notti/settimane *Vollyahmo reemahnayray meeneemo...nottee/setteemahnay*
We don't know yet	Non lo sappiamo di preciso *Non lo sahppeeahmo dee praycheezo*
Do you allow pets (cats/dogs)?	Sono permessi gli animali domestici (cani/gatti)? *Sono payrmayssee lly ahneemahlee domaysteechee (kahnee/gahttee)?*
What time does the gate/door open/close?	A che ora apre/chiude il cancello? *Ah kay orah ahpray/keeooday eel kahnchello?*
Could you get me a taxi, please?	Mi potrebbe chiamare un taxi? *Mee potraybbay keeahmahray oon tahxee?*
Is there any mail for me?	C'è posta per me? *Chay postah payr may?*

Camping equipment

(the diagram shows the numbered parts)

	luggage space	lo spazio per bagaglio	*lo spahzeeo payr bahgahllyo*
	can opener	apriscatole (m)	*ahpreeskahtolay*
	butane gas bottle	bombola a gas butano	*bombolah ah gahs bootahno*
1	pannier	sacca	*sahkkah*
2	gas cooker	fornello da campeggio	*fornayllo dah kahmpaydjeeo*
3	groundsheet	fondo della tenda	*fondo dayllah tayndah*
	mallet	martello di gomma	*mahrtayllo dee gommah*
	hammock	amaca	*ahmahkah*
4	jerry can	tanica	*tahneekah*
	campfire	fuoco	*fwoko*
5	folding chair	seggiolino pieghevole	*saydjoleeno peeaygayvolay*
6	insulated picnic box	borsa frigo	*borsah freego*
	ice pack	accumulatore (m) di ghiaccio	*ahkkoomoolahtoray dee geeahtcheeo*
	compass	bussola	*boossolah*
	corkscrew	cavatappi	*kahvahtahppee*
7	airbed	materassino gonfiabile	*mahtayrahsseeno gonfeeahbeelay*
8	airbed pump	pompa	*pompah*
9	awning	tenda	*tayndah*
10	sleeping bag	sacco a pelo	*sahkko ah paylo*
11	saucepan	pentola	*payntohlah*
12	handle (pan)	manico	*mahneeko*
	primus stove	fornello a spirito	*fornayllo ah speereeto*
	zip	chiusura lampo	*keeoozoorah lahmpo*
13	backpack	zaino	*dzaheeno*
14	guy rope	tirante (m) di tenda	*teerahntay dee tayndah*
15	storm lantern	lanterna a vento	*lahntayrnah ah vaynto*
	camp bed	brandina	*brahndeenah*
	table	tavolino	*tahvoleeno*
16	tent	tenda	*tayndah*
17	tent peg	picchetto	*peekkaytto*
18	tent pole	palo	*pahloh*
	thermos flask	il termos	*eel tayrmoss*
19	water bottle	borraccia	*borrahtchah*
	clothes peg	molletta	*mollayttah*
	clothes line	corda da bucato	*kordah dah bookahto*
	windbreak	paravento	*pahrahvaynto*
20	torch	torcia	*torchah*
	penknife	temperino	*taympayreeno*

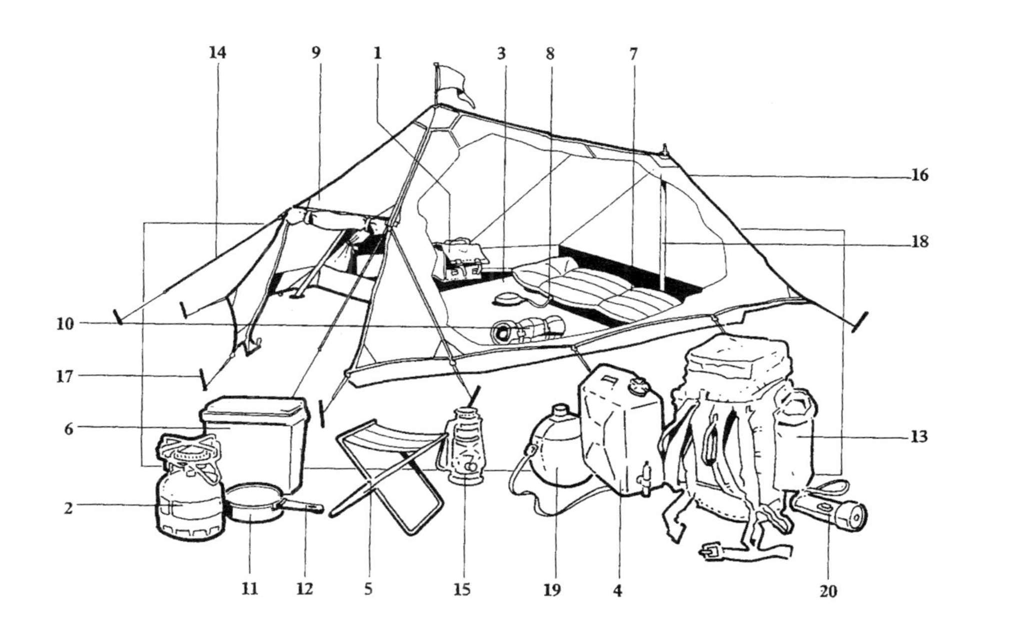
14
9
1
3
8
7
16
18
10
17
6
2
13
11
12
5
15
19
4
20

.2 Camping

See the diagram on page 69.

Scelga pure un posto	You can pick your own site
Le verrà indicato un posto	You'll be allocated a site
Ecco il numero del Suo posto	This is your site number.
Attacchi bene questo sulla macchina per favore	Please stick this firmly to your car
Non perda questa tesserina	You mustn't lose this card

Where's the manager?	Dov'è l'amministratore? *Dovay ay lahmmeenneestrahtoray?*
Are we allowed to camp here?	E' permesso fare il campeggio qui? *Ay payrmaysso fahray eel kahmpaydjo kwee?*
There are...of us and we have...tents	Siamo in...e abbiamo...tende *Seeahmo een...ay ahbbeeahmo...taynday*
Can we pick our own site?	Possiamo scegliere noi un posto? *Posseeahmo shayllyayhray noee oon posto?*
Do you have a quiet spot for us?	Ha un posto tranquillo per noi? *Ah oon posto trahnkweello payr noy?*
Do you have any other sites available?	Non c'è un altro posto libero? *Non chay oonahltro posto leebayro?*
It's too windy/sunny/ shady here.	C'è troppo vento/troppo sole/troppa ombra qui *Chay troppo vaynto/troppo solay/troppah ombrah kwee*
It's too crowded here	C'è troppa gente qui *Chay troppah jayntay kwee*
The ground's too hard/uneven	La terra è troppo dura/ineguale *Lah tayhrrah ay troppo doorah/eenaygwahlay*
Do you have a level spot for the camper/caravan/folding caravan?	Ha un posto piano per il nostro camper/la nostra roulotte/il nostro carrello tenda? *Ah oon posto peeahno payr eel nostro kahmper/lah nostrah roolot/eel nostro kahrrayllo tayndah?*
Could we have adjoining sites?	E' possibile avere posti vicini? *Ay posseebeelay ahvayray postee veecheenee?*
Can we park the car next to the tent?	E' permesso parcheggiare la macchina vicino alla tenda? *Ay payrmaysso pahrkaydjahray lah mahkkeenah veecheeno ahllah tayndah?*
How much is it per person/tent/caravan/car?	Quanto costa per persona/per una tenda/per una roulotte/per una macchina? *Kwahnto kostah payr payrsonah/payr oonah tayndah/payr oonah roolot/payr oonah mahkkeenah?*
Do you have chalets for hire?	Ha uno chalet da affittare? *Ah oono shahlay dah ahffeettahray?*
Are there any...?	Ci sono...? *Chee sono...?*

– hot showers?	Ci sono docce calde? *Chee sono dotchay kahlday?*
– washing machines?	Ci sono lavatrici? *Chee sono lahvahtreechee?*
Is there a...on the site?	Il campeggio ha...? *Eel kahmpaydjo ah...?*
Is there a children's play area on the site?	Il campeggio ha un parco giochi? *Eel kamppaydjo ah oon pahrko jokee?*
Are there covered cooking facilities on the site?	C'è un' area coperta per cucinare? *Chay oonahrayah kopayrtah payr koocheenahray?*
Can I rent a safe?	E' possibile prendere a noleggio una cassetta di sicurezza? *Ay posseebeelay prayndayray ah nolaydjo oonah kahssayttah dee seekooraytzah?*
Are we allowed to barbecue here?	E' permesso fare il barbecue? *Ay payrmaysso fahray eel bahrbaykeeoo?*
Are there any power points?	Ci sono delle prese elettriche? *Chee sono dayllay praysay aylayttreekay?*
Is there drinking water?	C'è acqua potabile? *Chay ahkwah potahbeelay?*
When's the rubbish collected?	Quando c'è la raccolta dei rifiuti? *Kwahndo chay lah rahkkoltah dayèe reefeeootee?*
Do you sell gas bottles (butane gas/ propane gas)?	Vende delle bombole di gas (gas butano/gas propano)? *Vaynday dayllay bombolay dee gahs (gahs bootahno/gahs propahno)?*

 .3 Hotel/B&B/apartment/holiday house

Do you have a single/ double room available?	Ha una camera singola/doppia? *Ah oonah kahmayhrah seengolah/doppeeah?*
per person/per room	per persona/per camera *payr payrsonah/payr kahmayhrah*
Does that include breakfast/lunch/dinner?	E' inclusa la prima colazione?/E' incluso il pranzo?/E' inclusa la cena? *Ay eenkloosah lah preemah kolahtzeeonay?/ Ay eenklooso eel prahntzo?/Ay eenkloosah lah chaynah?*
Could we have two adjoining rooms?	E' possibile stare in due camere vicine? *Ay posseebeelay stahray een dooay kahmayray veecheenay?*
with/without toilet/bath/shower	con/senza gabinetto/bagno/doccia *con/saynzah gahbeenaytto/bahneeo/dotchah*
facing the street	guarda sulla strada *gwahrdah soollah strahdah*
at the back	sul retro *sool raytro*
with/without sea view	che dà/che non dà sul mare *kay dah/kay non dah sool mahray*
Is there...in the hotel?	L'albergo ha...? *Lahlbayrgo hah...?*
Is there a lift in the hotel?	L'albergo ha l'ascensore? *Lahlbayrgo ah lahshaynsoray?*
Do you have room service?	C'è il servizio in camera? *Chay eel sayrveetzeeo een kahmayhrah?*

Could I see the room?	E' possibile vedere la camera? *Ay posseebeelay vahdayray lah kahmayrah?*
I'll take this room	Prendo questa *Prayndo kwaystah*

Il bagno e la doccia sono allo stesso piano/nella Sua camera	The toilet and shower are on the same floor/en suite
Prego, da questa parte	This way please
La Sua camera è al...piano, numero...	Your room is on the...floor, number...

We don't like this one	Questa qui non ci piace *Kwaystah kwee non chee peeahchay*
Do you have a larger/ less expensive room?	Ha una camera più grande/meno cara? *Ah oonah kahmayhrah peeoo grahnday/mayno kahrah?*
Could you put in a cot?	Potrebbe aggiungere un lettino per il bambino/la bambina? *Potraybbay ahdjoonjayray oon laytteeno payr eel bahmbeeno/lah bahmbeenah?*
What time's breakfast?	A che ora c'è la colazione? *Ah kay orah chay lah kolahtzeeonay?*
Where's the dining room?	Dov'è la sala da pranzo? *Dovay ay la sahlah dah prahntzo?*
Can I have breakfast in my room?	Mi potrebbe portare la prima colazione in camera? *Mee potraybbay portahray lah preemah kolahtzeeonay een kahmayhrah?*
Where's the emergency exit/fire escape?	Dov'è l'uscita di sicurezza/la scala di sicurezza? *Dovay ay loosheetah dee seekooraytzah/lah skahlah dee seekooretzah?*
Where can I park my car (safely)?	Dove posso parcheggiare la mia macchina (in un posto sicuro)? *Dovay posso pahrkaydjahray lah meeah mahkkeenah (een oon posto seekooro)?*
The key to room..., please	La chiave della camera...per favore *Lah keeahvay dayllah kahmayhrah...payr fahvoray*
Could you put this in the safe, please?	Posso mettere questo nella sua cassetta di sicurezza? *Posso mayttayray kwaysto naylla sooah kahssayttah dee seekooraytzah?*
Could you wake me at...tomorrow?	Mi potrebbe svegliare domani alle...? *Mee potraybbay svayllyahray domahnee ahllay...?*
Could you find a babysitter for me?	Mi potrebbe cercare una babysitter? *Mee potraybbay chayrkahray oonah bahbeeseettayr?*
Could I have an extra blanket?	Potrei avere un'altra coperta? *Potray ahvayhray oonahltrah copayrtah?*
What days do the cleaners come in?	Che giorno fanno le pulizie? *Kay jorno fahnno lay pooleetzeeay?*

When are the sheets/ towels/tea towels changed?	Quando cambiano le lenzuola/gli asciugamani/gli strofinacci? *Kwahndo kahmbeeahno lay layntzwolah/lly ahshoogahmahnee/lly strofeenahtchee?*

7.4 Complaints

We can't sleep for the noise	Non riusciamo a dormire per i rumori *Non reeoosheeahmo ah dormeeray payr ee roomoree*
Could you turn the radio down, please?	Può abbassare la radio? *Pwo ahbbahssahray lah rahdeeo?*
We're out of toilet paper	E' finita la carta igienica *Ay feeneetah lah kahrtah eejayneekah*
There aren't any.../ there's not enough...	Non ci sono/ci sono troppo pochi/e... *Non chee sono/chee sono troppo pokee/ay...*
The bed linen's dirty	La biancheria è sporca *Lah beeahnkayreeyah ay sporkah*
The room hasn't been cleaned.	La camera non è stata pulita *La kahmayrah non ay stahtah pooleetah*
The kitchen is not clean	La cucina non è pulita *Lah koocheenah non ay pooleetah*
The kitchen utensils are dirty	Gli utensili da cucina sono sporchi *Lly ootaynseelee dah koocheenah sono sporkee*
The heating isn't working	Il riscaldamento non funziona *Eel reeskahldahmaynto non foontzeeonah*
There's no (hot) water/electricity	Non c'è acqua (calda)/corrente *Non chay ahkwah (kahldah)/corrayntay*
...doesn't work/is broken	...non funziona/è rotto/a *...non foontzeeonah/ay rotto/ah*
Could you have that seen to?	Potrebbe farlo aggiustare? *Potraybbay fahrlo ahdjoostahray?*
Could I have another room/site?	Posso cambiare camera/posto per la tenda? *Posso kahmbeeahray kahmayra/posto payr lah tayndah?*
The bed creaks terribly	Il letto scricchiola terribilmente *Eel laytto skreekkeeolah tayrreebeelmayntay*
The bed sags	Il letto cede troppo *Eel laytto chayday troppo*
Could I have a board under the mattress?	Mi potrebbe dare una tavola da mettere sotto il materasso? *Mee potraybbay dahray oonah tahvolah dah mayttayray sotto eel mahtayrahsso?*
It's too noisy	C'è troppo rumore *Chay troppo roomoray*
There are a lot of insects/bugs	Ci sono molti insetti *Chee sono moltee eensayttee*
This place is full of mosquitos	E' pieno di zanzare *Ay peeayno dee zahnzahray*
– cockroaches	E' pieno di scarafaggi *Ay peeayno dee skahrahfahdjee*

.5 Departure

See also 8.2 Settling the bill

I'm leaving tomorrow. Could I settle my bill, please?	Domani parto. Mi potrebbe fare il conto adesso? *Domahny pahrto. Mee potraybbay fahray eel konto ahdaysso?*
What time should we vacate the room?	A che ora dobbiamo lasciare la camera? *Ah kay orah dobbeeahmo lahsheeahray lah kahmayhrah?*
Could I have my deposit/ passport back, please?	Mi potrebbe riconsegnare la caparra/il passaporto? *Mee potraybbay reekonsayneeahray lah kahpahrrah/eel pahssahporto?*
We're in a great hurry	Abbiamo molta fretta *Abbeeahrmo moltah frayttah*
Could you forward my mail to this address?	Può rispedirmi la posta a questo indirizzo? *Pwo reespaydeermee lah postah ah kwaysto eendeereetzo?*
Could we leave our luggage here until we leave?	Possiamo lasciare le nostre valigie qui finchè partiamo? *Posseeahmo lahsheeahray lay nostray vahleedjay kwee feenkay pahrteeahmo?*
Thanks for your hospitality	Grazie per l'ospitalità *Grahtzeeay payr lospeetahleetah*

Money matters

Money matters

● **In general,** banks are open to the public Monday to Friday from 8:30am to 1:30pm, and 2:30 to 4:30pm, but it is always possible to find an exchange office *(cambio)* open in larger towns or tourist centres. Proof of identity is usually required to exchange currency.

8.1 Banks

Where can I find a bank/an exchange office around here?	Scusi, c'è una banca/un'agenzia di cambio qui vicino? *Skoozee, chay oonah bahnkah/oonahjayntzeeah dee kahmbeeo kwee veecheeno?*
Where can I cash this traveller's cheque/giro cheque?	Dove posso incassare questo traveller cheque/assegno postale? *Dovay posso eenkahssahray kwaysto trahvayllayr shayk/ahssayneeo postahlay?*
Can I cash this...here?	E' possibile incassare qui questo/a... *Ay posseebeelay eenkahssahray kwee kwaysto/ah...?*
Can I withdraw money on my credit card here?	E' possibile prelevare qui dei soldi con una carta di credito? *Ay posseebeelay praylayvahray kwee dayee soldee con oonah kahrtah dee craydeeto?*
What's the minimum/maximum amount?	Qual'è la somma minima/massima? *Kwahlay ay lah sommah meeneemah/mahsseemah?*
Can I take out less than that?	E' possibile prelevare una somma minore? *Ay posseebeelay praylayvahray oonah sommah meenoray?*
I had some money cabled here. Has it arrived yet?	Ho fatto fare una rimessa per cablogramma. E' già arrivata? *Oh fahtto fahray oona reemayssah payr kahblograhmmah. Ay jah ahrreevahtah?*
These are the details of my bank in the UK	Ecco i dati della mia banca in Inghilterra *Ekko ee dahtee dayllah meeah bahnkah een Eengeeltayhrrah*
This is the number of my bank/giro account	Ecco il numero del mio conto in banca/conto corrente postale *Ekko eel noomayro dayl meeo konto een bahnkah/konto korrayntay postahlay*
I'd like to change some money	Vorrei cambiare dei soldi *Vorrayee kahmbeeahray dayee soldee*
– pounds into...	– sterline in... *– stayrleenay een...*
– dollars into...	– dollari in... *– dollahree een...*
What's the exchange rate?	Quant'è il cambio? *Kwahnto ay eel kahmbeeo?*
Could you give me some small change with it?	Mi potrebbe dare anche degli spiccioli per favore? *Mee potraybbay dahray ahnkay daylly speetchohlee payr fahvoray?*
This is not right	C'è un errore *Chay oonayrroray*

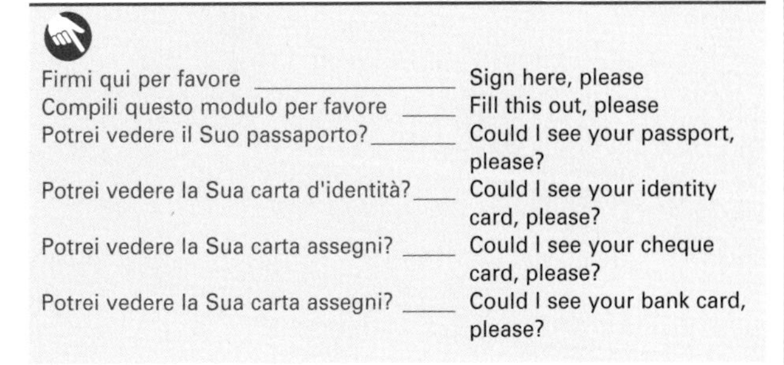

Firmi qui per favore ________ Sign here, please
Compili questo modulo per favore ____ Fill this out, please
Potrei vedere il Suo passaporto? ____ Could I see your passport, please?
Potrei vedere la Sua carta d'identità? ____ Could I see your identity card, please?
Potrei vedere la Sua carta assegni? ____ Could I see your cheque card, please?
Potrei vedere la Sua carta assegni? ____ Could I see your bank card, please?

8.2 Settling the bill

Could you put it on my bill?	Lo metta sul mio conto *Lo mayttah sool meeo konto*
Is service included?	Il servizio è compreso? *Eel sayrveetzeeo ay komprayso?*
Can I pay by...?	Potrei pagare con...? *Potrayee pahgahray kon...?*
Can I pay by credit card?	Potrei pagare con una carta di credito? *Potrayee pahgahray kon oonah kahrtah dee kraydeeto?*
Can I pay by traveller's cheque?	Potrei pagare con un traveller cheque? *Potrayee pahgahray kon oon trahvayller shayk?*
Can I pay with foreign currency?	Potrei pagare con soldi stranieri? *Potrayee pahgahray kon soldee straneeayree?*
You've given me too much/you haven't given me enough change.	Mi ha dato troppo di resto/Non mi ha dato abbastanza di resto *Mee ah dahto troppo dee raysto/Non mee ah dahto ahbbahstahnzah dee raysto*
Could you check this again, please?	Potrebbe verificare di nuovo? *Potraybbay vayhreefeekahray dee nwovo?*
Could I have a receipt, please?	Mi potrebbe dare una ricevuta per favore? *Mee potraybbay dahray oonah reechayvootah payr fahvoray?*
I don't have enough money on me.	Non mi bastano i soldi *Non mee bahstahno ee soldee*

Non accettiamo carte di credito/traveller cheque/valuta straniera	We don't accept credit cards/traveller's cheques/foreign currency

This is for you	Ecco a Lei *Aykkoh ah lay*
Keep the change	Tenga il resto *Tayngah eel raysto*

Post and telephone

Post and telephone

9.1 Post

For giros, see 8 Money matters

● **Major post offices** are open Monday to Saturday from 8:30am to 6 or 7pm. Smaller post offices open Monday to Friday, 8:30am to 2pm and on Saturdays from 8:30am to midday. Stamps *(francobolli)* can also be purchased at authorised tobacconists *(tabacchi)*. The cost of sending a letter depends on its weight and the cost of sending an air mail letter also depends on where it is being sent. The Italian postal service is notoriously inefficient.

francobolli stamps	telegrammi telegrammes	vaglia postali money orders
pacchi parcels		

Where is...?	Dov'è...? *Dovay ay...?*
– the nearest post office?	Dov'è l'ufficio postale più vicino? *Dovay ay looffeetcheeo postahlay peeoo veecheeno?*
– the main post office	Dov'è la posta centrale? *Dovay ay lah postah chayntrahlay?*
– the nearest post box?	Dov'è la buca delle lettere più vicina? *Dovay ay lah bookah dayllay layttayray peeoo veecheenah?*
Which counter should I go to...?	A quale sportello devo rivolgermi? *Ah kwahlay sportayllo dayvo reevoljayrmee?*
Which counter should I go to to send a fax?	Lo sportello per fare un fax, qual è? *Lo sportayllo payr fahray oon fahx, kwahlay?*
Which counter should I go to to change money?	Lo sportello per cambiare dei soldi, qual è? *Lo sportayllo payr kahmbyahray dayee soldee, kwahlay?*
Which counter should I go to to change giro cheques?	Lo sportello per i vaglia di conto corrente postale, qual è? *Lo sportayllo payr ee vahllyah dee konto korrayntay postahlay, kwahlay?*
Which counter should I go to to cable a money order?	Lo sportello per fare una rimessa cablografica, qual è? *Lo sportayllo payr fahray oonah reemayssah kahblograhfeekah, kwahlay?*
Which counter should I go to for poste restante?	Lo sportello per il fermo posta, qual è? *Lo sportayllo payr eel fayrmo postah, kwahlay?*
Is there any mail for me? My name's...	C'è posta per me? Il mio nome è...? *Chay postah payr may? Eel meeo nomay ay...*

Stamps

What's the postage for a...to...?	Quanti francobolli ci vogliono per un/uno...da spedire a/in...? *Kwahntee frahnkobollee chee vollyono payr oon/oonah...dah spaydeeray ah/een...?*
Are there enough stamps on it?	Bastano questi francobolli? *Bahstahno kwaystee frahnkobollee?*
I'd like [quantity] [value] stamps	Vorrei...francobolli da... *Vorrayee...frahnkobollee dah...*
I'd like to send this...	Vorrei spedire questo/a... *Vorrayee spaydeeray kwaysto/ah...*
– express	Vorrei spedire questo/a per espresso *Vorrayee spaydeeray kwaysto/ah payr ayspraysso*
– by air mail	Vorrei spedire questo/a per posta aerea *Vorrayee spaydeeray kwaysto/ah payr postah ahayrayah*
– by registered mail	Vorrei spedire questo/a per raccomandata *Vorrayee spaydeeray kwaysto/ah payr rahkkomahndahtah*

Telegram / fax

I'd like to send a telegram to...	Vorrei spedire un telegramma a... *Vorrayee spaydeeray oon taylaygrahmmah ah...*
How much is that per word?	Quanto costa per parola? *Kwahnto kostah payr pahrolah?*
This is the text I want to send	Ecco il testo che vorrei spedire *Ekko eel taysto kay vorray spaydeeray*
Shall I fill out the form myself?	Desidera che compili io il modulo? *Dayzeedayhrah kay kompeelee eeo eel modoolo?*
Can I make photocopies/ send a fax here?	E' possibile fare una fotocopia qui/spedire un fax da qui? *Ay posseebeelay fahray oonah fotokopeeah kwee/spaydeeray oon fahx dah kwee?*
How much is it per page?	Quanto costa per pagina? *Kwahnto kostah payr pahjeenah?*

9.2 Telephone

See also 1.8 Telephone alphabet

● **Direct international calls** can easily be made from public telephones using a phonecard available from tobacconists *(tabacchi)*, newspaper stands and vending machines in Telecom offices. Phonecards have a value of L 5,000, L 10,000 or L 15,000. Dial 00 to get out of Italy, then the relevant country code (UK 44; USA 1), city code and number. To make a reverse charge call from a public telephone, dial 170 for international and 15 for European countries. All operators speak English. When phoning someone in Italy, you will be greeted with *Pronto*.

Is there a phone box around here?	Senta, c'è una cabina telefonica qui vicino? *Sayntah, chay oonah kahbeenah taylayfoneekah kwee veecheeno?*
May I use your phone, please?	Scusi, potrei servirmi del Suo telefono? *Skoozee, potrayee sayrveermee dayl soo-o taylayfono?*
Do you have a (city/region) phone directory?	Ha un elenco telefonico della città di/della regione...? *Ah oonaylaynko taylayfoneeko dayllah cheettah dee..../dayllah rayjonay...?*
Where can I get a phone card?	Dove posso comprare una scheda telefonica? *Dovay posso komprahray oonah skaydah taylayfoneekah?*
Could you give me...?	Mi potrebbe dare...? *Mee potraybbay dahray...?*
– the number for international directory enquiries?	Mi potrebbe dare il numero dell'ufficio informazioni per l'estero? *Mee potraybbay dahray eel noomayro dayll ooffeecheeo eenformahtzeeonee payr laystayro?*
– the number of room...?	Mi potrebbe dare il numero della camera...? *Mee potraybbay dahray eel noomayro dayllah kahmayrah...?*
– the international access code?	Mi potrebbe dare il prefisso internazionale? *Mee potraybbay dahray eel prayfeesso eentayrnahtzeeonahlay?*
– the...(country) code?	Mi potrebbe dare il prefisso per il/la...? *Mee potraybbay dahray eel prayfeesso payr eel/lah...?*
– the trunk code for...?	Mi potrebbe dare il prefisso di...? *Mee potraybbay dahray eel prayfeesso dee...?*
– the number of [subscriber]...?	Mi potrebbe dare il numero dell' abbonato...? *Mee potraybbay dahray eel noomayro dayll ahbbonahto...?*
Could you check if this number's correct?	Potrebbe verificare se questo numero è giusto? *Potraybbay vayhreefeekahray say kwaysto noomayro ay joosto?*
Can I dial international direct?	E' possibile chiamare direttamente all'estero? *Ay posseebeelay keeahmahray deeraytttahmayntay ahllaystayro?*
Do I have to go through the switchboard?	Bisogna chiamare tramite il centralino? *Beezoneeah keeahmahray trahmeetay eel chayntrahleeno?*
Do I have to dial '0' first?	Bisogna prima fare lo zero? *Beezoneeah preemah fahray lo dzayro?*
Do I have to book my calls?	Bisogna prenotare la telefonata? *Beezoneeah praynotahray lah taylayfonahtah?*

Could you dial this number for me, please?	Mi potrebbe fare il seguente numero per favore? *Moo potraybbay fahray eel saygwayntay noomayro payr fahvoray?*
Could you put me through to.../extension..., please?	Mi potrebbe passare.../interno numero...per favore? *Mee potraybbay pahssahray.../eentayrno noomayro...payr fahvoray?*
I'd like to place a reverse charge call to...	Vorrei fare una telefonata a carico del destinatario, numero... *Vorrayee fahray oonah taylayfonahtah ah kahreeko dayl daysteenahtahreeo, noomayro...*
What's the charge per minute?	Quanto costa al minuto? *Kwahnto kostah ahl meenooto?*
Have there been any calls for me?	C'è stata una chiamata per me? *Chay stahtah oonah keeahmahtah payr may?*

The conversation

Hello, this is...	Pronto, sono... *Pronto, sono...*
Who is this, please?	Chi parla? *Kee pahrlah?*
Is this...?	Parlo con...? *Pahrlo kon...?*
I'm sorry, I've dialled the wrong number	Scusi, ho sbagliato numero *Skoozee, o zbahllyahto noomayro*
I can't hear you	Non La sento *Non lah saynto*
I'd like to speak to...	Vorrei parlare con... *Vorrayee pahrlahray kon...*
Is there anybody who speaks English?	C'è qualcuno che parla inglese? *Chay kwahlkoono kay pahrlah eenglaysay?*
Extension..., please	Mi passi l'interno numero... *Mee pahssee leentayrno noomayro...*

La vogliono al telefono	There's a phone call for you
Bisogna prima fare lo zero	You have to dial '0' first
Un attimo per favore	One moment, please
Non risponde nessuno	There's no answer
Il numero è occupato	The line's engaged
Vuole aspettare?	Do you want to hold?
Le passo...	Putting you through
Ha sbagliato numero	You've got a wrong number
In questo momento non c'è	He's/she's not here right now
Tornerà alle...	He'll/she'll be back at...
Questa è la segreteria telefonica di...	This is the answering machine of...

Could you ask him/her to call me back?	Potrebbe chiedergli/chiederle di richiamarmi? *Potraybbay keeaydayrlly/keeaydayrlay dee reekeeahmahrmee?*
My name's... My number's...	Il mio nome è...Il mio numero è... *Eel meeo nomay ay...Eel meeo noomayro ay...*
Could you tell him/her I called?	Gli/le dica che ho chiamato *Lly/lay deekah kay o keeahmahto*
I'll call him/her back tomorrow	Lo/la richiamerò domani *Lo/lah reekyahmayro domahnee*

Shopping

10 Shopping

● **Shops** are generally open Monday to Saturday from 9am to 1pm and 3:30 to 7:30pm or 4 to 8pm. Grocery shops may not re-open until 5pm and could stay open until 9pm in the summer. Shops, department stores and supermarkets usually close for a half day during the week - usually Monday morning, Thursday afternoon or Saturday afternoon. This varies from place to place.

---

alimentari
grocery shop
barbiere
barber's
bigiotteria
costume jewellery
calzature
footwear
calzolaio
cobbler
cartoleria
stationery shop
casalinghi
household goods
copisteria
typing agency
edicola
news-stand
enoteca
stock of vintage wines
erboristeria
herbalist's shop
farmacia
pharmacy
fioraio
florist
forno/fornaio
bakery
fruttivendolo
green grocer
gelateria
icecream shop
gioielleria
jeweller
grande magazzino
department store
istituto di bellezza
beauty salon
latteria
dairy (shop selling dairy products)
lavanderia
laundry
lavanderia a gettone/a secco
coin-operated laundry/dry cleaner
libreria
book shop
macelleria
butcher's shop
riparazione moto/biciclette
motorbike and bicycle repairs
mercato
market
merceria
haberdashery
negozio dell'usato
second-hand shop
negozio di abbigliamento
clothing shop
negozio di articoli da campeggio
camping supplies shop
negozio di articoli di fotografia
camera shop
negozio di articoli sportivi
sporting goods
negozio di biancheria per la casa
household linen shop
negozio di dischi
music shop (CDs, tapes etc)
negozio di elettrodomestici
household appliances (white goods)
negozio di frutta e verdura /fruttivendolo
fruit and vegetable shop
negozio di giocattoli
toy shop
negozio di strumenti musicali
musical instrument shop
negozio fai-da-te
DIY shop
oreficeria
goldsmith
orologeria
watches and clocks
ottico
optician
panetteria
baker's shop
parrucchiere
hairdresser
pasticceria
confectioner's/cake shop
pelletteria
leather goods
pellicceria
furrier
pescivendolo/ pescheria
fishmonger
polleria
poultry shop
profumeria
perfumery
salumeria
delicatessen
supermercato
supermarket
tabacchi
tobacconist
vivaio
nursery (plants)

10.1 Shopping conversations

Where can I get...?	Dove posso comprare...? *Dovay posso komprahray...?*
When is this shop open?	Quando è aperto questo negozio? *Kwahndo ay ahpayrto kwaysto naygotzeeo?*
Could you tell me where the...department is?	Mi potrebbe indicare il reparto...? *Mee potraybbay eendeekahray eel raypahrto...?*
Could you help me, please? I'm looking for...	Mi potrebbe aiutare? Cerco... *Mee potraybbay aeeootahray? Chayrko...*
Do you sell English/ American newspapers?	Vende dei giornali inglesi/americani? *Venday dayee jornahlee eenglaysee/ahmayreekahnee?*

La stanno servendo? — Are you being served?

No, I'd like...	No. Vorrei... *No. Vorrayee...*
I'm just looking, if that's all right	Sto solo guardando *Sto solo gwahrdahndo*

(Desidera) altro? — (Would you like) anything else?

Yes, I'd also like...	Sì, mi dia anche... *See, mee deeah ahnkay...*
No, thank you. That's all	No grazie, basta così *No grahtzeeay, bahstah cozee*
Could you show me...?	Mi potrebbe far vedere...? *Mee potraybbay fahr vaydayray...?*
I'd prefer...	Preferisco... *Prayfayreesko...*
This is not what I'm looking for	Non è quello che cerco *Non ay kwayllo kay chayrko*
Thank you. I'll keep looking	Grazie. Proverò da qualche altra parte *Grahtzeeay. Provayro dah kwahlkay ahltrah pahrtay*
Do you have something...?	Ha qualcosa di...? *Ah kwahlkosah dee...?*
– less expensive?	Ha qualcosa di meno caro? *Ah kwahlkosah dee mayno kahro?*
– smaller?	Ha qualcosa di più piccolo? *Ah kwahlkosah dee peeoo peekkolo?*
– larger?	Ha qualcosa di più grande? *Ah kwahlkosah dee peeoo grahnday?*
I'll take this one	Prendo questo/a qui *Prayndo kwaysto/ah kwee*
Does it come with instructions?	Ci sono le istruzioni per l'uso? *Chee sono lay eestrootzeeonee payr loozo?*
It's too expensive	E' troppo caro *Ay troppo kahro*

I'll give you...	Le posso dare... *Lay posso dahray...*
Could you keep this for me? I'll come back for it later	Me lo potrebbe tenere da parte? Verrò a prenderlo più tardi *May lo potraybbay taynayray dah pahrtay? Vayrro ah prayndayrlo peeoo tahrdee*
Do you have a bag? for me, please?	Ha un sacchetto? *Ah oon sahkkaytto?*
Could you giftwrap it, please?	Mi potrebbe fare una confezione regalo, per favore? *Mee potraybbay fahray oonah konfaytzeeonay raygahlo, payr fahvoray?*

Mi dispiace, questo non ce l'abbiamo	I'm sorry, we don't have that.
Mi dispiace, sono finiti/e	I'm sorry, we're sold out.
Mi dispiace, arriverà solo tra...	I'm sorry, it won't come back in until....
Paghi alla cassa	Please pay at the cash desk
Non accettiamo carte di credito	We don't accept credit cards.
Non accettiamo traveller cheques	We don't accept traveller's cheques.
Non accettiamo valuta straniera	We don't accept foreign currency.

10.2 Food

I'd like a hundred grams of..., please	Vorrei un etto di... *Vorrayee oon aytto dee...*
I'd like half a kilo/five hundred grams of...	Vorrei mezzo chilo/cinquecento grammi di... *Vorrayee maydzo keelo/cheenkwaychaynto grahmmee dee...*
I'd like a kilo of...	Vorrei un chilo di... *Vorrayee oon keelo dee...*
Could you...it for me, please?	Me lo potrebbe...? *May lo potraybbay...?*
– slice it/cut it up for me, please?	Me lo potrebbe affettare/tagliare a pezzi? *May lo potraybbay ahffayttahray/tahllyahray ah paytzee?*
– grate it for me, please?	Me lo potrebbe grattugiare? *May lo potraybbay grahttoojahray?*
Can I order it?	Potrei ordinarlo? *Potrayee ordeenahrlo?*
I'll pick it up tomorrow/ at...	Verrò a prenderlo domani/alle... *Vayrro ah prayndayrlo domahny/ahllay...*
Can you eat/drink this?	Si può mangiare/bere questo? *See pwo mahnjahray/bayhray kwaysto?*
What's in it?	Cosa c'è dentro? *Kosah chay dayntro?*

10.3 Clothing and shoes

I saw something in the window. Shall I point it out?	Ho visto qualcosa in vetrina. Vuole che glielo indichi? *O veesto kwahlkosah een vaytreenah. Vwolay kay lyeeaylo eendeekee?*
I'd like something to go with this	Vorrei qualcosa che vada bene con questo/a *Vorrayee kwahlkosah kay vahdah behnay kon kwaysto/ah*
Do you have shoes to match this?	Ha delle scarpe nello stesso colore di questo/a? *Ah dayllay skahrpay nayllo staysso koloray dee kwaysto/ah?*
I'm a size...in the UK	In Inghilterra la mia misura è... *Een Eengeeltayrrah lah meeah meezoorah ay...*
Can I try this on?	Posso provarlo/provarla? *Posso provahrlo/provahrlah?*
Where's the fitting room?	Dov'è il camerino? *Dovay ay eel kahmayreeno?*
It doesn't suit me	Non mi sta bene *Non mee stah bayhnay*
This is the right size	Questa è la misura giusta *Kwaystah ay lah meezoorah joostah*
It doesn't look good on me	Mi sta male *Mee stah mahlay*
Do you have this/ these in...?	Ha questo(a)/questi(e) in...? *Ah kwaysto(ah)/kwaystee(ay) een...?*
The heel's too high/low	Il tacco è troppo alto/basso *Eel tahkko ay troppo ahlto/bahsso*
Is this real leather?	E' pelle vera? *Ay payllay vayhrah?*
Is this genuine hide?	E' vero cuoio? *Ay vayhro kwoeeo?*
I'm looking for a...for a...year-old child	Cerco un/una...per un bambino/una bambina di...anni *Chayrko oon/oonah...payr oon bahmbeeno/oonah bahmbeenah dee...ahnnee*
I'd like a...	Vorrei un/una...di... *Vorrayee oon/oonah...dee...*
– silk	Vorrei un/una...di seta *Vorrayee oon/oonah...dee saytah*
– cotton	Vorrei un/una...di cotone *Vorrayee oon/oonah...dee kotonay*
– woollen	Vorrei un/una...di lana *Vorrayee oon/oonah...dee lahnah*
– linen	Vorrei un/una...di lino *Vorrayee oon/oonah...dee leeno*
At what temperature should I wash it?	A che temperatura va lavato/a? *Ah kay taympayrahtoorah vah lahvahto/ah?*
Will it shrink in the wash?	Si restringe con il lavaggio? *See raystreenjay kon eel lahvahdjo?*

Bucato a mano	Lavaggio a secco	Non stirare
Hand wash	Dry clean	Do not iron
Bucato in lavatrice	Non centrifugare	Stendere piatto
Machine washable	Do not spin dry	Lay flat

At the cobbler

Could you mend these shoes?	Mi può riparare queste scarpe? *Mee pwo reepahrahray kwaystay skahrpay?*
Could you resole/reheel these shoes?	Potrebbe risuolare queste scarpe/rifare i tacchi a queste scarpe? *Potraybbay reeswolahray kwaystay skahrpay/reefahray ee tahkkee ah kwaystay skahrpay?*
When will they be ready?	Quando saranno pronte? *Kwahndo sahrahnno prontay?*
I'd like..., please	Vorrei... *Vorrayee...*
– a tin of shoe polish	Vorrei una scatola di lucido da scarpe *Vorrayee oonah skahtolah dee loocheedo dah skahrpay*
– a pair of shoelaces	Vorrei un paio di lacci *Vorrayee oon paheeo dee lahtchee*

10.4 Photographs and video

I'd like a film for this camera, please	Vorrei una pellicola per questa macchina fotografica *Vorrayee oonah paylleekolah payr kwaystah mahkkeenah fotograhfeekah*
I'd like a cartridge, please	Vorrei una cassetta *Vorrayee oonah kahssayttah*
– a one twenty-six cartridge	Vorrei una cassetta centoventisei *Vorrayee oonah kahssayttah chayntovaynteesay*
– a slide film	Vorrei una pellicola diapositive *Vorrayee oonah paylleekolah deeahposeeteevay*
– a movie cassette, please	Vorrei una cassetta per cinepresa *Vorrayee oonah kahssayttah payr cheenaypraysah*
– a videotape	Vorrei una cassetta per videoregistrazione *Vorrayee oonah kahssayttah payr veedayo-rayjeestrahtzeeonay*
– colour/black and white	– a colori/bianco e nero *– ah koloree/beeahnko ay nayhro*
– super eight	– super otto *– soopayr otto*
– 12/24/36 exposures	– dodici/ventiquattro/trentasei pose *– dodeechee/vaynteekwahttro/trayntahsayèe posay*
– ASA/DIN number	– numero ASA/DIN *– noomayro ASA/DEEN*

Problems

Could you load the film for me, please?	Potrebbe mettermi il rullino nella macchina fotografica? *Potraybbay mayttayrmee eel roolleeno nellah mahkkeenah fotograhfeekah?*
Could you take the film out for me, please?	Potrebbe levare la pellicola dalla macchina fotografica? *Potraybbay layvahray lah paylleekolah dahllah mahkkeenah fotograhfeekah?*
Should I replace the batteries?	Devo cambiare le pile? *Dayvo kahmbyahray lay peelay?*
Could you have a look at my camera, please? It's not working	Potrebbe controllare la mia macchina fotografica? Non funziona più *Potraybbay kontrollahray lah meeah mahkkeenah fotograhfeekah? Non foontzeeonah peeoo*
The...is broken	....è guasto/a *....ay gwahsto/ah*
The film's jammed	La pellicola si è bloccata *Lah paylleekolah see ay blokkahtah*
The film's broken	La pellicola si è rotta *Lah paylleekolah see ay rottah*
The flash isn't working	Il flash non funziona *Eel flash non foontzeeonah*

Processing and prints

I'd like to have this film developed/printed, please	Vorrei far sviluppare/far stampare questa pellicola *Vorrayee fahr sveelooppahray/fahr stahmpahray kwaystah paylleekolah*
I'd like...prints from each negative	Vorrei...copie di ogni negativo *Vorrayee...copeeay dee onyee naygahteevo*
glossy/mat	lucido/opaco *loocheedo/opahko*
6x9	sei per nove *sayee payr novay*
I'd like to order reprints of these photos	Vorrei far fare un'altra ristampa di queste foto *Vorrayee fahr fahray oonahltrah reestahmpah dee kwaystay foto*
I'd like to have this photo enlarged	Vorrei far ingrandire questa foto *Vorrayee fahr eengrahndeeray kwaystah foto*
How much is processing?	Quanto costa lo sviluppo? *Kwahnto kostah lo sveelooppo?*
How much for printing?	Quanto costa la stampa? *Kwahnto kostah lah stahmpah?*
How much is are the reprints?	Quanto costa la ristampa? *Kwahnto kostah lah reestahmpah?*
How much is it for enlargement?	Quanto costa l'ingrandimento? *Kwahnto kostah leengrahndeemaynto?*
When will they be ready?	Quando saranno pronte? *Kwahndo sahrahnno prontay?*

.5 At the hairdresser's

Do I have to make an appointment?	Bisogna prendere un appuntamento? *Beezoneeah prayndayray oon ahppoontahmaynto?*
Can I come in straight away?	E' subito a mia disposizione? *Ay soobeeto ah meeah deesposeetzeeonay?*
How long will I have to wait?	Quanto devo aspettare? *Kwahnto dayvo ahspayttahray?*
I'd like a shampoo/ haircut	Vorrei farmi lavare/tagliare i capelli *Vorrayèe fahrmee lahvahray/tahllyahray ee kahpayllee*
I'd like a shampoo for oily/dry hair, please	Vorrei uno shampoo per capelli grassi/secchi *Vorrayee oono shahmpo payr kahpayllee grahssy/saykkee*
I'd like an anti-dandruff shampoo	Vorrei uno shampoo anti-forfora *Vorrayee oono shahmpo ahnteeforforah*
I'd like a colour-rinse shampoo, please	Vorrei uno shampoo colorante *Vorrayee oono shahmpo kolorahntay*
I'd like a shampoo with conditioner, please	Vorrei uno shampoo con balsamo *Vorrayee oono shahmpo kon bahlsahmo*
I'd like highlights, please	Vorrei i colpi di sole *Vorrayee ee kolpee dee solay*
Do you have a colour chart, please?	Ha una tabella dei colori, per favore? *Ah oonah tahbayllah dayèe koloree, payr fahvoray?*
I'd like to keep the same colour	Non vorrei cambiare colore *Non vorrayee kahmbeeahray koloray*
I'd like it darker/lighter	Li vorrei più scuri/più chiari *Lee vorrayee peeoo skooree/peeoo keeahree*
I'd like/I don't want hairspray	Vorrei/Non voglio la lacca *Vorrayee/Non vollyo lah lahkkah*
– gel	– il gel *– eel jayl*
– lotion	– la lozione *– lah lotzeeonay*
I'd like a short fringe	Vorrei una frangetta corta *Vorrayee oonah frahnjayttah kortah*
Not too short at the back	Non troppo corti dietro *Non troppo kortee deeayhtro*
Not too long	Non troppo lunghi *Non troppo loongee*
I'd like it curly/not too curly	Li vorrei ricci/non troppo ricci *Lee vorrayee reetchee/non troppo reetchee*
It needs a little/ a lot taken off	Me li tagli un po' più corti/molto più corti *May lee tahlly oon po peeoo kortee/molto peeoo kortee*
I'd like a completely different style/a different cut	Vorrei cambiare pettinatura/un taglio diverso *Vorrayee kahmbyahray paytteenahtoorah/oon tahleeo deevayrso*
I'd like it the same as in this photo	Vorrei un taglio come in questa foto *Vorrayèe oon tahllyo komay een kwaystah foto*

– as that lady's	– come quella signora – *komay kwayllah seeneeorah*
Could you put the drier up/down a bit?	Può alzare/abbassare un po'il casco? *Pwo ahltzahray/ahbbahssahray oon po eel kahsko?*
I'd like a facial	Vorrei una maschera per il viso *Vorrayee oonah mahskayhra payr eel veezo*

Come desidera che siano tagliati i capelli?	How do you want it cut?
Quale taglio ha in mente?	What style did you have in mind?
Quale colore desidera?	What colour did you want it?
Le va bene la temperatura?	Is the temperature all right for you?
Desidera leggere qualcosa?	Would you like something to read?
Desidera bere qualcosa?	Would you like a drink?
Le va bene così?	Is this what you had in mind?

– a manicure	la manicure – *lah mahneekooray*
– a massage	– un massaggio – *oon mahssahdjo*
Could you trim my..., please?	Vorrei che mi desse una spuntatina *Vorrayee kay mee dayssay oonah spoontahteenah*
– fringe?	– alla frangetta – *ahllah frahnjayttah*
– beard?	– alla barba – *ahllah bahrbah*
– moustache?	– ai baffi – *ahee bahffee*
I'd like a shave, please	Mi faccia la barba, per favore *Mee fahtchah lah bahrbah, payr fahvoray*
I'd like a wet shave, please	Vorrei essere raso con la lametta *Vorray ayssayray rahzo kon lah lahmayttah*

At the Tourist Information Centre

At the Tourist Information Centre

11.1 Places of interest

● **There are three main categories** of tourist office: regional, provincial and local. Regional offices are mainly concerned with planning and budgeting etc. Provincial offices (EPT or APT) usually have information on regions and towns. A good range of more specific local information about buses, museums, tours etc. is available at CIT and AAST offices. Tourist offices are generally open Monday to Friday, 8:30am to 12 or 1pm and 3pm to 7pm. Some also open on Saturdays and Sundays during the summer.

Where's the Tourist Information, please?	Senta, dov'è l'ufficio informazioni turistiche? *Sayntah, dovay ay looffeetcheeo eenformahtzeeonee tooreesteekay?*
Do you have a city map?	Ha una piantina della città, per favore? *Ah oonah peeahnteenah dayllah cheettah, pahr fahvoray?*
Where is the museum?	Dov`è il museo? *Dovay ay eel moosayo?*
Where can I find a church?	Dove posso trovare una chiesa? *Dovay posso trovahray oonah keeaysah?*
Could you give me some information about...?	Mi potrebbe dare qualche informazione su...? *Mee potraybbay dahray kwahlkay eenformahtzeeonay soo...?*
How much is this?	Quanto costa? *Kwahnto kostah?*
What are the main places of interest?	Quali sono i monumenti più interessanti da vedere? *Kwahlee sono ee monoomayntee peeoo eentayrayssahntee dah vaydayray?*
Could you point them out on the map?	Me li potrebbe indicare sulla pianta? *May lee potraybbay eendeekahray soollah pyahntah?*
What do you recommend?	Cosa ci consiglia? *Kosah chee konseellyah?*
We'll be here for a few hours	Ci fermeremo qui per qualche ora *Chee fayrmayraymo kwee payr kwahlkay orah*
We'll be here for a day	Ci fermeremo qui per un giorno *Chee fayrmayraymo kwee payr oon jorno*
We'll be here for a week	Ci fermeremo qui per una settimana *Chee fayrmayraymo kwee payr oonah saytteemahnah*
We're interested in...	Siamo interessati a... *Seeahmo eentayhrayssahtee ah...*
Is there a scenic walk around the city?	E' possibile seguire un itinerario turistico della città? *Ay posseebeelay saygweeray oon eeteenayrahreeo tooreesteeko dayllah cheettah?*
How long does it take?	Quanto dura? *Kwahnto doorah?*

Where does it start/end?	Dove comincia/finisce? *Dovay komeenchah/feeneeshay?*
Are there any boat trips?	E' possibile fare un giro in battello? *Ay posseebeelay fahray oon jeero een bahttayllo?*
Where can we board?	Dove possiamo imbarcarci? *Dovay posseeahmo eembahrkahrchee?*
Are there any coach tours?	E' possibile fare un giro della città in pullman? *Ay posseebeelay fahray oon jeero dayllah cheettah een poollmahn?*
Where do we get on?	Dove possiamo salire? *Dovay posseeahmo sahleeray?*
Is there a guide who speaks English?	C'è una guida che parla inglese? *Chay oonah gweedah kay pahrla englaysay?*
What trips can we take around the area?	Quali gite si possono fare nei dintorni? *Kwahlee jeetay see possono fahray nayee deentornee?*
Are there any excursions?	Ci sono delle escursioni? *Chee sono dayllay ayskoorseeonee?*
Where do they go?	Dove vanno? *Dovay vahnno?*
We'd like to go to...	Vogliamo andare a... *Vollyahmo ahndahray ah...*
How long is the excursion?	Quanto tempo dura l'escursione? *Kwahnto taympo doorah layskoorseeonay?*
How long do we stay in...?	Per quanto tempo ci fermeremo a...? *Payr kwahnto taympo chee fayrmayraymo ah...?*
Are there any guided tours?	Ci sono delle visite guidate? *Chee sono dayllay veeseetay gweedahtay?*
How much free time will we have there?	Quanto tempo libero avremo a disposizione? *Kwahnto taympo leebayro ahvraymo ah deesposeetzeeonay?*
We want to have a walk around/to go on foot	Vogliamo fare un giro a piedi *Vollyahmo fahray oon jeero ah peeaydee*
Can we hire a guide?	E' possibile avere una guida? *Ay posseebeelay ahvayray oonah gweedah?*
Can we book an alpine hut?	E' possibile prenotare dei rifugi alpini? *Ay poosseebeelay praynotahray dayee reefoojee ahlpeenee?*
What time does... open/close?	A che ora apre/chiude...? *Ah kay orah ahpray/keeooday...?*
What days is...open/closed?	Quali sono i giorni in cui...è aperto/a/chiuso/a? *Kwahlee sono ee jornee een kooee...ay ahpayrto/ah keeoozo/ah?*
What's the admission price?	Quanto costa un biglietto d'ingresso? *Kwahnto kostah oon beellyaytto deengraysso?*
Is there a group discount?	C'è uno sconto per gruppi? *Chay oono skonto payr grooppee?*
Is there a child discount?	C'è uno sconto per bambini? *Chay oono skonto payr bahmbeenee?*

Is there a discount for pensioners/senior citizens?	C'è uno sconto per anziani? *Chay oono skonto payr ahntzeeahnee?*
Can I take (flash) photos/can I film here?	Qui è permesso fotografare (con il flash)/filmare? *Kwee ay payrmaysso fotograhfahray (kon eel flash)/feelmahray?*
Do you have any postcards of...?	Avete cartoline di...? *Avaytay kahrtoleenay dee...?*
Do you have an English...?	Ha un/una...in inglese? *Ah oon/oonah...een eenglaysay?*
– catalogue?	– catalogo? *– kahtahlogo?*
– programme?	– programma? *– prograhmmah?*
– brochure?	– opuscolo? *– opooskolo?*

11.2 Going out

● **The main theatre season** is during the winter. Classical music concerts are performed throughout the year. Florence offers the *Maggio Musicale Fiorentino*, *La Scala* is Milan's famous opera house and *Umbria Jazz* takes place in *Perugia* in July. There is a very popular Italian film industry and most foreign films are dubbed into Italian. Venice offers an international film festival and the *Biennale*, a visual arts festival held every two years.

Do you have this week's/month's entertainment guide?	Ha il calendario delle manifestazioni e degli spettacoli di questa settimana/di questo mese? *Ah eel kahlayndahreeo dayllay mahneefaystatzeeonee ay daylly spayttahkkolee dee kwaystah saytteemahnah/dee kwaysto maysay?*
What's on tonight?	Che spettacoli ci sono stasera? *Kay spayttahkolee chee sono stahsayhrah?*
We want to go to...	Vorremmo andare a... *Vorraymmo ahndahray ah...*
What's on at the cinema?	Che film danno al cinema? *Kay feelm dahnno ahl cheenaymah?*
What sort of film is that?	Che tipo di film è? *Kay teepo dee feelm ay?*
– suitable for everyone	– per tutti *– payr toottee*
– not suitable for under 12s/under 16s	– vietato ai minori di dodici/sedici anni *– veeaytahto ayee meenoree dee dodeechee/saydeechee ahnnee*
– original version	– versione originale *– vayrseeonay oreejeenahlay*
– subtitled	– con sottotitoli *– kon sottoteetolee*
– dubbed	– doppiato *– doppeeahto*
Is it a continuous showing?	E' uno spettacolo continuato? *Ay oono spayttahkolo konteenooahto?*

What's on at...?	Che danno a...? *Kay dahnno ah...?*
– the theatre?	– al teatro? *– ahl tayahtro?*
– the opera?	– al teatro lirico? *– ahl tayahtro leereeko?*
What's happening in the concert hall?	Quale concerto danno al teatro? *Kwahlay konchayrto dahnno ahl tayahtro?*
Where can I find a good disco around here?	C'è una buona discoteca qui vicino? *Chay oonah bwonah deeskotaykah kwee veecheeno?*
Is it members only?	E' richiesta la tessera? *Ay reekeeaystah lah tayssayrah?*
Where can I find a good nightclub around here?	C'è un buon night qui vicino? *Chay oon bwon neeght kwee veecheeno?*
Is it evening wear only?	E' obbligatorio l'abito da sera? *Ay obbleegahtoreeo lahbeeto dah sayhrah?*
Should I/we dress up?	E' necessario un abito elegante? *Ay naychayssahreeo oon ahbeeto aylaygahntay?*
What time does the show start?	A che ora comincia lo show? *Ah kay orah komeenchah lo show?*
When's the next soccer match?	Quando è la prossima partita di calcio? *Kwahndo ay lah prosseemah pahrteetah dee kahlcho?*
Who's playing?	Chi gioca? *Kee jokah?*
I'd like an escort (m/f) for tonight	Stasera vorrei un accompagnatore/un'accompagnatrice *Stahsayhrah vorrayèe oon ahkkompahneeahtroray/ oonahkkompahneeatreechay*

11.3 Booking tickets

Could you book some tickets for us?	Ci potrebbe fare la prenotazione, per favore? *Chee potraybbay fahray lah praynotatzeeonay payr fahvoray?*
We'd like to book... seats/a table for...	Vogliamo...posti/un tavolo per... *Vollyahmo...postee/oon tahvolo payr...*
– seats in the stalls in the main section	Vogliamo...poltrone in platea in sala *Vollyahmo...poltronay een plahtayah een sahlah*
– seats in the circle	Vogliamo...posti in galleria *Vollyahmo...postee een gahllayryah*
– a box for...	Vogliamo un palco con...posti *Vollyahmo oon pahlko kon...postee*
– front row seats/a table for...at the front	Vogliamo...posti/un tavolo per...nelle prime file *Vollyahmo...postee/oon tahvolo payr...nayllay preemay foelay*
...seats in the middle/a table in the middle	Vogliamo...posti/un tavolo al centro *Vollyahmo...postee/oon tahvolo ahl chayntro*
...back row seats/a table at the back	Vogliamo...posti/un tavolo in fondo *Vollyahmo...postee/oon tahvolo een fondo*

Could I book...seats for the...o'clock performance?	E' possibile prenotare...posti per lo spettacolo delle...? *Ay posseebeelay praynotahray...postee payr lo spayttahkolo dayllay...?*
Are there any seats left for tonight?	Ci sono ancora biglietti per stasera? *Chee sono ahnkorah beellyayttee payr stahsayhrah?*
How much is a ticket?	Quanto costa un biglietto? *Kwahnto kostah oon beellyaytto?*
When can I pick up the tickets?	Quando posso ritirare i biglietti? *Kwahndo posso reeteerahray ee beellyayttee?*
I've got a reservation	Ho prenotato *O praynotahto*
My name's...	Il mio nome è... *eel meeo nomay ay...*

Per quale spettacolo vuole fare una prenotazione?	Which performance do you want to book for?
Che tipo di posto?	Where would you like to sit?
E' tutto esaurito	Everything's sold out
Sono rimasti solo posti in piedi	It's standing room only
Sono rimasti solo posti in galleria	We've only got circle seats left
Sono rimasti solo posti in loggione	We've only got upper circle (in the gods) seats left
Sono rimaste solo le poltrone in platea	We've only got stalls seats left
Sono rimasti solo posti nelle prime file	We've only got front row seats left
Sono rimasti solo i posti in fondo	We've only got seats left at the back
Quanti posti desidera?	How many seats would you like?
Deve ritirare i biglietti prima delle...	You'll have to pick up the tickets before...o'clock
Biglietti prego	Tickets, please
Ecco il suo posto	This is your seat
Siete seduti nel posto sbagliato	You are in the wrong seat

12 Sports

12 Sports

12.1 Sporting questions

Where can we... around here?	Dove possiamo...qui vicino? *Dovay posseeahmo...kwee veecheeno?*
Can I/we hire a...?	E' possibile prendere a nolo un/una...? *Ay posseebeelay praydayray ah nolo oon/oonah...?*
Can I/we take...lessons?	E' possibile prendere lezioni di...? *Ay posseebeelay prendayray laytzeeonee dee...?*
How much is that per hour/per day/How much is each one?	Quanto costa all'ora/al giorno/a lezione? *Kwahnto kostah ahllorah/ahl jorno/ah laytzeeonay?*
Do you need a permit for that?	Bisogna avere una licenza? *Beezoneeah ahvayray oonah leechaynzah?*
Where can I get the permit?	Dove posso ottenere questa licenza? *Dovay posso ottaynayray kwaystah leechaynzah?*

12.2 By the waterfront

Is it far (to walk) to the sea?	Per andare al mare, c'è molto (a piedi)? *Payr ahndahray ahl mahray chay molto (ah peeaydee)?*
Is there a...around here?	C'è un/una...qui vicino? *Chay oon/oonah...kwee veecheeno?*
– a swimming pool	C'è una piscina? *Chay oonah peesheenah?*
– a sandy beach	C'è una spiaggia di sabbia? *Chay oonah speeahdjah dee sahbbeeah?*
– a nudist beach	C'è una spiaggia per nudisti? *Chay oonah speeahdjah payr noodeestee?*
– mooring (place)/dock	C'è un molo d'attracco? *Chay oon molo dahttrahkko?*
Are there any rocks here?	Ci sono degli scogli qui? *Chee sono daylly skolly kwee?*
When's high/low tide?	Quando c'è l'alta marea/la bassa marea? *Kwahndo chay lahltah mahrayah/lah bahssah mahrayah?*
What's the water temperature?	Qual è la temperatura dell'acqua? *Kwahlay ay lah taympayrahtoorah dayllahkwah?*
Is it (very) deep here?	E' (molto) profondo qui? *Ay (molto) profondo kwee?*
Is it safe (for children) to swim here?	E' sicuro (per i bambini) fare il bagno qui? *Ay seekooro (payr ee bahmbeenee) fahray eel bahneeo kwee?*
Are there any currents?	Ci sono correnti? *Chee sono korrayntee?*
Are there any rapids/waterfalls along this river?	Questo fiume ha delle rapide/delle cascate? *Kwaysto feeoomay ah dayllay rahpeeday/kahskahtay?*

What does that flag/ buoy mean?	Cosa significa quella bandiera/quella boa? *Kosah seeneefeekah kwayllah bahndeeayrah/kwayllah boah?*
Is there a lifeguard on duty?	C'è un bagnino che sorveglia? *Chay oon bahneeno kay sorvellyah?*
Are dogs allowed here?	Sono permessi i cani? *Sono payrmayssee ee kahnee?*
Is camping on the beach allowed?	E' permesso fare il campeggio sulla spiaggia? *Ay payrmaysso fahray eel kahmpaydjo soollah speeahdjah?*
Can we light a fire?	E' permesso fare un fuoco? *Ay payrmaysso fahray oon fwoko?*

Zona di pesca Fishing waters	Solo con licenza Permits only	Divieto di surfing No surfing
Pericolo Danger	Divieto di balneazione No swimming	Pesca vietata No fishing

12.3 In the snow

Can I take ski lessons here?	E' possibile prendere delle lezioni di sci? *Ay posseebeelay prayndayray dayllay laytzeeonee dee shee?*
For beginners/ intermediates	Per principianti/di medio livello *Payr preencheepeeahntee/dee maydeeo leevello*
How large are the groups?	Quanti persone ci sono in un gruppo? *Kwahntay payrsonay chee sono een oon grooppo?*
What languages are the classes in?	In che lingua fanno lezione? *Een kay leengwah fahnno laytzeeonay?*
I'd like a lift pass, please	Vorrei uno skipass *Vorrayee oono skeepahss*
Where are the nursery slopes?	Dove sono le piste per i principianti? *Dovay sono lay peestay payr ee preencheepeeahntee?*
Are there any cross-country ski runs around here?	Ci sono piste di fondo qui vicino? *Chee sono peestay dee fondo kwee veecheeno?*
Have the cross-country runs been marked?	Sono indicate le piste di fondo? *Sono eendeekahtay lay peestay dee fondo?*
Are the...open?	Sono aperti...i/le? *Sono ahpayrtee...ee/lay?*
– the ski lifts...?	Sono aperti gli skilift? *Sono ahpayrtee lly skeeleeft?*
– the chair lifts...?	Sono aperte le seggiovie? *Sono ahpayrtee lay sedgeeoveeay*
– the runs...?	Sono aperte le piste? *Sono ahpayrtee lay peestay?*
– the cross-country runs...?	Sono aperte le piste di fondo? *Sono ahpayrtay lay peestay dee fondo?*

Sports 12

13 Sickness

Sickness

13.1 Call (fetch) the doctor

● **If you become ill** or need emergency treatment, it is better to go to Casualty *(pronto soccorso)* at your nearest hospital.

Could you call (fetch) a doctor quickly, please?	Mi chiami presto il medico, per favore *Mee keeahmy praysto eel maydeeko, payr fahvoray*
When does the doctor have surgery?	Quando riceve il medico? *Kwahndo reechayvay eel maydeeko?*
When can the doctor come?	Quando potrà venire il medico? *Kwahndo potrah vayneeray eel maydeeko?*
Could I make an appointment to see the doctor?	Mi potrebbe fissare un appuntamento con il medico? *Mee potraybbay feessahray oon ahppoontahmaynto con eel maydeeko?*
I've got an appointment to see the doctor at... o'clock	Ho un appuntamento con il medico alle... *O oon ahppoontahmaynto con eel maydeeko ahllay...*
Which doctor/pharmacy is on night/weekend duty?	Quale medico/farmacia è in servizio notturno/in servizio di fine settimana? *Kwahlay maydeeko/fahrmahcheeah ay een sayrveetzeeo nottoorno/een sayrveetzeeo dee feenay saytteemahnah?*

13.2 Patients' ailments

I don't feel well	Mi sento male *Mee saynto mahlay*
I'm dizzy	Ho il capogiro *O eel kahpojeero*
– ill	Sono ammalato/a *Sono ahmmahlahto/ah*
I feel sick (nauseous)	Ho la nausea *O lah nahoozayah*
I've got a cold	Sono raffreddato/a *Sono rahffrayddahto/ah*
It hurts here	Mi fa male qui *Mee fah mahlay kwee*
I've been sick (vomited)	Ho vomitato *O vomeetahto*
I've got...	Soffro di... *Soffro dee...*
I'm running a temperature of...degrees	Ho la febbre... *O lah faybbrayah...*
I've been...	Sono stato/a... *Sono stahto/ah...*
– stung by a wasp	Sono stato/a punto/a da una vespa *Sono stahto/ah poonto/ah dah oonah vayspah*
– stung by an insect	Sono stato/a punto/a da un insetto *Sono stahto/ah poonto/ah dah oon eensaytto*
– bitten by a dog	Sono stato/a morso/a da un cane *Sono stahto/ah morso/ah dah oon kahnay*

– stung by a jellyfish	Sono stato/a punto/a da una medusa *Sono stahto/ah poont/ah dah oonah maydoosah*
– bitten by a snake	Sono stato/a morso/a da una serpe *Sono stahto/ah morso/ah dah oonah sayrpay*
– bitten by an animal	Sono stato/a morso/a da una bestia *Sono stahto/ah morso/ah dah oonah baysteeah*
I've cut myself	Mi sono tagliato/a *Mee sono tahllyahto/ah*
I've burned myself	Mi sono bruciato/a *Mee sono broocheeahto/ah*
I've grazed/scratched myself (m/f)	Mi sono scorticato/a, graffiato/a *Mee sono skorteekahto/ah, graffeeahto/ah*
I've had a fall	Sono caduto/a *Sono kahdooto/ah*
I've sprained my ankle	Mi sono storto/a la caviglia *Mee sono storto/ah lah kahveellyah*
I'd like the morning-after pill	Vorrei la pillola del giorno dopo *Vorrayèe lah peellolah dayl jorno dopo*

13.3 The consultation

Quali disturbi ha?	What seems to be the problem?
Da quanto tempo ha questi disturbi?	How long have you had these complaints?
Ha sofferto già prima di questi disturbi?	Have you had this trouble before?
Ha la febbre? Quanti gradi?	Do you have a temperature? What is it?
Si spogli per favore	Get undressed, please
Si scopra il torace per favore	Strip to the waist, please
Può spogliarsi da questa parte	You can undress there
Si scopra il braccio sinistro/destro per favore	Roll up your left/right sleeve, please
Si sdrai qui, per favore	Lie down here, please
Fa male?	Does this hurt?
Respiri profondamente	Breathe deeply
Apra la bocca	Open your mouth

Patients' medical history

I'm a diabetic	Sono diabetico/a *Sono deeahbayhteeko/ah*
I have a heart condition	Soffro di disturbi di cuore *Soffro dee deestoorbee dee kworay*
I'm an asthmatic	Soffro di asma *Soffro dee ahsmah*
I'm allergic to...	Sono allergico/a a... *Sono ahllayrjeeko/ah ah...*
I'm...months pregnant	Sono incinta di...mesi *Sono eencheentah dee...maysee*

I'm on a diet	Seguo una dieta *Saygwo oonah deeaytah*
I'm on medication/ the pill	Prendo dei farmaci/la pillola contraccettiva *Prayndo dayee fahrmahchee/lah peellolah kontrahchaytteevah*
I've had a heart attack once before	Ho avuto già in passato un attacco cardiaco *O ahvooto jah een pahssahto oon ahttahkko kahrdeeahko*
I've had a(n)...operation	Mi hanno fatto un'operazione a... *Mee ahnno fahtto oonopayhrahtzeeonay ah...*
I've been ill recently	Sono stato/a ammalato/a di recente *Sono stahto/ah ahmmahlahto/ah dee raychayntay*
I've got a stomach ulcer	Soffro di un'ulcera gastrica *Soffro dee oonoolchayrah gahstreekah*
I've got my period	Ho le mestruazioni *O lay maystrooahtzeeonee*

The diagnosis

E' allergico/a a qualcosa?	Do you have any allergies?
Sta prendendo altri farmaci?	Are you on any medication?
Segue una dieta?	Are you on a diet?
E' incinta?	Are you pregnant?
E' stato/a vaccinato/a contro il tetano?	Have you had a tetanus injection?

Non è niente di grave	It's nothing serious
Ha una frattura al/alla...	Your...is broken
Ha una distorsione al/alla...	You've got a sprained...
Ha uno strappo al/alla...	You've got a torn...
Ha un'infezione	You've got an infection/ some inflammation
Ha un'appendicite	You've got appendicitis
Ha una bronchite	You've got bronchitis
Ha una malattia venerea	You've got a venereal disease
Ha l'influenza	You've got the flu
Ha avuto un attacco cardiaco	You've had a heart attack
Ha un'infezione (virale, batterica)	You've got a (viral/bacterial) infection
Ha una polmonite	You've got pneumonia
Ha una gastrite/un'ulcera	You've got gastritis/an ulcer
Ha uno strappo muscolare	You've pulled a muscle
Ha un'infezione vaginale	You've got a vaginal infection

Ha un'intossicazione alimentare	You've got food poisoning
Ha un'insolazione	You've got sunstroke
E' allergico a...	You're allergic to...
E' incinta	You're pregnant
Vorrei fare analizzare il Suo sangue/la Sua orina/le Sue feci	I'd like to have your blood/urine/stools tested
La ferita deve essere suturata	It needs stitches
La indirizzo da uno specialista/all'ospedale	I'm referring you to a specialist/sending you to hospital.
Bisogna far fare qualche radiografia	You'll need some x-rays taken
Può aspettare un attimo nella sala d'attesa, per favore?	Could you wait in the waiting room, please?
Deve essere operato/a	You'll need an operation

Is it contagious?	E' contagioso? *Ay kontahjozo?*
How long do I have to stay...?	Per quanto tempo devo rimanere...? *Payr kwahnto taympo dayvo reemahnayray...?*
– in bed	– a letto? *– ah laytto?*
– in hospital	– all'ospedale? *– ahllospaydahlay?*
Do I have to go on a special diet?	Devo seguire una dieta? *Dayvo saygweeray oonah deeaytah?*
Am I allowed to travel?	Mi è permesso viaggiare? *Mee ay payrmaysso veeahdjahray?*
Can I make another appointment?	Potrei fissare un nuovo appuntamento? *Potrayee feessahray oon nwovo ahppoontahmaynto?*
When do I have to come back?	Quando devo ritornare? *Kwahndo dayvo reetornahray?*
I'll come back tomorrow	Ritorno domani *Reetorno domahny*
How do I take this medicine?	Come devo prendere questa medicina? *Comay dayvo prayndayray kwaystah maydeecheenah?*

Deve ritornare domani/fra...giorni	Come back tomorrow/in...days' time.

13.4 Medication and prescriptions

How many capsules/ drops/injections/ spoonfuls/tablets each time?	Quante capsule/gocce/iniezioni/ cucchiaiate/compresse alla volta? *Kwahntay kahpsoolay/gotchay/ eeneeaytzeeonee/kookkeeaheeahtay/ komprayssay ahllah voltah?*
How many times a day?	Quante volte al giorno? *Kwahntay voltay ahl jorno?*

I've forgotten my medication At home I take...	Mi sono dimenticato/a le medicine. A casa prendo... *Mee sono deementeekahto/ah lay maydeecheenay. A kahza prayndo...*
Could you make out a prescription for me, please?	Mi potrebbe scrivere una ricetta? *Mee potraybbay skreevayray oonah reechayttah?*

Le prescrivo degli antibiotici/uno sciroppo/un tranquillante/degli analgesici	I'm prescribing antibiotics/a mixture/a tranquillizer/pain killers
Bisogna che si riposi	Have lots of rest
Non può uscire	Stay indoors
Non può alzarsi	Stay in bed

capsule
capsules
compresse
tablets
condurre a termine la cura
finish the course
cucchiaio/cucchiaino
spoonful/teaspoonful
iniezioni
injections
per...giorni
for...days

far sciogliere in acqua
dissolve in water
gocce
drops
inghiottire
swallow (whole)
ogni...ore
every...hours
pomata
ointment
prendere
take

prima di ogni pasto
before meals
queste medicine influiscono sull'abilità di guida
this medication impairs your driving
solo per uso esterno
external use only
spalmare
rub on
...volte al giorno
...times a day

13.5 At the dentist's

Do you know a good dentist?	Conosce un buon dentista? *Konoshay oon bwon daynteestah?*
Could you make a dentist's appointment for me? It's urgent	Mi potrebbe prendere un appuntamento urgente dal dentista? *Mee potraybbay prayndayray oon ahppoontahmaynto oorjenahtay dahl daynteestah?*
Can I come in today, please	Posso venire oggi, per favore? *Posso vayneeray odjee payr fahvoray?*
I have a (terrible) toothache	Ho (un) mal di denti (terribile) *O (oon) mahl dee dayntee (tayrreebeelay)*
Could you prescribe/ give me a painkiller?	Mi potrebbe prescrivere/dare un analgesico? *Mee potraybbay prayskreevayray/dahray oon ahnahljeezeeko?*
I've got a broken tooth	Ho un dente spezzato *O oon dayntay spaytzahto*
My filling's come out	Ho perso un'otturazione *O payrso oonottoorahtzeeonay*
I've got a broken crown	Si è rotta la capsula *See ay rottah lah kahpsoolah*

I'd like/I don't want a local anaesthetic	Vorrei essere curato/a con/senza anestesia locale *Vorrayee ayssayhray koorahto/ah kon/ saynzah ahnaystayzeeah lokahlay*
Could you do a temporary repair?	Mi potrebbe curare adesso in modo provvisorio? *Mee potraybbay koorahray ahdaysso een modo provveezoreeo?*
I don't want this tooth pulled	Non voglio un'estrazione *Non vollyo oonaystrahtzeeonay*
My denture is broken. Can you fix it?	Ho rotto la dentiera. La può aggiustare? *O rotto lah daynteeayhrah. Lah pwo ahdjoostahray?*

Qual è il dente che Le fa male?	Which tooth hurts?
Ha un ascesso	You've got an abscess.
Le devo fare una cura canalare	I'll have to do a root canal
Le faccio un'anestesia locale	I'm giving you a local anaesthetic
Devo estrarre/fare un'otturazione/ limare questo dente	I'll have to pull/fill/file this tooth
Devo trapanarlo	I'll have to drill it
Apra la bocca	Open wide, please
Chiuda la bocca	Close your mouth, please
Si sciacqui la bocca	Rinse, please
Sente ancora dolore?	Does it hurt still?

14

In trouble

In trouble

14.1 Asking for help

Help!	Aiuto! *Ayooto!*
Fire!	Al fuoco! *Ahl fwoko!*
Police!	Polizia! *Poleetzeeah!*
Quick/Hurry!	Presto! *Praysto!*
Danger!	Pericolo! *Payreekolo!*
Watch out!	Attenzione! *Attayntzeeonay!*
Stop!	Alt!/Stop! *Ahlt!/Stop!*
Be careful!/Go easy!	Attenzione!/Piano! *Attayntzeeonay!/Peeahno!*
Get your hands off me!	Giù le mani! *Joo lay mahnee!*
Let go!	Lascia! *Lahshah!*
Stop thief!	Al ladro! *Ahl lahdro!*
Could you help me, please?	Mi potrebbe aiutare? *Mee potraybbay aheeootahray?*
Where's the police station/emergency exit/fire escape?	Dov'è la questura/l'uscita di emergenza/la scala di sicurezza? *Dovay ay lah kwaystoorah/loosheetah dee aymayrjayntzah/lah skahlah dee seekooraytzah?*
Where's the nearest fire extinguisher?	Dov'è un estintore? *Dovay ay oonaysteentoray?*
Call the fire brigade!	Chiami i pompieri! *Keeahmee ee pompeeayhree!*
Call the police!	Chiami la polizia! *Keeahmee lah poleetzeeah!*
Call an ambulance!	Chiami un'ambulanza! *Keeahmee oonahmboolahntzah!*
Where's the nearest phone?	Dov'è un telefono? *Dovay ay oon taylayfono?*
Could I use your phone?	Potrei servirmi del Suo telefono? *Potrayee sayrveermee dayl soo-o taylayfono?*
What's the emergency number?	Qual è il numero dei servizi di emergenza? *Kwahlay ay eel noomayro dayee sayrveetzee dee aymayrjayntzah?*
What's the number for the police?	Qual è il numero della polizia? *Kwahlay ay eel noomayro dayllah poleetzeeah?*

14.2 Loss

I've lost my wallet/purse	Ho perso il portafoglio/portamonete *O payrso eel portahfollyo/portahmonaytay*
I lost my...here yesterday	Ieri ho dimenticato qui... *Eeayree oh deemayteekahto kwee...*
I left my...here	Ho lasciato qui il mio.../la mia... *O lahsheeahto kwee eel meeo.../lah meeah...*
Did you find my...?	Ha trovato il mio /la mia...? *Ah trovahto eel meeo /lah meeah...?*
It was right here	Stava qui *Stahvah kwee*
It's very valuable	E' molto prezioso/a *Ay molto praytzeeozo/ah*
Where's the lost property office?	Dov'è l'ufficio oggetti smarriti? *Dovay ay looffeetcheeo odjayttee smahrreetee?*

14.3 Accidents

There's been an accident	C'è stato un incidente *Chay stahto ooneencheedayntay*
Someone's fallen into the water	Qualcuno è caduto nell'acqua *Kwahlkoono ay kahdooto nayllahkwah*
There's a fire	C'è un incendio *Chay ooneenchayndyo*
Is anyone hurt?	Ci sono dei feriti? *Chee sono dayee fayhreetee?*
(Nobody) someone has been injured	(Non) ci sono dei feriti *(Non) chee sono day fayhreetee*
Someone's still trapped inside the car/train	C'è ancora qualcuno intrappolato dentro la macchina/il treno *Chay ahnkorah kwahlkoono eentrahppolahto dayntro lah mahkkeenah/eel trayno*
It's not too bad. Don't worry	Non è grave. Non si preoccupi *Non ay grahvay. Non see prayokkoopee*
Leave everything the way it is, please	Lasci tutto così com'è, per piacere *Lahshee tootto kozee komay ay, payr peeahchayray*
I want to talk to the police first	Vorrei parlare prima alla polizia *Vorrayee pahrlahray preemah ahllah poleetzeeah*
I want to take a photo first	Vorrei prima fare una foto *Vorrayee preemah fahray oonah foto*
Here's my name and address	Ecco il mio nome e il mio indirizzo *Ekko eel meeo nomay ay eel meeo eendeereetzo*
May I have your name and address?	Potrei sapere il Suo nome e il Suo indirizzo? *Potrayee sahpayray eel soo-o nomay ay eel soo-o eendeereetzo?*
Could I see your identity card/your insurance papers?	Potrei vedere la Sua carta d'identità/i documenti dell'assicurazione? *Potrayee vaydayray lah sooah kahrtah deedaynteetah/ee dokoomentee dayllasseekoorahtzeeonay?*

Will you act as a witness?	Accetta di testimoniare? *Ahtchayttah dee taysteemoneeahray?*
I need this information for insurance purposes	Ho bisogno di questi dati per via dell'assicurazione *O beezoneeo dee kwaystee dahtee payr veeah dayllahsseekoorahtzeeonay*
Are you insured?	E' assicurato/a? *Ay ahsseekoorahto/ah?*
Third party or comprehensive?	Responsabilità civile o assicurazione completa? *Raysponsahbeeleetah cheeveelay o ahsseekoorahtzeeonay komplaytah?*
Could you sign here, please?	Firmi qui, per favore *Feermee kwee, payr fahvoray*

14.4 Theft

I've been robbed	Sono stato/a derubato/a *Sono stahto/ah dayroobahto/ah*
My...has been stolen	Hanno rubato il mio.../la mia... *Ahnno roobahto eel meeo.../lah meeah...*
My car's been broken into	Mi hanno forzato la macchina *Mee ahnno fortzahto la mahkkeenah*

14.5 Missing person

I've lost my child/ grandmother	Ho perso mio figlio/mia figlia/mia nonna *O payrso meeo feellyo/meeah feellyah/ meeah nonnah*
Could you help me find him/her?	Mi potrebbe aiutare a cercarlo/cercarla? *Mee potraybbay aheeootahray ah chayrkahrlo/chayrkahrlah?*
Have you seen a small child?	Ha visto un bambino/una bambina? *Ah veesto oon bahmbeeno/oonah bahmbeenah?*
He's/she's...years old	Ha...anni *Ah...annee*
He/she's got...hair	Ha i capelli... *Ah ee kahpayllee...*
short/long/blond/red/ brown/black/grey/curly/ straight/ frizzy	corti/lunghi/biondi/rossi/bruni/neri/grigi/ ricci/lisci/crespi *kortee/loongee/beeondee/rossee/broonee/ nayree/ greejee/reetchee/krayspee*
– a ponytail	– con la coda di cavallo *– kon lah kodah dee kahvahllo*
– plaits	– con le trecce *– kon llay traytchay*
– a bun	– con una crocchia *– kon loonah crokkeeah*
He's/she's got blue/brown/green eyes	Ha gli occhi azzurri/bruni/verdi *Ah lly okkee ahdzoorree/broonee/vayrdee*
He/she's wearing swimming trunks/hiking boots	Porta un costume da bagno/gli scarponi *Portah oon kostoomay dah bahneeo/lly skahrponee*
with/without glasses, carrying/not carrying a bag	con/senza occhiali, (non) porta una borsa *kon/saynzah okkeeahlee, (non) portah oonah borsah*

He/She is tall/short	È alto/a, basso/a *Ay ahlto/ah, bahsso/ah*
This is a photo of him/her	Ecco una sua foto *Ekko oonah sooah foto*
He/she must be lost	Deve essersi perso/a *Dayvay ayssayrsee payrso/ah*

14.6 The police

An arrest

Documenti prego	Your (vehicle) documents, please
Ha superato il limite di velocità	You were speeding
E' vietato parcheggiare qui	You're not allowed to park here
Non ha messo soldi nel parcometro/ parchimetro	You haven't put money in the 'Pay and display'/ parking meter
I fari della sua macchina non funzionano	Your lights aren't working
Le devo fare una multa di....	That's a L.....fine
Paga direttamente?	Do you want to pay on the spot?
Deve pagare subito	You'll have to pay on the spot

I don't speak Italian	Non parlo l'italiano *Non pahrlo leetahleeahno*
I didn't see the sign	Non ho visto quel cartello *Non o veesto kwayl kahrtayllo*
I don't understand what it says	Non capisco cosa c'è scritto *Non kahpeesko kosah chay skreetto*
I was only doing... kilometres an hour	Andavo soltanto a...chilometri all'ora *Ahndahvo soltahnto ah...keelomaytree ahllorah*
I'll have my car checked	Farò controllare la macchina *Fahro kontrollahray lah mahkkeenah*
I was blinded by oncoming lights	Sono stato/a abbagliato/a *Sono stahto/ah ahbbahllyahto/ah*

Dov'è successo?	Where did it happen?
Cosa ha perso?	What's missing?
Cosa hanno rubato?	What's been taken?
Potrei avere la Sua carta d'identità?	Could I see your identity card/some identification?
A che ora è successo?	What time did it happen?
Ci sono dei testimoni?	Are there any witnesses?
Firmi qui, per favore	Sign here, please
Desidera un interprete?	Do you want an interpreter?

At the police station

I want to report a collision/missing person/rape	Vorrei denunciare uno scontro/uno smarrimento/uno stupro *Vorrayee daynooncheeahray oono skontro/ oono zmahrreemaynto/oono stoopro*
Could you make a statement, please?	Può fare una dichiarazione scritta, per favore? *Pwo fahray oonah deekeeahrahtzeeonay skreettah, payr fahvoray?*
Could I have a copy for the insurance?	Mi dia una copia per l'assicurazione *Mee deeah oonah kopeeah payr lahsseekoorahtzeeonay*
I've lost everything	Ho perso tutto *O payrso tootto*
I've no money left, I'm desperate	Non ho più soldi, sono disperato/a *Non o peeoo soldee, sono deespayrahto/ah*
Could you lend me a little money?	Mi potrebbe prestare qualcosa? *Mee potraybbay praystahray kwahlkosah?*
I'd like an interpreter	Vorrei un interprete *Vorrayee ooneentayrprayhtay*
I'm innocent	Sono innocente *Sono eennochayntay*
I don't know anything about it	Non ne so niente *Non nay so neeayntay*
I want to speak to someone from the British/ American/ Australian embassy	Vorrei parlare con qualcuno dell'ambasciata Britannica/Americana/ Australiana *Vorrayee pahrlahray con kwahlkoono dayllahmbahshahtah Breetahnneekah/ Ahmayreekahnah/Ahoostrahleeahnah*
I want a lawyer who speaks...	Vorrei un avvocato che parli... *Vorrayee oonahvvokahto kay pahrlee...*

15

Word list

Word list English - Italian

● **The following word list** is meant to supplement the chapters in this book. Verbs are indicated by the word "verb" and where the gender of a noun is not clear, the word is followed by (m) or (f).

Some of the words not contained in this list can be found elsewhere in the book, eg. alongside the diagrams of the car, bicycle and camping equipment. Many food items can be found in the Italian-English list in chapter 4.7

A

about	circa	*cheerkah*
above, up	sopra	*soprah*
abroad	all'estero	*ahllaystayro*
accident	incidente (m)	*eencheedayntay*
adder	vipera	*veepayrah*
address	indirizzo	*eendeereetzo*
admission	ingresso	*eengraysso*
admission price	prezzo del biglietto	*praytzo dayl beellyaytto*
advice	consiglio	*konseellyo*
after	dopo	*dopo*
afternoon	pomeriggio	*pomayreedjo*
aftershave	il dopobarba	*eel dopobahrbah*
again	di nuovo	*dee nwovo*
against	contro	*kontro*
age	età	*aytah*
Aids	Aids (m)	*ayeeds*
air conditioning	aria condizionata	*ahreeah kondeetzeeonahtah*
air sickness bag	busta per vomitare	*boostah payr vomeetahray*
aircraft	aeroplano	*ahayroplahno*
airport	aeroporto	*ahayroporto*
alarm	allarme (m)	*ahllahrmay*
alarm clock	sveglia	*svayllyah*
alcohol	le bevande alcoliche	*lay bayvahnday ahlkoleekay*
all the time	di continuo	*dee konteenoo-o*
allergic	allergico	*ahllayrjeeko*
alone	solo	*solo*
always	sempre	*saympray*
ambulance	ambulanza	*ahmboolahntzah*
amount	somma	*sommah*
amusement park	il 'luna' park	*eel 'loonah' pahrk*
anaesthetize (verb)	anestetizzare	*ahnaystayteetzahray*
anchovy	acciuga	*ahtchoogah*
angry	arrabbiato	*ahrrahbbeeahto*
animal	animale (m)	*ahneemahlay*
ankle	caviglia	*kahveellyah*
answer	risposta	*reespostah*
ant	formica	*formeekah*
anti-diarrhhoea tablets	medicina astringente	*maydeecheenah ahstreenjayntay*

antibiotics	gli antibiotici	*lly ahnteebeeoteechee*
antifreeze	antigelo	*ahnteejaylo*
antique	antico	*ahnteeko*
antiques	gli oggetti antichi	*lly odjayttee ahnteekee*
anus	ano	*ahno*
apartment	appartamento	*ahppahrtahmaynto*
aperitif	aperitivo	*ahpayreeteevo*
apple	mela	*maylah*
apple juice	succo di mela	*sookko dee maylah*
apple pie	torta di mele	*tortah dee maylay*
apple sauce	passato di mele	*pahssahto dee maylay*
appointment	appuntamento	*ahppoontahmaynto*
apricot	albicocca	*ahlbeekokkah*
April	aprile (m)	*ahpreellay*
architecture	architettura	*ahrkeetayttoorah*
area	i dintorni	*ee deentornee*
arm	braccio	*brahtcheeo*
arrive (verb)	arrivare	*ahrreevahray*
arrow	freccia	*fraytchah*
art	arte (f)	*ahrtay*
artery	arteria	*ahrtayreeah*
artichokes	i carciofi	*ee kahrchofee*
article	articolo	*ahrteekolo*
artificial respiration	la respirazione artificiale	*lah rayspeerahtzeeonay ahrteefeechahlay*
arts and crafts	artigianato	*ahrteejahnahto*
ashtray	il portacenere	*eel portahchaynayray*
ask (verb)	chiedere	*keeaydayray*
asparagus	gli asparagi	*lly ahspahrahjee*
aspirin	aspirina	*ahspeereenah*
assault	la violazione	*lah veeolahtzeeonay*
at home	a casa	*ah kahsah*
at night	la/di notte	*lah/dee nottay*
at the back	in fondo	*een fondo*
at the end/at the rear	in fondo	*een fondo*
at the front (theatre etc)	nelle prime file	*nayllay preemay feellay*
at the front	di fronte	*dee frontay*
at the latest	al massimo/al più tardi	*ahl mahsseemo/ ahl peeoo tahrdee*
aubergine	melanzana	*maylahntzahnah*
August	agosto	*ahgosto*
automatic (car)	macchina con il cambio automatico	*mahkkeenah kon eel kahmbeeo ahootomahteeko*
automatic	automatico	*ahootomahteeko*
automatic shutter release	autoscatto	*ahootoskahtto*
autumn	autunno	*ahootoonno*
avalanche	valanga	*vahlahngah*
awake	sveglio	*svayllyo*
awning	tenda da sole	*tayndah dah solay*

B

baby	bambino/a	*bahmbeeno/ah*
baby food (jars of)	gli omogeneizzati	*lly omojaynayeedzahtee*
babysitter	la/il baby-sitter	*lah/eel baybeeseettayr*
back	schiena	*skeeaynah*
bacon	pancetta	*pahnchayttah*
bad	cattivo/male	*kahtteevo/mahlay*
bad/serious	grave	*grahvay*
bag	borsa	*borsah*
baker	panetteria	*pahnayttayreeah*
balcony (theatre)	galleria	*gahllayreeah*
balcony (to building)	il balcone	*eel bahlkonay*
ball	il pallone	*eel pahllonay*
ballet	balletto	*bahllaytto*
ballpoint pen	la biro	*lah beero*
banana	banana	*bahnahnah*
bandage	fascia	*fahsheeah*
bank (river)	riva	*reevah*
bank	banca	*bahnkah*
bar (café)	il bar	*eel bahr*
bar (drinks cabinet)	il bar	*eel bahr*
barbecue	il barbecue	*eel bahrbaykeeoo*
basketball (to play)	giocare a pallacanestro	*jokahray ah pahllahkahnaystro*
bath	bagno	*bahneeo*
bath towel	asciugamano da bagno	*ahshoogahmahno dah bahneeo*
bathing cap	cuffia da bagno	*cooffeeah dah bahneeo*
bathing cubicle	cabina	*kahbeenah*
bathing suit	il costume da bagno	*eel kostoomay dah bahneeo*
bathroom	bagno	*bahneeo*
battery (car)	batteria	*bahttayreeah*
battery	pila	*peellah*
beach	spiaggia	*speeahdjah*
beans	i fagioli	*ee fahjolee*
beautiful	bello	*bayllo*
beauty parlour	istituto di bellezza	*eesteetooto dee bayllaytzah*
bed	letto	*laytto*
bee	ape (f)	*ahpay*
beef	manzo	*mahnzo*
beer	birra	*beerrah*
beetroot	barbabietola	*bahrbahbeeaytolah*
begin (verb)	cominciare	*komeencheeahray*
beginner	il/la principiante	*eel/lah preencheepeeahntay*
behind	dietro	*deeaytro*
belt	cintura	*cheentoorah*
berth	cuccetta	*kootchayttah*
better	meglio	*mayllyo*
bicarbonate of soda	bicarbonato	*beekahrbonahto*
bicycle	bicicletta	*beecheeklayttah*
bicycle pump	pompa della bicicletta	*pompah dayllah beecheeklayttah*

bicycle/motorcycle repairs	riparazioni motociclette e biciclette	*reepahrahtzeeonee motocheeklayttay ay beecheeklayttay*
bikini	il bikini	*eel beekeenee*
bill	conto	*konto*
billiards, to play	giocare a biliardo	*jokahray ah beellyahrdo*
birthday	compleanno	*komplayahnno*
biscuit	biscotto	*beeskotto*
bite (verb)	mordere	*mordayray*
bitter	amaro	*ahmahro*
black	nero	*nayro*
bland	insipido	*eenseepeedo*
blanket	coperta	*kopayrtah*
bleach (verb)	ossigenare	*osseejaynahray*
blister	vescica	*vaysheekah*
blond	biondo	*beeondo*
blood	il sangue	*eel sahngway*
blood pressure	la pressione (del sangue)	*lah praysseeonay (dayl sahngway)*
blouse	camicetta	*kahmeechayttah*
blow dry (verb)	asciugare con il fon	*ahshoogahray kon eel fon*
blue	azzurro	*ahdzoorro*
boat	barca	*bahrkah*
body	corpo	*korpo*
body milk	il latte per il corpo	*eel lahttay payr eel korpo*
bone	osso	*osso*
bonnet	cofano	*kofahno*
book	libro	*leebro*
book (verb)	prenotare	*praynotahray*
booked	prenotato	*praynotahto*
booking office	ufficio prenotazioni	*ooffeecheeo praynotahtzeeonee*
bookshop	libreria	*leebrayreeah*
boot (car)	il baule	*eel bahoolay*
border	frontiera	*fronteeayrah*
bored (be)	annoiarsi	*ahnnoeeahrsee*
boring	noioso	*noeeozo*
born	nato	*nahto*
borrow	prendere in prestito	*prayndayray een praysteeto*
botanical garden	orto botanico	*orto botahneeko*
both	tutti e due	*toottee ay dooay*
bottle-warmer	lo scaldabiberon	*lo skahldah beebayron*
bottle (baby)	il biberon	*eel beebayron*
bottle	bottiglia	*botteellyah*
box (theatre)	palco	*pahlko*
box	scatola	*skahtolah*
boy	ragazzo	*rahgahtzo*
bra	reggiseno	*raydjeesayno*
bracelet	braccialetto	*brahtchahlaytto*
braised	stufato	*stoofahto*
brake	freno	*frayno*

brake fluid	liquido dei freni	*leekweedo dayee fraynee*
brake oil	olio dei freni	*oleeo dayee fraynee*
brass	ottone (m)	*ottonay*
bread	il pane	*eel pahnay*
break (one's...)	rompersi (la...)	*rompayrsee (lah...)*
breakdown recovery	soccorso stradale	*sokkorso strahdahlay*
breakfast	la (prima) colazione	*lah (preemah) kolahtzeeonay*
breast	petto	*paytto*
bridge	il ponte	*eel pontay*
bring (verb)	portare	*portahray*
brochure	opuscolo	*opooskolo*
broken	rotto	*rotto*
brother	fratello	*frahtayllo*
brown	marrone	*mahrronay*
bruise	livido	*leeveedo*
brush	spazzola	*spahtzolah*
Brussels sprouts	i cavoletti di Bruxelles	*ee kahvolayttee dee Brooxayls*
bubble bath	il bagno schiuma	*eel bahneeo skeeoomah*
bucket	secchio	*saykkeeo*
bug	insetto	*eensaytto*
building	edificio	*aydeefeecho*
buoy	boa	*boah*
burglary	furto (con scasso)	*foorto (kon skahsso)*
burn	bruciatura	*broochahtoorah*
burn (verb)	bruciare	*broochahray*
burnt	bruciato	*broochahto*
bus	autobus (m)	*ahootoboos*
bus station	la stazione degli autobus	*lah stahtzeeonay daylly ahootoboos*
bus stop	fermata dell'autobus	*fayrmahtah dayll-ahootoboos*
business trip	viaggio d'affari	*veeahdjo dahffahree*
busy	occupato	*okkoopahto*
butane camping gas	bombola a gas butano	*bombolah ah gahs bootahno*
butcher	macellaio	*mahchayllaheeo*
butter	burro	*boorro*
buttered roll	panino (con burro)	*pahneeno (kon boorro)*
button	il bottone	*eel bottonay*
buy (verb)	comprare	*komprahray*
by airmail	via aerea	*veeah ahayrayah*

C

cabbage	cavolo	*kahvolo*
cabin	capanna	*kahpahnnah*
cake	torta	*tortah*
cake (small)	pasticcino	*pahsteetcheeno*
cake shop	pasticcieria	*pahsteetcheeayreeah*
call (verb)	telefonare/chiamare	*taylayfonahray/ keeahmahray*
call (verb)	chiamare	*keeahmahray*
called, to be	chiamarsi	*keeahmahrsee*

camera	macchina fotografica	*mahkkeenah fotograhfeekah*
camp (verb)	campeggiare	*kahmpedjahray*
camp shop	il mini-market	*eel meenee-mahrkayt*
camp site	campeggio	*kahmpaydjo*
camper	il camper	*eel kahmper*
camping guide	guida dei campeggi	*gweedah dayee kahmpedjee*
camping permit	permesso di campeggiare	*payrmaysso dee kahmpedjahray*
canal boat	battello	*bahttayllo*
cancel (verb)	annullare	*ahnnoollahray*
candle	candela	*kahndaylah*
canoe	canoa	*kahnoah*
canoe (verb)	andare in canoa	*ahndahray een kahnoah*
car	macchina	*mahkkeenah*
car documents	i documenti della macchina	*ee dokoomayntee dayllah mahkkeenah*
car seat	il sedile	*eel saydeellay*
car trouble	panne	*pahnnay*
carafe	caraffa	*kahrahffah*
caravan	la roulotte	*lah roolot*
cardigan	il cardigan	*eel cahrdeegahn*
careful	attenzione	*ahttayntzeeonay*
carriage (railway)	il vagone	*eel vahgonay*
carriageway	carreggiata	*kahrraydjhahtah*
carrot	carota	*kahrotah*
carton (cigarettes)	stecca (di sigarette)	*stekkah (dee seegahrayttay)*
cartridge	cassetta	*kahssayttah*
cash desk	cassa	*kahssah*
casino	casinò	*kahzeeno*
cassette	cassetta	*kahssayttah*
castle	castello	*kahstayllo*
cat	gatto	*gahtto*
catalogue	catalogo	*kahtahlogo*
cathedral	la cattedrale	*lah kahttaydrahlay*
cauliflower	il cavolfiore	*eel kahvolfeeoray*
cave	grotta	*grottah*
CD	il compact (disk)	*eel kompahkt (deesk)*
celebrate (verb)	far festa	*fahr faystah*
cellotape	nastro adesivo	*nahstro ahdayzeevo*
cemetery	cimitero	*cheemeetayro*
centimetre	centimetro	*chaynteemaytro*
central heating	riscaldamento centrale	*reeskahldahmaynto chayntrahlay*
centre	centro	*chayntro*
chain	catena	*kahtaynah*
chair	sedia	*saydyeeah*
chambermaid	cameriera	*kahmayreeayrah*
chamois (leather)	camoscio	*kahmosho*
champagne	lo champagne	*lo shahmpahn*
change	resto	*raysto*
change (verb)	cambiare	*kahmbeeahray*

change the baby's nappy (verb)	cambiare il pannolino	*kahmbeeahray eel pahnnoleeno*
change the oil (verb)	cambiare l'olio	*kahmbeeahray loleeo*
chapel	cappella	*kahppayllah*
charter flight	volo charter	*volo chahrtayr*
chat up (verb)	fare la corte	*fahray lah kortay*
check (verb)	controllare	*kontrollahray*
check in (verb)	fare il check in	*fahray eel chaykeen*
cheers	cin cin	*cheen cheen*
cheese (tasty, mild)	formaggio (saporito, delicato)	*formahdjo (sahporeeto, dayleekahto)*
chef	capo	*kahpo*
cheque	assegno	*ahssayneeo*
cheque card	carta assegni	*kahrtah ahssaynyee*
cherries	le ciliege	*lay cheelleeayjay*
chess (to play)	(giocare a) scacchi	*(jokahray ah) skahkkee*
chewing gum	il chewing gum	*eel chayweeng goom*
chicken	pollo	*pollo*
chicory	cicoria	*cheekoreeah*
child	bambino	*bahmbeeno*
child's seat (bicycle)	seggiolino	*saydjeeoleeno*
chilled	fresco	*fraysko*
chin	mento	*maynto*
chips	le patate fritte	*lay pahtahtay freettay*
chocolate	cioccolata	*chokkolahtah*
chocolate (a)	cioccolatino	*chokkolahteeno*
choose (verb)	scegliere	*shayllyayray*
chop	braciola	*brahcholah*
christian name	il nome	*eel nomay*
church	chiesa	*keeayzah*
cigar	sigaro	*seegahro*
cigar shop	tabacchi (m)	*tahbahkkee*
cigarette	sigaretta	*seegahrayttah*
cigarette paper	le cartine	*lay kahrteenay*
cine camera	cinepresa	*cheenaypraysah*
circle	cerchio	*chayrkeeo*
circus	circo	*cheerko*
city hall	municipio	*mooneecheepeeo*
city map	pianta	*peeahntah*
classical concert	concerto di musica classica	*konchayrto dee moozeekah klahsseekah*
clean	pulito	*pooleeto*
clean (verb)	pulire	*pooleeray*
clear	chiaro	*keeahro*
clearance	svendita	*svayndeetah*
closed	chiuso	*keeoozo*
closed off (road)	chiuso al traffico	*keeoozo ahl trahffeeko*
clothes	i vestiti	*ee vaysteetee*
clothes hanger	ometto	*omaytto*
clothes peg	molletta da bucato	*mollayttah dah bookahto*
clothing	abbigliamento	*ahbbeellyahmaynto*
coach	il pullman	*eel poollmahn*
coat	soprabito/cappotto	*soprahbeeto/kahppotto*
cockroach	lo scarafaggio	*lo skahrahfahdjo*

cocoa	cacao	*kahkaho*
cod	merluzzo	*mayrlootzo*
coffee	il caffè	*eel kahffay*
coffee filter	filtro del caffè	*feelltro dayl kahffay*
cognac	il cognac	*eel koneeahk*
cold (adj)	freddo	*frayddo*
cold	il raffreddore	*eel rahffrayddoray*
cold cuts	gli affettati	*lly ahffettahtee*
colleague	il/la collega	*eel/lah kollaygah*
collision	lo scontro	*lo skontro*
cologne	eau de toilette (f)	*o day twahlayt*
colour	il colore	*eel koloray*
colour pencils	le matite colorate	*lay mahteetay kolorahtay*
colour TV	il televisore a colori	*eel taylayveezoray ah koloree*
colouring book	album (m) da colorare	*ahlboom dah kolorahray*
comb	il pettine	*eel paytteenay*
come	venire	*vayneeray*
come back (verb)	ritornare	*reetornahray*
compartment	lo scompartimento	*lo skompahrteemaynto*
complaint (med)	disturbo	*deestoorbo*
complaint	reclamo	*rayklahmo*
complaints book	libro reclami	*leebro rayklahmy*
completely	del tutto	*dayl tootto*
compliment	complimento	*kompleemaynto*
compulsory	obbligatorio	*obbleegahtoryeeo*
concert	concerto	*konchayrto*
concert hall	sala dei concerti	*sahlah day konchayrtee*
concussion	la commozione cerebrale	*lah kommotzeeonay chayraybrahlay*
condensed milk	il latte condensato	*eel lahttay kondaynsahto*
condom	preservativo	*praysayrvahteevo*
congratulate (verb)	congratulare	*kongrahtoolahray*
connection	collegamento	*kollaygahmaynto*
constipation	stitichezza	*steeteekaytzah*
consulate	consolato	*konsolahto*
consultation	la consultazione	*lah konsooltahtzeeonay*
contact lens	la lente a contatto	*lah layntay ah kontahtto*
contact lens solution	liquido per lenti a contatto	*leekweedo payr layntee ah kontahtto*
contagious	contagioso	*kontahdjozo*
contraceptive	anticoncezionale (m)	*ahnteekonchaytzee-nahlay*
cook (verb)	cucinare	*koocheenahray*
cook	cuoco/a	*kwoko/ah*
copper	il rame	*eel rahmay*
copy	copia	*kopeeah*
corkscrew	il cavatappi	*eel kahvahtahppee*
corn flour	fecola di mais	*faykolah dee mahees*
corner	angolo	*ahngolo*
correct	giusto	*joosto*
correspond (verb)	corrispondere	*korreespondayray*
corridor	corridoio	*korreedoeeo*
costume	il costume	*eel kostoomay*

cot	lettino per il bambino	*laytteeno payr eel bahmbeeno*
cotton	il cotone	*eel kotonay*
cotton wool	il cotone idrofilo	*eel kotonay eedrofeello*
cough	la tosse	*lah tossay*
cough mixture	lo sciroppo per la tosse	*lo sheeroppo payr lah tossay*
counter	banco	*bahnko*
country	campagna	*kahmpahneeah*
country code	prefisso	*prayfeesso*
countryside	il paese	*eel pahaysay*
courgette	zucchina	*dzookkeenah*
course	cura	*koorah*
cousin	cugino/a	*koogeeno/ah*
crab	granchio	*grahnkeeo*
cream	panna	*pahnnah*
cream/ointment (med)	pomata	*pomahtah*
credit card	carta di credito	*kahrtah dee kraydeeto*
crisps	le patatine	*lay pahtahteenay*
croissant	il cornetto	*eel kornaytto*
cross-country run	pista da fondo	*peestah dah fondo*
cross-country skiing	fare dello sci di fondo	*fahray dayllo shee dee fondo*
cross-country skis	gli sci da fondo	*lly shee dah fondo*
cross (the road) (verb)	attraversare (la strada)	*ahttrahvayrsahray (lah strahdah)*
crossing (sea)	traversata	*trahvayrsahtah*
cry (verb)	piangere	*peeahnjayray*
cubic metre	metro cubo	*maytro koobo*
cucumber	cetriolo	*chaytreeolo*
cuddly toy	giocattolo di pelouche	*jokahttolo dee payloosh*
cuff links	i gemelli	*ee jemayllee*
culottes	la gonna pantaloni	*lah gonnah pahntahlonee*
cup	tazza	*tahtzah*
curly	riccio	*reetcheeo*
current	la corrente	*lah korrayntay*
cushion	cuscino	*koosheeno*
custard	crema	*kraymah*
customary	in uso	*een oozo*
customs	dogana	*dogahnah*
customs check	controllo doganale	*kontrollo dogahnahlay*
cut (verb)	tagliare	*tahllyahray*
cutlery	le posate	*lay pozahtay*
cycling	ciclismo	*cheekleesmo*

D

dairy produce	i latticini	*ee lahtteecheenee*
damaged	danneggiato	*dahnnaydjahto*
dance (verb)	ballare	*bahllahray*
dandruff	forfora	*forforah*
danger	pericolo	*payreekolo*
dangerous	pericoloso	*payreekoloso*
dark	scuro	*skooro*
daughter	figlia	*feellyah*

dawn	alba	*ahlbah*
day	giorno	*jorno*
day before yesterday	l'altro ieri	*lahltro eeayree*
dead	morto	*morto*
dear/expensive	caro	*kahro*
decaffeinated	decaffeinato	*daykahffayeenahto*
December	dicembre (m)	*deechaymbray*
deck chair	la sdraio	*lah zdraheeo*
declare (verb)	dichiarare	*deekeeahrahray*
deep	profondo	*profondo*
deep sea diving	gli sport subacquei	*lly sport soobahkwayee*
deepfreeze	il surgelatore	*eel soorjaylahtoray*
degrees	i gradi	*ee grahdee*
delay	ritardo	*reetahrdo*
delicious	ottimo	*otteemo*
dentist	il/la dentista	*eel/lah daynteestah*
dentures	dentiera	*daynteeayrah*
deodorant	il deodorante	*eel dayodorahntay*
department	reparto	*raypahrto*
department store	grande magazzino	*grahnday mahgahdzeeno*
departure	partenza	*pahrtaynzah*
departure time	ora di partenza	*orah dee pahrtaynzah*
depilatory cream	crema depilatoria	*kraymah daypeellahtoreeah*
deposit (verb)	deposito	*daypozeeto*
deposit	caparra	*kahpahrrah*
dessert	il dolce	*eel dolchay*
destination	la destinazione	*lah desteenahtzeeonay*
develop	sviluppare	*sveellooppahray*
diabetic	diabetico	*deeahbeteeko*
dial (verb)	fare	*fahray*
diamond	il diamante	*eel deeahmahntay*
diarrhoea	diarrea	*deeahrrayah*
dictionary	dizionario	*deetzeeonahreeo*
diesel	gasolio	*gahzoleeo*
diesel oil	olio per motori diesel	*oleeo payr motoree deesayl*
diet	dieta	*deeaytah*
difficulty	difficoltà	*deeffeekoltah*
dine (verb)	cenare	*chaynahray*
dining room	sala da pranzo	*sahlah dah prahntzo*
dining/buffet car	carrozza ristorante	*kahrrotza/ reestorahntay*
dinner	cena	*chaynah*
dinner jacket	lo smoking	*lo smokeeng*
direction	la direzione	*lah deeraytzeeonay*
directly	direttamente	*deerayttahmayntay*
dirty	sporco	*sporko*
disabled	disabile	*deezahbeellay*
disco	discoteca	*deeskotaykah*
discount	lo sconto	*lo skonto*
dish	piatto	*peeahtto*
dish of the day	piatto del giorno	*peeahtto dayl jorno*
disinfectant	il disinfettante	*ll deeseenfettahntay*

distance	distanza	*deestahntzah*
distilled water	acqua distillata	*ahkwah deesteellahtah*
disturb (verb)	disturbare	*deestoorbahray*
disturbance	disturbo	*deestoorbo*
dive (verb)	tuffarsi	*tooffahrsee*
diving	gli sport subacquei	*lly sport soobahkwayee*
diving board	trampolino	*trahmpoleeno*
diving gear	attrezzatura da sub	*ahttraytzahtoorah dah soob*
divorced	divorziato	*deevortzeeahto*
DIY-shop	negozio fai-da-te	*negotzeeo fahee-dah-tay*
dizzy (be)	avere il capogiro	*ahvayray eel kahpogeero*
do (verb)	fare	*fahray*
doctor	medico	*maydeeko*
dog	il cane	*eel kahnay*
doll	bambola	*bahmbolah*
domestic	domestico	*domaysteeko*
done (cooked)	cotto	*kotto*
door	porta	*portah*
double	doppio	*doppeeo*
down	giù	*joo*
draught	esserci corrente	*ayssayrchee korrayntay*
draughts (play)	giocare a dama	*jokahray ah dahmah*
dream (verb)	sognare	*soneeahray*
dress	vestito	*vaysteeto*
dressing gown	vestaglia	*vaystahllyah*
drink (verb)	bere	*bayray*
drinking chocolate	cacao	*kahkaho*
drinking water	acqua potabile	*ahkwah potahbeellay*
drive (verb)	guidare	*gweedahray*
driver	autista (m/f)	*ahooteestah*
driving licence	la patente (di guida)	*lah pahtayntay (dee gweedah)*
drought	siccità	*seetcheetah*
dry (verb)	asciugare	*ahshoogahray*
dry	secco	*saykko*
dry clean (verb)	lavare a secco	*lahvahray ah sekko*
dry cleaner's	lavanderia a secco	*lahvahndayreeah ah saykko*
dry shampoo	lo shampoo in polvere	*lo shahmpo een polvayray*
dummy	succhiotto	*sookkeeotto*
during	durante	*doorahntay*
during the day	di giorno	*dee jorno*

E

ear	orecchio	*oraykkeeo*
ear, nose and throat (ENT) specialist	otorinolaringoiatra	*otoreenolahreengoee-ahtrah*
earache	il mal d'orecchio	*eel mahl dorekkeeo*
eardrops	le gocce per le orecchie	*lay gotchay payr lay oraykkeeay*
early	presto	*praysto*

earrings	gli orecchini	*lly oraykkeenee*
earth	terra	*tayrrah*
earthenware	ceramica	*chayrahmeekah*
east	est	*ayst*
easy	facile	*fahcheellay*
eat (verb)	mangiare	*mahnjahray*
eczema	eczema (m)	*aykzaymah*
eel	anguilla	*ahngweellah*
egg	uovo	*wovo*
elastic band	elastico	*aylahsteeko*
electric	elettrico	*aylayttreeko*
electricity	la corrente	*lah korrayntay*
embassy	ambasciata	*ahmbahshahtah*
emergency brake	freno d'emergenza	*frayno demayrjayntzah*
emergency exit	uscita di sicurezza	*oosheetah dee seekooraytzah*
emergency number	numero d'emergenza	*noomayro daymayrjayntzah*
emergency phone	telefono d'emergenza	*taylayfono dee aymayrjayntzah*
emergency triangle	triangolo d'emergenza	*treeahngolo daymayrjayntzah*
emery board	limetta per le unghie	*leemayttah payr lay oongeeay*
empty	vuoto	*vwoto*
engaged (busy)	occupato	*okkoopahto*
England	Inghilterra	*eengeelltayrrah*
English	inglese	*eenglaysay*
enjoy (verb)	godere	*godayray*
envelope	busta	*boostah*
error	errore (m)	*ayrroray*
escort	accompagnatrice (f)	*ahkkompahneeah-treechay*
evening (in the)	di sera	*dee sayrah*
evening wear	abito da sera	*ahbeeto dah sayrah*
event	avvenimento	*ahvvayneemaynto*
everything	tutto	*tootto*
everywhere	dappertutto	*dahppayrtootto*
examine (verb)	visitare	*veeseetahray*
excavation	gli scavi	*lly skahvee*
excellent	eccellente	*aytchayllayntay*
exchange (verb)	cambiare	*kahmbeeahray*
exchange office	ufficio cambio	*ooffeecho kahmbeeo*
exchange rate	tasso di cambio	*tahsso dee kahmbeeo*
excursion	escursione (f)	*ayskoorseeonay*
excuse me	mi scusi	*mee skoozee*
excuse/pardon me	scusi	*skoozee*
exhibition	mostra	*mostrah*
exit	uscita	*oosheetah*
expenses	le spese	*lay spaysay*
expensive	caro	*kahro*
explain (verb)	spiegare	*speeaygahray*
express	diretto	*deeraytto*
external	esterno	*aystayro*
eye	occhio	*okkeeo*

eye drops	le gocce per gli occhi	*lay gotchay payrlly okkee*
eye shadow	ombretto	*ombraytto*
eye specialist	oculista (m/f)	*okooleestah*
eyeliner	eye-liner (m)	*aheellaheenayr*

F

face	faccia	*fahtchah*
factory	fabbrica	*fahbbreekah*
faith	la fede	*lah fayday*
fall (verb)	cadere	*kahdayray*
family	famiglia	*fahmeellyah*
famous	famoso	*fahmoso*
farm	fattoria	*fahttoreeah*
farmer	agricoltore	*ahgreekoltoray*
fashion	moda	*modah*
fast	presto	*praysto*
father	il padre	*eel pahdray*
fault	colpa	*kolpah*
fax (verb	spedire un fax	*spaydeeray oon fahx*
February	febbraio	*faybbraheeo*
feel (verb)	sentire	*saynteeray*
feel sick (verb)	avere la nausea	*ahvayray lah nahoozayah*
fence	cancello	*kahnchayllo*
ferry	traghetto	*trahgaytto*
fever	la febbre	*lah faybbray*
fill (verb)	otturare (un dente)	*ottoorahray (oon dayntay)*
fill out (verb)	compilare	*kompeellahray*
filling	otturazione (f)	*ottoorahtzeeonay*
film (photographic)	rullino	*roolleeno*
film	il film	*eel feellm*
filter	filtro	*feelltro*
find (verb)	trovare	*trovahray*
fine (delicate)	fine	*feenay*
fine	multa	*mooltah*
finger	dito	*deeto*
fire	fuoco	*fwoko*
fire (accident)	incendio	*eenchayndeeo*
fire brigade	i pompieri/i vigili del fuoco	*ee pompee-ayree/ee veejeellee dayl fwoko*
fire escape	scala di sicurezza	*skahlah dee seekooraytzah*
fire extinguisher	estintore (m)	*aysteentoray*
first	primo	*preemo*
first aid	pronto soccorso	*pronto sokkorso*
first class	prima classe	*preemah klahssay*
fish (verb)	pescare	*peskahray*
fish	il pesce	*eel payshay*
fishing rod	canna da pesca	*kahnnah dah payskah*
fitness centre	palestra	*pahlaystrah*
fitness training	il fitness	*eel feetness*
fitting room	camerino	*kahmayreeno*
fix (verb)	aggiustare	*ahdjoostahray*
flag	bandiera	*bahndeeayrah*

flash	il flash	*eel flash*
flash bulb	lampada flash	*lahmpahdah flash*
flash cube	cubo flash	*koobo flahsh*
flat	appartamento	*ahppahrtahmaynto*
flea market	mercato delle pulci	*mayrkahto dayllay poolchee*
flight	volo	*volo*
flight number	numero del volo	*noomayro dayl volo*
flood	inondazione (f)	*eenondahtzeeonay*
floor	piano	*peeahno*
flour	farina	*fahreenah*
flu	influenza	*eenflooayntzah*
fly-over	viadotto	*veeahdotto*
fly (verb)	andare in aereo	*ahndahray een ahayrayo*
fly (insect)	mosca	*moskah*
fog	nebbia	*naybbeeah*
foggy (be)	esserci nebbia	*ayssayrchee naybbeeah*
folkloristic	folcloristico	*folkloreesteeko*
follow (verb)	seguire	*saygweeray*
food	cibo	*cheebo*
food poisoning	intossicazione (f) alimentare	*eentosseekahtzeeonay ahleemayntahray*
foodstuffs	gli alimentari	*lly ahleemayntahree*
foot	il piede	*eel peeayday*
for hire	a nolo	*ah nolo*
forbidden	vietato	*veeaytahto*
forehead	la fronte	*lah frontay*
foreign	straniero	*strahnyayro*
forget (verb)	dimenticare	*deemaynteekahray*
fork	forchetta	*forkayttah*
form	modulo	*modoolo*
fort	fortezza	*fortaytzah*
forward (verb)	spedire	*spaydeeray*
fountain	fontana	*fontahnah*
fragrant	aromatizzato	*ahromahteedzahto*
frame (for glasses)	montatura	*montahtoorah*
franc	franco	*frahnco*
free (of charge)	gratis	*grahtees*
free	libero	*leebayro*
free time	tempo libero	*taympo leebayro*
freeze (verb)	gelare	*jaylahray*
French	francese	*frahnchaysay*
French bread	filoncino	*feelloncheeno*
fresh	fresco	*fraysko*
Friday	il venerdì	*eel vaynayrdee*
fried	fritto	*freetto*
friend	amico/a	*ahmeeko/ah*
friendly	gentile	*jaynteellay*
frightened (be)	avere paura	*ahvayray pahoorah*
fringe	frangetta	*frahnjayttah*
fruit	frutta	*froottah*
fruit juice	succo di frutta	*sookko dee troottah*
frying pan	padella	*pahdayllah*
full	pieno	*peeayno*
fun	divertimento	*deevayrteemaynto*

G

gallery	galleria	*gahllayreeah*
game	gioco	*joko*
garage	il garage	*eel gahrahdj*
garbage bag	sacco per i rifiuti	*sahkko payr ee reefeeootee*
garden	giardino	*jahrdeeno*
gastroenteritis	la gastroenterite	*lah gahstroayntayreetay*
gauze	garza idrofila	*gahrdzah eedrofeellah*
gear	marcia	*mahrchah*
gel	il gel	*eel jayl*
German	tedesco	*taydaysko*
get off	scendere	*shayndayray*
gift	regalo	*raygahlo*
gilt	dorato	*dorahto*
ginger	lo zenzero	*lo dzayndzayro*
girl	ragazza	*rahgahtzah*
girlfriend	amica	*ahmeekah*
giro cheque	assegno postale	*ahssayneeo postahlay*
giro pass	carta assegni	*kahrtah ahssaynee*
glacier	ghiacciaio	*geeahtcheeaeeo*
glass (tumbler)	il bicchiere	*eel beekkeeayray*
glass (wine)	vetro	*vaytro*
glasses	gli occhiali	*lly okkeeahlee*
glove	guanto	*gwahnto*
glue	colla	*kollah*
gnat	zanzara	*dzahndzahrah*
go	andare	*ahndahray*
go back (verb)	ritornare	*reetornahray*
go for a walk (verb)	fare una passeggiata	*fahray oonah pahssaydjeahtah*
go out (verb)	uscire	*oosheeray*
goat's cheese	formaggio caprino	*formahdjo kahpreeno*
gold	oro	*oro*
golf (play)	giocare a golf	*jokahray ah golf*
golf course	campo da golf	*kahmpo dah golf*
gone	sparito	*spahreeto*
good afternoon	buongiorno	*bwonjorno*
good evening	buonasera	*bwonahsayrah*
good morning	buongiorno	*bwonjorno*
good night	buonanotte	*bwonahnottay*
goodbye	addio	*ahddeeo*
gram	grammo	*grahmmo*
grandchild	il/la nipote	*eel/lah neepotay*
grandfather	nonno	*nonno*
grandmother	nonna	*nonnah*
grape	uva	*oovah*
grape juice	succo d'uva	*sookko doovah*
grapefruit	pompelmo	*pompaylmo*
grave	tomba	*tombah*
grease	grasso	*grahsso*
green	verde	*vayrday*
green card	carta verde	*kahrtah vayrday*
greet (verb)	salutare	*sahlootahray*
grey	grigio	*greejo*
grill (verb)	grigliare	*greellyahray*

grilled	alla griglia	*ahllah greellyah*
grocer	gli alimentari	*lly ahleemayntahree*
ground	terra	*tayrrah*
group	gruppo	*grooppo*
guest house	la pensione	*lah paynseeonay*
guide (book)	guida	*gweedah*
guide (person)	guida	*gweedah*
guided tour	visita guidata	*veeseetah gweedahtah*
gynaecologist	ginecologo	*jeenaykologo*

H

hair	i capelli	*ee cahpaylly*
hairbrush	spazzola	*spahtzolah*
hairdresser	il parrucchiere	*eel pahrrookkeeayray*
hairpins	le forcine	*lay forcheenay*
hairspray	lacca	*lahkkah*
half	metà	*maytah*
half full	pieno a metà	*peeayno ah maytah*
half/middle	mezzo	*maydzo*
ham (boiled)	prosciutto (cotto)	*proshootto (kotto)*
ham (raw)	prosciutto (crudo)	*proshootto (kroodo)*
hammer	martello	*mahrtayllo*
hand	la mano	*lah mahno*
hand brake	freno a mano	*frayno ah mahno*
hand-glider	deltaplano	*dayltahplahno*
handbag	borsa	*borsah*
handkerchief	fazzoletto	*fahtzolaytto*
handmade	fatto a mano	*fahtto ah mahno*
happy	felice	*fayleechay*
harbour	porto	*porto*
hard	duro	*dooro*
hat	cappello	*kahppayllo*
have a light (verb)	avere da accendere	*ahvayray dah ahtchayndayray*
hayfever	la febbre da fieno	*lah febbray dah feeayno*
hazelnut	nocciola	*notcholah*
head	testa	*taystah*
headache	il mal di testa	*eel mahl dee testah*
health	la salute	*lah sahlootay*
health food shop	erboristeria	*ayrboreestayreeah*
hear (verb)	sentire	*saynteeray*
hearing aid	apparecchio acustico	*ahppahraykkeeo ahkoosteeko*
heart	il cuore	*eel kworay*
heart patient	malato di cuore	*mahlahto dee kworay*
heat	il caldo	*eel kahldo*
heater	riscaldamento	*reeskahldahmaynto*
heavy	pesante	*payzahntay*
heel	calcagno	*kahlkahneeo*
heel (shoe)	tacco	*tahkko*
hello, goodbye	ciao	*chaho*
helmet	casco	*kahsko*
help (verb)	aiutare/dare una mano	*aeeootahray/dahray oonah mahno*
help	aiuto	*aheeooto*

helping (of food)	la porzione	*lah portzeeonay*
herbal tea	infuso	*eenfooso*
herbs	le erbe aromatiche	*lay ayrbay ahromahteekay*
here	qui	*kwee*
herring	aringa	*ahreengah*
high	alto	*ahlto*
high tide	alta marea	*ahltah mahrayah*
highchair	il seggiolone	*eel saydjeeolonay*
hiking boots	gli scarponi	*lly skahrponee*
hip	anca	*ahnkah*
hire	prendere a nolo	*prayndayray ah nolo*
historic town centre	centro storico	*chayntro storeeko*
hitchhike (verb)	fare l'autostop	*fahray lahootostop*
hobby	hobby (m)	*obbee*
hold-up	colpo di mano	*kolpo dee mahno*
holiday (public)	giorno festivo	*jorno faysteevo*
holiday park	villaggio turistico	*veellahdjeeo tooreesteeko*
holidays	le vacanze	*lay vahkahntzay*
homesickness	nostalgia	*nostahljeeah*
honest	onesto	*onaysto*
honey	il miele	*eel meeayllay*
horizontal	orizzontale	*oreedzontahlay*
horrible	orribile	*orreebeellay*
horse	cavallo	*kahvahllo*
hospital	ospedale (m)	*ospaydahlay*
hospitality	ospitalità	*ospeetahleetah*
hot-water bottle	borsa dell'acqua calda	*borsah dayllahkwah kahldah*
hot, warm	caldo	*kahldo*
hotel	albergo	*ahlbayrgo*
hour	ora	*orah*
house	casa	*kahsah*
household items	i casalinghi	*ee kahsahleengee*
houses of parliament	palazzo del parlamento	*pahlahtzo dayl pahrlahmaynto*
housewife	casalinga	*kahsahleengah*
how far?	quanto è lontano?	*kwahnto ay lontahno?*
how long?	quanto tempo?	*kwahnto taympo?*
how much?	quanto?	*kwahnto?*
hundred grams	etto	*aytto*
hungry (be)	avere fame	*ahvayray fahmay*
hurricane	uragano	*oorahgahno*
hurry	fretta	*frayttah*
husband	marito	*mahreeto*
hut	cabina	*kahbeenah*
hyperventilation	iperventilazione (f)	*eepayrvaynteellah-tzeeonay*

I

ice (cubes)	ghiaccio	*gheeahtcheeo*
ice skate (verb)	pattinare	*pahtteenahray*
icecream	gelato	*jaylahto*
idea	idea	*eedayah*
identify (verb)	identificare	*eedaynteefeekahray*
identity card	carta d'identità	*kahrtah deedaynteetah*

ignition key	la chiave d'accensione	*lah keeahvay dahtchaynseeonay*
ill	malato	*mahlahto*
illness	malattia	*mahlahtteeah*
imagine (verb)	immaginarsi	*eemmahjeennahrsee*
immediately	subito	*soobeeto*
import duty	tassa d'importazione	*tahssah deemportahtzeeonay*
impossible	impossibile	*eemposseebeellay*
in	in	*een*
in love with (be)	essere innamorato di	*essayray eennahmorahto dee*
included	incluso	*eenklooso*
indicate (verb)	indicare	*eendeekahray*
indicator	indicatore (m) di direzione	*eendeekahtoray dee deeraytzeeonay*
inexpensive	a buon mercato	*ah bwon mayrkahto*
infection (viral, bacterial)	infezione (f) (virale, batterica)	*eenfetzeeonay (veerahlay, bahttayreekah)*
inflammation	infiammazione (f)	*eenfeeahmmahtzeeo-nay*
information	informazione (f)	*eenformahtzeeonay*
information office	ufficio informazioni	*ooffeecheeo eenformahtzeeonee*
injection	iniezione (f)	*eenyeetzeeonay*
injured	ferito	*fayreeto*
inner ear	orecchio interno	*oraykkeeo eentayrno*
inner tube	camera d'aria	*kahmayrah dahreeah*
innocent	innocente	*eennochayntay*
insect	insetto	*eensaytto*
insect bite	puntura d'insetto	*poontoorah deensaytto*
insect repellant	insettifugo	*eensaytteefoogo*
inside	dentro	*dayntro*
insole	soletta	*solayttah*
insurance	assicurazione (f)	*ahsseekoorahtzeeonay*
intermission	intervallo	*eentayrvahllo*
international	internazionale	*eentayrnahtzeeonahlay*
interpreter	interprete (m/f)	*eentayrpraytay*
intersection, crossing	incrocio	*eenkrocheeo*
introduce (verb)	presentare	*praysayntahray*
invite (verb)	invitare	*eenveetahray*
iodine	(tintura di) iodio	*(teentoorah dee) eeodeeo*
Ireland	Irlanda	*Eerlahndah*
iron (metal)	ferro	*fayrro*
iron (verb)	stirare	*steerahray*
iron	ferro da stiro	*fayrro dah steero*
ironing board	tavolo da stiro	*tahvolo dah steero*
island	isola	*eezolah*
Italian	italiano	*eetahleeahno*
itch	prurito	*prooreeto*

J

jack	il cric	*eel kreek*
jacket	giacca	*jahkkah*
jam	marmellata	*mahrmayllahtah*
January	gennaio	*jaynnaheeo*
jar	barattolo	*bahrahttolo*
jaw	mascella	*mahshayllah*
jellyfish	medusa	*maydoosah*
jeweller	gioielleria	*joeeayllayreeah*
jewellery	i gioielli	*ee joyayllee*
jog (verb)	fare il footing	*fahray eel footeeng*
joke	lo scherzo	*lo skayrtzo*
juice	succo	*sookko*
July	luglio	*loolyo*
jumble sale	vendita di beneficenza	*vayndeetah dee baynayfeechayntzah*
jump leads	cavetto del caricabatteria	*kahvetto dayl kahreekahbahttayree-ah*
jumper	il maglione	*eel mahllyonay*
June	giugno	*jooneeo*

K

key	la chiave	*lah keeahvay*
kilo	chilo	*keello*
kilometre	chilometro	*keellomaytro*
kind	simpatico	*seempahteeko*
king	il re	*eel ray*
kiss (verb)	baciare	*bahcheeahray*
kiss	bacio	*bahcheeo*
kitchen	cucina	*koocheenah*
knee	ginocchio	*jeenokkeeo*
knee socks	i calzettoni	*ee kahltzettonee*
knife	coltello	*koltayllo*
knit	lavorare a maglia	*lahvorahray ah mahleeah*
know (verb)	sapere	*sahpayray*

L

lace	pizzo	*peetzo*
ladies toilet	gabinetto per signore	*gahbeenaytto payr seeneeoray*
lake	lago	*lahgo*
lamp	lampada	*lahmpahdah*
land (verb)	atterrare	*ahttayrrahray*
lane	corsia	*korseeah*
language	lingua	*leengwah*
lard	lardo	*lahrdo*
large	grande	*grahnday*
last	ultimo	*oolteemo*
last night	ieri notte	*eeayree nottay*
late	tardi	*tahrdee*
later	più tardi	*peeoo tahrdee*
laugh (verb)	ridere	*reedayray*
launderette	lavanderia	*lahvahndayreeah*

law	diritto	*deereetto*
laxative	lassativo	*lahssahteevo*
leather	la pelle/cuoio	*lah payllay/kwoeeo*
leather goods	pelletteria	*payllayttayreeah*
leave (verb)	partire	*pahrteeray*
leek	porro	*porro*
left (on the)	a sinistra	*ah seeneestrah*
left	sinistra	*seeneestrah*
left luggage	deposito bagagli	*daypozeeto bahgahlly*
leg	gamba	*gahmbah*
lemon	il limone	*eel leemonay*
lend	prestare	*praystahray*
lens	obiettivo	*obeeaytteevo*
lentils	le lenticchie	*lay laynteekkyeeay*
less	meno	*mayno*
lesson	la lezione	*lah laytzeeonay*
letter	lettera	*layttayrah*
lettuce	lattuga	*lahttoogah*
level crossing	passaggio a livello	*pahssahdjeeo ah leevayllo*
library	biblioteca	*beebleeotaykah*
lie (verb)	mentire	*maynteeray*
life guard	bagnino	*bahneeno*
lift (hitchhike)	passaggio	*pahssahdjo*
lift (in building)	ascensore (m)	*ahshaynsoray*
lift (ski)	seggiovia	*saydjeeoveeah*
light (not dark)	chiaro	*keeahro*
light (not heavy)	leggero	*ledjayro*
lighter	accendino	*ahtchayndeeno*
lighthouse	faro	*fahro*
lightning	il fulmine	*eel foolmeenay*
like (verb)	piacere	*peeahchayray*
line	linea	*leenayah*
linen	lino	*leeno*
lipstick	rossetto	*rossaytto*
liquorice	liquerizia	*leekwayreetzeeah*
listen (verb)	ascoltare	*ahskoltahray*
literature	letteratura	*layttayrahtoorah*
litre	litro	*leetro*
little	poco	*poko*
live (verb)	abitare	*ahbeetahray*
live together (verb)	vivere insieme	*veevayray eenseeaymay*
lobster	aragosta	*ahrahgostah*
local	locale	*lokahlay*
lock	serratura	*sayrrahtoorah*
long	lungo	*loongo*
look (verb)	guardare	*gwahrdahray*
look for (verb)	cercare	*chayrkahray*
lorry	il camion	*eel kahmeeon*
lose (verb)	perdere	*payrdayray*
loss	perdita	*payrdeetah*
lost (be)	perdersi	*payrdayrsee*
lost	perso	*payrso*
lost item	oggetto smarrito	*odjaytto zmahrreeto*

lost property office	ufficio oggetti smarriti	*ooffeecheeo odjayttee smahrreetee*
lotion	la lozione	*lah lotzeeonay*
loud	forte	*fortay*
love	amore (m)	*ahmoray*
love (verb)	amare	*ahmahray*
low	basso	*bahsso*
low tide	bassa marea	*bahssah mahrayah*
LPG	il gas liquido	*eel gahs leeqweedo*
luck	fortuna	*fortoonah*
luggage	i bagagli	*ee bahgahlly*
luggage locker	armadietto	*ahrmahdeeaytto*
lunch	pranzo	*prahntzo*
lungs	i polmoni	*ee polmonee*

M

macaroni	i maccheroni	*ee mahkkayronee*
madam	signora	*seeneeorah*
magazine	rivista	*reeveestah*
mail	posta	*postah*
main post office	posta centrale	*postah chayntrahlay*
main road	strada maestra	*strahdah mahaystrah*
make an appointment (verb)	fissare un appuntamento	*feessahray oon ahppoontahmaynto*
make love	fare l'amore	*fahray lahmoray*
makeshift	provvisorio	*provveezoreeo*
man	uomo	*womo*
manager	il direttore	*eel deerayttoray*
mandarin	mandarino	*mahndahreeno*
manicure	manicure	*mahneekooray*
map	pianta/mappa	*peeahntah/mahppah*
marble	marmo	*mahrmo*
March	marzo	*mahrtzo*
margarine	margarina	*mahrgahreenah*
marina	porto turistico	*porto tooreesteeko*
market	mercato	*mayrkahto*
marriage	matrimonio	*mahtreemoneeo*
married	sposato	*sposahto*
marry (verb)	sposarsi	*sposahrsee*
mass	messa	*mayssah*
massage	massaggio	*mahssahdjo*
mat	opaco	*opahko*
match	partita	*pahrteetah*
matches	i fiammiferi	*ee feeahmmeefayree*
May	maggio	*mahdjo*
maybe	forse	*forsay*
mayonnaise	la maionese	*lah maheeonaysay*
mayor	sindaco	*seendahko*
meal	pasto	*pahsto*
mean (verb)	significare	*seeneefeekkahray*
meat	la carne	*lah kahrnay*
medication	farmaco	*fahrmahko*
medicine	medicina	*maydeecheenah*
meet (verb)	conoscere	*konoshayray*
melon	il melone	*eel maylonay*
member (be a)	essere socio	*essayray socho*

menstruate (verb)	avere le mestruazioni	*ahvayray lay maystrooahtzeeonee*
menstruation	la mestruazione	*lah maystrooahtzeeonee*
menu	il menù	*eel maynoo*
menu of the day	il menù del giorno	*eel maynoo dayl jorno*
message	messaggio	*mayssahdjo*
metal	metallo	*maytahllo*
meter (in cab)	tassametro	*tahssahmaytro*
metre	metro	*maytro*
migraine	emicrania	*aymeekrahneeah*
mild (tobacco)	leggero	*ledjeeayro*
milk	il latte	*eel lahttay*
millimetre	millimetro	*meelleemaytro*
mince	la carne tritata	*lah kahrnay treetahtah*
mineral water	acqua minerale	*ahkwah meenayrahlay*
minute	minuto	*meenooto*
mirror	lo specchio	*lo spekkeeo*
miss (verb)	mancare	*mahnkahray*
missing (be)	essere sparito	*essayray spahreeto*
missing (be) (verb)	mancare	*mahnkahray*
mistake	lo sbaglio	*lo sbahllyo*
mistaken (be)	sbagliarsi	*sbahllyahrsee*
misunderstanding	malinteso	*mahleentayzo*
modern art	arte moderna	*ahrtay modayrnah*
moment	attimo/momento	*ahtteemo/momaynto*
monastery	monastero	*monahstayro*
Monday	il lunedì	*eel loonaydee*
money	i soldi	*ee soldee*
month	il mese	*eel maysay*
moped	motorino	*motoreeno*
morning-after pill	pillola del giorno dopo	*peellolah dayl jorno dopo*
morning (in the)	la mattina	*lah mahtteenah*
mosque	moschea	*moskayah*
motel	il motel	*eel motayl*
mother	la madre	*lah mahdray*
motor cross	il motocross	*eel motocross*
motorbike	la moto(cicletta)	*lah moto(cheeklayttah)*
motorboat	motoscafo	*motoskahfo*
motorway	autostrada	*ahootostrahdah*
mountain	montagna	*montahneeah*
mountain hut	rifugio alpino	*reefoojo ahlpeeno*
mountaineering	alpinismo	*ahlpeeneesmo*
mouse	topo	*topo*
mouth	bocca	*bokkah*
much/many	molto/molti	*molto/moltee*
multi-storey car park	parcheggio a pagamento	*pahrkedjeeo ah pahgahmaynto*
muscle	muscolo	*mooskolo*
muscle spasms	i crampi muscolari	*ee krahmpee mooskolahree*
museum	museo	*moozayo*
mushrooms	i funghi	*ee foonghee*
music	musica	*moozeekah*
musical	il musical	*eel moozeekahl*

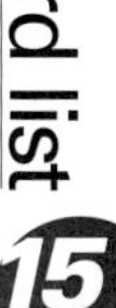

mussels	le cozze	*lay kotzay*
mustard	la senape	*lah saynahpay*

N

nail (on hand)	unghia	*oongeeah*
nail	chiodo	*keeodo*
nail polish	lo smalto per le unghie	*lo smahlto payr lay oongheeay*
nail scissors	le forbicine per unghie	*lay forbeecheenay payr oongheeay*
naked	nudo	*noodo*
nappy	pannolino	*pahnnoleeno*
National Health Service	servizio sanitario	*sayrveetzeeo sahneetahreeo*
nationality	nazionalità	*nahtzeeonahleetah*
natural	naturale	*nahtoorahlay*
nature	natura	*nahtoorah*
naturism	naturismo	*nahtooreezmo*
near	presso	*praysso*
nearby	vicino	*veecheeno*
necessary	necessario	*nechayssahreeo*
neck	collo	*kollo*
nectarine	la pescanoce	*lah peskahnochay*
needle	ago	*ahgo*
negative	negativa	*naygahteevah*
neighbours	i vicini	*ee veecheenee*
nephew	il nipote	*eel neepotay*
never	mai	*mahee*
new	nuovo	*nwovo*
news	le notizie	*lay noteetzeeay*
news stand	edicola	*aydeekolah*
newspaper	il giornale	*eel jornahlay*
next	prossimo	*prosseemo*
next to	accanto a	*ahkkahnto ah*
nice	piacevole/bello/buono	*peeahchayvolay/ bayllo/bwono*
niece	la nipote	*lah neepotay*
night	la notte	*lah nottay*
night duty	servizio notturno	*sayrveetzeeo nottoorno*
night-club	il locale notturno	*eel lokahlay nottoorno*
nightclub	il night	*eel naheet*
nightlife	vita notturna	*veetah nottoornah*
no-one	nessuno	*nessoono*
no	no	*no*
no overtaking	divieto di sorpasso	*deeveeayto dee sorpahsso*
noise	il rumore	*eel roomoray*
nonsense	le sciocchezze	*lay shokkaytzay*
nonstop	senza scalo	*saynzah skahlo*
normal	normale	*normahlay*
north	nord	*nord*
nose	naso	*nahzo*
nose drops	le gocce per il naso	*lay gotchay payr eel nahzo*
notepaper	carta da lettere	*kahrtah dah layttayray*
nothing	niente	*neeayntay*

November	novembre (m)	*novaymbray*
nowhere	da nessuna parte	*dah nessoonah pahrtay*
nudist beach	spiaggia per nudisti	*speeahdjah payr noodeestee*
number	numero	*noomayro*
number plate	targa	*tahrgah*
nurse	infermiera	*eenfayrmeeayrah*
nutmeg	la noce moscata	*lah nochay moskahtah*
nuts	le noci	*lay nochee*

O

October	ottobre (m)	*ottobray*
odometer	il contachilometri	*eel kontahkeellomaytree*
off-licence	enoteca	*aynotaykah*
off (of food)	andato a male	*ahndahto ah mahlay*
offer (verb)	offrire	*offreeray*
office	ufficio	*ooffeecheeo*
oil (vegetable)	olio di semi	*oleeo dee saymee*
oil	olio	*oleeo*
oil level	livello dell'olio	*leevayllo daylloleeo*
ointment	pomata	*pomahtah*
ointment for burns	pomata contro le ustioni	*pomahtah kontro lay oosteeonee*
okay	d'accordo	*dahkkordo*
old	vecchio	*vaykkeeo*
olive oil	olio d'oliva	*oleeo doleevah*
olives	le olive	*lay oleevay*
omelette	frittata/omelette (f)	*freettahtah/omaylayt*
on	su/sopra	*soo/soprah*
on board	a bordo	*ah bordo*
oncoming car	veicolo che viene in senso contrario	*vayeekolo kay veeaynay een saynso kontrahryeeo*
one-way traffic	senso unico	*saynso ooneeko*
onion	cipolla	*cheepollah*
open	aperto	*ahpayrto*
open (verb)	aprire	*ahpreeray*
open air (in the)	all'aperto	*ahllahpayrto*
opera	opera	*opayrah*
operate (verb)	operare	*opayrahray*
operator (telephone)	il/la centralinista	*eel/lah chayntrahleeneestah*
operetta	operetta	*opayrayttah*
opposite	di fronte a	*dee frontay ah*
optician	ottico	*otteeko*
orange	arancia	*ahrahnchah*
orange (adj)	arancione	*ahrahncheeonay*
orange juice	spremuta d'arancia	*spraymootah dahrahnchah*
order	ordinazione (f)	*ordeenahtzeeonay*
order (verb)	ordinare	*ordeenahray*
other	altro	*ahltro*
other side	lato opposto	*lahto opposto*
outing	gita	*jeetah*
outside	fuori	*foohoree*

overtake (verb)	sorpassare	*sorpahssahray*
oysters	le ostriche	*lay ostreekay*

P

packed lunch	la colazione al sacco	*lah kolahtzeeonay ahl sahkko*
pain	il dolore/il male	*eel doloray/eel mahlay*
painkiller	analgesico	*ahnahljayzeeko*
paint	la vernice	*lah vayrneechay*
painting (art)	pittura	*peettoorah*
painting (object)	quadro	*kwahdro*
palace	palazzo	*pahlahtzo*
pan	padella/pentola	*pahdayllah/payntolah*
pancake	la crèpe	*lah krayp*
pants (ladies')	lo slip	*lo sleep*
pants, briefs	le mutande	*lay mootahnday*
panty liner	il salvaslip	*eel sahlvahsleep*
paper	carta	*kahrtah*
paraffin oil	olio di paraffina	*oleeo dee pahrahffeenah*
parasol	ombrellone (m)	*ombrayllonay*
parcel	pacchetto	*pahkkaytto*
parents	i genitori	*ee jayneetoree*
park	parco	*pahrko*
park (verb)	parcheggiare	*pahrkaydjeeahray*
parking space	parcheggio	*pahrkaydjeeo*
parsley	prezzemolo	*praytzaymolo*
part (spare)	pezzo di ricambio	*paytzo dee reekahmbeeo*
partner	il/la partner	*eel/lah pahrtner*
party	festa	*faystah*
passable	transitabile	*trahnseetahbeellay*
passenger	passeggero	*pahssaydjayro*
passport	passaporto	*pahssahporto*
passport photo	la foto tessera	*lah foto tessayrah*
patient	il/la paziente	*eel/lah pahtzeeentay*
pavement	il marciapiede	*eel mahrcheeahpeeayday*
pay (verb)	pagare	*pahgahray*
peach	pesca	*payskah*
peanuts	le noccioline	*lay notcheeoleenay*
pear	pera	*payrah*
peas	i piselli	*ee peezayllee*
pedal	il pedale	*eel pedahlay*
pedestrian crossing	attraversamento pedonale	*ahttrahvayrsahmaynto paydonahlay*
pedicure	il/la pedicure	*eel/lah paydeekooray*
pen	penna	*paynnah*
pencil	matita	*mahteetah*
penis	il pene	*eel paynay*
pepper (red, green)	il peperone (rosso, verde)	*eel paypayronay (rosso, vayrday)*
pepper	il pepe	*eel paypay*
performance	lo spettacolo/la rappresentazione	*lo spayttahkolo/lah rahppraysayntahtzeeo-nay*

perfume	profumo	*profoomo*
perm (verb)	fare la permanente	*fahray lah payrmahnayntay*
perm	la permanente	*lah payrmahnayntay*
permit	licenza	*leechaynzah*
person	persona	*payrsonah*
personal	personale	*payrsonahlay*
petrol	benzina	*bayndzeenah*
petrol station	il distributore di benzina	*eel deestreebootoray dee bayndzeenah*
pets	gli animali domestici	*lly ahneemahlee domaysteechee*
pharmacy	farmacia	*fahrmahcheeah*
phone (verb)	telefonare	*taylayfonahray*
phone (tele-)	telefono	*taylayfono*
phone box	telefono pubblico	*taylayfono poobbleeko*
phone directory	elenco telefonico	*aylaynko taylayfoneeko*
phone number	numero di telefono	*noomayro dee taylayfono*
photocopier	la copiatrice	*lah copeeahtreechay*
photocopy (verb)	fotocopiare	*fotokopeeahray*
photocopy	fotocopia	*fotokopeeah*
photograph	la foto	*lah foto*
photograph (verb)	fotografare	*fotograhfahray*
pick up (verb)	andare/venire a prendere	*ahndahray/vayneeray ah prayndayray*
pickled	sott'aceto	*sottahchayto*
picnic	il picnic	*eel peekneek*
piece of clothing	capo di vestiario	*kahpo dee vaysteeahreeo*
pier	molo	*molo*
pigeon	il piccione	*eel peetcheeonay*
pill (contraceptive)	pillola (anticoncezionale)	*peellolah (ahnteekonchaytzeeo-nahlay)*
pillow	il guanciale	*eel gwahncheeahlay*
pillowcase	federa	*faydayrah*
pin	lo spillo	*lo speello*
pineapple	ananas (m)	*ahnahnahs*
pink	rosa	*rozah*
pipe	pipa	*peepah*
pipe tobacco	tabacco da pipa	*tahbahkko dah peepah*
pity	peccato	*pekkahto*
place of interest	monumento	*monoomaynto*
plan, map	la piantina	*lah peeahnteenah*
plant	pianta	*peeahntah*
plasters	i cerotti	*ee chayrottee*
plastic	plastica	*plahsteekah*
plastic bag	busta di plastica	*boostah dee plahsteekah*
plate	piatto	*peeahtto*
platform	binario	*beenahreeo*
play (a)	opera teatrale	*opayrah tayhahtrahlay*
play (verb)	giocare	*jokahray*
playground	parco giochi	*pahrko jokee*
playing cards	le carte da gioco	*lay kahrtay dah joko*

pleasant	piacevole	*peeahchayvolay*
please	per favore	*payr fahvoray*
please (verb)	piacere	*peeahchayray*
pleasure	il piacere	*eel peeahchayray*
plum	prugna	*prooneeah*
pocketknife	temperino	*taympayreeno*
point (verb)	indicare	*eendeekahray*
poison	veleno	*vaylayno*
police	polizia	*poleetzeeah*
police station	questura	*kwaystoorah*
policeman	il vigile	*eel veejeellay*
pond	lo stagno	*lo stahneeo*
pony	il pony	*eel ponee*
pop concert	concerto pop	*konchayrto pop*
population	la popolazione	*lah popolahtzeeonay*
pork	la carne di maiale	*lah kahrnay dee maheeahlay*
port	(vino di) porto	*(veeno dee) porto*
porter (hotel)	portinaio	*porteeonaheeo*
porter (railway)	facchino	*fahkkeeno*
post code	il codice postale	*eel kodeechay postahlay*
post office	ufficio postale	*ooffeecheeo postahlay*
postage	affrancatura	*ahffrahnkahtoorah*
postbox	buca delle lettere	*bookah dayllay layttayray*
postcard	cartolina	*kahrtoleenah*
postman	postino	*posteeno*
potato	patata	*pahtahtah*
poultry	il pollame	*eel pollahmay*
powdered milk	il latte in polvere	*eel lahttay een polvayray*
power point	presa elettrica	*prayzah aylayttreekah*
power walking	podismo	*podeezmo*
pram	carrozzina	*kahrrotzeenah*
prawns	i gamberetti	*ee gahmbayrayttee*
prefer (verb)	preferire	*prefayreeray*
preference	preferenza	*prefayrayntzah*
pregnant	incinta	*eencheentah*
present (gift)	regalo	*regahlo*
present (in time)	presente	*prayzayntay*
press (verb)	pigiare	*peejahray*
pressure	la pressione	*lah praysseeonay*
price	prezzo	*praytzo*
price list	listino prezzi	*leesteeno praytzee*
print (verb)	stampare	*stahmpahray*
print	copia	*kopeeah*
probably	probabilmente	*probahbeellmayntay*
problem	il problema	*eel problaymah*
profession	la professione	*lah professeeonay*
programme	il programma	*eel prograhmmah*
pronounce (verb)	pronunciare	*pronoonchahray*
propane camping gas	bombola a gas propano	*bombolah ah gahs propahno*
prune	prugna secca	*prooneeah saykkah*
pudding	budino	*boodeeno*

pull a muscle (verb)	avere uno strappo muscolare	*ahvayray oono strahppo mooskolahray*
pull out (a tooth) (verb)	estrarre (un dente)	*estrahrray (oon dayntay)*
pure	puro	*pooro*
purple	viola	*veeolah*
purse	il portamonete/ borsellino	*eel portahmonaytay/ borsaylleeno*
push (verb)	spingere	*speenjayray*
puzzle	il puzzle	*eel poodzlay*
pyjamas	il pigiama	*eel peejahmah*

Q

quarter	quarto	*kwahrto*
quarter of an hour	quarto d'ora	*kwahrto dorah*
queen	regina	*rayjeenah*
question	domanda	*domahndah*
quick	presto	*praysto*
quiet	tranquillo	*trahnkweello*

R

radio	la radio	*lah rahdeeo*
railways	le ferrovie	*lay fayrroveeay*
rain (verb)	piovere	*peeovayray*
rain	pioggia	*peeodjah*
raincoat	impermeabile (m)	*eempayrmayahbeellay*
raisin	uva secca	*oovah saykkah*
rape	lo stupro	*lo stoopro*
rapids	rapida	*rahpeedah*
raspberries	i lamponi	*ee lahmponee*
raw	crudo	*kroodo*
raw vegetables	le verdure crude	*lay vayrdooray krooday*
razor blades	le lamette	*lay lahmayttay*
read	leggere	*ledjayray*
ready	pronto	*pronto*
receipt (till)	lo scontrino	*lo skontreeno*
receipt	ricevuta	*reechayvootah*
recipe	ricetta	*reechayttah*
reclining chair	sedia a sdraio	*saydeeah ah sdraheeo*
recommend (verb)	consigliare	*konseellyahray*
rectangle	rettangolo	*rayttahngolahray*
red	rosso	*rosso*
red wine	vino rosso	*veeno rosso*
reduction	lo sconto	*lo skonto*
refrigerator	frigorifero	*freegoreefayro*
regards	(tanti) saluti	*(tahntee) sahlootee*
region	la regione	*lah rayjonay*
registered	raccomandato	*rahkkomahndahto*
registration (car)	libretto di circolazione	*leebraytto dee cheerkolahtzeeonay*
relatives	i parenti	*ee pahrayntee*
reliable	affidabile	*ahffeedahbeellay*
religion	la religione	*lah rayleejonay*
rent (verb)	affittare	*ahffeettahray*
rent out (verb)	affittare	*ahffeettahray*

Word list 15

repair (verb)	aggiustare	*ahdjoostahray*
repairs	le riparazioni	*lay reepahrahtzeeonee*
repeat (verb)	ripetere	*reepaytayray*
report	il verbale	*eel vayrbahlay*
responsible	responsabile	*raysponsahbeellay*
rest (verb)	riposare	*reepozahray*
restaurant	il ristorante	*eel reestorahntay*
retired	pensionato	*paynseeonahto*
return (ticket)	andata e ritorno (f)	*ahndahtah ay reetorno*
reverse (vehicle) (verb)	fare marcia indietro	*fahray mahrchah eendeeaytro*
rheumatism	reumatismo	*rayoomahteezmo*
rice	riso	*reezo*
riding (horseback)	andare a cavallo	*ahndahray ah kahvahllo*
riding school	maneggio	*mahnaydjeeo*
right	destra	*daystrah*
right (on the)	a destra	*ah daystrah*
ripe	maturo	*mahtooro*
risk	rischio	*reeskeeo*
river	il fiume	*eel feeoomay*
road	strada	*strahdah*
roasted	arrostito	*ahrrosteeto*
rock	roccia	*rotchah*
roll (bread)	panino	*pahneeno*
rolling tobacco	tabacco per sigarette	*tahbahkko payr seegahrayttay*
roof rack	il portapacchi	*eel portahpahkkee*
room	camera	*kahmayrah*
room number	numero della camera	*noomayro dayllah kahmayrah*
room service	servizio in camera	*sayrveetzeeo een kahmayrah*
rope	corda	*kordah*
rosé	rosato	*rozahto*
roundabout	rotatoria	*rotahtoreeah*
route	itinerario	*eeteenayrahreeo*
rowing boat	barca a remi	*bahrkah ah raymee*
rubber	gomma	*gommah*
rubbish (silly things)	le sciocchezze	*lay shokkaytzay*
rucksack	lo zaino	*lo dzaheeno*
rude	scortese	*skortayzay*
ruins	le rovine	*lay roveenay*
run into (verb)	incontrare	*eenkontrahray*

S

sad	triste	*treestay*
safari	il safari	*eel sahfahree*
safe (adj)	sicuro	*seekooro*
safe	cassetta di sicurezza	*kahssayttah dee seekooraytzah*
safety pin	spilla di sicurezza	*speellah dee seekooraytzah*
sail (verb)	fare della vela	*fahray dayllah vaylah*
sailing boat	barca a vela	*bahrkah ah vaylah*
salad	insalata	*eensahlahtah*
salami	il salame	*eel sahlahmay*
sale	i saldi	*ee sahldee*

salt	il sale	*eel sahlay*
same	lo stesso	*lo staysso*
sandy beach	spiaggia di sabbia	*speeahdjah dee sahbbeeah*
sanitary pads	gli assorbenti	*lly ahssorbayntee*
sardines	le sardine	*lay sahrdeenay*
satisfied	contento	*kontaynto*
Saturday	sabato	*sahbahto*
sauce	sugo	*soogo*
sausage	salsiccia	*sahlseetchah*
savoury	saporito	*sahporeeto*
say (verb)	dire	*deeray*
scarf	sciarpa	*shahrpah*
scenic walk	itinerario turistico	*eeteenayrahreeo tooreesteeko*
school	scuola	*skwolah*
scissors	le forbici	*lay forbeechee*
scooter	scooter	*skootayr*
scorpion	lo scorpione	*lo skorpeeonay*
Scotland	Scozia	*Scotzeeah*
scrambled eggs	le uova strapazzate	*lay wovah strahpahtzahtay*
screw	la vite	*lah veetay*
screwdriver	il cacciavite	*eel kahtchahveetay*
sculpture	scultura	*skooltoorah*
sea	il mare	*eel mahray*
seasick (be)	avere il mal di mare	*ahvayray eel mahldeemahray*
seat	posto (a sedere)	*posto (ah saydayray)*
second-hand	usato	*oozahto*
second	secondo	*saykondo*
secretion (med)	la secrezione	*lah saykraytzeeonay*
sedative	il tranquillante	*eel trahnkweellahntay*
see (verb)	vedere	*vedayray*
semi-skimmed	parzialmente scremato	*pahrtzeeahlmayntay skraymahto*
send (verb)	spedire	*spaydeeray*
sentence	la frase	*lah frahzay*
September	settembre (m)	*sayttaymbray*
service (church)	la funzione religiosa	*lah foontzeeonay rayleejozah*
service	servizio	*sayrveetzeeo*
serviette	tovagliolo	*tovahllyolo*
set (of hair) (verb)	mettere in piega	*mayttayray een peeaygah*
sewing thread	filo da cucire	*feello dah koocheeray*
shade	ombra	*ombrah*
shallow	poco profondo	*poko profondo*
shampoo	lo shampoo	*lo shahmpo*
shark	lo squalo	*lo skwahlo*
shave (verb)	farsi la barba	*fahrsee lah bahrbah*
shaver	rasoio	*rahzoyeeo*
shaving brush	pennello da barba	*paynnayllo dah bahrbah*
shaving cream	crema da barba	*kraymah dah bahrbah*
shaving soap	il sapone da barba	*eel sahponay dah bahrbah*

sheet	lenzuolo	*laynzwolo*
sherry	Sherry	*Shayrree*
shirt	camicia	*kahmeechah*
shoe	scarpa	*skahrpah*
shoe polish	lucido da scarpe	*loocheedo dah skahrpay*
shoe shop	calzature	*kahltzahtooray*
shoelace	laccio	*lahtcheeo*
shoemaker	calzolaio	*kahltzolaheeo*
shop	negozio	*negotzeeo*
shop (verb)	fare la spesa	*fahray lah spayzah*
shop assistant	commessa/o	*kommayssah/o*
shop window	vetrina	*vaytreenah*
shopping centre	centro commerciale	*chayntro kommayrchahlay*
short	corto/breve	*korto/brayvay*
short circuit	cortocircuito	*kortocheerkweeto*
shoulder	spalla	*spahllah*
show	lo spettacolo	*lo spayttahkolo*
shower	doccia	*dotcheeah*
shutter	otturatore (m)	*ottoorahtoray*
side	lato	*lahto*
sieve	setaccio	*saytahtcho*
sign	cartello	*kahrtayllo*
sign (verb)	firmare	*feermahray*
silence	silenzio	*seellayntzeeo*
silver	argento	*ahrjaynto*
silver-plated	placcato in argento	*plahkkahto een ahrjaynto*
simple	semplice	*saympleechay*
single (ticket)	andata	*ahndahtah*
single (unmarried)	singolo	*seengolo*
single	singolo	*seengolo*
sir	il signore	*eel seeneeoray*
sister	sorella	*sorayllah*
sit (verb)	sedere	*saydayray*
size	misura/ taglia	*meezoorah/ tahllyah*
ski (verb)	sciare	*sheeahray*
ski boots	gli scarponi da sci	*lly skahrponee dah shee*
ski goggles	gli occhiali da sci	*lly okkeeahlee dah shee*
ski instructor	maestro di sci	*mahaystro dee shee*
ski lessons/class	la lezione di sci	*lah laytzeeonay dee shee*
ski lift	lo ski-lift	*lo skee-leeft*
ski pants	i pantaloni da sci	*ee pahntahlony dah shee*
ski pass	lo ski pass	*lo skee pahss*
ski slope	pista da sci	*peestah dah shee*
ski stick	racchetta	*rahkkayttah*
ski suit	completo da sci	*complayto dah shee*
ski wax	sciolina	*sheeoleenah*
skin	la pelle	*lah payllay*
skirt	gonna	*gonnah*
skis	paio di sci	*paheeo dee shee*
sleep (verb)	dormire	*dormeeray*

sleeping car	la carrozza letto	*lah kahrrotzah laytto*
sleeping pills	i sonniferi	*ee sonneefayree*
slide	diapositiva	*deeahpozeeteevah*
slip	la sottoveste	*lah sottovaystay*
slip road	corsia di accelerazione	*korseeah dee ahtchaylayrahtzeeonay*
slow	lento	*laynto*
slow train	il locale	*eel lokahlay*
small	piccolo	*peekkolo*
small change	moneta	*monaytah*
smell (verb)	puzzare	*pootzahray*
smoke	fumo	*foomo*
smoke (verb)	fumare	*foomahray*
smoked	affumicato	*ahffoomeekahto*
smoking compartment	scompartimento per fumatori	*skompahrteemaynto payr foomahtoree*
snake	la serpe	*lah sayrpay*
snorkel	il boccaglio	*eel bokkahllyo*
snow (verb)	nevicare	*nayveekahray*
snow	la neve	*lah nayvay*
snow chains	le catene da neve	*lay kahtaynay dah nayvay*
soap	il sapone	*eel sahponay*
soap powder	il sapone in polvere	*eel sahponay een polvayray*
soccer	calcio	*kahlcho*
soccer match	partita di calcio	*pahrteetah dee kahlcho*
socket	presa di corrente	*prayzah dee korrayntay*
socks	i calzini	*ee kahltzeenee*
soft drink	bibita/ bevanda	*beebeetah/ bevahdah*
sole (fish)	sogliola	*sollyolah*
sole (shoe)	suola	*swolah*
solicitor	avvocato	*ahvvokahto*
someone	qualcuno	*kwahlkoono*
sometimes	talvolta	*tahlvoltah*
somewhere	da qualche parte	*dah kwahlkay pahrtay*
son	figlio	*feellyo*
soon	presto	*praysto*
sorbet	sorbetto	*sorbaytto*
sore	ulcera	*oolchayrah*
sore throat	il mal di gola	*eel mahl dee golah*
sorry	scusami/mi scusi	*skoozahmee/mee skoozee*
sort	tipo	*teepo*
soup	zuppa	*dzooppah*
source	la sorgente	*lah sorjayntay*
south	il sud	*eel sood*
souvenir	il souvenir	*eel sooovayneer*
spaghetti	gli spaghetti	*lly spahgayttee*
spanner	la chiave fissa/la chiave per bulloni	*lah keeahvay feessah/lah keeahvay payr boollonee*
spare	di riserva	*dee reesayrvah*
spare parts	i pezzi di ricambio	*ee paytzee dee reekahmbeeo*

spare wheell	ruota di scorta	*rwotah dee skortah*
speak (verb)	parlare	*pahrlahray*
special	straordinario	*strahordeenahreeo*
specialist	lo specialista	*lo spaychahleestah*
specialty	specialità	*spaycheeahleetah*
speed limit	il limite di velocità	*eel leemeetay dee vaylocheetah*
spell (verb)	dire come si scrive	*deeray komay see skreevay*
spicy	piccante	*peekkahntay*
splinter	scheggia	*skaydjeeah*
spoon, spoonful	cucchiaio	*kookkeeaheeo*
sport (play)	fare dello sport	*fahray dayllo sport*
sport	lo sport	*lo sport*
sports centre	centro sportivo	*chayntro sporteevo*
spot	posto/luogo	*posto/lwogo*
sprain (verb)	slogarsi	*slogahrsee*
spring	primavera	*preemahvayrah*
square	quadrato	*kwahdrahto*
square (town)	piazza	*peeahtzah*
square metre	metro quadro	*maytro kwahdro*
squash (to play)	giocare a squash	*jokahray ah sqoo-osh*
stadium	lo stadio	*lo stahdeeo*
stain	macchia	*mahkkeeah*
stain remover	lo smacchiatore	*lo smahkkeeahtoray*
stainless steel	acciaio inossidabile	*ahtcheeaheeo eenosseedahbeellay*
stairs	scala	*skahlah*
stalls	platea	*plahtayah*
stamp	francobollo	*frahnkobollo*
start (an engine) (verb)	accendersi/mettere in moto	*ahtchayndayrsee/ mayttayray een moto*
station	la stazione	*lah stahtzeeonay*
statue	statua	*stahtooah*
stay (in hotel) (verb)	essere alloggiato	*essayray ahllodjeeahto*
stay (verb)	rimanere	*reemahnayray*
stay	soggiorno	*sodjorno*
steal (verb)	rubare	*roobahray*
stench	puzzo	*pootzo*
sting (verb)	pungere	*poonjayray*
stitch (med) (verb)	suturare	*sootoorahray*
stitch (verb)	cucire	*koocheeray*
stock, broth	brodo	*brodo*
stockings	le calze	*lay kahltzay*
stomach	lo stomaco/pancia	*lo stomahko/pahnchah*
stomach ache	il mal di stomaco/ pancia	*eel mahl dee stomahko/pahnchah*
stomach cramps	i crampi allo stomaco	*ee krahmpy ahllo stomahko*
stools	le feci	*lay faychee*
stop (bus/train)	fermata	*fayrmahtah*
stop (verb)	fermarsi	*fayrmahrsee*
stopover	lo scalo	*lo skahlo*
storm	tempesta	*taympaystah*
straight	liscio	*leesheeo*
straight ahead	sempre dritto	*saympray dreetto*

straw	cannuccia	*kahnnootchah*
strawberries	le fragole	*lay frahgolay*
street	strada	*strahdah*
street side	lato della strada	*lahto dayllah strahdah*
strike	lo sciopero	*lo shopayro*
strong	forte	*fortay*
study (verb)	studiare	*stoodeeahray*
stuffing	ripieno	*reepeeayno*
subscriber's number	numero dell'abbonato	*noomayro dayllahbbonahto*
subtitled	con sottotitoli	*kon sottoteetolee*
succeed (verb)	riuscire	*reeoosheeray*
sugar	lo zucchero	*lo dzookkayro*
sugar lump	zolletta di zucchero	*dzolayttah dee dzookkayro*
suit	abito/completo	*ahbeeto/komplayto*
suitcase	valigia	*vahleedjah*
summer	estate (f)	*aystahtay*
summertime	ora legale	*orah laygahlay*
sun	il sole	*eel solay*
sun hat	cappello di paglia	*kahppayllo dee pahllyah*
sunbathe	prendere il sole	*prayndayray eel solay*
Sunday	domenica	*domayneekah*
sunglasses	gli occhiali da sole	*lly okkeeahlee dah solay*
sunset	tramonto	*trahmonto*
sunstroke	insolazione (f)	*eensolahtzeeonay*
suntan lotion	olio solare	*oleeo solahray*
supermarket	supermercato	*soopayrmayrkahto*
surcharge	supplemento	*soopplaymaynto*
surf (verb)	fare il surf	*fahray eel soorf*
surf board	tavola da surf	*tahvolah dah soorf*
surgery	ambulatorio	*ahmboolahtoreeo*
surname	il cognome	*eel koneeomay*
surprise	sorpresa	*sorprayzah*
swallow (verb)	inghiottire	*eengeeotteeray*
swamp	la palude	*lah pahlooday*
sweat	il sudore	*eel soodoray*
sweet	caramella	*kahrahmayllah*
sweet (adj)	dolce	*dolchay*
sweetcorn	granturco	*grahntoorko*
sweet dreams	sogni d'oro	*sonyee doro!*
sweeteners	la saccarina	*lah sahkkahreenah*
swim (verb)	nuotare/fare il bagno	*nwotahray/fahray eel bahneeo*
swimming pool	piscina	*peesheenah*
swimming trunks	lo slip/il costume da bagno	*lo sleep/eel kostoomay dah bahneeo*
swindle	truffa	*trooffah*
switch	interruttore (m)	*eentayrroottoray*
synagogue	sinagoga	*seenahgogah*

T

table	tavolino	*tahvoleeno*
table tennis	ping-pong	*peeng-pong*
tablet	compressa	*komprayssah*
take (verb)	prendere	*prayndayray*
take (time) (verb)	durare	*doorahray*
talcum powder	talco	*tahlko*
talk (verb)	parlare	*pahrlahray*
tall	alto	*ahlto*
tampons	i tamponi	*ee tahmpony*
tanned	abbronzato	*ahbbronzahto*
tap	rubinetto	*roobeenaytto*
tap water	acqua del rubinetto	*ahkwah dayl roobeenaytto*
taste (verb)	assaggiare	*ahssahdjeeahray*
tax free shop	negozio duty-free	*naygotzeeo dootee-free*
taxi	il taxi	*eel tahxee*
taxi stand	posteggio dei taxi	*postedjeeo day tahxee*
tea	il tè	*eel tay*
teapot	teiera	*tayeeayrah*
teaspoon	cucchiaino	*kookkeeaheeno*
teat	tettarella	*tayttahrayllah*
telegram	il telegramma	*eel taylaygrahmmah*
telephoto lens	teleobiettivo	*taylayobeeaytteevo*
television set	il televisore	*eel taylayveezoray*
telex	il telex	*eel taylayx*
temperature	temperatura	*taympayrahtoorah*
temporary filling	otturazione provvisoria	*ottoorahtzeeonay provveezoreeah*
tender	tenero	*taynayro*
tennis (to play)	giocare a tennis	*jokahray ah taynnees*
tennis ball	palla da tennis	*pahllah dah taynnees*
tennis court	campo da tennis	*kahmpo dah taynnees*
tennis racket	racchetta da tennis	*rahkkayttah dah taynnees*
tenpin bowling	bowling	*boleeng*
tent	tenda	*tayndah*
tent peg	picchetto	*peekkaytto*
terminal (bus/tram)	il capolinea	*eel kahpoleenayah*
terribly	terribilmente	*tayrreebeellmayntay*
thank (verb)	ringraziare	*reengrahtzeeahray*
thank you	grazie	*grahtzeeay*
thank you very much	mille grazie	*meellay grahtzeeay*
thaw (verb)	sgelare	*sjaylahray*
the day after tomorrow	dopodomani	*dopodomahny*
theatre	teatro	*tayahtro*
theft	furto	*foorto*
there	là	*lah*
thermal bath	le terme	*lay tayrmay*
thermometer	termometro	*tayrmomaytro*
thick	spesso	*spaysso*
thief	ladro	*lahdro*
thigh	coscia	*koshah*
thin	magro	*mahgro*
things	roba	*robah*
think (verb)	pensare	*paynsahray*

third	terzo	*tayrtzo*
thirsty, to be	avere sete	*ahvayray saytay*
this afternoon	questo pomeriggio	*kwaysto pomayreedjo*
this evening	stasera	*stahsayrah*
this morning	stamattina	*stahmahtteenah*
thread	filo	*feello*
throat	gola	*golah*
throat lozenges	le pasticche per la gola	*lay pahsteekkay payr lah golah*
throw up (verb)	vomitare	*vomeetahray*
thunderstorm	il temporale	*eel taymporahlay*
Thursday	il giovedì	*eel jovaydee*
ticket	biglietto	*beellyetto*
tidy (verb)	mettere in ordine	*mayttayray een ordeenay*
tie	cravatta	*krahvahttah*
tights	la calzamaglia/il collant	*lah kahltzahmahlleeah/ eel kollahnt*
time	tempo	*taympo*
times	volte	*voltay*
timetable	orario	*orahreeo*
tin	lattina	*lahtteenah*
tip	mancia	*mahnchah*
tissues	i fazzoletti di carta	*ee fahtzolayttee dee kahrtah*
toast	il brindisi	*eel breendeezee*
toast (bread)	il pane tostato	*eel pahnay tostahto*
tobacco	tabacco	*tahbahkko*
toboggan	il toboga	*eel tobogah*
today	oggi	*odjee*
toe	dito (del piede)	*deeto (dayl peeayday)*
together	insieme	*eenseeaymay*
toilet	bagno/ gabinetto	*bahneeo/ gahbeenaytto*
toilet paper	carta igienica	*kahrtah eejayneekah*
toilet seat	sedile del water	*saydeellay dayl vahtayr*
toiletries	gli articoli da toletta	*lly ahrteekoly dah tolayttah*
tomato	pomodoro	*pomodoro*
tomato ketchup	il ketchup	*eel kaytchoop*
tomato purée	salsina di pomodoro	*sahlseenah dee pomodoro*
tomato sauce	sugo di pomodoro	*soogo dee pomodoro*
tomorrow	domani	*domahnee*
tongue	lingua	*leengwah*
tonic water	acqua tonica	*ahkwah toneekah*
tonight	stanotte	*stahnottay*
too much	troppo	*troppo*
tools	gli arnesi	*lly ahrnaysee*
tooth	il dente	*eel dayntay*
toothache	il mal di denti	*eel mahl dee dayntee*
toothbrush	lo spazzolino da denti	*lo spahtzoleeno dah dayntee*
toothpaste	dentifricio	*daynteefreechoo*
toothpick	lo stuzzicadenti	*lo stootzeekahdayntee*
top up (verb)	riempire	*reeaympeeray*
total	totale	*totahlay*
tough	duro	*dooro*

tour	giro della città	*jeero dayllah cheettah*
tour guide	accompagnatore (m) turistico	*ahkkompahneeahtoray tooreesteeko*
tourist class	la classe turistica	*lah klahssay tooreesteekah*
Tourist Information office	ufficio informazioni turistiche	*ooffeecho eenformahtzeeonee tooreesteekay*
tourist menu	il menù turistico	*eel maynoo tooreesteeko*
tow (verb)	trainare	*traheenahray*
tow cable	cavo di traino	*kahvo dee traheeno*
towel	asciugamano	*ahshoogahmahno*
tower	la torre	*lah torray*
town	città	*cheettah*
toys	i giocattoli	*ee jokahttolee*
traffic	traffico	*trahffeeko*
traffic light	semaforo	*saymahforo*
trailer tent	il carrello tenda	*eel kahrrayllo tayndah*
train	treno	*trayno*
train ticket	biglietto (del treno)	*beellyaytto (dayltrayno)*
train timetable	orario ferroviario	*orahreeo fayrroveeahreeo*
translate (verb)	tradurre	*trahdoorray*
travel (verb)	viaggiare	*veeahdjahray*
travel agent	agenzia viaggi	*ahjayntzeeah veeahdjee*
travel guide	guida turistica	*gweedah tooreesteekah*
traveller	il viaggiatore	*eel veeahdjahtoray*
traveller's cheque	assegno turistico	*ahssayneeo tooreesteeko*
treacle/syrup	melassa/lo sciroppo di melassa	*maylahssah/lo sheeroppo dee maylahssah*
treatment	trattamento	*trahttahmaynto*
triangle	triangolo	*treeahngolo*
trim (verb)	accorciare	*ahkkorchahray*
trip	gita/viaggio	*jeetah/veeahdjo*
trousers/shorts	i pantaloni (lunghi, corti)	*ee pahntahlony (loongee/kortee)*
trout	trota	*trotah*
trunk call	interurbana	*eentayroorbahnah*
trunk code	prefisso	*prayfeesso*
trustworthy	fidato	*feedahto*
try on (verb)	provare	*provahray*
tube	tubetto	*toobaytto*
Tuesday	il martedì	*eel mahrtaydee*
tumble drier	asciugatore	*ahshoogahtoray*
tuna	tonno	*tonno*
tunnel	galleria	*gahllayreeah*
turn	volta	*voltah*
TV	la TV	*lah TeeVoo*
tweezers	pinzetta	*peentzayttah*
tyre (bicycle)	il copertone	*eel kopayrtonay*
tyre pressure	la pressione delle gomme	*lah praysseeonay dayllay gommay*

U

ugly	brutto	*brootto*
umbrella	ombrello	*ombrayllo*
under	giù/sotto	*joo/sotto*
underground	il metrò	*eel maytro*
underground railway system	metropolitana	*maytropoleetahnah*
underground station	la stazione del metrò	*lah stahtzeeonay dayl maytro*
underpants	le mutande	*lay mootahnday*
understand (verb)	capire	*kahpeeray*
underwear	biancheria intima	*beeahnkayreeah eenteemah*
undress (verb)	spogliarsi	*spollyahrsi*
unemployed	disoccupato	*deesokkoopahto*
uneven	ineguale	*eenaygwahlay*
university	università	*ooneevayrseetah*
unleaded	senza piombo	*saynzah peeombo*
urgent	urgente	*oorjayntay*
urgently	d'urgenza	*doorjayntzah*
urine	orina	*oreenah*
use (verb)	usare	*oozahray*
usually	il più delle volte	*eel peeoo dayllay voltay*

V

vacate (verb)	lasciare libero/a	*lahshahray leebayro/ah*
vaccinate (verb)	vaccinare	*vahtcheenahray*
vagina	vagina	*vahjeenah*
vaginal infection	infezione vaginale (f)	*eenfetzeeonay vahjeenahlay*
valid	valido	*vahleedo*
valley	la valle	*lah vahllay*
valuable	prezioso	*praytzeeozo*
van	il furgone	*eel foorgonay*
vanilla	vaniglia	*vahneellyah*
vase	vaso	*vahzo*
vaseline	vaselina	*vahzayleenah*
veal	vitello	*veetayllo*
vegetable soup	il minestrone	*eel meenaystronay*
vegetables	verdura	*vayrdoorah*
vegetarian	vegetariano	*vayjaytahreeahno*
vein	vena	*vaynah*
vending machine	il distributore automatico	*eel deestreebootoray ahootomahteeko*
venereal disease	malattia venerea	*mahlahtteeah vaynayrayah*
via	per	*payr*
video recorder	il videoregistratore	*eel veedayorayjeestrah-toray*
video tape	videocassetta	*veedaeeokahssayttah*
view	il panorama	*eel pahnorahmah*
village	il paese	*eel pahaysay*
visa	visto	*veesto*
visit (verb)	visitare	*veezeetahray*
visit	visita	*veezeetah*

vitamins, vitamin tablets	le vitamine	*lay veetahmeenay*
volcano	vulcano	*voolkahno*
volleyball	pallavolo	*pahllahvolo*
vomit (verb)	vomitare	*vomeetahray*

W

wait (verb)	aspettare	*ahspayttahray*
waiter	il cameriere	*eel kahmayreeayray*
waiting room	sala d'attesa	*sahlah dahttayzah*
waitress	cameriera	*kahmayreeayrah*
wake up (verb)	svegliare	*svayllyahray*
Wales	Galles	*Gahllays*
walk	passeggiata/ giro a piedi	*pahssaydjeeahtah/ jeero ah peeaydee*
walk (verb)	fare due passi	*fahray dooay pahssee*
wallet	il portafoglio	*eel portahfollyo*
wardrobe	guardaroba	*gwahrdahrobah*
warn (verb)	avvisare/chiamare	*ahvveezahray/ keeahmahray*
warning	avviso	*ahvveezo*
wash	lavare	*lahvahray*
washing-powder	detersivo	*daytayrseevo*
washing	bucato	*bookahto*
washing line	corda da bucato	*kordah dah bookahto*
washing machine	la lavatrice	*lah lahvahtreechay*
wasp	vespa	*vayspah*
water	acqua	*ahkwah*
water ski (verb)	fare lo sci nautico	*fahray lo shee nahooteeko*
waterfall	cascata	*kahskahtah*
waterproof	impermeabile (m)	*eempayrmayahbeellay*
wave-pool	piscina con movimento a onda marina	*peesheenah kon moveemaynto ah ondah mahreenah*
way	modo	*modo*
way (on the)	per strada	*payr strahdah*
way	la direzione	*lah deeraytzeeonay*
we	noi	*noee*
weak	debole	*daybolay*
weather	tempo	*taympo*
weather forecast	bollettino meteorologico	*bollaytteeno maytayorolodjeeko*
wedding	le nozze	*lay notzay*
Wednesday	il mercoledì	*eel mayrkolaydee*
week	settimana	*saytteemahnah*
weekend	il fine-settimana	*eel feenay saytteemahnah*
weekend duty	servizio di fine-settimana	*sayrveetzeeo dee feenay-saytteemahnah*
welcome	benvenuto	*baynvaynooto*
well	bene	*baynay*
west	ovest (m)	*ovayst*
wet/damp	umido	*oomeedo*
wetsuit	muta	*mootah*
what/how?	come?	*komay?*

what?	che (cosa)?	*kay (kosah)?*
wheel	ruota	*rwotah*
wheelchair	sedia a rotelle	*saydeeah ah rotayllay*
when?	quando?	*kwahndo?*
where?	dove?	*dovay?*
which?	quale?	*kwahlay?*
whipped cream	panna montata	*pahnnah montahtah*
white	bianco	*beeahnko*
who?	chi?	*kee?*
wholemeal	integrale	*eentaygrahlay*
wholemeal bread	il pane integrale	*eel pahnay eentaygrahlay*
why?	perchè?	*payrkay?*
wide-angle lens	il grandangolare	*eel grahndahngolahray*
widow	vedova	*vaydovah*
widower	vedovo	*vaydovo*
wife	la moglie	*lah mollyay*
wind	vento	*vaynto*
windbreak	paravento	*pahrahveento*
windmill	mulino	*mooleeno*
window (car)	portiera	*porteeayrah*
window	finestrino/finestra	*feenaystreeno/ feenaystrah*
window pane	vetro	*vaytro*
windscreen wiper	tergicristallo	*tayrjeekreestahllo*
wine	vino	*veeno*
wine list	lista dei vini	*leestah dayee veeny*
winter	inverno	*eenvayrno*
witness	il/la testimone	*eel/lah taysteemonay*
woman	donna	*donnah*
wonderful	delizioso/bellissimo	*dayleetzeeozo/ baylleesseemo*
wood	legno	*layneeo*
wool	lana	*lahnah*
word	parola	*pahrolah*
work	lavoro	*lahvoro*
working day	giorno feriale	*jorno fayreeahlay*
worn	logoro	*logoro*
worried	preoccupato	*prayokkoopahto*
wound	ferita	*fayreetah*
wrap (verb)	incartare	*eenkahrtahray*
wrist	polso	*polso*
write (verb)	scrivere	*skreevayray*
write down (verb)	scrivere	*skreevayray*
writing pad (squared/lined)	blocco (a quadretti/a righe)	*blokko (ah kwahdrayttee/ah reegay)*
writing paper	carta da lettere	*kahrtah dah layttayray*
written	per iscritto	*payr eeskreetto*
wrong	sbagliato	*sbahllyahto*

Y

yacht	lo yacht	*lo eeot*
year	anno	*ahnno*
yellow	giallo	*jahllo*
yes	sì	*see*

yes, please	volentieri	*volaynteeayree*
yesterday	ieri	*eeayree*
yoghurt	lo iogurt	*lo eeogoort*
you	Lei/tu	*layee/too*
you too	altrettanto	*ahltrayttahnto*
youth hostel	ostello della gioventù	*ostayllo dayllah jovayntoo*

Z

zip	la chiusura lampo	*lah keeoozoorah lahmpo*
zoo	lo zoo	*lo dzo*

Basic grammar

There are two genders in Italian, masculine (m) and feminine (f). This applies to nouns, articles (the/a) and adjectives.

1 Definite article

The form of the definite article (English '**the**') depends on the sound at the beginning of the word following it:

	Singular	Plural
m	**il** bambino	I bambini (before a consonant)
m	**lo** zio/**lo** studente	**gli** zii/**gli** studenti (before z or s+consonant)
m	**l'**animale	**gli** animali (before a vowel)
f	**la** casa	**le** case (before a consonant)
f	**l'**amica	**le** amiche (before a vowel)

2 Indefinite article

Depending on the sound of the following word, the indefinite article (English '**a**' or '**an**',) is:

m	**un** bambino/ **un** animale	(before a consonant or a vowel)
m	**uno** zio/**uno** studente	(before z or s+consonant)
f	**una** casa	(before a consonant)
f	**un'**amica	(before a vowel)

The plural of the in definite article (English '**some**') are:

m	**dei** bambini	(before consonant)
m	**degli** zii/**degli** studenti	(before z or s+consonant)
f	**delle** bambine/ **delle** amiche	(before a consonant or a vowel)

3 Nouns

In general:

Nouns ending in **-o** are masculine. To form the plural change **-o** to**-i**: (vin**o**-vin**i**)

Nouns ending in **-a** are feminine. To form the plural change **-a** to **-e**: (birr**a**- birr**e**)

Nouns ending in **-e** are either masculine or feminine. Learn each individually. To form the plural change **-e** to **-i**: il pied**e** **(m)** - **i** pied**i**; la nott**e** **(f)** - le nott**i**

Some nouns are irregular:
la mano (hand) is feminine
il problema (problem) is masculine

Nouns ending in **-ista** can be either masculine or feminine:
il/la dentista; **il/la** pianista

4 Adjectives

Adjectives tend to go after the noun they refer to. They must agree with the noun they accompany, both in gender (masculine/feminine) and in number (singular/plural).

	Singular	Plural
m	**un ragazzo italiano**	**dei ragazzi italiani**
m	**uno studente italiano**	**degli studenti italiani**
(m	**un tavolo grande**	**dei tavoli grandi)**
f	**una ragazza italiana**	**delle ragazze italiane**
f	**una stanza grande**	**delle stanze grandi**
(f	**una stazione vicina**	**delle stazioni vicine)**

5 Possessive adjectives

A possessive adjective agrees in gender and in number with the noun whch follows it, and not with the 'owner' as in English. It is usually preceded by the definite article:

	masculine		feminine	
	singular	plural	singular	plural
my, mine	**il mio**	**i miei**	**la mia**	**le mie**
your, yours	**il tuo**	**i tuoi**	**la tua**	**le tue**
his, her, hers, its	**il suo**	**i suoi**	**la sua**	**le sue**
our, ours	**il nostro**	**i nostri**	**la nostra**	**le nostre**
your, yours	**il vostro**	**i vostri**	**la vostra**	**le vostre**
their, theirs	**il loro**	**i loro**	**la loro**	**le loro**

6 Personal pronouns

Since verb endings are normally sufficient to indicate who is doing the action, io, tu, lei, lui, etc. are only used for emphasis or to avoid confusion.

I	**io**
you (singular and familiar)	**tu**
he	**lui**
she,you (formal)	**lei**
we	**noi**
voi (you, plural)	**voi**
they	**loro**

7 Verbs

Regular verbs follow one of three patterns, depending on their endings in the infinitive.

	-are	**-ere**	**-ire**
infinitive	**comprare** (to buy)	**prendere** (to take)	**dormire** (to sleep)
(io)	**compro**	**prendo**	**dormo**
(tu)	**compri**	**prendi**	**dormi**
(lui/lei)	**compra**	**prende**	**dorme**
(noi)	**compriamo**	**prendiamo**	**dormiamo**
(voi)	**comprate**	**prendete**	**dormite**
(loro)	**comprano**	**prendono**	**dormono**